Continue

Right Click on the Appalachian Trail

Phillip Valentine

"With God as his constant companion and a host of fascinating characters looping in and out along the way, Phillip Valentine chronicles a truly unique recovery journal of his 6 month, 189 day journey from Georgia to Maine on the Appalachian Trail. The 12 Steps merge seamlessly with the 5,528,570 footsteps taken on the trail. Millions of steps, thousands of lessons learned, countless prayers offered. And with each and every step, gratitude abounding. An entertaining, enlightening, and inspiring guide that reveals the depth and breadth of the word 'recovery.'"

Kathy Ketcham

"What a delightful read. And what a cast of characters! It felt like I was on the journey with you and enmeshed in the Trail culture, which really is a world of its own by your account."

Bill White

Dedicated to Mom and Dad

Table of Contents

Forward 3

In Remembrance 4

Introduction 5

Prologue 6

The Call 8

MARCH 10

APRIL 36

MAY 69

JUNE 108

JULY 147

AUGUST 186

SEPTEMBER 252

Epilogue 286

A Note from Sandy 289

Acknowledgments 292

Gear List 293

Stuff I Had the Entire Hike 295

Daily Log 296

Forward

I'm humbled and honored to write this forward for my friend Phil or "Right Click," as he was dubbed on the Appalachian Trail. Learning what Phil encountered on the grueling hike, the storms he faced, how he overcame fear, and what it took to complete the journey gave me a new understanding and appreciation for the challenges Phil met and how he persevered. I reflected on my own life and the trials I've faced. The daily log of experiences Phil writes about reveals the power of faith, friendship, and family.

I know Phil through the recovery space and am reminded of my recovery journey and the significant roles others had in my sobriety. The support Phil received from his fellow hikers, his family, and those he met along the way helped give him the strength to continue each day.

Although I've not experienced what it takes to hike the AT, I've experienced climbing mountains and the feeling of wanting to give up, but instead was able to reach summits with the encouragement of fellow climbers and by reminding myself to take one step at a time. In the pages of Phil's story, I found the motivation to climb mountains still to come on the path ahead. Overwhelming emotions well up when standing on top of a mountain, and that particular moment can change lives. At difficult times, I draw upon the memories of what it took and know I have the inner strength to face and conquer whatever it is I'm up against.

I am in awe of what Phil endured during the punishing and demanding thru-hike; it makes me wonder if I could do it. Who knows, maybe one day, I'll give the AT a try. You've planted a seed for me and, most likely, for many who read this excellent book.

Congratulations, my friend, on an accomplishment few will ever experience and to remind us that we can do things we never thought possible.

Scott Strode, Founder and National Executive Director of The Phoenix

In Remembrance

Russ Wilson - my sponsee, friend, and "brother," passed far too early on June 28, 2014, at just 55 years old; my privilege and profound comfort to have Russ in my ear the entire way.

♥ ♥ ♥

Colter Abely - died in a single-car accident on August 18, 2012, at just 21 years old. I carried his copper-infused bracelet the entire way, his parents Brian and Chaleen, two of my biggest supporters. Brian's words at my sending-off party set the tone for the whole of the journey, and I'd repeat them often, "You'll figure it out."

♥ ♥ ♥

Jimmy McCracken - the younger brother of my dear friend Rick "McPackin" McCracken, died on Christmas Eve, 2014, due to chronic alcoholism. After Jimmy did not respond to any phone calls, Rick found him lying in a pool of blood, locked alone in his home. Jimmy's few stints in Alcoholics Anonymous never sustained his recovery. I carried one of Jimmy's 24-hour coins until I lost it somewhere on the trail. Rick hiked with me in Vermont and New Hampshire for several days.

Introduction

On October 18, 1987, I stood in the birthing room of Rockville General Hospital mesmerized by the in and out motion of a newborn baby's tongue. Transfixed, I cradled my first daughter in my arms. Her infant eyes burned their way into the depths of my soul and cut through the drug-induced haze. At the time, I was wildly strung out on cocaine; my drug dealer delivered an eight-ball to my car's glove compartment for me to get through the 22-hour delivery. I'm not proud of that fact; I will never be proud of it. But after working a program of recovery since December 28, 1987, I am no longer ashamed.

And that has made all the difference in the world.

Prologue

On a flawless spring day in Connecticut, I drove slowly, aimlessly northwards, toward Ellington and Somers, relishing the cornfields, barns, and homes on the back roads. I absorbed the news, just diagnosed with Stage 4 oropharyngeal cancer – tongue cancer.

A few weeks earlier, I checked in at the doctor's office because of some pesky swollen glands; they didn't hurt, and I didn't feel sick, but they bothered me. A physician's assistant put me on antibiotics. Three weeks later, the swollen glands still loomed large. I returned to the doctor's office. This time, a real doctor touched my neck and his eyes filled with concern. He immediately ushered me out of the room, down the hall, and stood me in front of an x-ray machine. After the procedure, I asked.

"Doc, what are you looking for?" I knew enough to be concerned.

"Dark masses in your chest. But there are none." He was relieved. I was relieved too.

"I want you to go see a surgical oncologist."

A few days later, with warranted trepidation, Sandy and I drove to the cancer doc, a crusty old man who hassled me. Why? With no bedside manner, he laid me on a table, stabbed one of my swollen nodes with a needle, and spattered the mess onto a glass slide. From across the room, he griped.

"Damn, I got to stick him again!"

The nurse shot me a look of "oh dear." He stuck me again. A few minutes later, he informed me.

"We'll call you with the results."

On March 19, 2010, the doctor called. Cancer. No longer a considerable surprise, but the news was quite sobering. Ironic for a guy who had been clean and sober for more than two decades.

"Sandy, I think I need to be alone for a bit."

"Sure, honey, that's a good idea. I need some time too."

I went for a drive. I called Enrique while on the road; he lost a leg complement to childhood cancer. He listened. He agreed that cancer sucked. I ended the conversation knowing I didn't have many options.

"God, you must have something in mind."

A line from the Serenity Prayer, ingrained from hundreds upon hundreds of Alcoholics Anonymous meetings, came to mind.

"God grant me the serenity to accept the things I cannot change."

I found it odd that I never once protested, "why me?" Instead, I asked, "why not me?" If I proclaimed to be a man of faith, a man of integrity, and a man who worked a program of recovery daily, then I'd show my sphere of influence what it looked like when I faced a trial.

In the following months, I endured two inpatient chemo stays, a feeding tube installation that led to two other hospital stays, thirty-nine radiation treatments, and more chemotherapy that left me emaciated, hairless, and shaken—but cured. During the treatment, I struggled with the decision to begin narcotic medication. I didn't want to jeopardize my sobriety, but eventually, the pain decided for me. I tapered off the opioids more quickly than the doctors recommended when the treatment ended. I shook apart from nerve damage, withdrawal, and anxiety for the next several weeks.

Faith got me through. Sandy got me through. My family, co-workers, employer, AA sponsor, and many prayers got me through.

One day at a time, I survived.

The Call

In the winter of 2011, after enduring the worst treatment and weaning off all medication but still prone to anxiety and full body tremors, I lay in bed and wondered what the day would bring. I heard someone or something speak to me. I recognized The Voice. I heard it a few times previously in my life.

"I want you to hike the Appalachian Trail."

"God, is that you?"

"I want you to hike the Appalachian Trail."

"Stop messing with me."

"I want you to hike the Appalachian Trail."

"The whole thing?"

"Yes, the whole thing."

With warmth and humor in the response, not a command, it felt like an invitation to go on an adventure. The thought of a massive undertaking like an Appalachian Trail thru-hike resonated deep within. It thrilled me. I dragged myself out of bed and found Sandy.

"Sandy, I've got to tell you something. I think God just called me to walk the Appalachian Trail."

"The whole thing?"

"Yes."

"How long will this take?"

"About six months."

"That's nice, honey. When do you think God wants you to do this?"

"I don't know. How about March 19, 2015?"

I picked a date five years from the day I received the cancer diagnosis.

"That's nice, honey."

I sensed her skepticism.

In the following months, I turned this audacious idea around and around in my mind. It consumed me. It distracted me from my recent ordeal. It gave me purpose. I wasn't much of a hiker. I wasn't much of a woodsman. I had only gone on one backpacking trip about forty years earlier.

But I knew I could walk.

Over the next few years, I read books by people who thru-hiked the Appalachian Trail. The more I read, the more the idea grew. I learned much about what to expect and what gear to acquire. The more I knew, the more I wanted to give it a shot. To Sandy's credit, she read some of the books too.

I prepared. I acquired the gear. I hiked around town. I made arrangements. It came time to inform my employer that I'd be leaving for at least six months. I went to a Connecticut Community for Addiction Recovery (CCAR) Board of Directors meeting in May of 2013, nervous but steadfast. As executive director of CCAR, I planned to let them decide on whether or not I would be placed on leave or terminated, prepared to walk out unemployed and left to figure out how to cover my salary. However, much to my amazement, during the discussion, they decided that if I could put a face on recovery during the hike, they'd support me. Part of CCAR's mission, putting a face on recovery meant offering myself as living proof that recovery from addiction is real. They saw this hike as an opportunity for CCAR. The bottom line – the CCAR Board would keep me on the payroll. In absolute awe, I drove home. I never considered that option.

"Sandy, guess what?"

"What?" She asked with trepidation.

"They're going to pay me to go on the hike."

"What? Really? Oh wow. This just got real."

Up to this point, she thought the financial factor would keep me off the trail.

"Right?"

We spent the next twenty-two months getting ready. When the day rolled around for me to fly to Georgia to start my hike, Sandy was prepared for me to go. We drove to Bradley Airport near Hartford, CT.

"You've talked about this every day for four years. You are not allowed to come back for thirty days. Goodbye, honey. I love you."

With that, she kissed me, hopped in the car, and left me on the curb. I watched her drive away. I knew she left quickly because of our tears.

MARCH

Continue

I woke up way before the alarm. I didn't sleep well. It took me a few seconds to realize where I was. Oh yeah, the guest room of Neil and Lori in an Atlanta suburb. The anxiety immediately hit me deeply, smack dab in the gut. One of their dogs used his nose to push open my door.

"Good morning, Leon. Today's the day, Leon. Thursday, March 19, 2015. Today's the day I start north on the Appalachian Trail. Today is a big day."

Leon wagged his tail, happier about it than I.

I looked at my pack leaning against the dresser. I had poured through all my stuff several times, packed and re-packed. Neil said she'd mail back the things I decided not to take. Will I have everything I need?

Still dark, I checked my phone. The weather did not alleviate my apprehension— rain, wind, and temperature in the 40s were forecast for north Georgia all day.

"Figures."

Leon tilted his head.

I crawled out of bed, dressed in my hiking clothes, and heard some commotion upstairs. The other two dogs, Buddy and Jade, were up too. I ate breakfast despite my growing nausea. We took the dogs for a walk then Neil and I climbed into her vehicle for the two-hour drive north. Jade accompanied us.

It was dark. It rained. The wind blew. That pretty much described my emotional state. Maybe I should just have her drive me to the airport? I shut that thought down. My stomach churned. Was I going to puke? I squelched that too. As the day grew brighter, the terrain grew rougher. My anxiety heightened. I remembered to ask Neil to stop so I could get an Aquafina water bottle to match the threads on my Sawyer water purification filter.

The GPS led us to the Springer Mountain parking lot. Soon we turned onto a dirt road, the road slick and curvy with steep drop-offs. Thank God for German engineering. Neil was calm and enjoyed the challenge. Thank God because I was anything but calm. I shook.

We arrived at the parking lot; the sight of a few vehicles comforted me. We donned our rain gear and let Jade run free. I stepped onto the Appalachian Trail. The

AT greeted me with a surge of energy. It felt like an electric current thrummed underneath the trail. My spirit connected immediately to it.

"Do you feel that, Neil?"

"Feel what?"

"Never mind…"

We headed south to the Springer Mountain summit, just under a mile. I took in the rain, the trees, the rocks, and the trail. After a few minutes, I saw a guy coming our way.

"Hello, are you a thru-hiker?"

"No! I'm a ridge runner!" He said gruffly and a tad rudely.

"Oh." I thought, "what the hell is a ridge runner?" I knew so little. I felt so inadequate. The trail felt so powerful. It felt too big for me.

"What did I get myself into?" I mumbled.

Lost in this mood, Neil strolled behind me. I looked down at the trail. A grayish-green tent in motion floated down the path when I looked up. What the heck? I looked more closely. No, it was a person, a woman. When our eyes caught, she smiled from ear to ear. Her smile distracted me from thoughts of inadequacy and anxiety. Another thought occurred to me immediately.

"If this woman (she may be crazy) is enjoying this, then I might be OK too."

"Hi, I'm Right Click. Are you thru-hiking?" I managed.

"Yes. I'm thru-hiking." Still smiling, only her face visible in a sea of ripstop nylon.

"Do you have a trail name?"

"Not yet; I'm Kristin."

We chatted and parted ways, but our interaction calmed me. I met someone as foolish as me. Neil affirmed this.

"See? You're not alone."

Jade streaked through the woods. At least the dog enjoyed himself. Neil and I reached the summit with a few others. Springer Mountain didn't feel like much of a mountain. Yet, I choked up with emotion. On the hallowed ground, I stood on the southern terminus of the Appalachian Trail. I found the old plaque on a rock. Along with an engraving of a hiker, the plaque had a message for me.

APPALACHIAN TRAIL
GEORGIA TO MAINE

A Footpath for Those who seek Fellowship with the Wilderness

The GEORGIA APPALACHIAN TRAIL CLUB

I touched the plaque in the rain, fog, wind, and cold. I had envisioned this moment for years. Tears filled my eyes.

"I'm here. I'm actually here."

After all the planning and preparation, I had accomplished my goal. My goal was never to finish the Appalachian Trail. My goal was to start. In the movie Knight and Day, Tom Cruise's character Roy Miller tells Cameron Diaz, "Someday is a very dangerous word. It's a code word for never."

My someday had come. I scheduled this adventure and worked toward it for four years. I looked for the logbook and found it tucked away in a metal drawer in the rock. I signed the book. Neil, Jade, and I headed back down to the parking lot. I faced my moment of truth. This would be my last chance to call the whole thing off. I thought about it. I joked about it.

"Hey Neil, how about a ride home? To Connecticut?"

She laughed. "You can do it. I believe in you."

The rain and the frigid wind escalated. I hefted my heavy pack onto my shoulders and tightened my waist belt.

"Goodbye, Neil. Good-bye Jade. You're a good dog. Thanks again, Neil."

I hugged her tightly and then watched her drive away. I stood in the parking lot, clutched my trekking poles, and choked back tears (again). I felt alone, abandoned, bewildered, and completely incapable. I shivered even though I wore almost all the clothes in my possession. I considered all my options. I couldn't quit now, could I? I couldn't just stand here. I bowed my head and asked for help. I heard a whispered reply, barely audible through the tumult.

"Continue."

Tested Early

The rain poured down. Heavy winds shook the trees. The trail muddied. This was all new to me. Although frightened and unsure, I relished my first steps. The more I walked, the more my spirits lifted. I loved the trail. The white blazes beckoned. The woods intrigued and inspired me.

I met a few other hikers. A young couple sat in the pouring rain on the side of the trail. The woman suffered from a painful knee. Only a few miles from the start, the man hastily transferred gear from her pack to his. It didn't look good for them. I trudged on.

I labored under the weight of my pack. It took me all day to reach Hawk Mountain Shelter, 8.1 miles from Springer Mountain. I averaged a little over 1 mile per hour. I spotted many tents set up on the flat ground near the shelter. I stuck my nose in. People way younger than me made quite a commotion. The distinct smell of marijuana wafted in the air. Several seemed quite happy to be high and out of the rain.

"Do you want us to make room for you?"

Not seeing how this would even be physically possible, I replied.

"No, thank you."

'You want some of this?"

A young man extended a burning bowl. I thought about it briefly. The last time I smoked marijuana resulted in an unpleasant paranoid reaction; more than two decades ago.

"No. Thank you. No, I'm going to set up back there somewhere."

The kid nodded as if to say, "It's cool, man. Whatever."

That would be ironic; twenty-seven years of recovery blown on the first day. I looked around for a tent site, plenty to choose from. I found a flat spot and set it up in the rain. At the time, I had no idea how good a place I had found. I'd realize it later when the flat ground came at a premium. It took me a long time to assemble the tent and stake it out. The rain made the process challenging. Finally, I crawled inside, squirmed out of my wet clothes, inflated my Neotherm mattress, and rolled out my sleeping bag. I sought warmth and comfort. Only in the early evening I immediately snuggled in to deny my anxiety and isolation. I tend to shut down in response to stress. This day was stressful – a long car ride, a goodbye, a beginning, challenging weather, and a sobriety test. The warmth and comfort of my bed allowed me to doze off.

I woke up an hour or so later. I thought I should be ravenous after a long hike in harsh conditions. But I wasn't. I should have just gone back to sleep. I didn't want to go outside to cook; too cold and wet. So, on my first night, I proceeded to do something stupidly dangerous. I fired up my JetBoil inside my tent (not even the vestibule), cooked a seasoned side of rice, and mixed a foil pack of tuna with it. One forkful, and I gagged. Horrible! I spent an hour trying to consume most of it. I couldn't. I looked at the leftovers.

"What the hell do I do with this?"

And now I needed to pee, urgently. But where? Still light out, many tents nearby and people stuffed in the shelter, I considered my options. I came up with a solution. I could pee and get rid of the leftovers at the same time.

13

I donned my yellow Crocs and blue Marmot rain jacket, crawled out of my cozy shelter, and stood up. The rain had subsided, but water still dripped from the bare trees. I shivered. I headed towards the privy with my JetBoil of food skillfully hidden under my jacket. I hoped no one would notice. As I arrived, the "Solid Waste Only" sign surprised me. Pooping only? I quickly scraped the rice and tuna crap into the hole. Then I peed in it anyway. I walked back to my tent with my head held low and ashamed. I broke two rules in one trip to the privy. Lost in my guilt, I rounded the shelter and spotted Kristin.

Still draped in grayish green ripstop nylon, she stood outside the shelter cooking mashed potatoes. She correctly used her stove. Again, she greeted me with a smile. I hid my anxiety and my empty JetBoil. As we talked, I sensed she genuinely enjoyed this lifestyle. She was comfortable and calm. I was not. I shuffled back to my tent, disgraced.

Once inside, I listened to the unfamiliar night sounds. One question beleaguered me and kept me from sleeping deeply.

"Phillip, what have you gotten yourself into?"

May 1988

"Phillip, what have you gotten yourself into?"

Frightened, I sat in the car and gawked at the people gathered outside a church. Some smoked cigarettes. Some engaged in conversation. Some hugged. I didn't recognize or know any of them.

My daughter was seven months old. I hadn't used any substance since December. Repressed feelings frequently surfaced, and I couldn't predict which ones would come up. My marriage suffered. We participated in counseling. The therapist firmly recommended my attendance at Alcoholics Anonymous (AA) meetings.

At almost 8:00 pm, more people showed up. I opened the car door. I stood up. I faced my fear and took my first step toward the door. After several more steps, I crossed the threshold and entered a brave new world. I talked to no one and sat down in a chair.

I became aware of my surroundings. Some people smiled. I noticed the light in the eyes. That light stoked my curiosity. My eyes settled on a banner in the front of the room. For the first time, I read the Twelve Steps.

1. We admitted we were powerless over alcohol—that our lives had become unmanageable.

2.   Came to believe that a Power greater than ourselves could restore us to sanity.

3.   Made a decision to turn our will and our lives over to the care of God *as we understood Him*.

4.   Made a searching and fearless moral inventory of ourselves.

5.   Admitted to God, to ourselves, and to another human being the exact nature of our wrongs.

6.   Were entirely ready to have God remove all these defects of character.

7.   Humbly asked Him to remove our shortcomings.

8.   Made a list of all persons we had harmed and became willing to make amends to them all.

9.   Made direct amends to such people wherever possible, except when to do so would injure them or others.

10. Continued to take a personal inventory and when we were wrong promptly admitted it.

11. Sought through prayer and meditation to improve our conscious contact with God *as we understood Him*, praying only for knowledge of His will for us and the power to carry that out.

12. Having had a spiritual awakening as the result of these steps, we tried to carry this message to alcoholics and to practice these principles in all our affairs.

It became apparent that God was the answer, according to AA. Over the years, many people have described how they bristled against and stoutly resisted this idea. Not me.

I read the steps. My mind absorbed them. A new and welcomed peace settled over me. This made sense. I couldn't stay clean and sober on my own. I needed help. I quietly exhaled.

"Thank God."

Settling In

I opened my eyes to the morning light. I listened for rain – no pattering on the tent. I extracted myself from my warm sleeping bag, pulled on some damp clothes, and snuggled in my puff jacket. I unzipped the tent, crawled out, and stood in the fresh air. After a few deep breaths of the cool Georgia air, I fired up my stove and boiled some water for tea. I ate a Pop-Tart. I noticed the area had mainly emptied. A few people milled about, but they soon headed down the side trail back to the AT. It didn't take me too long to realize that most thru-hikers got up very early. I wasn't going to be in the majority. My best sleeping happened in the dawn hours. I needed my sleep.

It took me too long to pack up. I had yet to figure out where to put everything in my huge and heavy Osprey Aether 70 backpack (the pack alone weighed more than five pounds). I arranged my sleeping bag, sleeping pad, tent, and three stuff sacks (one for clothes, one for food, and one for miscellaneous stuff) and cinched all the straps down. I did not know how you fill your pack affects how it rides on your body.

Before I left, though, I had one more thing to do. I put it off for as long as I could. I needed to poop. I grabbed my toilet paper and headed to the privy. Before pulling my pants down, I scanned the area to ensure no one watched, even though the structure fully enclosed me. Nervously, I completed the chore. I stood up, greatly relieved in more ways than one. I headed back to my site.

I stowed away the toilet paper, hefted the pack on my shoulders, and cinched the belt. I checked the area. It looked good, just like I left it. One of the last to go, I became acutely aware of my inexperience. Again. I headed back to the AT. Up ahead, I saw some familiar gray-green ripstop nylon. Kristin. I fell in behind her. I pestered her with questions.

"How was your night?"

"Good."

"Mine was not good. I didn't sleep well. What did you have for breakfast?"

"A little oatmeal."

"How far are you going today?"

"I'll see. The next shelter is seven point seven miles away." She responded precisely.

"Sounds good to me. Do you mind if I hike a little while with you?"

"Not at all."

Kristin answered all my questions with patience and kindness. I learned we thought similarly about mileage. Kristin finished the El Camino de Santiago in Spain the previous fall, but that trail damaged her feet. She wondered how far she could go each day. She wanted to keep her mileage lower early on. I did too, but not because of my feet. I wasn't in excellent shape. My body needed to acclimate and grow stronger gradually. I worried about my knees and ankles. When she mentioned her feet, I started thinking about my feet. Then I spiraled to my shoulders; they ached from the heavy pack. My back started to hurt a little too. Yeah, my 55-year-old body concerned me. Could it handle this?

Kristin and I had a natural rapport, and boy, was I grateful. A much more experienced hiker than I, she helped me shake off some of the loneliness and anxiety.

We hit some hills. I hiked up until I ran out of breath, stopped, rested, caught my wind, then began again. I'd repeat this pattern over and over. Not Kristin. She'd keep the same pace up. Slower than my pace, she could maintain it, and she'd often be first to the top. She'd keep the same speed on the flats and the downs. She impressed me. Her pace was rock steady.

Kristin, remarkably, connected with anyone. She listened superbly. People opened up to her immediately. They appreciated her friendliness and attention. With a great sense of humor, she discussed any topic. Kristin was rock steady in another way; she was unflappable. I tried to shake her up. I consider stirring people's pots one of my gifts, but no luck with her. Warm and welcoming, Kristin made many friends along the way, none more significant than Paradox. We first met Paradox as we left Hawk Mountain Shelter just eight miles into our journey.

"Hi, I'm Right Click."

"Hi. Paradox." She said warily. She checked us out.

"I'm Kristin."

"Hi."

We asked if she wanted to join us. She said something about waiting for her mom. I thought she just blew us off. No big deal. Little did I know what a profound role she'd have in this adventure. There were many people on the trail. Hundreds of hikers were determined to make it to Katahdin. They all sported different reasons for hiking, different approaches, different gear, different attitudes, and different personalities. As people attempting a thru-hike, we were all different, but we all had a common goal. Katahdin. Most of them would not make it.

Shortly after we wished Paradox a good hike, Kristin asked me, "How did you get the name Right Click?"

I recalled an evening several months before I set out on the trail. I had dreamt vividly. God made his presence known when hiking in some mountains with several other people. He boldly declared from the heavens,

"THOU SHALT BE CALLED RIGHT CLICK!"

God spoke to me in King James English and capital letters! Before the dream, I contemplated several trail names, most associated with recovery from alcohol and other addictions. Most trail names come from the experience on the trail; my plan until God intervened with Right Click. Really? I didn't like it. I thought the name strange. I had not considered anything like it. But who was I to deny the name God dubbed me? I knew I would use it. When I told Sandy about it, she questioned my mental stability. I told her it made sense because my right knee clicked, especially going uphill. It didn't hurt; it just clicked. Before I left, Dr. Veltri examined my right knee. I wanted assurance that it wasn't injured. He didn't think it would be a problem. Finally, my son Matthew affirmed the name.

"Dad, things have been clicking right along since you've been planning this."

Indeed, when I signed shelter journals (which wasn't often), I used "*Right Click Clicking Right Along.*" But when Kristin asked me, I replied.

"Because my right knee clicks going uphill."

"Oh."

She chuckled. I'd tell her the real reason several weeks later. I didn't tell her (and many others) the whole truth behind my name because I didn't want her to dismiss me. Looking back, I lacked some courage.

That day while we hiked, Kristin listened to my recovery story with no apparent judgment. I learned about her. She walked the Appalachian Trail while her husband served in the US Army in Korea. She grew up on a farm in Pennsylvania with two brothers. A chemical engineer by schooling, she had held various jobs that served to fuel her passion for hiking.

The second evening at Gooch Mountain Shelter, less than sixteen miles down the trail, I staked out my tent, blew up my mattress, and rolled out my sleeping bag in slightly less time. I showed some progress, not perfection. Kristin set up a few yards away. A weird guy with a dog set his tarp and hammock down the hill from me. He had long black hair parted in the middle. He sported a longish black beard. He declared himself a guide and liked to talk about his wilderness skills. He and another lady led a group of several hikers north on a thru-hike. A wiry dog accompanied him. I didn't like how he or his dog skulked around.

I ate dinner over at Kristin's site since the crowded shelter didn't have additional cooking space. Again, I prepared food I didn't want. It only took me two days to come to an epiphany. I whined about it.

"Why didn't I get food that I like to eat? I can't stand this crap. I have never eaten a rice side in my life, and I decide to eat it out here?"

Kristin laughed. "That's pretty stupid Right Click. You should have thought about that."

"Right?" I agreed. After dinner, I returned to my tent and lay down. It felt good. My muscles ached. I took most of the day to hike just under eight miles. I shattered no mileage records. Physically fatigued and slightly more relaxed, I slept better than the previous night.

On the third morning, Kristin called me over to show me something. I walked over as I munched on a Pop-Tart. I liked Pop-Tarts.

"Look Right Click."

She pointed to her shoe outside her tent, now filled with nuts. Some creature (probably a mouse) robbed people and stashed the bounty in her shoe. She beamed. Little magical moments like this would become commonplace. Kristin's example of appreciating the wonder in small things inspired me to do the same.

We planned to hike to Lance Creek. This left us in the range of Neel Gap, our first hostel. My right shoulder screamed in pain by the time I reached camp. I dropped my pack and could barely move my arm. I had not packed the weight evenly, and I had not used the backpack's harness straps correctly. But I didn't know that at the time. In addition, two toes on my right foot shrieked at me every step, even in camp—just three days in, severe discomfort set in. I whined about my physical woes as we sat around a fire that evening. Fellow thru-hiker Cindy Loppers dropped some sage advice that I remembered to Maine.

"Hey Cindy, does anything hurt when you hike?"

"Yeah, all the time. But I just walk through it." That proved true. Every day I hiked; some part of my body hurt.

Nothing to it; just walk through it.

Shedding

By the fourth day, I came to a sobering realization.

"Too damn heavy, this pack on my back."

I sighed as I rested again, going uphill. My food weighed me down. My prior research led me to conclude that thru-hikers needed two pounds of food daily. To be safe, I carried five days' worth or ten pounds. I planned to get to Neel Gap in four days but packed an extra day of food "just in case." Carrying additional items you *might* need, kills thru-hikes. After three full days on the trail, I still had more than eight pounds of food. I hungered not. Early on, physical exertion stole my appetite. Nothing in my food bag appealed to me. For example, I carried five small Ziplocks of trail mix (raisins, peanuts, and M&M's) that I couldn't even look at. Yuck. I'm a reasonably tall guy, 6'3, and I started the trail at 254 pounds. In high school and college, back in the late '70s, I weighed a whopping 165 pounds soaking wet. Now, my body stored an ample supply of energy. My body tried to educate me.

"Stop putting food in; let's burn what we already have!"

I hiked enthusiastically to Mountain Crossings at Neel Gap. I arrived very cold and wet, but instead of taking a shower, warming up, and getting dry, I went straight to the outfitters and asked for a shakedown. Under Pretzel's guidance, I made piles of gear on the floor. He analyzed my entire pack, item by item. With great respect, he offered suggestions of things to send home. Pliable, the discard pile grew —fleece jacket, rope to hang food, shovel, rain pants, stuff sack for my sleeping bag, GoPro camera, waterproof matches, bear whistle, and more. Once he saw I wasn't the defensive type, he joked about some of the items. For example, Pretzel told me the surest way to draw a bear into camp was to hang food from a tree. He slept with his food.

He declared, "Possession is nine-tenths of the law."

Next, he suggested a new backpack. What? So, I tried one, a ULA Catalyst pack nearly three pounds lighter than the Osprey! My pack weight dropped thirteen pounds. Ecstasy ripped through me. Smiling from ear to ear, positively glowing, I settled in at the hostel.

Amused at my giddiness, Kristin asked, "Right Click, are you OK?"

"I am. I am. I feel free. I am an unfettered soul!" I danced.

She shook her head. "You're nuts." It was not unkind.

I showered in a tiny dark stall and dressed in spare clothes. I found a top bunk in the bunk room. I soon concluded that I probably wouldn't spend too much time in hostels; too hard to sleep. The guy below showed me his spreadsheet for his hike. He planned how many miles he had to do each day, when and where to pick up mailed food drops, where he was going to stay... It must have taken days and days to create that itinerary. As he explained all this to me, I thought,

"What happens when something materializes and makes the itinerary useless?"

Thoughts about my recovery surfaced. I turned a recovery slogan over and over in my head - One Day At A Time (ODAAT). I remembered first seeing that on bumper stickers in either red or blue with silver lettering surrounded by a glittering silver border. Once I attended Alcoholics Anonymous meetings, I connected the bumper stickers to the slogans posted on the walls. Now, I lived my entire life in recovery, one day at a time. That philosophy brought me through a divorce, emotional turmoil, job upheaval, wedding days, birthdays, court trials, cancer treatment, and Appalachian Trail preparation. One day at a time was the only way I knew how to approach the trek. I had faith that each day would take care of itself. For me, fear sometimes appeared as control. If I could control you or the outcome, fear would abate. That didn't work because fear always won unless I supplanted fear with faith. Control issues surface in a variety of manners. And maybe that was the itinerary guy's way of dealing with anxiety and the uncertainty of life on the trail.

Men and women share the same space in most hostels. Kristin bunked near a man who slept amidst a mountain of stuff. Some whispered, "homeless." People often used the hostels and the hiker boxes to live. Hiker boxes collect gear that other hikers jettison. They always contain some food items. That night, I delighted in getting rid of all the food I had brought from Connecticut. I made quite a commotion. People snatched up the beef jerky, the bags of trail mix, and the rice and potato side dishes. Kristin thought I should not get rid of all that food.

"No worries, Rock Steady! I stocked up at the store with things I like to eat." She shook her head, smiled, said nothing, and ate her peanuts.

I found the song Rock Steady (The Whispers version, not the Bad Company version) and played it on my iPhone. She sat cross-legged on a top bunk, ate more peanuts, smiled, and shook her head "no." Other hikers laughed. Some sang. I officially dubbed Kristin "Rock Steady." She rejected it outright. But to her dismay, the trail name eventually stuck.

When the lights went out, the itinerary guy fell asleep. Sort of. He battled all night long against a severe case of undiagnosed sleep apnea. He snored voraciously. His breath stopped and started. He rattled the bunk. Morning took a long time coming. Kristin experienced the same, a full hostel, a boisterous place.

Even though I hit the trail sleep deprived, I felt a new freedom. My lighter pack enabled me to hike with less strain. While the weight came off my back, another type of weight lifted off my shoulders. I let go of some of the emotional and mental burdens I carried onto the trail; the responsibilities of stressful work life and the obligations of helping to manage a very active home. Let Go and Let God – another recovery axiom functioned here. With this lighter load, I felt I saved my thru-hike; going deep into the trail became a real possibility. As I hiked with this new sensation, the first grains of confidence sprouted. I still had much "figuring out" to do, but I took great strides in the first four days.

Good for me.

Emotional Detox

With the lighter emotional load, my thoughts drifted back to 25 years before the thru-hike. I mowed the front yard and both side yards—time to start the backyard. I took a few passes across the lawn near the house. The following path would take me near my daughter's sandbox. She recently turned two.

I shut down the lawnmower. I regarded the sandbox warily. The last few times I moved the sandbox, a garter snake slid out from under and startled me. I didn't want to be surprised.

I slid my fingers under the sandbox, grasped the underside, and slid the box so I could mow around it. Sure enough, a garter snake scurried out from under and sped away toward safety. I leaped upwards. I yelled. I hit the ground and stomped back to the lawnmower.

Anger unexpectedly began to build. I fumed. The anger mutated into a rage. I furiously focused on people, places, and things that boiled me. Like steam from a teapot, the rage forced its way out. I began to growl with ferocity as I mowed the backyard. For an hour, I growled, thinking no one could hear me over the noise of the lawn mower.

When I finished and stepped inside the kitchen, my wife (at the time) cowered, white with fear.

"What's wrong with you?" She probed cautiously.

I did not know.

I know now. I experienced a bout of an emotional detox. Without warning, many pent-up emotions no longer anesthetized by drink or drugs burst forth. The feelings often did not align with the current situation and were way too intense. I've learned it's common for many people early in recovery (the first five years). I didn't know that either. It's only through training recovery coaches that I discovered the concept.

Emotional detox lightened my load. I probably would have returned to drinking and drugging to suppress the feelings if I didn't. It was painful but necessary. And it did have its consequences. My wife (and I) did not know that emotional detox indicated a normal part of the recovery process.

After a little more than three years of recovery, we divorced.

Dumbass

Still, two toes on my right foot hurt. I was concentrating on my foot. I came upon the young couple I saw on my first day. She still took every step in much pain. I admired their tenacity. I checked in with them.

When the man discovered my hometown, he began to call me "Manchester!" He said it with enthusiasm! I heard it as "MAN CHEST AH!" The trail named me

22

"Manchestah," but God reigned supreme in dubbing me. I liked "Manchestah," though.

After hanging with them for a bit, I headed up the trail. Every step sent a fiery jolt up my leg. I made it to Wolf Laurel Top; I sat on a log and looked over the Georgia hills. Time for lunch. Rock Steady joined me. I yanked off my boots and socks to air my feet out. The two toes next to my pinky toe were so sore. I touched them and winced.

"Damn it!"

I noticed the toenails were long. I dug out my toenail clippers. I trimmed them and put my footwear back on. When I took the first step, I felt complete and immediate relief.

"Oh my God, Rock Steady! My toes don't hurt. I don't believe it."

"I bet you'll cut your toenails from now on."

I waited for her to add "dumbass." I would have, but she was a lot nicer than me. I am a dumbass. I make no bones about it. Maybe Dumbass would have been the best, most appropriate trail name.

"Hi there. What's your trail name?"

"Dumbass. But that's not just my trail name. I'm called that all the time."

I endured hours and hours of needless pain because my toenails were too long. Dumbass.

Paradox

Paradox caught up with us. I don't remember when or how she joined us; she just did. Twenty-five years old, married for three years, I describe her as stealthy. As we hiked, we talked. Our conversation made its way to soccer. She humbly recalled her scholastic career as a big, fast, strong striker. My respect for her grew. I coached youth soccer for many years. We talked about gear. Her footwear gave her trouble. She started in boots, and they produced severe blisters. She walked on. She carried all types of first aid; if we didn't have it, Paradox would cheerfully dig into her massive pack and fish it out. She carried much weight but never weighed her pack; she didn't want to know.

Once I got to know her, she was anything but a paradox. Naturally humble, quietly confident, she did not seek attention. When we were in groups, she tended to listen. Although cautious, her eyes absorbed everything; behind the façade of timidity lay a foundation of tenacity. When spoken to, always friendly. It didn't take long for us to communicate without a word. One glance, and she knew what I thought. I could do the same with her. She had radar that instantaneously detected bullshit or arrogance in another person. She'd then immediately distance herself from that person. Although quick to assess with uncanny accuracy, Paradox carried an enormous capacity for love, so I believe it sometimes frightened her.

Paradox started the trail with her mom, who never got going because of a medical problem. Equipped with a satellite and GPS, her husband tracked her as an added security measure; he knew her location at all times. She kept a digital camera within easy reach and took thousands of pictures. Her mom and dad hung around the first week or two and met her at road crossings. They worried a bit, but I did not. She was tough, well well-equipped, optimistic, and determined. I did not meet anyone on the trail, man or woman, more determined and with more strength (physically and mentally). I had doubts about my ability to finish, so I checked in with her.

"Paradox, what do you think your chances are of finishing?"

"What?'

She stopped, turned around, and checked my eyes to see if I was serious. She quickly registered that I was.

"Right Click, I am going to finish. No. Matter. What."

She said the last three words very slowly.

She said it with such intensity that I felt a pang of guilt for asking the question. I believed her.

Low Power

After a meager seven miles on the first night out of Neel Gap, I set up camp with Rock Steady, Paradox, and Stix. Stix, another young woman who had left the hostel simultaneously, carried a remarkable story. With serious physical injuries in her past (a broken back, for example), Stix shouldered a huge, heavy, disorganized pack. She labored under it but owned a sweet, tender demeanor and a wonderful sense of humor. That evening, we built a small campfire. We ate and chatted about things and learned more about each other. We retired to our tents, and I heard others whispering on their phones. I called Sandy. I told her about my day with hardly any stress in my communication. She listened easily. I told her whom I hiked with and now shared a campsite with.

"Are there any men on the trail?" She asked with a trace of resentment.

"Yes." An awkward silence followed.

"I don't know why I'm surprised. You work with women all the time."

24

True. As executive director of CCAR, a non-profit focusing on recovery from alcohol and other addictions, my work world is predominantly female. I worked for years with primarily women. I'm married to a woman. I have three daughters (and two sons). I've learned to be comfortable with women. That wasn't always the case. Up until my late 20's, I could barely hold a conversation with a woman. Now I hiked with three.

Later that night, I woke up as I rolled over—my vision filled with light dancing on the nylon ceiling of my tent. In the quiet, I became disoriented. My breath quickened. What was that? It took me a while to identify the light as fire. With urgency, I unzipped my tent and stuck my head out. One of the sticks in the campfire had flared up a bit, still ensconced in the fire ring, nothing to cause alarm. It was not a forest fire bearing down on me—no motion or sound from the other three tents. I took the opportunity to walk into the woods and relieve myself against a tree. I tried to make as little noise as possible. Every sound amplified, and the stream of pee hitting the ground sounded thunderous; I desperately did not want to wake anyone.

I crawled back into my tent and lay down on my back. I listened to see if I had disturbed anyone. I did not hear a thing. I watched the firelight flick against the tent ceiling. I checked my phone. I didn't have much battery left, and I had used up my portable charger. My phone was my security blanket. I needed to get it charged, and I needed to find a different power source to carry. The thought of my phone running out of juice made me anxious. I needed to do something about that.

The next day as I traveled north through the Georgia woods, I absorbed the forest. Maybe the forest absorbed me. Not in bloom yet, no leaves on the trees; it felt open and alive. The trail consisted of mostly deep brown Georgia dirt and brown leaves. We climbed up. We climbed down. I did not appreciate the softness of the track at the time. Even though I started to connect with nature, my thoughts incessantly returned to the low battery on my phone. It rented too much space in my head.

We traveled our personal best to date, more than eleven miles. Near the end of the day, the four of us stacked up at a stream to fill our water bottles. We wanted to find a place to settle down. It did not look promising. The rocky terrain slanted steeply for the last few miles with no apparent change. This ground made setting up one tent, never mind four, impossible. With not much daylight left, my anxiety rose. Still learning how to interpret the AT Guide, I checked it. The trail profile displayed lots of tiny squiggles. I know now that meant a reasonable possibility of rocks, lots of rocks. It showed we were about seven-tenths of a mile from Blue Mountain Shelter, but we all agreed that seemed too far. We were too tired.

Rock Steady pulled out her iPhone. "Let me check Guthook."

"Wait. What? What's that?"

"It's an app of the trail. It's got GPS, so it knows exactly where we are."

It took a few minutes for her phone to power on (she kept it off), find a signal, and load the app.

"It looks like there might be a flat spot, just up there."

She pointed up the trail. She showed us on the phone. Paradox concurred. We shouldered our packs, headed up the trail, and sure enough, we were on flat ground in a matter of minutes; others had camped before here too.

The three ladies set up on one side of the trail and I on the other. As we ate, I floated the idea of going into town the next day. I did not tell them about my growing anxiety about my phone. Perhaps that would have been a good idea; they were all logical and practical, and they would understand. But they said they had enough food, stayed in a hostel a couple of nights ago, and their clothes were mostly clean, so they would skip it. They had no problem if I decided to go.

Busy Living or Busy Dying

The following day, we walked about three miles to a road where trail magic awaited. According to the AT guide, my ticket to town in the form of a shuttle picked up hikers here. I summoned my courage and bid farewell to Rock Steady, Stix and Paradox, not knowing if I'd see them again. I hopped onto the short bus and headed into Hiawassee, GA. Not sure why my internal urge to go into town intensified. I pushed it aside. I found it striking that there were enough thru-hikers to justify a bus going back and forth from the trailhead. I got dropped off at the Budget Inn. I stepped into the office and immediately sensed something ominous. The manager shook visibly. I didn't know why. I paid my fee and walked to my crappy room. - old, worn, no electrical outlet covers, light bulbs out, no drain covers. I sighed. Was this better than my tent? Maybe. I stripped and hopped in the shower. The hot water and soap soothed my anxiety. Feeling better, I got dressed. I glanced out the window— the parking lot filled with emergency vehicles. I went outside. I saw the manager sitting outside the office. I walked over.

"Hey, what's going on?"

"Guy killed himself. Hiker. I found him. Right in that room over there. Just before you came in."

"Oh no. That's awful. I bet you didn't sign up for that...."

"No, sir. I did not."

I let him talk, and when the talking subsided, we just sat together and watched the activity. I later learned that the suicide victim, an older white man, had checked in a few days earlier. He checked out that morning but never left. Hotel California? In his 50's, attempting a thru-hike, he killed himself in a particularly gruesome way. He walked down the street to the hardware store, bought a utility knife, returned to his room, and slit his throat while lying on the bed. The manager walked in on that scene. I could not imagine it. The irony and the gravity of the situation settled on me.

I believe God called me to this place at this time, but I'm not sure why. Was it just to sit with the manager? Was it a lesson in gratitude for all I have been given? Or could it be "but for the grace of God, there go I"? I posted an Instagram picture of all the emergency vehicles in the parking lot. Maybe someone else needed to see it?

As I sat quietly with the manager, I thought about my recent experience with death. Five years earlier, I dwelt in the cancer ward. Grateful when compared to others, I only had four hospital admissions that totaled twenty-two days. During that time, I made observations. First, I didn't want to be transferred to the rooms with the fake wood floors at the back of the ward. That's where people died. Second, people were busy living or busy dying (to borrow a line from The Shawshank Redemption). A few times a day, I'd escape my bed and walk (more like a shuffle) around the quadrangle with my IVs in tow. On one circuit, I met this young woman, bandanna wrapped around her head, as she shuffled in the other direction. Our eyes met, hers ablaze. She smiled warmly, greeted me, and we exchanged some pleasantries. She was busy living, yet she died a couple of days later.

From my bed, I'd listen to others complain, scream for more pain medicine, and demand nurse attention as they shared their misery. Yet they were not in any immediate danger of death. Still, others gave up. I learned that some people use their cancer diagnosis as a legitimate way to check out. Nobly and permanently.

They were busy dying.

I wondered about the guy in the motel room. How much pain did he bear? I imagined the courage it took to do what he did. I never seriously thought about killing myself with all I had been through. Many years ago, when I turned my life over to the care of God, I made my choice. I am busy living.

Was the dead thru-hiker at peace? I hoped so.

Power Restored

The hiker bus pulled into the Budget Inn parking lot.

"Here's my ride."

The manager nodded. I hopped on and rode to Walmart. Other hikers went to resupply. I had enough food. I needed a better portable battery. I walked to the back of the store to the electronics area. I talked with a young kid behind the counter about what I needed. A tall, skinny guy with long hair, a beard, tattooed arms, and impressive gages sporting a Walmart vest interrupted.

"You hiking the trail?"

"Um yeah."

Abruptly and with authority, he directed, "This is what you need. This will charge your phone four, maybe five times."

He reached under the counter, placed a small box in front of me, and returned to his task. I trusted him. I took the box, paid at the register, and waited for the bus. I purchased a Pocket Juice Max 7800. Some super ultralight wonks will say it's too heavy. Other hikers who want to be entirely off-grid will say it's unnecessary. I say it served me well. I had reliable power for my iPhone for the entire hike.

Later that evening, I walked to a popular restaurant and ordered the most expensive item on the menu, a rib-eye steak dinner for $19. I chuckled at the low Georgia prices. I couldn't find that price anywhere in Connecticut. As I waited for my food, I noticed a German dude sitting at a table; I met him on the trail. On a long, steep ascent, I had stopped to rest and sat on a rock. With an unobstructed view down the path, I spotted this guy. Dressed in head-to-toe black spandex, he attacked the ascent with powerful, long strides. I could hear the exertion as he grunted up the hill toward me. He stopped on the trail, just a few feet away. Intimidated at the time, I extended a cautious greeting.

"Hi. How are you?"

He paused for a moment, looked at me, and said, "This is haaaaaaard."

He said it with bewilderment like he had not considered it before.

"Yes, it is." The best I could come up with as I sat on my weak ass.

He nodded in agreement and started again. He strode up the mountain. I watched until he disappeared around a bend. It left a lasting impression.

Now in the restaurant, I asked him how he was doing. He hesitated and, with some sorrow, told me his knee gave out, and he had to go home. Surprised and saddened, I said sorry and wished him luck.

Lesson noted. Physical prowess did not necessarily mean a completed thru-hike. That encouraged me. My mind and attitude would be my power source. I controlled that.

Not much else.

Frightened

On my eighth day on the trail, I walked alone. The new power source comforted me; my phone's battery would remain charged. Most of the time, I kept my iPhone 6s on airplane mode to save power while allowing me to use the camera.

Minor things on the trail started to intrigue me. I noticed tufts of grass sprouting along each side of the trail. The grass flourished where hiker trekking poles aerated the soil. It didn't grow anywhere else that I could see. The green grass outlined the brown footpath charmingly. I tuned into the enchantment of the woods even more. After ten miles or so, I thought it was time to set up camp. I felt good. I came upon a well-used stealth site with some light left in the day. Do I hike longer? I decided Sassafras Gap would suffice for the night. I hoped someone might come along and set up too, but no. As darkness fell, I camped alone. I listened to the owls as I drifted off to sleep. Their companionship soothed my spirit. I grew to appreciate owls profoundly, especially their voice.

I woke up at about 3:00 am to pee. I drank a couple of quarts of water at dinner. In this early stage of the journey, getting out to pee proved to be an ordeal. I struggled to find my headlamp, unzip the sleeping bag (zipper #1), put on crocs, unzip the mesh (zipper #2), reach out and unzip the vestibule (zipper #3), then stagger to a standing position and wobble a suitable distance away without falling on very sore, uncooperative legs. On this night at Sassafras Gap, my headlamp hit nothing but quickly moving fog. Cold rain spat down, carried by a brisk wind. I stood up, shivered, and took a few steps. It wouldn't take much to get completely disoriented. I made sure my tent stayed within range of my headlamp. I let go of my liquid load and shook off, but my nerves jangled. At that moment, a thought leaped into my mind and genuinely disturbed me.

Ax murderer?

No. What would an ax murderer be doing up here in the middle of the night in thick fog?

Big animal of the predatory type?

No. I was confident I would not be eaten in the Georgia woods.

This particular notion dug in and flustered me. I rapidly became terrified. I dove back into my tent, knocked off my crocs, zipped all three zippers quickly, snuggled into my bag, curled into a fetal position, and shook. A full-fledged panic attack beckoned me from the shadows. I willed myself to sleep. I tried not to think about the one force that could kill me out here. I could only whisper the word. I could not speak it out loud.

"Zombies."

Move a Muscle

I woke up the following day and checked myself for bite marks. As far as I could tell, I had not fallen prey to zombies. Still human, I hiked another day to the Plumorchard Gap shelter. I found a nice, flat spot behind the shelter and set up my tent. At dinnertime, I wandered back to the shelter and cooked some food. I met a hiker named Parking Lot. As you might have guessed, he didn't hike very far. Since the night would be below freezing, he told me to sleep with my Sawyer Squeeze (water filter) in my bag.

"If a Sawyer freezes, then it won't work anymore."

"Really?"

I didn't read that in any of my preparation. I slipped the Sawyer Squeeze in when I settled in my sleeping bag. Just in case. When I woke in the morning, a dusting of snow coated the ground. I packed my stuff and froze my fingers. After a hot breakfast of oatmeal and tea, I set off on my own. Again.

I came upon Chip. I passed him, but he tried to keep up and continue a conversation with me. Older and less seasoned than me (hard to believe), Chip gave a new meaning to the word "novice." He and I crossed the first state border, from Georgia to North Carolina. One state down; thirteen to go. After I hiked eleven miles, the longest stint to date, I camped at Deep Gap with the guy. I watched Chip try to set up his tent. He made me feel like an expert as he fumbled and groaned. When done, his tent looked like it might topple over. That's hard to do. Backpacking tents are designed for simplicity. Chip ended up being the guy I came closest to punching out, but we formed an uneasy alliance for now. I ate dinner, and with darkness settling in, I called home from my tent. Sandy told me about the cold weather expected at Deep Gap.

"How cold?"

"In the teens. Or lower."

"Wait. What?"

I felt another panic attack begin to form. A deep freeze at Deep Gap? How poetic. It sounded like an appropriate place to die. My sleeping bag, rated at $9°$, served me well to this point, but this approached a danger zone. Usually, I'm not prone to worry. I ended the call with Sandy and started to worry. I was obsessed with the impending cold. I put on my puff jacket and snuggled in. Nearby, I heard long moans from Chip's tent. I didn't want to know what they might mean. They grew in volume. Then they quieted. I hoped they were deep yawns before he slept. Although not toasty warm, I slept intermittently. It got into single digits that night.

I woke in the morning light, not eager to get out of the sleeping bag. I tried to fire up my JetBoil, but the fuel had gotten so cold that it separated and burned poorly. Who knew? First Sawyer Squeezes, now fuel? I wanted some hot tea and oatmeal. Fortunately, Chip let me borrow his all-season fuel, and I got some warm food.

Again, packing up proved excruciatingly difficult in the sub-freezing temperature. My fingers didn't work well. All my joints felt stiff and creaky. The intense cold made it easy for me to wonder what I was doing. I took some solace as I watched Chip. He fumbled with everything. He made it clear how much he hated the cold. He slept a lot less than me. I almost felt bad for him. Almost.

I started to walk, and my attitude improved. Over the previous 27 years, my recovery program trained me that if I "moved a muscle, I'd change a thought."

My mind drifted back to the spring of 2011. Intense chemotherapy, radiation, and narcotic withdrawal rendered me fraught with anxiety – the period before God invited me to this hike. My AA sponsor, Rick, called and listened to me describe my condition.

"I'm coming over."

It was a statement, not a question. He sat with me for a bit and assessed my situation.

"Get your jacket. We're going out to lunch."

Again, it wasn't a request.

"I'm not hungry. And I can't chew or swallow."

"I don't care. You're going out."

He dragged me out reluctantly. I watched him eat. We talked intermittently, but I felt better when he dropped me back home.

"Move a muscle and change a thought," he said. Then he drove away and left me in my driveway.

A half-mile down the trail, I loosened up. I warmed up much more eager to take on the day. I reflected on how far I had come already. I repeated the words out loud to no one in particular.

"Move a muscle, change a thought."

Bitter or Better

On my eleventh evening on the trail, I set up at Betty Creek Gap with many other people. Chip set his tent in a tiny area amid the Three Wise Men, who had arrived

31

much earlier. Surprised that Chip set up where he did, they questioned his sanity but appreciated his audacity. By now, I expected it. Clueless and utterly unaware of his surroundings and unwritten protocol, Chip saw a flat spot and claimed it. Describes Chip in a nutshell.

I tucked into a cozy flat site enclosed by rhododendrons. Like every night prior, I dialed Sandy. We enjoyed our evening conversations. We talked about things besides the children and the house schedule. I looked forward desperately to the call; it made my day. Here at Betty Creek Gap, I had "no service." Eager to tell her about my longest hike to date (more than twelve miles), the disappointment embittered me. I had thought about Sandy and my kids all day; my heart ached for them. I felt isolated again. I felt disconnected even though other people camped nearby. I struggled with my sour mood.

As I lay there, my thoughts drifted to 1991 when divorce disrupted me, the only time in my life when I experienced two full-blown anxiety attacks. I once visited my daughter in the house I no longer lived in. The stress overcame me. It felt like an impending heart attack. My heart beat wildly. I prepared to die. I didn't, but I fled. I made some excuse and bolted out of there, barely able to draw a breath.

I gradually calmed down. A few days later, at the Tuesday night AA meeting, I raised my hand and shared about the divorce. I thought I spoke from the heart when I just complained. After the meeting, I stood, and a large, intimidating, stern-looking, bald man walked over. He wanted to say something.

"Yes?"

He pointed his finger in my face, heat behind his words. "You can get bitter. Or you can get better. The choice is yours!"

I nodded, slightly terrified. He walked away and out the door. Gradually, the initial fear turned into a slow boil. My bruised ego simmered into steam. I stayed pissed off for a few days until I realized he was right. What road did I want to take? Bitter? Or Better? I wanted to get better.

I asked that guy to be my AA sponsor a few months later. Rick and I are the best of friends today.

Lying in my tent on a remote site on the AT, I faced the same decision. Do I get bitter over no cell coverage? Or do I get better? This time, bitter emerged as the better choice. I fell asleep with a bad attitude and a bad taste in my mouth.

Thunder and Lightning

Sometime after midnight, I woke to the sound of thunder. I listened intently as the thunder grew louder. I watched the lightning intensify. Soon, the storm rampaged just a few feet above me. Lightning didn't appear in a flash; it materialized as circles through the tent's roof. Rain hammered the tent as my heart hammered in my chest. At every thunder crash, my hands flew instinctually to cover my ears. I flipped on my headlamp and checked for leaks. The tent held—a few backsplashes under the vestibule but nothing serious. I turned off the lamp. I laid back down. I took a few deep breaths. I tried to calm myself in the pandemonium. I thought,

"OK, Phillip, what are your options?"

The clear answer? None. I certainly could not run to someplace safer. Stuck in place, I prayed.

"God, I am completely in Your hands. Your will, not mine, be done. And I know You're pretty busy with this magnificent storm, but if it's not too much of a bother, I could use a little help. I'm pretty scared."

After I finished, peace enveloped me. Instantaneously. I did not resist. I accepted it. I felt cradled, comforted in a protective cocoon of love. Amid a wild tempest, I fell back asleep, deeply asleep. The next day, I woke fully rested. I thought about what had happened that night. No longer bitter, I understood awe, not only of God's power but also of God's love.

Others at the campsite discussed the storm animatedly. We survived. I chose not to talk about my experience with God.

Invigorated by the fresh mountain air and sunshine, I strode another twelve-plus miles. My body started to acclimate to the regimen. My legs liked the exercise. With my mind in a better place, I headed to Franklin, North Carolina, and checked in at the Sapphire Inn. Many other hikers graced the inn. Cindy Loppers and Chip waved warm hellos. I unlocked my door on the first floor, dumped my stuff on one of the double beds, stripped out of my sweaty, stinky clothes, and headed for the shower. After getting cleaned up, I joined a bunch of hikers on a shuttle to resupply.

On the bus, a guy named Walkabout held court. He thru-hiked a few years earlier in the year of rain, where it rained almost every day, especially in New England, Vermont, known as Ver-Mud. He chatted with some other hikers. I listened intently. He spoke with authority garnered from experience. He offered sensible suggestions. The topic got to keys to complete a thru-hike. He relayed nothing unique – perseverance, attitude, etc. Walkabout mentioned that he found it better to take Neros instead of zeros. A Nero is when you walk some miles into town, resupply, maybe stay the night, then get back on the trail the following day. A zero day is a day where you do not hike: you walk zero miles. Walkabout talked frankly about hikers he predicted would quit soon. I wondered what he saw in me, so I asked.

"You think I'll make it?"

He sized me up quickly.

"You? I'm not worried about you. You'll make it. Guys our age have a different mindset. We've been through a lot already. You'll make it."

Walkabout said this as a matter of fact, without any doubt. Still, I didn't fully believe him. But his words helped me down the trail. I remembered that brief exchange several times when I doubted my ability.

Thank you, Walkabout.

I woke the following day and considered taking my first zero to rest my aching body. Or should I take a Nero? I had hiked some miles for twelve straight days and had covered 109.8 trail miles. I had kept to my game plan – single-digit miles until my body adapted. Yet, I felt guilty when I thought about spending two nights in the Sapphire Inn.

Why did guilt surface?

I define one of my character defects as laziness, or in Biblical terms, sloth. I always think I can do more and have more in me to give. Sandy, my children, and my colleagues at work don't believe this about me… but that notion is deeply rooted in me. So even though I needed and welcomed rest, I felt like I *should* be on the trail. I called Sandy in the morning, and she was OK with a zero; she encouraged it. I decided to stay. Chip didn't want to stay another night, but he didn't want to leave either. He hung around my room until the manager chased him away. Too cheap to pay for a ride back to the trail, Chip set off down the road. I'd later find out he walked more than ten miles to get back to the trailhead.

The following morning, I experienced an unexpected emotional response to the day of rest. I no longer wanted to get back out on the trail. I felt sorry for myself. I felt the path was too big and too hard for me. I quietly prayed for guidance.

When I finished, I checked my email. I had turned off all my accounts, except for one I created just for the trail. Only a handful of people could access this account. Sandy, just minutes before, sent me a link to a video testimony from my son Joshua. I clicked on the link. He recorded a video clip for a school assignment. I listened to him respond to my battle with cancer and how it affected and influenced him. Tears flowed as I absorbed the positive impact my ordeal and ultimate victory had on his life.

34

Just what I needed at precisely the right time, I shouldered my pack and waited for the shuttle to take me back to the trailhead. No way I could quit after that message. God found another way to encourage me.

Continue, I did.

APRIL

Animal's Bucket

On this stretch of trail, I didn't hike with a crew; I hiked solo. I used the time to "figure stuff out." The North Carolina "Bald" experience rewarded me. I had no conception of a Bald until I walked on them on the trail. They are hills (or mountains) with no trees on top, so the views are fantastic. I loved the way the clearly defined dirt trail meandered through the grass. I could see the course ahead for long stretches for the first time. I arrived at Siler Bald. The side trail to the summit beckoned me. I shrugged off my pack and enjoyed the unencumbered hike to the top. The view inspired me. Several minutes passed while I gazed at the surrounding mountains. Still early spring, the trees had not blossomed. I slowly pirouetted in place and immersed myself in the 360-degree view. A day hiker joined me and snapped a couple of pictures for me. I strolled back down quickly.

I chatted briefly with Young Gun, who rigged his tarp in a grove of trees. That would be his spot for the afternoon and evening, a glorious spot. I told him so. Young Gun strummed a small guitar. I would interact with Young Gun for almost the entire journey.

Later that day, alone, I sat down for a rest and a snack. After a few minutes, I started back up the trail. Cindy Loppers sat just a few hundred yards ahead. I sat down with her and said hello. As we talked, Animal came along carrying a 5-gallon plastic bucket. He put the pail down and took a seat on it. Curious, I asked him about it.

"What's in the bucket?"

Animal glared at me. Anger flashed across his face. Cindy Loppers tensed. Then Animal sensed my genuine curiosity. He relaxed.

"I carry stuff in it, and it has many uses. I mostly carry food and don't have to go into towns often."

He went on in detail about cost savings and other benefits of carrying the pail. Animal also talked about his previous successful thru-hike. He politely excused himself, picked up his bucket, and headed north.

"Right Click, I can't believe he was so nice to you. I've seen him get angry when people ask him about his bucket." Cindy Loppers confided.

"Hey, I was just curious. I was. I don't think I could carry one, but it seems to work for him."

"Hike your own hike, right?"

I agreed with her and continued. I got to the Wayah Bald tower. Animal perched on the wall outside the stone tower. We took in the incredible view, basking in the late afternoon light, when Animal whispered.

"Hear that? I hear a bear."

"You do?" I whispered back. I desperately wanted to see a bear.

"Yeah. And I think I see it right down there." He pointed.

I heard a rustle, but I didn't see anything.

"I don't see it."

"It's gone now. It's moving away."

I didn't know if Animal played me. Or was I just too inexperienced to see? I liked Animal. I admired his willingness to be different. So, I didn't challenge him. I let it go. I'd see Animal once more in Damascus, where a bum knee drove him off the trail.

Devil's Trail Magic

I went down to the Wayah Bald Shelter and spent an uneventful night sleeping comfortably in the tent. The next day, I walked past Rocky Bald and came to a steep descent down into Tellico Gap, a distance of one point seven miles. At first, I welcomed the downhill stretch, but soon my legs revolted. Both knees throbbed. I often stopped to alleviate the pain. When I reached the bottom, my right knee sent searing jolts through my system with every step. My left knee followed with slightly less intensity. If this kept up, I wouldn't be long for the trail. I had prepared mentally and knew there would be times I'd suffer, but another thing to experience it. I far underestimated the intensity. Incredibly grateful to hit bottom, I stumbled into a little dirt parking lot.

That's where So Way and Little Diablo set up trail magic. So Way seemed friendly enough, but something gnawed at me about him. He offered a fried egg, bologna, and cheese sandwich with a smile. I gratefully accepted, but I passed on the fried bologna.

I dropped my pack near a rock. Using the rock as a backrest, I sat on the ground and propped my knees on my pack. My right knee had swollen. I hoped elevating it would alleviate some discomfort. I would assume this position often while I rested. Occasionally, I'd use a tree and extend my legs up the trunk to drain the blood out of

37

my feet. It worked. I dug some Vitamin I (ibuprofen) out of my pack and swallowed a couple with gulps of water.

I watched So Way cook over a small fire. He loved to talk. I found myself eerily drawn into his monologue. So Way, an accomplished hiker (by his description), labeled his lifestyle extreme. He shared his RV, a converted Subaru Legacy station wagon, with Little Diablo. Her appearance matched her moniker, the first Goth hiker I ran into. So Way hiked with less weight than anyone I met. He proudly called himself hiker trash, a term I would grow to loathe. So Way lived off the grid. He claimed that in a couple of years, he would attempt another thru-hike starting at Springer Mountain with just the clothes on his back and a knife. He thought he could acquire all necessary gear and food from hiker boxes along the way. He, like Walkabout, talked about Nero days instead of zero days. This year he'd be a southbounder (SOBO). He claimed to be a cairn builder and assured me that when I got up north, I would see his work. He spoke with authority bred from experience. For some reason, in his presence, I felt self-conscious and inadequate.

Two of The Three Wise Men, Flutter and All's Well, stumbled in as I struggled to stand upright. The third Wise Man, Gasper, quit already. So Way offered egg sandwiches. With their arrival, So Way's spell on me broke. I stood up and quickly bid them all farewell.

As I hiked up the hill and away from that disorienting conversation, I tested my right knee, stiff but manageable. I took time to process what I had just heard. I wouldn't say I liked it. I engaged in some positive self-talk. As I encouraged myself, I let my healthy fear of the trail turn into respect. I could deal with respect. Fear could kill this hike. It took me hours, but I gradually shook the encounter off.

I would learn that another hiker I met, MKat, descended into Tellico Gap just behind me that day. His knees ached too. But instead of continuing, he pulled out his cell phone, called for a ride into town, booked a flight, and flew home to Texas. I ate dinner with MKat a couple of nights earlier. A gracious, friendly man, MKat recently retired. An AT thru-hike was on his bucket list, something he always wanted to do. He told Cindy Loppers he was in too much pain, that there was no more fun in it for him, so he left. MKat ended his journey after 129 miles. The news upset me. I thought he owned all the right stuff to make it—good attitude, great sense of humor, confidence, no time constraints, determination, and knowledge.

Damn. I wondered if he talked with So Way and Little Diablo.

I ran into So Way again in Vermont in August. Sure enough, headed south, he had acquired another young woman to hike with. This woman looked seriously high on powerful drugs; she lurched down the trail and growled about getting tacos. The look

38

in her blazing blue eyes could best be described as feral. So Way sported a wry smile when she talked about going into town to destroy tacos. His eyes betrayed him when he inquired.

"Look at my pet tiger. Would you like one?"

Um. No. Not into being a ringmaster. That seems to be your line of work.

Uphill Exert, Downhill Hurt

I believe I coined the phrase "uphill exert, downhill hurt." But who knows? I could have heard it somewhere. On my way up to the Wesser Bald shelter, the exertion provided temporary relief from knee pain. After almost eleven miles, I settled in for the night. I looked ahead to the next day. I planned to reach the NOC (Nantahala Outdoor Center), a well-known spot on the AT. However, the infamous descent into the NOC took a heavy toll on thru-hikers. My right knee felt shoddy and was still swollen; I hoped it would cooperate. I went to sleep with some trepidation but resigned that I had little choice but to continue.

A long downhill stretch of seven miles stood in the way of reaching the NOC. After three miles, my knee honestly acted up. I winced with every step. To make matters worse, my right calf seized repeatedly. Each time it cramped, it rendered me nearly immobile. I took one step with my left leg and dragged my right leg behind me. My turn to slowly lurch down the trail, I wondered if this could be the end. Did I blow out my knee? If I was not hurt, I could have finished the hike in three hours. After seven hours, I made it to the NOC, where hot food, a few Cokes, lodging, and an outfitter awaited me. But before I settled in, I took the weight off my back, found a bench near the river, sat down, and elevated my aching knee on a wall. I people-watched and waved to some other thru-hikers. I sat there for more than an hour and just chilled. Finally, hunger and thirst drove me to get back on my feet. Cautiously, I stood. The pain had diminished, and thankfully my right calf stopped seizing. I found the office, checked in, and got myself a bunk for the night.

The AT Guide showed that climbing out of the NOC was also very tough. Concerned, I called my son Joshua, who was in school to pursue an athletic training degree, and asked about my knee. He suggested RICE – Rest, Ice, Compression, Elevation. He said it didn't sound like an injury, just overuse and a bad case of tendonitis. I rested my knee for the rest of the day. I got some ice. I wrapped it, and I elevated it. I employed RICE for the entire hike whenever I could, though thru-hiking is not conducive to the R - rest. I had a fabulous dinner with Tank and his girlfriend in the restaurant overlooking the river.

I hobbled back to the bunkhouse. I shared the room with two young kayakers from Alabama. They talked enthusiastically about their love of white water. As I packed my gear the following day, I looked out the window and saw Chip headed up the trail. He didn't have his trekking poles with him. That was odd. Maybe he let them go. I took my time and got a late morning start up and out of the NOC. My right knee, although tender, functioned well enough. On the trail for thirty minutes, I saw a familiar purple puff coat headed toward me. It was Chip.

"What's up, Chip?"

"Hey, Right Click. I left my trekking poles. It took me over an hour to realize I didn't have them."

"Oh. That sucks." I did not mention that I noticed he left without them.

"Hey. Where's your pack?" I asked.

"I left it on the trail. I took it off when I realized I had to come back."

"Oh. See you up the trail."

My knees liked uphill a lot better than down. On an "easy" day, I climbed 6.5 steep miles up to the next shelter. Done, my knee swelled slightly, with the pain minimal. At the shelter, I sat near the stream and doused my knee with cold water, as close to "ice" as possible.

Wrong Way

I decided I could live with painful tendonitis in the knee. The following day, I took 600 mg of Vitamin I (ibuprofen) with my breakfast to control the pain and swelling.

"Just walk through it," I recalled the words of Cindy Loppers.

As I walked, my knee loosened up. I gobbled a midday meal at a shelter and turned left back onto the AT. I noticed Mona with her dog Gertrude, an enormous bloodhound. She smoked a cigarette and sat on a rock that looked eerily familiar. Did I see that exact rock before?

I learned more about Mona later on. Her husband recently died of cancer. Her cousin had just lost his wife to a heroin overdose; now, he recovered in rehab for his heroin addiction. Mona's sad eyes matched those of her bloodhound. Gertrude did not listen well but in a friendly way. She wandered off, found something to roll in, and paid no attention to Mona's calls. The trail might serve to heal Mona. It helps to cure many. I passed Mona and hiked some more.

I encountered Giggly Goose as he walked toward me.

"Hey, why are you going south?" He asked.

"I'm not," I responded.

"Yes, you are."

"No way… Am I?"

"Yes, you are."

I remembered I passed Giggly Goose while we headed north hours earlier. He could be right. There are spots on the AT where you could be headed north according to the compass but southbound toward Springer Mountain. In one of those spots, he convinced me. Embarrassed, I turned around. I had hiked in the wrong direction for nearly an hour. My confidence took a hit. The trail humbled me again. I vowed to be more careful. As I trudged back, I reflected on how many times I took a wrong turn in life but got back on track.

However, I would go the wrong way one more time.

Fidelity in Fontana

I spotted Fontana Dam, the next milestone, through the trees as I descended. I hiked into the last stop before the fabled Smokies. I walked by the "Fontana Hilton,"; perhaps the best-known shelter on the AT situated right on the water and known as a place to party. I saw it but did not check it out. I walked right by to the Fontana Dam Visitor Center. I called for a ride to Fontana Lodge, a beautiful resort. I got picked up soon enough. I held on a little too tightly as my body responded involuntarily to the van's speed. At the resort, several hikers hung out in the lobby.

After several days and nights in the woods, the Fontana Lodge offered all the comforts I had left behind. The Fontana Lodge beckoned visitors with big, puffy lodge-like furniture, a classic lodge with sturdy stonewalls and wood beams. The spacious rooms are comfortable, with a large bathroom, wifi, and cable TV. I checked the front desk to see if my package from home had arrived. It had not. Too bad, maybe it would come the next day.

I ate a satisfying dinner alone in the lodge's restaurant while I scrolled through Facebook and Instagram. After a surprisingly good night's sleep in one of the double beds, I ate breakfast and headed to the general store. I stepped out of the store with plastic bags filled with my purchases into the misty, drizzly, cool atmosphere. As I meandered back up the hill to the lodge, my back suddenly seized. I could not straighten up; the pain was so intense that I could barely breathe. After several attempts to catch my breath, I took a few steps gingerly. Frightened, I shuffled back to my room and lay down.

Just rest, Phillip. Just relax."

I took more ibuprofen. A fleeting thought passed that taking so much ibuprofen might not be a good idea. At that moment, I didn't care; I needed to relieve the back pain. I dozed off. I woke up a bit better. I dragged myself out of my room and found many people in the lobby, primarily thru-hikers. The off-season for the lodge, so thru-hikers generated a high percentage of their business in early April.

The last few weeks provided a deep immersion into the hiking culture. I began to feel a part of it, no longer a curious observer but a willing participant. I connected quickly with other hikers. I appreciated the transparency, generosity, and care for one another. For example, at the small Laundromat down the hill near the general store, a bunch of us gathered to wash our clothes. While the clothes washed and dried, we talked honestly and openly. Every conversation mattered. People seemed much more willing to share intimately. I loved it. I rarely found this in other circles. The rooms of recovery came closest to matching this culture. Even though a novice in many aspects of thru-hiking, I felt welcomed and valued. This materialized in all the conversations with other people in the Fontana Lodge.

I met Flutter, and All's Well in the lobby, and we agreed to dine together. Before that, I checked in with the front desk, and my package had arrived. Now I faced a dilemma. I wanted to stay another night for a few reasons. The weather sucked, and I didn't want to go out in the rain. The UConn women's basketball team was on that night, and I longed to watch them vie for another national championship. My knee and now my back were still pretty sore. But I couldn't justify spending more money on another night. Maybe if I shared the room, it would be palatable. It would cut the rate in half.

Cindy Loppers was in the lodge, but she was not checked in. She said she couldn't afford this place. I could offer her one of my beds. The idea came from a place of generosity; rooms were priced out of the range of many thru-hikers. Plus, it would help me out of my quandary. But deep down, I knew it wasn't a good idea, even though I had innocent intentions. She was married. I was married. What could go wrong?

Yeah, I know.

But I ran the idea past Sandy anyway. That wasn't a good idea either. She made it clear that it was my decision. She also made it clear where she stood. I decided not to even bring the subject up with Cindy Loppers.

After the UConn women won, I slept, thinking about my conversation with Sandy. She had thought about it too. Sandy sent me an email the following day.

From: Sandy Valentine
> Date: April 7, 2015 at 6:58:25 AM EDT
> Subject: Thoughts

Good morning,

Writing to you since I don't think you have cell range. I checked out your spending, and aside from the pack, you've been spending about $200 a week. Some of the meals in town seem high $$. You still have about $300 on your credit card from the original overpayment I made.

As for room sharing, the voices in my head have the following answers:

Your wife - go ahead if you want to, but there is no coming back from infidelity with me, and you are putting yourself in a slippery place given the situation - miles away, outdoors all the time, abstinence, free spirits, no one who knows you back home.

Mother of your children - what message does that send to your kids - especially since even off campus, Josh is committed to living in accordance with God-honoring behaviors. How would they feel that you were sharing intimate surroundings with another woman? A mistake when you are feeling vulnerable would tear our family up.

Your champion on the Battalion - you've put our family in a very public place, and with social media, the wrong message could get out there - rightly or wrongly. And I couldn't help but carry the shame of it.

You'd be saving $30-$40. Money you'd easily spend on lunch at home.

There is a theme here. If YOU want to save money, share with a guy. If someone else needs to save money, seems like it is their issue.

I'll admit, part of me is angry you even asked - putting the decision in my hands. Doesn't mean I don't love you or support you. You are typically in conversation with women at work all week - who adore you. I'm sure it's a very comfortable place to be. And I'm sure they enjoy you - you are funny, encouraging, and strong. But, how about building up those man relationships? lol

I've got a light meeting day today, so we can talk if you have time.

Love and peace, Sandy

After reading this, I thanked God I was married to Sandy.
And I wondered if I would ever stop being a dumbass.

A Glimpse into My Future

At dinner that night, more people from the hiking community joined our table. Sobo, short for southbounder, commanded the stage at our table. Near the finish of his thru-hike, I gawked at his crazed eyes and thought "lunatic" might be an apt description. Was I looking into my future? Rail thin, Sobo sported a typical thru-hiker shaggy beard. He ate like a pro. Another guy bought dinner for him and encouraged him to eat. Sobo ate three cheeseburgers, downed three beers, and dessert too. Was he putting on a show? Could this be real?

He fascinated me.

"Sobo, I have extra food from a care package in my room. I'm not going to take it with me. Do you want it?"

"YES! YES!"

I jumped in my chair at the voracity of his response. Nervous, I led him down the hall to my room, never having been alone with a hunger-crazed thru-hiker. I hoped he was harmless.

He was.

He scooped up everything I offered. Everything. He accepted with complete and sincere gratitude. I was more than glad to share. I had plenty to eat. I certainly didn't want to carry all of it. Sandy would be happy that her package went to good use too.

The following day, I met Flutter, and All's Well (two men) in the lobby. We had agreed to hike for a few days together. We got a ride back to the Fontana Dam Visitor Center under sunny skies, walked over the dam, made a right turn, and headed into the Smokies.

Flutter and Gaspering

Grateful to meet and talk with another person in recovery, Flutter earned his name on the trail. Whenever he was asked what his trail name was, he'd say,

"I don't have one; I'm trying to fly under the radar."

Some creative thru-hiker used the acronym FUTR (Fly Under The Radar), but that translated to Futter, so the "l" was added to make it Flutter. I don't think Flutter liked the name much, but it stuck. Highly extroverted, Flutter did everything but fly under the radar. He'd be the first to welcome someone into camp, start a conversation, and offer advice. Loud, friendly, curious, and opinionated, he ascertained that his way was the best. I hiked with him for many miles until I couldn't anymore.

One of the Three Wise Men mentioned earlier, Flutter, was the youngest at age 50. All's Well, in his 60's, a retired minister wielded a beautiful soul and heart. Peace exuded from him. His wife followed along in their pickup truck and trailer, serving as their home for the past seven years. He'd last just a few more days until we reached Clingman's Dome, a distance of two hundred miles. In his 70's, Gasper lasted one hundred miles (the oldest of the Three Wise Men). He acquired his trail name because of how he breathed – not a good omen for a thru-hiker. Gasper hiked slowly, stopped often, and carried way too much water. He irritated the other two Wise Men when he stopped to remove sticks, branches, and sometimes rocks from the trail. He repeatedly blocked other hikers while he groomed the path. Again, this did not bode well for Gasper to complete a thru-hike.

Later, Flutter and I created a game to tribute Gasper. As we walked along, we used our trekking poles to knock sticks off the path. An official "Gasper" consisted of one continuous motion with a trekking pole; breaking stride was forbidden. I became skilled in the art of Gaspering. Sticks flew off my pole deep into the woods on either side. Placing the tip of the trekking pole correctly to fling the stick off the trail took hours of practice. Professional Gaspers drew attention to the flying stick with a shout of…

"Gasper!"

The cries of "Gasper" paid homage to our fallen comrade. I'd gasper for two thousand miles and came close to achieving mastery. Initially, as Flutter and I developed our craft, we used two basic strokes, forehands and backhands. My left-handed backhand stroke was the weakest, while my right-handed backhand stroke set records. In North Carolina, I established a personal best of 63' 7" with one gasper. I took gaspering to a new level when I successfully attempted a behind-the-back maneuver. Soon enough, though, young people came and took over the sport. The 25-year-old Paradox dominated with more speed, grace, power, and accuracy off both sides than I could even imagine. Alas, Gaspering, too, is a young person's game.

Smokies

Flutter, All's Well, and I entered Great Smoky National Park. I previously registered online and carried my paper with me. The park rules demand that hikers stay in shelters. If the shelter fills, then you are allowed to camp nearby. No stealth camping is permitted. This proved to be challenging. No. It proved to be a pain in the ass.

45

I discovered I hiked a lot faster than my new traveling companions. I reached the Shuckstack fire tower first. The Twins had just come down. I looked up at a rickety steel structure.

"Do I want to go up there?"

"Sure you do!" One of the Twins encouraged.

"I might not get another chance. Right?"

I left my pack at the bottom of the access trail and climbed the rise to the tower. I hesitated at the foot of the stairs. A Seals and Croft tune ponged from side to side in my mind.

"We may never pass this way again...."

I sang it softly out loud to calm my nerves as I slowly scaled the tower step by step. The view from the top took my breath away. Or maybe I was so frightened I couldn't breathe. I took a few pics and a couple of selfies; not a stretch to put on a fearful face. I didn't stay up there long. Two minutes maybe? More than enough. I took extreme caution coming back down; not a fan of fire towers.

On the first day in the Smokies, I hiked five point six miles to Birch Spring Gap, the only designated campsite (no shelter) in the park. I arrived at camp first, the entire hike uphill. Flutter and All's Well showed up much later. Flutter and I set our tents near each other. All's Well set up his hammock. For the first time, I used the bear cables installed at the site to hang my food. A warm night, I slept with both sides of the tent open. I woke to shouts and raucous laughter in the middle of the night. Two young women came in the dark, hung their food, and the cable snapped. Flutter heard the noise and hoped for a bear. He scrambled out of his tent to take photos. He came back disappointed. I didn't budge. I barely opened my eyes. I just wanted to sleep. I heard the complete story the following day over breakfast. I also discovered that when my food bag hit the ground, some mayonnaise packets burst. What a mess. From that point forward, I packaged all my condiments in a separate Ziploc.

I'd find out later that this campsite closed a few weeks later due to bear activity. Two months later, I'd also read that a black bear grabbed a kid out of his hammock at 10:30 at night by the kid's head! The incident happened in the Smokies just a few miles from this site. The boy's dad jumped on the bear and punched him in the face to get the bear to drop the kid. The 16-year-old boy had bite marks and lacerations on his face. They hiked five miles to a lake, and a helicopter picked them up. Rangers later killed a bear they thought might be the culprit. A DNA test proved it to be the wrong bear. The kid munching bear still roams the Smokies. The boy made a full recovery.

Over the next three days, we hiked 10.8, 6.3, and 7.5 miles, not very big days. Several factors played into the low mileage. I kept my miles low to let my tender knee heal. The two other guys were not prone to big miles. The terrain did not lend itself to big miles either. The AT Guide had many squiggles that reflected tough going with many PUDs (Pointless Ups and Downs).

Then the rain came.

Park rangers hung giant tarps over the entrance to keep the elements out of the three-sided shelters. Most shelters sported two levels, jammed with hikers. I blew up my air mattress when I rolled in and claimed my sliver of board space. I positioned myself on the lower level near the entrance when I had to get up and pee. No upper level for me; old Right Click would not negotiate ladders in the dark. The upper level served those much younger than I. Even so, one young female hiker stepped off the upper level and crashed face-first into stone. From the account told by a Ridge Runner, this was the worst accident he had witnessed in all his years working the AT.

The Smokies shelter restrictions accomplished a few things. It kept camping in specific areas and lessened the "damage" to the woods. Although, as I hiked through the Smokies, I doubted hikers could do as much damage as the woolly adelgid, an invasive insect from Asia. It destroyed massive tracts of forest. Giant hemlocks lay on the ground in vast areas. At times, I felt like I walked through a war zone. The devastation silenced me. As I padded along, I nurtured a deep respect for the forest. I tapped into deep suffering, not human in origin. Was there a lesson in this? Something about the ability of a tiny insect to take down the mighty hemlock?

Another outcome of having the hiker community pile up in shelters is forced connections. I talked to the person who slept two inches from me. I conversed with many hikers. I started to know some of the people on the trail. I felt natural affiliations with some and others I wanted to avoid. Some of these relationships would last a lifetime. Just three weeks into the adventure, I witnessed the formation of hiking "crews." I traveled with Flutter and All's Well, but I yearned to catch up with Rock Steady and Paradox. They matched up with me better. I guessed the two ladies might be in front of me, but I did not know.

The long, arduous climbs in the Smokies typically would have been rewarded with spectacular views, but not now. I climbed and climbed in the fog and mist, reached a summit, and stared off into a white void. The sensation kicked in a touch of vertigo and made me unsteady on my feet. I would quickly move on. The wet weather shortened breaks considerably, and I covered good ground.

All's Well's attitude deteriorated. Rain, wind, and crowded shelter sleeping wore him down. A retired pastor, he quickly engaged people with a warm smile and welcoming demeanor. Before the Smokies, his wife met him and took his hiking partners back home to their RV, a very appealing way to hike the AT. All's Well lost access to his RV through the Great Smoky National Park. He stayed in overcrowded shelters because of limited road access. Most of our clothes and gear were wet. I felt lucky to have some merely damp camp clothes. It took a particular breed and attitude to endure long periods of rain. I recalled something Rock Steady told me back in Georgia.

"You see what a person is made of after hiking five straight days in the rain."

I resisted the depression. I believed I could get through anything "one day at a time." I maintained a relatively positive mental attitude compared to those around me.

At night, I endured cavernous snoring (Flutter notorious among the culprits) while wedged between foreign bodies. Sleep deprived, I did not wish to emerge from my warm, dry sleeping bag, only to put on wet, cold shorts, shirt, socks, and shoes. Besides, how do you do this in a shelter full of people? I hid under my sleeping bag and kept my naked time to an extreme minimum. Once I stepped back out on the trail, my attitude constantly improved. I embraced the suck. In the rain, the woods radiated with beautiful, peaceful energy.

One day, I caught up to Flutter and All's Well, who had left the shelter earlier. The rain poured down. The wind whistled. We stood near the top of a mountain in an open spot. The grass waved in the wind. Excited, I yelled.

"Isn't this awesome? I love this weather! It's great to be out here!"

As water poured off their hats, they looked at me like I needed to be institutionalized. I think I interrupted them in the middle of a rant.

"OK, Right Click…"

I hesitated. Their looks of anger caught me off guard.

"OK. See you down the trail. Enjoy the hike."

All's Well still scowled, but now Flutter looked confused. Then Flutter broke into a smile.

"You're nuts!" He laughed.

I think he appreciated my perspective. He knew from his years in recovery that we have choices in how we view a given situation. We always have the option of bitter or better. On this day, I chose better.

On the fifth day in the Smokies, we faced a short three-mile hike to Clingman's Dome, the highest point on the Appalachian Trail. Luckily, the weather cleared. The observation deck looked like a flying saucer from below. I wound my way up the ramp to the stunning view. The wind astonished me when it knocked me off balance.

48

Wispy clouds streaked by at eye level, carried by the brisk wind. The cold air and heavy wind didn't let us stay on top for too long. We trekked to the parking lot and waited for All's Well's wife. We drove into Gatlinburg and stopped at an outfitter. Several hikers browsed through the store, including a young, athletic man, Cruise Control.

"See that guy?" Flutter whispered to me and pointed.

"Yeah."

"All's Well, and I came to a spot, and we didn't know how we would get up. Cruise Control came along. He asked me what the matter was. I said that we didn't know how to climb up this ledge. Cruise Control said, like this. And he went up in three steps! Then he disappeared and left us there."

Flutter laughed. Cruise Control was 6'6", young and athletic, with huge, powerful legs built for hiking.

"Yeah, it must be nice to be young."

We settled on a spot for a hot meal, then drove to the campground where All's Well parked his RV. We took turns taking showers. Masters Sunday, they allowed me to watch Jordan Spieth cruise to victory. That night I shared a full-sized pullout couch with Flutter. In all my planning, it never occurred to me that I'd spend a night in the same small bed with a very hairy man who snored heavily. Sandy would enjoy hearing about this.

Over breakfast at Waffle House, All's Well told us that he decided on "taking a break." Neither Flutter nor I were surprised. After 199.9 miles, All's Well retired from his thru-hike. He never came back to the trail in 2015. For him (this is my opinion), the level of discomfort became intolerable. I respect that. To finish the hike, one needed to make peace with pain.

We said our goodbyes at the parking lot. We watched him drive off. All's Well and Flutter had been together since Springer Mountain. Flutter and I, now a crew of two, started in overcast skies. The rain came again. It poured for two days continuously. The trail morphed into a stream. Even soaked to the skin, I didn't mind hiking in the rain. Other experiences taught me that rain clouds have silver linings. For example, I like the beach in the rain. It's a great time to fish. Plus, most people disappear indoors. Back in my professional golf days, when it rained, the golf course cleared out and became a prime time to play. Some hikers simply hated the rain.

Flutter one of them.

49

Hiker Lingerie

On the third day, as a crew of two, we started early and arrived at a shelter to eat lunch. We had hiked just under eight miles. I ate and suited back up, ready to go another eight miles to the next shelter, my longest hike to date. I felt good. The rain kept me on the move. I didn't loiter.

But Flutter did not suit up. He was done. Cold, wet, tired, and grouchy, he would not move on. I wanted to go. But bitterly, against my better judgment, I stayed. The shelter started to fill up. Flutter and I claimed our spots, but we'd soon be wedged in like sardines. Everyone stunk with sweaty wetness. Gear hung from every available nail, but none of it dried.

A woman came in mid-afternoon frantic about reserving space in the shelter. She raced more than twenty miles to get to this shelter early; the previous night, there were thirty or more people crammed in a shelter designed for sixteen.

"Yes, there is still plenty of room." Flutter, a self-appointed greeter and shelter keeper, informed her.

"Good. Good."

She impressed me that she did more than twenty miles early in the day. There weren't too many people doing big miles through the Smokies. She claimed a spot on the second level and said some other guys followed her. She stripped down to a thin black t-shirt, short shorts, socks, and camp shoes. Her soaking wet clothes clung to her. Not wearing underwear of any sort, the low temperature (40's) turned her high beams on.

As he did with everyone, Flutter started a conversation with the woman in hiker lingerie, although more enthusiastically and animated than usual. Amused, I listened to Flutter prod her with questions. Her name? Beast Bison. Why? Her spirit animal is a bison, and she hiked like a beast. Soon she shut Flutter down. As the shelter filled up, she hung out in her hiker lingerie. My entertainment consisted of watching other hikers check her out and attempt conversation. She shut them all down efficiently and with frigid precision. I did not try to talk with her.

Beast Bison refused to put on dry, warm clothes. Flutter offered her his puff coat (of course he did). She preferred shivering for a few hours. Her wet garments would dry more quickly on her body. Soon, her traveling male companions showed, tongues hanging out from the exertion of trying to keep up with her for twenty-plus miles. Soon, their tongues hung out for other reasons. They, too, did their best to coddle her. She didn't have any of it. The queen ordered her loyal servants to do her bidding. Beast Bison looked down her nose at everyone. If there's such a thing as hiker trash,

50

maybe she thought of herself as hiker royalty? Eventually, Beast Bison determined her clothes were dry enough to change into warmer gear under cover of her sleeping bag. She left very early in the morning, long before I woke up.

In the Smokies, people raced to get to the next campsite so they could first pick a tent site or a prime location in the shelter. People got up before the sun, ate no breakfast, and packed up quickly and on the trail just as the sky started to lighten. They hiked, looking over their shoulder—too much pressure for me. If I earned a less desirable spot to sleep, no big deal. Flutter did not share the same schedule as me. He was an early morning hiker, early into camp kind of guy. Our two patterns would clash later.

Flutter and I hiked out of the Smokies and spent a night at the Standing Bear, my second night in a hostel. It would be my last. I didn't have a horrible night; I just wasn't a fan of the partying. People smoked weed and drank alcohol. My recovery depends on complete abstinence from alcohol and other drugs. But I'm OK with other people imbibing. A line I stole from somewhere goes like this,

"I don't have a problem with alcohol, only if I drink it."

It was hard to sleep with a lot of smoking and drinking. When it quieted down, snoring surfaced. Some talked in their sleep. Others coughed and sneezed. Some got up to pee and turned the lights on. They moaned and groaned. They got up early and made a commotion while they packed. I found so many people in one spot unappealing. I wished I had a crew who thought like me. I wondered about Rock Steady, Paradox, and Stix.

I sat in Standing Bear's kitchen after a restless night. I had just finished my meal when Beast Bison sat at the table next to me. Her Highness barely acknowledged my presence. She sat down with postcards and began writing.

"That's unusual."

"What is?" Beast Bison asked.

"You're writing handwritten notes. Not too many people do that anymore. I'm sure they'll be appreciated."

"Thank you."

She replied icily. She looked down at her postcard and continued writing. She effectively shut me down, just like all the others. I would not run into Beast Bison again. She probably finished weeks and weeks ahead of me.

Perfectly Flat

Snowbird Mountain proved to be a formidable climb. I moved ahead of Flutter. I ran into a North Carolina trail maintenance crew on the way up. I pictured myself volunteering for some trail maintenance in the future. One guy offered some conversation. He said,

"North Carolina is perfectly flat." He paused. He waited for a reaction.

"That's bullshit." I took the bait.

Deadpan, he replied. "Yep, it's 50% up and 50% down, perfectly flat."

I laughed. Having just reviewed the AT Guide, I knew a long uphill lay ahead. I asked, "What's the trail like up ahead?".

"Let's put it this way; the easiest part is behind you."

I laughed again. I believed him. Right; the easiest part was behind me. I reflected on that comment many times, repeated it to others, and realized those words harbored some profound wisdom. Yet, the opposite is also true.

"The hardest part is behind you."

I flipped these ideas. I tossed them around in my head. I thought about expectations. What I thought of the trail behind me set my expectations of the trail ahead of me. The trail never changed; it is what it is. My attitude constantly changed, however. Eventually, I accepted the trail and took it one step at a time. I didn't always do this well, as you'll read about later.

A few months later, Just Doug shared a beautiful quote from Warren Doyle, a trail legend I'd meet and talk with in New Hampshire.

"Don't fight the trail. You have to flow with it. Time, distance, terrain, weather, and the Trail itself cannot be changed. You have to change. Don't waste any of your energy complaining over things you have no control over. Instead, look to yourself and adapt your mind, heart, body and soul to the Trail."

Finally, out of the restrictions in the Smokies, I enjoyed the freedom to camp where I wanted. I heard one smaller shelter in the Smokies welcomed thirty-seven people on one particularly stormy night. I also heard stories of people being rejected when they hiked to one with the claim that "there's no room." It sucked to walk a long way over rough terrain and terrible conditions, reach your home for the night, and be rejected. I am not a fan of selfishness. No one had the right or power to say who could stay and who couldn't.

I might not have liked the rules, but I respected them. Many hikers felt they were above the rules, or the restrictions didn't apply, and they were entitled to do whatever they wanted. For example, hikers brazenly brought their dogs into the Great Smoky National Park, where no dogs were allowed. One hiker, Mama Moab, claimed her dog was a service dog. She trained her dog to detect anaphylactic shock. People questioned whether or not that was true. Other hikers complained loud and long about how the rules sucked and that they infringed on their right to freedom.

If you don't like the rules, hike somewhere else.

Gorilla Rock

After ten miles, Flutter and I looked for a place to camp. We found a beautiful flat area near a large rock that looked eerily like a gorilla head. That evening, I texted co-workers who hosted our CCAR Annual Volunteer Recognition Dinner. Suddenly, distant gunshots interrupted my text messaging. I became nervous as the shots got closer.

"Hey Flutter, think we should do something?" I called to Flutter in his tent.

I thought we might move or have a plan if they came closer. Somehow, he thought this question ridiculous, so he ridiculed me from his enclave.

"What am I supposed to do? I have a little knife I could fight them off with."

"Do you think we should move?" We were camped near an old forest road. More ridicule followed.

"We could move near that big rock… like I wanted to before and hide there."

Jeez. I shut up. The gunshots faded away. But this story would not. Whenever we got into camp, and with others present, the ex-Marine would tell the story of how I asked about the gunshots. Flutter touted an arsenal of stories, most designed to highlight his expertise or another person's incompetency. Now on the list of the latter, it stung every time. But I didn't say anything. I should have; that's on me. I slowly started to separate from him mentally and emotionally. I separated from him physically as much as I could too. During the day, I'd hike ahead or let him get ahead.

One day, out in front of me, he arrived first at some incredible trail magic on the other side of Max Patch. A large group of thru-hikers from the previous year provided hot food, snacks, beer, soda, and juices. I feasted. As I sat in a camp chair, I listened to a story. One hiker came to the trail magic station, looked at all the drinks, and complained.

"Why isn't there any wine?"

In response to this "complaint," a young man volunteered to get some. He hiked a couple of miles back to his car, drove several miles more, purchased wine, and carried the wine back to her. The story shocked me. Talk about entitlement. Talk about arrogance. Talk about a complete lack of gratitude and respect. I started to understand why the thru-hiker reputation is often tarnished.

Hiker Trash

I first saw the term "hiker trash" when I prepped for the Appalachian Trail. It appeared in many accounts written by thru-hikers. I heard it many, many times on the trail. Some hikers used it with great affection and great pride. I winced any time anyone used it. I think it's rotten. I refused to say it or acknowledge it. I understand it's a term of endearment for some. Not for me. Yeah, my body stunk, and my clothes were discolored with grime. But I never considered myself trash. I never thought of other hikers as trash. Trash implies an unwanted, useless item destined for discard and abandonment. Trash is usually carted away and dumped with other trash. At best, trash may be recycled and, at worst, incinerated. I don't see that as the fate of thru-hikers; no life is a throwaway.

What is the perception of the non-hiking world when it sees the term "hiker trash"? It can't be favorable. Or honorable.

Additionally, trash possesses little power, whereas hikers hold tremendous personal power. The people I met who completed the thru-hike are worthy of incredible respect and honor, not to be called trash.

That's my feeble attempt to rid the hiking world of this derogatory term.

After the Max Patch trail magic experience, fully fueled, Flutter and I pushed on. After more than eleven miles, around 4:30, Flutter got anxious to find camp. His internal alarm sounded; time to stop. I just hit my stride. We hiked on.

"What about here?" Flutter pointed to a spot not worth consideration.

Ten minutes later, "What about here?" He pointed at a rocky area.

"No."

"What about here?" He pointed to an area overgrown and filled with fallen trees.

"Seriously? Come on. Let's keep going. There will be better places."

"You don't know that."

I did know that. Five minutes later, he asked again. "What about here?"

I looked at the worst one yet. Finally, I stopped dead in my tracks. Irritation dripped from every word.

54

"Look, if you want to camp here, go ahead. You can meet me in the morning. You are up way before me anyway."

I remained calm.

"No. We can keep going," He said, obviously frustrated.

We crossed a road and headed up a hill a few minutes later. Flutter groaned. He hated uphill.

"Right Click, maybe we could camp back down there."

"No. I'm not going back."

At the top, I found a flat spot with a used fire ring in a small grove of pines off the trail about thirty yards—stealth camping at its finest. If I were on my own, I would have hiked a couple more hours, but I took one for the "team." Flutter's mood improved once he pitched his tent and began eating. I didn't talk much but responded to him politely. Inwardly, I seethed. Still early for me, I crawled into my tent, my mood darker than outside.

Hot Springs

Ironically, with my mood simmering, we hiked into Hot Springs. I liked Hot Springs. The sidewalks donned AT blazes proudly. Scheduled to meet a fellow man in recovery and take a few opportunities to talk recovery and CCAR, Flutter and I stopped in a restaurant, ate a big breakfast, and waited for Richie T.

I faced an awkward moment. What do I do with Flutter? I could tell by his mannerisms that he expected to go along. Realizing his vulnerability and sensing he did not want to be left on his own appealed to my natural soft spot. I called and talked with Richie, so Flutter spent the next two days with me off the trail. We stayed in a beautiful home. I conveyed the message to a couple of addiction treatment providers and met the Chief of Police in a small North Carolina town. Flutter worked through some awkward moments but learned a few things about what I do in the recovery field. Grateful for the time off trail, I expressed my gratitude to Richie as he drove us back to Hot Springs.

Once in town, I communicated via text with Rock Steady. She was not in Hot Springs yet. I didn't know how that happened. When did I pass her? But she'd be in Hot Springs that day. I looked forward to that. So, instead of getting back on the trail immediately, I stalled. I told Flutter I wanted to see Rock Steady hoping he'd move on. But he stayed. We hung out in town. We ate at the same restaurant. We got our pictures taken for the Hiker Yearbook. I talked with many other hikers.

55

I stopped in the local outfitter to inquire about a rubber seal for my Sawyer water filter; mine wore out. I wanted to buy a new one. Instead, when I asked about a new seal, I got lectured. According to the guy behind the counter, my seal needed replacement because I screwed the filter down too tightly.

"OK."

"Look, Sawyer asked me to tell everyone."

OK, but did you have to be a dick about it? I didn't say that, but I certainly thought it. Then he gave me one, no charge. Maybe because Sawyer gave them out for free, he made customers pay in other ways. After my encounter with the outfitter, I received a text from Rock Steady. She had just arrived at the hostel at the other end of town. I left Flutter and walked down to see her. I stepped into the hostel and called for her.

"Down here!" I heard the familiar voice.

I made my way down the hall and found her. She had just put her pack down in her room. She had one shoe off. Her pants were unzipped (she had hiking shorts underneath). We picked up right where we left off and chatted excitedly. As we talked, Baltimore Jack showed up and immediately displayed a keen interest in Rock Steady that she would subsequently deny. Ignoring the subtle hints, Baltimore Jack showed no interest in leaving. His eyes drifted to her unzipped pants. After several awkward minutes, he left. I kidded her about her new admirer.

"You're full of shit, Right Click." It was not unkind.

I found out later that Baltimore Jack cooked her breakfast the following day. From what I gathered, she quickly understood his intentions better.

Rock Steady, happily married, often talked and for long periods with her husband in Korea, readily apparent they were very, very close and heartwarming to witness. During their fourteen years of marriage, they were together only about half the time (seven years). She spent time in other countries with her husband when the Army allowed her. This year, after his deployment ended, he joined her in New England, adopted the trail name "Latch," and finished the trail together. Unfortunately, I never met him.

Sandy and I adapted to my "deployment." In the evening, I looked forward to our conversations. With a lot of my burden shed, I delighted in our talks about "mundane" things, things we used to talk about but hadn't for a long time. Before the trail, our conversations usually centered on two topics; our children or urgent issues that needed to be addressed. Naturally, defenses surfaced. The trail stripped all of them away. After our conversations ended, I felt refreshed, loved, and hopeful. Sandy supported me like no other.

Rock Steady spent the night in Hot Springs. Flutter, and I eventually moved on. Rock Steady indicated she'd catch up. We hiked for a couple of short days. Now my other knee, my left knee, acted up and hit me with sharp, intense jolts of pain. I could have walked through it, but I used it as an excuse to stop and wait for her. I wanted company besides Flutter. I stopped at Spring Mountain Shelter after just four point four miles. Flutter did not say much as we set up early. He talked with other hikers while I kept watching the trail.

Late in the afternoon, Rock Steady and Stix emerged from the woods. Thrilled to see them both, I showed them our area near the shelter. They set up, and we ate a meal together. We shared several stories. The night turned cold and windy, but I slept comfortably.

Condiment Rules (1991)

Reenergized and enthused by new hiking companions, I willingly walked through the left knee pain. Flutter, Rock Steady, and I stopped at Mom's, a rundown, ramshackle establishment. True to her style, Stix traveled slowly and followed way behind. I ordered two hot dogs. Moms did not have ketchup available for hot dogs, a policy I fully supported. The husband, gone to purchase more food, did not allow ketchup. Mom told us all about this. He assured that his establishment aligned with the Federal Food and Drug Administration Condiment Rules, last revised in 1991. Excerpts from the code are reprinted here with permission.

> Article 28A: 102-3d: Allowable condiments on hot dogs include mustard, relish, onions, mayo, and chili. Ketchup (catsup) is not allowed. Use of ketchup on a hot dog is strictly prohibited and may be punishable by a fine and/or imprisonment.

> Article 28A:102-3e: All condiments are allowed on hamburgers.

It surprised me that no one I talked to had heard of the Condiment Rules, never mind, followed them. In my house, the rules are common knowledge. Other hikers found the code quite contentious. Unfortunately, I debated many times with several individuals on the merits of the Condiment Rules. Many argued and even violated the code by insisting that ketchup is allowable. For example, Rock Steady flaunted this belief in public and brazenly smothered her hot dog with the banned substance. To this day, I remain appalled.

I'm grateful I consumed extra nourishment at Moms. We planned a big day, over fifteen miles, to the Jerry Cabin Shelter. Looking at the guide, the trail went by places with the ominous names of Whiterock Cliff and Blackstack Cliffs. The AT Guide had this note:

Bearwallow Gap, Jerry Miller Trail to east, Firescald bypass to west reconnects with AT 1.5 miles north. AT between bypass points is rocky and strenuous.

The previous night, we had read the note and wondered about it. What did it mean?

We found out.

When the AT Guide says *rocky and strenuous*, it means *ridiculously rocky and strenuous*. I slowed way down. Flutter and Rock Steady accompanied me. I scrambled up and down steep rock faces in the most challenging stretch. For the first time, I used my hands to pull myself up and let myself down. Rugged hiking and spectacular views inspired me to pen this note in my AT Guide, "Best day on AT so far."

During this segment, the trail traversed a high ridge. I loved it, but my feet did not. I had no idea why my feet started screaming in pain. I do now. My boots "broke" on the rough terrain. They finally failed with more than five hundred miles on my Merrell Moab Ventilators soles. I could feel every small rock and stick with every step. My toes blistered again. I eventually replaced them in Damascus but endured another hundred miles of discomfort. From that point forward, I knew exactly when my boots failed, and I'd look to replace them immediately.

Nurse

I covered more than thirty miles in two days. I had planned on accumulating longer mile totals each day. Now, I hit double digits regularly. I thoroughly enjoyed hiking with Flutter, Rock Steady, and Stix. The two ladies soothed my uneasy relationship with Flutter.

Stix carried much weight in her pack. She powered through several injuries. She needed her great sense of humor because she hiked slowly and fell more than usual. Stix carried a small single-person tent. When we packed up in the morning, the rest of us got our gear together from outside our tent. Flutter stacked up all his components – tent, pad, sleeping bag, clothes sack, etc., then very precisely loaded his pack. He'd eat quickly and be ready to go long before anyone else. Stix didn't make an appearance until she was prepared to go. She emerged from her tent fully dressed,

58

packed, and the last thing she did was stuff her tent in her pack, a good process, particularly during morning rain.

On my thirty-seventh day on the AT, I set my sights on Hogback Ridge Shelter. During the day, the crew gradually spaced apart as usual. We "walked alone together" and knew we'd meet up at breaks or at the final destination for the day. I hiked all day in high heat and humidity. With two miles left to the shelter, my vision blurred, then doubled. I attributed it to exertion, fatigue, and dehydration. But it still made me nervous. It made walking problematic, mainly down grades. I'd learn to cope with double vision. It became a constant companion as my hike progressed.

Lost in my thoughts, a hiker came up behind me. Not an unusual occurrence, I let him pass.

"Hi, I'm Nurse." He offered as he passed.

"I'm Right Click. Good to meet you."

"Where you from?"

"Connecticut."

"Really? Where in Connecticut?"

"Manchester."

"What? Me too! What high school?"

"Manchester High School."

"No way. What year?"

I'm a proud member of the class of '77."

"WHAT? Me too!" He stopped and turned around. I stopped too. As we eyeballed each other, we searched our memory banks. We had no recollection of each other. We both thought the same thing.

"What are the chances of meeting someone from your high school graduating class while thru-hiking the Appalachian Trail?"

My conversation with Nurse took my mind off my medical condition on the way to the shelter. We talked about our hometown, the people we knew, the neighborhoods we grew up in, and what we were doing now. Nurse traveled ultra-light with minimal food and gear. He could cover some ground. Once at the shelter, we took some pics together to commemorate the moment. Flutter made his way in, then Rock Steady, but Stix did not show.

Long after dark, settled in my tent, Stix came into camp. Stix was often the caboose of our 4-person crew, but something must have happened for her to be so far behind. It did. In the middle of the day, her nose started to bleed badly, and she

59

couldn't get it to stop. When it finally did, she rested for a while, putting her behind us by 2-3 hours.

Being a dad, I dealt continually with my natural protective tendencies. Stix (and Paradox) were my trail daughters. I balanced my tendency to jump in and fix something by allowing them to "hike their own hike." When Stix came in, I struggled not to jump out of my tent to help her set up and ensure she was OK. She set up right next to me and assured me she was okay. She was tough! I brought her some water if she needed it.

"Thank you, Right Click."

It didn't help that the following day brought heavy rain; packing in the downpour was not fun, a real test of your attitude. Stix was still sound asleep by the time I started down the trail, so I woke her and let her know we were moving ahead.

"OK. I'll catch you."

I did not share my doubts. The weather improved, and the spectacular view encouraged me when I climbed Big Bald. I stood in awe of my surroundings. We hung out there for an hour and enjoyed the warm spring sunshine. Stix made it to the view, settled in, and conversed easily with everyone. One guy paid particularly close attention to her; Stix was not appreciative. However, in an idyllic setting and day, I heard someone say,

"It's not about the miles; it's about the smiles."

I appreciated that sentiment. I'd say it often, but always with the awareness that I wouldn't finish the hike if I didn't do the miles.

Wrong Way Again

I took a break at a shelter late in the afternoon with Rock Steady and Flutter. Two section hikers told us they planned to stay the night there. Their gear dried in the sun and hung from various tree branches and bushes. The previous night's rain left all our gear damp. I pulled some of my gear out and laid it out. Flutter, Rock Steady, and I discussed the pros and cons of staying put.

"It's early," I said.

"But it's a nice spot, and I'm tired. We've gone pretty far today." Flutter chimed in. His response was expected.

"Let's keep going." Rock Steady wanted to keep moving. Not surprisingly, daily mileage goals motivated her. She also liked to use most of the daylight.

Once again, I butted up against competing perspectives and desires. This happened consistently. Sometimes, I got my way. Sometimes, I capitulated. Many

60

times, my selfishness ruled my action. Way more opinionated than I liked, I could be pretty difficult. The spoiled brat in me jumped up and down and shouted until I got my way. If I didn't get it, I pouted. Have you ever seen a fifty-five-year-old man pout? Not pretty.

This particular evening, I had already unpacked my stuff, so I sat on the fence. I could stay, or I could go.

"Should I stay, or should I go now? Should I stay, or should I go now? If I stay, it could be trouble. If I go, it could be double." I sang the song out loud; the day-hikers just looked at me.

Flutter wanted to stay. Rock Steady would move whether we went with her or not. She would hike her hike. Flutter decided to follow her. His reluctance showed as he moped down the approach trail to the shelter. He pouted pretty well too. Cool with the decision to continue, I told them I'd pack up and meet them at a campsite a few miles up the trail. I got all my gear together, checked the area one last time, and made my way down the approach trail back to the AT. I turned left. I walked for several minutes. A sour feeling germinated in my gut. Something was not right. I hiked quickly and knew I should have caught Rock Steady.

"Have I been here before?" I asked myself.

I remembered I had come down off Big Bald into the shelter. I kept walking. The idea that I may be going south instead of north grew. Anxiety sprouted. I spied a big rock with a makeshift campsite.

"Shit. Oh, SHIT!"

I knew for sure. I got angry. I turned around and headed in the correct direction. I traveled more than half a mile the wrong way. Again. I felt sick. Several minutes later, I passed the shelter. Everything looked familiar, the day hikers still there. I could see them through the underbrush. I hoped they didn't see me. I beat myself up for making such a stupid, careless, embarrassing error; Flutter and Rock Steady far ahead of me now.

"Damn it!" I vowed never to do that again.

"Where were you?" Rock Steady asked when I finally got to the site.

"I went the wrong way out of the shelter."

They sensed my humiliation. To their credit, they didn't laugh too long or too loud. Stix never made it to this campsite. We hoped she was ok.

Erwin

Stix caught us at a break the next day. She stayed at the shelter where I took the wrong turn. We hoped to make it to town today to resupply and launder our clothes. After more than thirteen miles, I arrived in Erwin. Sometimes, I ended up in a town and said, "What the heck?" Erwin, Tennessee one of those towns for me.

Flutter and I shared a room at the Super 8. Rock Steady and Stix shared another. AWOL's guide indicated a laundry on-premise. The owner (not fond of thru-hikers) said he took the washing machine out after one day. It got used so much that it broke. It seemed to be a moneymaker if it generated that much business. But what do I know?

That evening, while I waited in the lobby for the crew to show up for dinner, a very drunk Spider came in. He shouted obscenities, cursed out the owners, and raged in general. His buddy, equally drunk, dragged him back to their room. Several hikers I came in contact with had severe alcohol problems. To my utter disbelief, a couple of female trail "angels" took care of these guys. They gave them rides. They let them stay in their homes. I heard stories of smashed cars, violent puking episodes, and dangerous drunken treks. They told stories with great gusto and bawdy laughter. To me, they were not funny. I often shuddered. In one yarn described with welcomed enthusiasm, this hiker stole someone's car, returned it to the house (where they were guests) with a smashed fender, and did not have any recollection about how it happened. The people listening laughed uproariously. I did not. No wonder hostel and hotel owners are fed up with hikers. Like anything else, a small percentage of the hiking population ruins the reputations of all other hikers. The most likely to call themselves "hiker trash" are the ones most likely to be loud, rude, disrespectful, and more prone to damage other peoples' property.

Blackouts frighten me today. That wasn't always the case, however. I endured my share. I'm not proud of them. And I certainly don't think of them as funny. They are extremely dangerous. I don't mean to sound like a prohibitionist. I'm not. I am in recovery and lived through my share of treacherous escapades. I consider myself blessed to be alive. I know that, just for today, I cannot safely consume alcohol, so I have chosen not to consume any since 1987.

My crew showed up, and we left the hotel before the drunken AT Holes caused more of a scene. Sunday night, four of us headed to a barbeque place across town. My mouth watered. Just before we got to the train tracks, the signal lit up. We waited fifteen minutes for the train to pass. We walked another fifteen minutes to find the barbeque place closed on Sundays. What? In Erwin, everything is closed on Sundays.

62

We hung our heads and headed back to the hotel. We had passed a McDonald's and a Huddle House on the way to the closed barbeque.

By now, famished and not appreciative of all the walking in town, we approached the railroad tracks again.

"Oh no, another train."

But this one stopped on the track, blocked the road, and started moving back and forth slowly. The couplings caught and caused a horrific metallic bang that drove me to duck and cringe every time. I'm not a fan of loud noises. My companions thought that quite humorous. I did not. We could see our restaurants just seventy-five yards away. I contemplated a dash between the cars and over the couplings, but I had no idea if this was safe or legal. We waited forty-five minutes. Finally, the train moved, and we sprinted to the Huddle House. I ordered three meals and ate them all.

The following day, some more discord hit our lovely traveling foursome. The Super 8 provided a continental breakfast of cereal, waffles, and muffins. I craved eggs. I let the other three know I'd meet them in the lobby if they were interested in a Huddle House breakfast. I stepped into the lobby, and Rock Steady sat eating her breakfast. Not a big breakfast eater, she declined the Huddle House. Earlier, Flutter gave me the impression that he wanted to go to the Huddle House, but he changed his mind in the lobby.

"We should eat here. It's free." Free a crucial factor for Flutter.

"No. I don't want this. I want eggs. I'm going to get hot food. Eat here. I'm a big boy. I can go by myself."

My decision upset Flutter. He did not understand why I would go against group consensus. He particularly didn't understand why I would choose to pay for food with free food readily available. His attitude became condescending. I do not respond well to condescension. Rock Steady watched with an interested smirk. This entertained her. As far as she was concerned, if I wanted to eat breakfast at the Huddle House, go for it. She certainly didn't take it personally—no big deal. As for Stix, she still slept.

I stomped out of the hotel, aggravated. I walked a few yards to the restaurant. I consumed a big, wonderful, protein and calorie-laden feast. The three of them came by as I finished up. We headed into town to do laundry. The tension between Flutter and me mounted. I could feel it in the strained conversation.

I'm sure he could too.

In the grand scheme of life, or if I were back in my everyday life, this interaction would carry little or no importance. I pondered why my relationship with Flutter affected me profoundly and adversely. I didn't have an answer, except maybe my walls were lowering, and I was reacting to heightened vulnerability.

The trail made me vulnerable. I'd later realize what a fantastic gift this was.

Chip Crosses the Line

I wonder why I attract certain types of people; true my entire life. I befriend the unpopular, the weird, and the strange. Or they befriend me. Maybe I fit that mold too. Chip personified this type of character. The first I met him, I concocted a fictitious, creepy background story. It went something like this. He lived in a rundown cabin on an isolated country lot with his mother. A shed in the back concealed a trapdoor on the floor… Let your imagination run from there.

The real story about Chip intrigued me too. The report came from his lips, so I took it with a grain of salt. A retired community college teacher, his social skills could, at best, be described as awkward and, at worst, offensive. I never figured out exactly what was wrong with the guy. The trail name I suggested for him was Phineas J. Whoopee, after the professor from the Tennessee Tuxedo cartoon. However, it didn't stick, and Chip didn't like it because Professor Whoopee was smart. Chip was not.

Besides the other difficulties I experienced while I hiked with him, Chip had trouble with his pack all the time with no idea how to use the straps. As time went on, his diet deteriorated. He ate at irregular intervals. He carried an odd assortment of foods. He lost too much weight too quickly. Several million Chip brain cells perished along the trail.

"Chip, you need nutrition," I said to him often. Other hikers said it to him too.

This became a common saying when anyone said something stupid. Over my 189 days, it became apparent that I often needed nutrition. Not exempt from saying some pretty senseless things, one day, during a car ride into a town, I declared,

"I want bacons and egg."

To combat the cold, Chip wore a pretty feminine purple puff coat. He wore that coat when we took photos at the GA-NC border. With his head wrapped in a bandanna, he resembled an elderly woman.

Chip talked with anyone and everyone. He offended many of them. He'd do stupid stuff, too, when he picked up Rock Steady's water and drank it. Didn't ask. Didn't say anything. He took a giant slug out of her water bottle and put it down like it was the most natural thing in the world. She fumed. He violated an unspoken code. Crossed the line.

64

He could be hilarious too. Sometimes intentionally, sometimes not. He told a story of how he fell off the side of the trail. He landed on his back. His huge pack held him in the bushes like a turtle flipped on its back. It took him nearly an hour to struggle out of his pack, scramble up the hill and get back on the trail. Another time he fell and crunched his head on a rock. He bled for a while. On another night, he got drunk and passed out on the side of the trail, wrapped in his purple puff coat. People walked by and poked him to see if he was alive.

We made our way out of Erwin, and a couple of nights later, many hikers gathered around a fire; our tents were scattered around the shelter. Several others chose to sleep in the shelter. I joined the group and listened to stories. I shared that I was excited to have my eighteen-year-old daughter join me in a few days. She had just finished her first year of college and wanted to accompany me for a few weeks. The people agreed this was very cool. I did too. Then Chip, with a straight face, asked,

"What tent is she going to sleep in? Yours or mine?"

A pall fell upon the group. Jaws dropped. People tensed for a fight. Was he this clueless? Or was he genuinely sinister? Either notion caused me to smolder. I replied with a calm that terrified even me.

"She will have her own tent, and it won't be anywhere near you." I got up and walked away.

I found out that before his community college teaching career, he held positions at two different high schools, but the schools "removed" him because of inappropriate behavior. He shared this with several of us. Yet he lasted twenty-seven years in a community college. He taught electrical engineering (or something like that) but couldn't operate his phone. I am usually a pretty forgiving man. I believe in redemption. In this case, I had no forgiveness and no respect. In my mind, he crossed the line. I couldn't let him back.

I encountered Chip occasionally from then on, but I kept my distance. He openly yellow-blazed (taking a car to skip sections of the trail), a practice commonly frowned upon by most thru-hikers. To my knowledge, he hiked *most* of the way to Mount Greylock in Massachusetts and called it quits.

It helped to hike with people with similar attitudes as mine. I preferred to take my time in the morning and walk later into the evening. I'm not a night hiker, but I don't mind setting up as the sun goes down. I also found out I preferred to camp in excellent spots. How do I define a nice location? In the summer, I liked to be up high for more chance of a cooling breeze. A view is nice but not necessary. The ideal site was flat, preferably with no large roots or rocks. My skill progressed to where I mastered setting up on sketchy sites. I made it work as long as I found a small flat place to lie down. My preferred surfaces, in order, were pine needles, then dirt, then grass, and finally leaves. Gravel, rock, and wood platforms sucked; I did my best to avoid them. In Maine, we found campsite heaven – soft pine needles under pine trees next to water. I knew what I liked because I stayed in places I didn't.

One afternoon, Flutter grumbled (again) about stopping for the night. He referenced the Appalachian Trail Conservancy guide, Rock Steady, and I used the AT Guide. As mentioned earlier, Rock Steady downloaded the Guthook app. In all our guides, no camping is denoted for several miles. We started looking for a stealth site: easily recognizable with nice flat worn areas and stone fire rings. Other times I just threw down where I could. We came across an old fire road. I didn't like it, but I said, "OK."

I tried to tap titanium stakes into the gravel surface—what a pain in the ass. My tent did stand freely with trekking poles, but the poles I carried did not fit; my tent required stakes. I blew up my Therm-a-Rest NeoAir XTherm sleeping pad. Forty-one breaths later, I laid on it and did not feel any gravel, sticks, roots, or acorns under—my mattress, my one luxury item well worth it.

Located in a nondescript section of woods, this site lacked imagination. We could have done better. I wondered about a nearby telephone pole with a street lamp. I wondered if it would click on. It did not.

However, all campsites *looked* precisely the same inside my buttoned-up Tarptent Double Rainbow. But they all *felt* different. Again, if I were alone, I would have gone on. Again, I compromised for the sake of the group. However, I realized I needed the group more than they needed me.

Overmountain Storm

On the way to Overmountain Shelter, Paradox caught up with us. She spent a few days with her husband. I still didn't know her well. Five of us ate lunch at the highest shelter on the trail, Roan High Knob Shelter. Paradox set up her camera and took one of my favorite pictures of the five of us through a remote from her phone. When we climbed up, the temperature hovered in the sixties. When we finished lunch, a cold biting wind hit the mountain and brought snow flurries. As we hiked away, massive black clouds, lightning flashes, and thunder rumbles accompanied us. Fortunately, the wet weather stayed away. When we arrived at Overmountain Shelter, a well-known shelter converted from an enormous barn, I donned most of my layers. It had turned chilly.

I checked out the barn. It didn't look too inviting to me. The group set up inside. I eyed the large grass field out in front with an incredible view.

"I think I'm going to set up out there. This doesn't look too comfortable for me."

"Why would you do that, Right Click? It's so much easier to set up in here."

Flutter gave me his unsolicited opinion. More condescension dripped from his comment. Paradox gave me a look that I interpreted as,

"I agree with you, but I'm resigned to staying here."

"Probably, but I think it will be quieter out there." Flutter didn't argue with that.

One other tent occupied the field. Thirty-five to forty hikers spread out on the lower and upper levels inside the barn. My companions set up on the upper level. As I trudged back outside, several emotions welled up. One I identified as fear. I ventured out, basically alone and unsure of my decision. Another emotion was excitement; this was an excellent place to camp with an incredible view. I also experienced a touch of abandonment.

"Why didn't they come out here with me?"

I pushed those away and dove into determination. I tried to convince myself.

"I know what's best for me."

I set my tent one hundred yards from the barn. I posted pics on Instagram, called Sandy, turned off the lights, and snuggled in.

Later, I woke to the weather thrashing my tent. The storm we skirted earlier in the day roared in and carried cold, wind, and ice. The wind whistled underneath the vestibule. I unstaked them, drew them in close, and tried to button up the tent as best I could to be warmer inside. This failed miserably. The wind sent the sides a-flapping so loudly it made sleep impossible. I lay in my bag and listened to the wind howl and the sleet batter the tent's walls. I felt anxiety rise.

"What do I do now? Do I pack up and run for the shelter of the barn? Could I even pack up without getting soaked and hypothermic? Once I got to the barn, how would I navigate through all those people in the pitch dark?"

I grumbled to myself. Multiple options ping-ponged around in my head. Finally, I ventured out into the tempest to restake the tent as designed. The wind raged. What a wild night! A ring of ice about two inches deep piled up around my tent. I quickly pulled the vestibules taut, staked them down, and scurried back inside. The wind still whistled underneath, but the flapping stopped. I could situate myself to tolerate the wind. I dozed off with the noise dramatically reduced and snug in my cozy down bag.

The storm subsided the following day. I packed up. Sheepishly I made my way to the barn to eat breakfast with the crew. I expected they had a much better night than I did. Wrong. None of them slept well. They managed short naps. The cold wind blasted through the wide cracks in the walls. The frigid air assailed them through the floor. They attempted to sleep in a windy refrigerator, much more miserable than I. I didn't see that coming. During the night, I wasn't miserable; my tent was the better choice (even with the struggles). Right then and there, a glimmer of trust flickered. Quiet confidence replaced the deep-seated doubt. This confidence differed from arrogance. This confidence rose from experience, not knowledge. After we shared stories, did I detect a slight nod of approval from Paradox?

Of course, Flutter told another story. According to him, he saved a day-hiker from hypothermia. This guy wore cotton clothes (including blue jeans) that got wet on the trek to the shelter. He brought a very light sleeping bag. Last year, they came on the same weekend with the warm weather. This guy woke up shivering desperately. Flutter wrapped him in some of his gear. Many other people chipped in to keep him warm enough to survive the night. It wouldn't be the first time I witnessed thru-hikers sharing their expertise and gear with others. The hiking community took care of one another.

I cherished this level of care.

MAY

Humping over Hump Mountain

We started that morning in damp, drizzly, cool conditions. The crew stretched out as we headed up Hump Mountain. I wondered how mountains got their names. Hump Mountain? My mind drifted to strange spaces. The higher we climbed, the wilder the weather was. Soon, I could barely see through the wind, ice, and fog. Icicles formed perpendicular to the ground. They speared off plants and rocks. I pulled off my gloves, got my iPhone, and took pictures and videos. My fingers numbed immediately. I attempted to get the phone back in a plastic Ziplock and missed. I watched the phone drop, screen first, onto a sharp rock, to my horror. It made a sickening sound when it hit. I stood there for several seconds and just looked at the phone.

"Oh no."

I reached down slowly, picked the phone up, and pressed the button. It worked. There was a ding in the Otter Box smack dab in the middle of the screen, but the phone still worked! I love products that work the way they are supposed to. Consider me a fan of Otter Box; if I had extra cash, I'd buy stock.

The AT Guide said that "NoBo (Northbound) have several false summits" up Hump Mountain. It certainly did. In these conditions, I couldn't see very far ahead. I kept on the move. Flutter, Rock Steady, and I stayed pretty close together. Stix fell behind. Paradox, as became her trademark, stayed behind in camp and took her time. She liked to see how big a lead she could give us and still catch us.

When conditions got "bad," I rose to the occasion. I didn't mind hiking in them. Others complained a lot. Hey, if John Muir climbed a 300-foot tree in a raging storm, I could walk a few miles. I made it to the actual summit, one step at a time. It took a lot longer than expected. The trail got rougher on the way down. On the descent, the weather slowly improved. I passed some young day hikers in shorts and t-shirts on their way up.

"Do you have any other clothes?"

"No. Why?"

"It's all ice, wind, and rain up there."

"We'll be fine."

"OK." Off they went climbing Hump Mountain. Oh, to be young and dumb again.

Wet rocks, roots, and mud slowed me down, but I hit the North Carolina – Tennessee border, another state down. Three of us arrived about the same time, the weather better. We chatted with trail maintenance guys. Paradox showed up grinning. She loved being out on the trail. She bore awful news, though; Stix fell and twisted her ankle. We waited for her at the sign. She finally limped in, eyes filled with pain and tears. We took the obligatory group picture at the state line sign. We divvied up her stuff into our packs and lightened her load considerably. She was reluctantly grateful. Again, another example of how a trail family cared unconditionally for one another. We hiked three more miles to the road, called for a ride, and ducked into the Roan Mountain Bed & Breakfast.

I contemplated the drastic shift in my environment over a short period. Just a few hours earlier, cold, wet, dirty, and stinky with ice clutched to my beard. Now warm, dry, clean, and headed to a barbeque joint to feast. This often happened on the trail.

Rock Steady and Paradox did not eat with us at the BBQ joint; instead, they went to a quaint gourmet pizza place. The crew began to splinter. I didn't like it. I wanted us to stay together. However, Rock Steady and Paradox set a precedent. They hiked their own hike. Part of me respected their resolve, but mostly my heart ached. I did my best not to let them see the latter. I surprised myself with how much I cared for the two of them and how much I enjoyed their company.

The following day, we prepared for a long day, about fifteen miles to a campsite. Warm sunshine, blue skies, and lush green hills made for a beautiful hike. I stopped for a break and showed Flutter how big my pants had become. I lost several inches from my gut. With plenty to lose, the fat melted off my body. Amused, Flutter offered to take a pic. He did.

Shortly after that, I rested at the four-hundred-mile mark next to a wide, shallow stream that meandered over gravel, a peaceful place. Thigh Gap sat down with his dog. Other hikers also stopped; four hundred miles was a big deal. We all agreed on that. From time to time, I chatted with Thigh Gap, a mellow fellow, probably from the weed he smoked. Once, he and I sat and ate lunch on the top level of a shelter in the Smokies. He fished out a joint, lit up, took an impressive long toke, and held it for an equally remarkable long time.

"Do you want a hit?"

He asked while holding his breath, his voice an octave higher. He extended the joint toward me.

"No, thank you. That's not my thing."

70

"Cool." He still held his breath.

In the spirit of returning the favor, I asked him if he wanted a bite-size Snickers. I held it in my palm for him. He looked at it. He continued to gaze at it. The gesture became awkward when he did not reply. A minute passed. He still gazed. I still held it in my palm. I realized how stoned he must be. I slowly smiled, more than curious, fascinated. Another minute passed. I became more interested. Then another. Thigh Gap seemed frozen in time. Two more minutes passed without anyone saying anything. After more than five minutes, Thigh Gap broke free from his trance and looked at me. He responded to my smile with a smile of his own. He said slowly,

"Yes. Thank you." He reached slowly and gently removed the Snickers from my hand.

"Well done, Grasshopper," I whispered.

I liked Thigh Gap. My spirit lifted when I saw him at the 400-mile marker.

Later that day, after more than thirteen miles, I stepped out onto a road with Stix, her ankle sore and her mood sour. Flutter matched the mood of Stix. They did not want to hike anymore. We waited briefly for Rock Steady and Paradox. The five of us discussed the pros and cons of staying in this less-than-ideal location. Should we venture ahead?

We scouted down the road a little way and found a side road not used much. Stix and Flutter liked it and decided to stay. Stix didn't care if we moved on. Flutter implored us all to stay together. Seeing no movement on a decision, he began to unpack. He made his choice. Rock Steady and Paradox conversed privately. I knew from the look on Rock Steady's face that they decided to leave. Now my turn. At that moment, I did not have any desire to camp with Flutter, especially in his obnoxious mood. Then I looked at Stix. She hurt. My soul's soft spot chimed in gently. I stayed.

Off went the two ladies.

Setting up on the gravel road frustrated me. The gravel repelled my tent stakes. My irritation threatened to boil over. I calmed myself as I ate dinner with Stix. She appreciated that I stayed with her. Flutter, just a few feet away, non-communicative. He ate his dinner ferociously and disappeared into his lair. Great. As the sun set, mosquitoes hummed in our ears and struck our flesh. Stix said good night. With no cell service in this gully, I set off down the road to look for a signal to call home. I didn't get through.

I camped next to two people, yet loneliness permeated my soul.

The Witches

I woke up early. I headed down the road from the trail to find a good spot for a morning constitutional (poop). I walked past something in the woods that I couldn't identify: some shelter or an alien spacecraft. As I walked by, my pace quickened. I urgently needed to address this bodily function. On the way back, I investigated the strange structure. I determined it was a hunting blind and quickly decided not to dwell here too long. I returned to camp; Flutter was gone. Fueled by irritation, I soon outpaced him on the uphill. I found Rock Steady and Paradox still in their tents just off the trail, pitched on leaves. They didn't find a very nice site either. As I chatted with them about their night, Flutter stomped by. He grunted something to express his displeasure, more drama. Yet compared to the "real world," this was nothing. After a few minutes, I said goodbye. We agreed to meet later on.

As I walked, I meditated a bit on the term "real world"? Was the real world back home? Or was the real world out here on the trail? I pondered deep questions to keep my mind off my feet. Blistered and sore, the pain eroded my sunny disposition (please note the sarcasm). They slowed me down. My broken boots caused more harm than good. By the end of the day, everyone but Stix passed me. I hobbled to Dennis Cove Road, my attitude sour. The rooms of recovery taught me to be aware of when H.A.L.T. (Hungry, Angry, Lonely, and Tired) manifested. Any of these conditions needed attention. All four at once could threaten a person's recovery. Thoughts of H.A.L.T. flickered through my mind as I gazed down the road. I felt all four. The crew made plans to stay at the Black Bear Resort, a little way down this road. Angrily, I thought...

"How far do I have to go? Damn it!"

At that moment, a mini-van stopped and rolled down the passenger side window.

"You going to Black Bear?"

"Yes, I am."

"Want a ride? I own the place."

"Yes, I do!"

I chucked my pack in the back and climbed in. Just a few yards down the road, Rock Steady sat on a rock. I asked the driver to stop. She looked surprised, then spied me sitting in the passenger seat. Her face lit up with the famous Rock Steady smile.

"Rock Steady, what are you doing?'

"Waiting for you. I should have known you'd get a ride."

She climbed in too. Her simple act of kindness heartened me. She had that way about her. She portrayed a strong independent woman, but when least expected, she would do something amazingly kind and considerate. The edge came off my poor H.A.L.T. attitude. Two minuscule acts of kindness affected me greatly. All of a sudden, I felt like butter - on a roll.

Later that afternoon, we piled into a Black Bear minivan and got a ride into "town," where I spent a lot of money at McDonald's. That's hard to do. Somehow, Thigh Gap and his dog made it to the same McDonald's. Thigh Gap feasted inside with his dog tied up outside. Poor girl. We brought our food back to the Black Bear, but Flutter couldn't wait. He devoured his food on the ride back. He ate a double cheeseburger in two bites as the rest of us watched in astonishment.

Back at a picnic table, we discussed foot care. I needed new boots; my feet were in rough shape. I hoped to get them in Damascus, fifty miles away. I received word that Samantha planned to meet me there in just two days. Could I get there on two hikes of twenty-five miles each in two days? Allegedly, the trail flattened into Damascus. I wanted to give it a go, but my highest two-day total up to this point was only thirty miles.

That night five of us tucked into four bunks in our little cabin. The following day, I got up and packed before everyone else woke up. As I returned to the trail, I contemplated my unwarranted feelings of abandonment. I had experienced this a few times already. And now, I abandoned the crew. I rationalized that I had to meet my daughter, a heroic mission. It was, to some extent, but I also wanted to see what I had. How hard could I push myself?

The trail treated me poorly from the Black Bear; the section around Laurel Falls was steep and rugged. My feet ached. I climbed a big unnamed mountain and then descended into Watauga Lake. I read signs that said you couldn't use shelters or camp for a 13-mile stretch because of a "troublesome" bear. Great. Immediately, I became more alert. I hiked along the lakeshore while keeping a wary eye out for a troublesome bear. Soon, I heard splashing in the water. Not a bear. No. Bears don't laugh. Three lady hikers in various stages of undress splashed in the water. I called these three "The Witches" (one of them was named Witch).

"Hey, Right Click! Want to join us?" One of them called from the water, flattered they knew my name.

I entertained the invitation. Did I *want* to? Yeah, I wanted to. One old married guy with three young women. Sure. I wanted to. Hot, tired, feet aching. Sure. I wanted to…

But I replied, "No thanks, got to keep moving."

So, I did. I wrestled with that encounter for a few minutes and assured myself I had done the right thing. I patted myself on the back for my righteousness. As I cruised along a flat stretch, I thought about my hiking prowess. I could do this. Confidence surged, but the trail retaliated. My left trekking pole hit a hidden log, bounced into my path, and I tripped over it. As I face-planted instantly, my body scorpioned. I spat dirt out and checked my face. No blood. Nothing broken, nothing sprained. I stood up and gave myself a once over. I continued down the trail, utterly humbled.

Late in the day, I arrived at a shelter. I covered eighteen miles. Hikers hung around eating and relaxing. I stopped and talked for a bit. They assumed I was there for the night. When I told them I was going on, eyebrows raised, but they wished me well. An hour later, darkness settled in. I dug out my headlamp. Situated on a steep, rock and rhododendron-laden trail, I slowly picked my way through a tunnel of plant life in the pitch black with only a single lamp to guide the way. Completely spooked. I thought,

"Why didn't I just stop at the last shelter? Why?"

All senses on full alert, I recoiled at the sounds around me. Leaves rustled; twigs snapped. I breathed heavily. I grunted often. I moaned every time I conjured up a fantastic beast. I shivered at the thought of zombies.

"Damn!"

I pushed panic aside and focused on the task at hand. I finally worked my way out of the rhododendron tunnel. What was that up ahead? Some kind of light. As I drew closer, I saw a firelight with campers around it. And I knew them! There sat Wolf Pine, Tink, Shits, and Giggles (I kid you not).

Shaken but relieved, I asked, "Mind if I camp with you guys?"

"Not at all, Right Click! Make yourself at home."

Extremely grateful for the warm welcome and the sanctuary, I set up across the trail on a relatively flat spot. I joined them at the fire. My jangled nerves started to calm, sitting with friendly people. Later, back in my tent, exhausted with sleep imminent, I checked my guide. I hiked just over twenty miles, my longest mileage day to date. But I still had thirty miles to walk to reach Damascus. Well, that wasn't going to happen.

I never hiked in the dark again on the AT.

Sami Time

As I started, I thought about my options; reaching Damascus was no longer realistic for 55-year-old legs in worn-out boots. I could let Sami stay a night alone in Damascus; not a good choice either. I decided to walk to the next road, TN 91, and see what happened. I got there at midday, still twenty miles short. Sami texted me that she had arrived in town and safely checked in at the Montgomery Homestead.

I sat down next to the road and dug out the AT Guide. I found the number for a shuttle driver named Gypsy Dave. I called him on my cell. He said he'd pick me up in twenty minutes. Gypsy Dave, a former thru-hiker, amused me with his story of how REI sold him eighty-one pounds of ultralight gear. With eighty-one pounds on his back, he barely made it to Mountain Crossings (the same place I lightened my load). Gypsy Dave gave me a thorough tour of Damascus before he dropped me off at the Montgomery Homestead. I told him my daughter waited for me, but I don't think he put it all together until he dropped me off.

"What? She's here already?"

"Ummm… yeah. I told you that."

"I'm sorry. I wouldn't have shown you everything in town."

"No problem, I enjoyed it."

I did, but I desperately wanted to see someone from my family. It had been a long time, in fact, the longest I had gone without seeing anyone from my family ever. Inside the bed and breakfast, I called,

"Sam?"

From upstairs, "Dad?"

My heart swelled when I heard her voice. I had gotten pretty good at pushing aside, maybe even ignoring, all the love associated with my family, too powerful to deal with on the trail. Part of me feared it. But now, seeing Sam, it all welled up, leaving me speechless. As I hugged her close and wept, I sensed "perfection," similar to the feeling I had during the thunderstorm. The Bible calls it a "peace that surpasses all understanding." Her desire to hike with her dad moved me. She brought encouragement. My journey would continue.

I hugged her, not caring that my stench might overpower her. To her credit, she didn't say anything or wrinkle her nose. I checked out our room. With my standards significantly lowered, this room was rated at the luxurious level. I talked and talked. She looked at me in awe and amusement.

Sami had not backpacked at all. Ever. I outlined an itinerary, go back to TN 91 and hike the twenty miles into Damascus over two days. One night in the woods, the second night back in town. Then we could re-assess, rest if needed, and make any adjustments to our gear.

But first, I showered. Then off to get some new boots. At the outfitters, a guy talked me into Oboz boots with Superfeet insoles. I wanted another pair of Merrell Moab Ventilators. The store on the main street didn't have them. I entertained a thought while I tried on the Oboz that the Merrells weren't broken; why am I fixing the problem? I wore Merrells for the last several years. They were super comfortable right out of the box. I loved their cushion, lightweight, and soles that had incredible grip. But switch I did, a decision I would soon regret.

Gypsy Dave gave Sami and me a ride back to the trailhead in the morning. Our first steps together on the Appalachian Trail took us through a gate into a cow pasture. An entire herd of cows walked with us. She laughed. We took pictures together. Sam took her first video as we melded with a pack of cows.

Welcome to the trail Sami.

She loved it, the day warm and bright. We cruised along easily, and by early evening we arrived at our planned destination, Abington Gap Shelter, a distance of more than eleven miles, a big day for a first day. As we descended the hill, I saw my crew eating dinner at the shelter's picnic table. I barked. I am part canine. I sport a realistic bark. They all turned. They knew my bark.

"Right Click!"

I strode downhill, eager to introduce my daughter. The hiking community welcomed her with enthusiasm. We sat at the picnic table in front of the shelter and ate with them. She fit in perfectly. She sat between Stix and Paradox, heartwarming to see. The three of them connected immediately. My friends continued north after dinner to leave them a shorter distance into Damascus the next day. I tried to convince them to stay, but no, they had their plan. We'd see them the next day in town.

Several people camped nearby. Cindy Loppers stopped and said hello. Sam and I set up our tents next to each other. Sam seemed comfortable. She set up her tent quickly. She liked my trail family. As we reviewed the day, I reflected on my emotions, proud that she hiked so far, willingly, on her very first day. The companionship of one of my children comforted me. Some concerns surfaced too. With her, I assumed more responsibility for keeping her safe. I've always been a dad who allowed my kids to take reasonable risks. How else does one grow? Sandy and I adopted the parenting perspective that we are not raising children; we are raising adults. The Appalachian Trail provided a tremendous opportunity for my daughter to grow personally. I sat on the ground next to her, thinking about these things. I

76

marveled at the clarity in my mind. But mostly, I basked in the warmth of our relationship.

As far as my feet, they still protested, and my new boots still hadn't passed muster. The next day, the long downhill hike into Damascus tortured Sami; her thighs screamed in protest. That night, she could barely walk. We decided to take a zero; my feet and Sami's legs needed some healing time. Rock Steady, Paradox, and Stix stayed in town too. Flutter headed home for Mother's Day, so he'd be gone for a few days. He'd also have to make up some serious ground to catch us. I'd like to say I was sorry to see him go, but I cannot.

Creeper Trail Blues

Damascus, the first town in Virginia, serves as a significant milestone for Appalachian Trail hikers. Gypsy Dave told me that if you can walk the four hundred seventy miles from Springer Mountain to Damascus, your body has what it takes to complete the entire trail. An interesting thought; not sure I agree with it, but it encouraged me at the time.

Damascus also hosts Trail Days yearly, a gigantic AT hiker reunion in May. We arrived one week before Trail Days 2015. We had many discussions among the crew if we should attend Trail Days. Paradox and Rock Steady wanted to. I did not. I couldn't understand why I would hike out for a week, get a ride back into town where thousands of people would be crammed into an area designed for a few hundred, then need to get back north to the trailhead. If we could stay ahead of the Trail Days bubble, the trail would be less crowded. Eventually, the two ladies decided to skip Trail Days too.

Damascus attracts tourists to the Creeper Trail, a famous rail trail. Local businesses drove people to the top, rented them a bike, then people coasted downhill back into town. On our zero day, Rock Steady, Sami, and I paid our fees, hopped in the truck, and were soon perched on bikes about to coast downhill for seventeen miles. After using just my feet for fifty days, getting on a bicycle provoked uncertainty. Rock Steady and Sami rode the bikes gracefully and confidently. Not me. I wobbled behind them and used the brake frequently. It took me some time to acclimate to the speed. Sam laughed loud and hard at my ineptitude.

"Come on, Dad, you can do it!"

She managed through fits of giggles. Sam and Rock Steady chattered as I coasted behind. A beautiful trail; I saw why so many people rode it.

That evening Paradox's parents took us out to dinner; they hailed from my generation. I reflected on that for a while as we waited for our food. This dinner would be the last time I would see Stix. Understandably, she wanted to stay in town; her ankle hurt severely. She would soon go home. Impressed she toughed it out for so long; I'd miss her sense of humor and resolve. It turns out she hiked for two hundred miles on a broken ankle. She made the right call.

Sam and I headed out of town the following day with Rock Steady and Paradox behind us. They said they'd catch up. About four and a half miles out of town, the trail crossed US 58. We read a sign posted on a tree about a bridge being out and an AT detour. We followed the detour and ended up back on the Creeper Trail. Sam and I headed up it. After thirty minutes or so, we couldn't locate any white blazes. The farther we went, the more concerned I became. I knew the AT reconnected with the Creeper Trail ahead, but still, I fretted. The hot day and gravel trail made walking hard on our feet, more demanding than if we had walked in the woods. Cyclists streamed by and filled the air with dust. After a couple more miles, we ate lunch off the trail next to a stream. We made our way through some long grass to some appealing rocks streamside to sit on. Sam jumped back when she saw a furry creature lying in the grass. She gasped.

'Dad, what's this?"

I looked. I just walked right by a sleeping fawn. We took some pictures quietly, left it alone, and got our aching feet in the cold water while we ate. The new Obozs were better blister-wise, but not so much for overall ache. Thinking we were off the AT annoyed me, but I made the most of it. We would not have encountered the fawn.

Further up the Creeper Trail, getting more hot, more tired, we reached a little ice cream shop. Sitting at the table were The Witches. Glad to see other hikers; I asked them if we were still on the AT.

"You're serious?"

"Yes, I'm serious."

"Uh, no, Right Click. You must have missed the turnoff. We chose to come this way."

Oh no. I listened as they explained that the AT turned left off the Creeper Trail just 50 yards from where the AT detoured onto it. Sam and I hadn't seen it. That was miles ago. Sam looked at me.

"Do we go back?" I asked.

"Whatever you want to do."

78

I didn't want to go back. But should I? Did I just compromise my thru-hike? Would I be labeled a blue blazer? A blue blazer is someone who takes shortcuts. "Damn it!"

I could tell from her eyes that she didn't want to go back, but she would if I decided to. She went inside the store to get us cold Cokes. I pondered the situation and explored the options. I could stay on the Creeper Trail and reconnect with the AT in a few miles. The distance hiked would be about the same. Or we could go back over the ground we just walked and hit the trail at the point we missed. This would take a lot of time and several additional miles. As we drank the Cokes, I decided we hadn't intentionally hiked up the Creeper Trail, an honest error. I'd learn later that several hikers missed the poorly marked detour. We went back to the Creeper Trail and moved on. Finally, we found the AT, deeply relieved to see white blazes again. But we still had more than three miles to a shelter. I asked Sam if she wanted to find a spot now or continue. She wanted to go on—tough girl.

We walked many miles on a hot, hard-surfaced, dusty Creeper Trail and several more on the AT when we arrived late at Lost Mountain Shelter. While pitching our tents, Sam revealed the heat rash on her legs, and I winced. I hurt for my daughter. She said her feet ached from the long gravel walk. She asked with deep discouragement in her voice,

"Why do people do this?"

Feeling very tired after nearly sixteen miles, discouraged and frustrated about marring the integrity of my hike, I had no answer for her. We ate dinner with several other hikers. Sam, immediately embraced again by the hiker community, actively participated in a conversation with Jester and Jokes leading the discussion. I observed her spirit lighten a bit. With names like that, how could Sam not be engaged and amused?

The trail provided the right people at the right time.

Girl on Fire

I internally monitored Sami's reaction to the previous day; her original enthusiasm dampened. Our destination loomed twelve miles away, the Thomas Knob Shelter. The trail took us out of the woods to Whitetop Mountain and Buzzard Rock. On a brilliantly bright, refreshing day, the panoramic views elicited gasps of awe and wonder. We shrugged off our packs and nestled into some of "nature's memory foam," ate, and enjoyed the view. Sam wandered off on her own and explored Buzzard Rock. I saw her visibly relax, letting nature wash over her, the clouds so close it seemed you could reach up and let them flow through your fingers. I left her alone, evident that she was in communion with God. I trusted God would make Himself known in a way that touched my daughter's soul. He certainly did that with me. We stayed for more than an hour. Other hikers came and went. Given her reaction yesterday, I thought she might not last long and decide to go home. But not now. Here, the trail imposed its will upon her. It spoke to her. I said nothing to her.

On our way down from Whitetop, I led the way when we came to an enchanted forest. Revitalized by our experience and view from Whitetop, I chattered about how magical this place was, and then....

"Aaaaahhh!"

I tumbled off the trail as my left ankle rolled. Lying in the weeds, I clutched my ankle. Sam held back a smile.

"Not funny, Sam!"

That did it. She laughed. OK, maybe it was funny. A thought flittered around that my new Oboz boots might have had something to do with it. I pushed that aside. Not much I could do about it now. I got on my feet and started again but much more carefully.

As I hobbled along those first few yards, I asked, "Sam, what would you have done if I had broken my ankle?"

Without missing a beat, she replied, "Just pin a note on you, keep going and let Rock Steady and Paradox deal with you."

"WHAT?" We both laughed. She inherited my sense of humor.

We came to a road and saw other hikers at the trunk of a car, a sign of trail magic. Papa Bear stood talking with a couple. We met him earlier. From my conversation with him, I knew he had about one year in recovery from alcoholism. A young man in his early twenties, he timidly held an ice-cold beer unopened in his right hand. He knew about my recovery and seemed grateful to see me.

"Right Click, do you want this?" He asked shakily. He knew I didn't. He quietly cried for help.

"No, thank you."

Then I whispered to him.

"Just hand it back. Tell him you've changed your mind and don't feel like a beer right now. It's OK; you won't offend him."

Papa Bear took the suggestion, handed the beer back, and the trail angel responded graciously, a definitive moment for Papa Bear. We crossed the road, and I talked with him for a bit, grateful that God arranged the "coincidence." I offered Papa Bear some other methods to politely decline alcoholic drinks.

80

"I'm allergic to alcohol. Every time I drink it, I break out in handcuffs."

"One beer is too many; one hundred is not enough."

We shared some laughter as we climbed part way up a long uphill grade. Sami and I took another break. Papa Bear moved on. We faced a four-mile climb that skirted Mount Rogers. I wanted to eat a snack and rest before we took it on.

After our break, Sam took the lead. Her pace gradually quickened. I could sense she wanted to go faster but didn't want to leave me. I called out to her and asked her to wait up. I caught up. When she turned, I saw *the look* in her eyes. Her eyes blazed, opened vast, brilliant blue, her soul on fire. I had seen this in her before when she nurtured children in Tijuana. The look caught me off guard but looks like that are ferociously contagious. She knew I knew. We connected soul to soul, God with us. I said simply,

"Go, my child. Go."

And off she went, earphones in. I did my best to keep up, but not going to happen. I passed Papa Bear at a good clip.

"What's up with Sam? She flew by me. I thought I was going pretty fast."

"She's feeling it. I'm doing my best, so she doesn't get too far in front of me. And she was worried that she'd slow me down."

Papa Bear laughed.

"See ya!"

Sam blistered four uphill miles. I witnessed the birth of a hiker. She slowed down near the top and waited for me at a half-mile side trail up to the summit of Mount Rogers.

"Sam, do you want to go up there? It is the highest peak in Virginia."

"Nah."

Most thru-hikers limit how far they go off trail for something - a view, shelter, water, or food. Some love to bag mountain peaks. Not me. My limit soon became two-tenths of a mile. I'd go that far. Three-tenths? Debatable. Four-tenths? No way. The trek up to the summit of Mt. Rogers was five-tenths. I was not going, not happening, and I had no desire to hike an extra mile at the end of a long day.

The area around Thomas Knob Shelter boasted magnificent views, but the shelter itself faced away from the view, so we scouted for a site. Food Truck and She Wee Dee camped on the sloping ground with the best view but no room for us. After several minutes, we made our way back down the trail to an open, grassy spot with a wondrous vista. We made a water run relatively far from our site and bumped into Rock Steady and Paradox on our way back from the spring. Trail family mini-reunions always generated enthusiasm and laughter. Their two tents were set fifty yards from us. They invited us to dinner at their place; the area just south of the Grayson Highlands rocks was magical. As we chatted and laughed over our food, the four of us shared the same feeling of reverence and awe. Sami revealed her discouragement from the previous day.

"I couldn't understand why people do this. I do now." She beamed.

Things changed so quickly on the trail. One night I thought about going home; the next night, I thought I could stay on the trail forever. As the sun set and the chill settled in, we built a fire. Besides almost setting Paradox's puff coat ablaze when I added a dead branch with pine needles, this evening registered as mystical. We laid down, backs on the grass, listened to the fire crack, and considered the brilliance of the stars in silence. Sparks sprayed from the fire occasionally rode the hot air currents into the dark sky. I silently thanked God for this experience. Eventually, the cold ground and the fatigue of a twelve–mile, primarily uphill day took their toll. We said good night and made our way back to our tents. Before settling, Sami offered me two words.

"Thanks, Dad."

I choked back emotion. Tears pooled in my eyes.

"You're welcome." All I could muster.

Charlize and Her Friends

A piercing whisper roused me from a deep sleep early the following day.

"Right Click, Sam! Get up! Right Click, Sam! Get up!" Paradox persisted.

"Ponies!"

Half asleep, I slipped on my yellow Crocs, donned my black puff coat, and stumbled into the crisp cool morning, the sun just about to rise. Wild ponies had come to visit. Down the slope, Rock Steady sat in the entranceway to her tent with a tan pony's nose in her face. The pony started to chew on her expensive Cuban fiber tent. Rock Steady didn't take any crap, especially from a precocious pony. She rebuked that pony, coupled with a slap on the snout. Among the dozen ponies, a few adorable foals wandered about.

We hung out with the wild ponies for more than an hour, taking photos and videos. Rock Steady, the farm girl, tried to lie across the back of a pony I dubbed Charlize Theron because of the pony's gorgeous blond mane. Charlize wanted no part of it and shrugged her off. So much for obeying park rules about not messing around with the ponies.

82

We slowly got our stuff together and ambled north through the Grayson Highlands. We encountered the ponies all along the way. Charlize followed us. An obnoxious black and white pony, slightly rowdy and aggressive, stuffed his nose into my shorts pocket to get at a Snickers wrapper. We stopped several times and enjoyed their company. When the trail offered unique experiences, we reveled in them. We may never pass this way again.

Later, we crossed the five-hundred-mile mark, a special milestone for me. I crossed it with three wonderful people – Sam, Rock Steady, and Paradox. Hard to comprehend that I had walked 500 miles, I considered the fifty-four days it took to do it. Still, more than three-quarters of the trail loomed ahead. We managed eleven miles to the Old Orchard Shelter despite stopping for frequent pony photo opportunities. As we cooked dinner, a thunderstorm rolled in, and we dove into our tents. After the storm passed, happy with her bowl of mac and cheese prepared just in time, Sam spoke from her tent. She echoed her thoughts from the previous night.

"Thanks again, Dad, this is amazing. I am so glad I came out here."

Night of the Nazgul

The four of us became a closely-knit pack; three remarkable women and me. I recalled how Sandy found it "interesting" that I hiked with women.

"Aren't there any men on the trail?"

Yet, my daughter formed powerful bonds with Paradox and Rock Steady. They treated her with respect, dignity, and unconditional love. They cared for her. As the miles went by, our care for one another deepened. We laughed a lot. We teased each other. We discussed options easily.

We traveled with many people. The shelters and campsites filled up. In hiker jargon, it's called being in a bubble, which was undoubtedly the case when we strode into Trimpi Shelter. The Family Von Trapp (my name for them) filled the small-sized shelter. The group of ten forced people to find sites on steep, rocky, and heavily wooded land surrounding the shelter. The one well-worn area would soon host many tents. Dash, one of the Von Trapps, hung his hammock in the middle of us all. The Witches came in after dark.

Rumored haunted, I scanned the area around Trimpi Shelter for ghosts, demons, or any other signs of paranormal activity. No signs; everything seemed peaceful. But this place scared the shit out of me. Shortly after nightfall, I woke to a mechanical roar in the distance, with most hikers sound asleep. It grew louder. And louder. The noise intensified. It moved toward us. It hovered above us. I screamed, but no one could hear me. The blare forced me to bury my head in my hands. The earth reverberated. I screamed louder. Was it going to land on us? It passed overhead slowly. But pass it did. My head vibrated. My ears rang as the din slowly receded into the distance.

"What the hell was that?" I yelled from my tent.

Someone responded. "Fighter jet."

Maybe. I wasn't so sure. I checked my sleeping bag. Good. I didn't soil it. I thought it might have been a Nazgul*. They make heads vibrate in pain. My head ached viciously. So did a Dementer.

"Military aircraft? Out here? What the hell?"

Whatever it was, I didn't like it. Fatigue eventually drove the fright away, and my frazzled nerves slowly unjangled. I thanked God. I drifted off to sleep with a final thought.

"Nazgul. Definitely. Nazgul. This place is haunted…." I asked Sam about it the next morning.

"What noise, Dad?"

"Come on, Sam. Really?"

She hadn't heard a thing.

Stranger Kindness

The three ladies and I got a ride from the Mount Rogers Visitor Center into Marion, VA, low on food but high on sweat, filth, and stink. We took care of ourselves at the Econolodge. The following day, Flutter texted us that he'd like to see us on his way back to Damascus. Flutter left us a few days earlier to visit his wife and dog. He also wanted to be with his mom on Mother's Day. He met us at our Econolodge, brought some homemade beef jerky, and gave us a ride to Walmart.

I tolerated Flutter in low doses. On this day, I genuinely appreciated his act of kindness. Besides, his time off trail left him sixty miles behind us. He couldn't possibly catch up with us, could he? Little did I know. On the way back to the hotel, we spotted a familiar purple puff jacket standing smack dab in the middle of the busy road. Chip gesticulated at the traffic and talked to no one in particular. We all ducked, not wanting him to see us. We said goodbye to Flutter at the Econolodge and returned to the trail. The weather heated up. We set our sights on a campsite thirteen miles away. Late in the afternoon, I walked ahead of Rock Steady, coming down a gentle hill into a meadow, when….

"AAaaaaaaaaaaaaahhhhh!!!"

I wandered a few inches off the path, found a hole, and my left ankle rolled over. Before I careened into the weeds, I felt a sickening pop. Rock Steady caught up to me and giggled.

"What's so funny?"

She tried to stifle the laughter. She could not.

"You looked like you just dove into the weeds.... It was ridiculous." More giggles.

I looked at the helium balloons tied to her pack courtesy of Paradox and Sam to celebrate her birthday (for the record, I'm not that thoughtful). As I lay there clutching my ankle, I resentfully thought,

"Who looks ridiculous?"

I picked myself up and tried to put some weight on it. Not good. I hobbled down the hill. We planned to eat at a well-known AT stop, the Barn Restaurant. We spotted it; many backpacks lined up outside. I shuffled in. Bitter because of the pain, I muttered,

"This place is not known for its décor," I commented on the austerity.

I sat down, put my foot on a chair, and felt my boot tighter as my ankle swelled. I called Sandy. Since I fell off my new Oboz boots twice, maybe she could send me a pair of my original boots (Merrell Moab Ventilators) to Pearisburg, our next town stop? She said she would. Unlike the rest of my crew, Sandy expressed genuine concern.

Now what? As we ate dinner, I weighed all my options. Adept at situation analysis, I sorted through my options.

Option 1: Hike to the next campsite about two miles away on a sprained ankle.

Option 2: Stop and rest somewhere nearby. The hotel across the street?

Option 3: With Interstate 81 just a few yards away, stick out my thumb and go home.

I hated being a burden to other hikers, yet when I stood up to go to the men's room, I didn't think hiking any further that day was a viable option. I jettisoned option one. Even though we stayed inside the night before, the ladies agreed to check out the Relax Inn (yes, that's the place's name) down the street. I made my way, slowly, to it.

No room at the inn. Putting most of my weight on my one good leg, I wondered about a stable in the back.

Option 4: I asked if we could set up our tents in the lovely flat grassy area behind the inn.

85

The manager shot us a look, but he reluctantly agreed. The area looked inviting, the grass longer than ideal but flat. Eager to get off my foot, I scanned for a place to set up. Then the first tractor-trailer truck thundered by just fifty yards away. We caught the eyes of each other; we all knew. At first, I got angry, but then the ladies started to snicker. Partly frustrated, mostly punchy, I laughed too. The anger and frustration ebbed.

Option 5: Go back and talk to the manager. Are there any other places to stay nearby? With rooms available?

Yes. A Comfort Inn five miles down the road. Most other hikers would have moved on and left me to my own devices. Not Paradox and Rock Steady. Not sure what Sam might have done, but she didn't have much choice, did she?

They decided to stick with the old guy, just one of the reasons I respected, cared for, and loved these ladies too. Now that we had chosen Option 5, how do we get to the Comfort Inn? Again, three choices surfaced: walk, taxi or hitch. Walking was not possible, and cabs were expensive. Paradox came through with a variation on the third option. She walked to the gas station next door and used some amazing but previously unrevealed charm. She sweet-talked this lovely gentleman into giving us all a ride. The four of us, plus the driver, squeezed into a compact car, packs and all. I got the passenger seat. On the trip to the Comfort Inn, he told us where he lived five separate times. Uh oh. Then he drove right by the hotel. He turned around and pulled in front. We thanked him. He offered to pick us up the following day and take us back to the trail. We politely declined. Smitten with Paradox, she sent him off with one more enchanting smile. He seemed dazed but eventually got his bearings and drove away.

"I didn't know you could do that?"

"Do what Right Click?" She said with a mischievous grin.

"Uh-huh."

The night manager tried to get us into two rooms, but by now, it was dark, well past hiker midnight, and I just wanted a place to lie down and ice my ankle. Four of us crammed into one room with two double beds. In the lobby, we met another guy who tried to hike the trail several years ago. People helped him during his hike, and he wanted to give back. He became concerned about my ankle and wanted to help. I politely declined.

As I sat on the bed, ankle iced, Paradox left the room to call Dan. Rock Steady, Sam, and I got ready for bed. Paradox returned more than an hour later with a

86

Walmart bag in tow. She did not speak to Dan. Our trail angel hiker friend gave her a ride to a local Walmart, where he bought me an ankle brace. The following morning, this guy gave us a ride back to the trailhead. He couldn't fit all four of us in his vehicle, so he made two trips. He sincerely expressed gratitude for the opportunity to help. As we said goodbye, I could not help but be encouraged by this man's generosity.

People, often inspired by our quest, wanted to be a small part of it. Sandy experienced the same sentiment at home. People helped her while I hiked.

In 2010, during cancer treatment, I learned a valuable lesson. Weak and emaciated, I kept up with my chores as best I could. I didn't want help, but I could use it. Pride played a factor. My dear friend Nate asked if he and some guys from church could do some lawn work.

"That's OK, Nate. I got it."

I didn't want to impose. Thankfully Nate did not have any of it. He gently but firmly persuaded me with this response.

"Phil, you have been a blessing to many. Don't deprive us of the opportunity to be a blessing to you. It's our turn."

I replied meekly. "Ok."

Sincerely grateful, they mulched the beds around the house, cut the lawn, and pruned the shrubs. I've always had difficulty accepting love and care.

The following day, I set out with my ankle firmly braced (thank God, Paradox, and the trail angel) and loaded up on a high dose of ibuprofen. Yeah, it hurt, but walkable. My mood elevated for another reason; on May 15, 2015, I recorded my 10,000th day in recovery (more than 27 years). I kept the knowledge of this significant milestone to myself, deeply grateful that I had been blessed with so many days alcohol and drug-free. My life has evolved wondrously ever since. What did I have to complain about? A slightly sore ankle was not an actual problem. I eventually walked through it. With my crew's resolute attitude and support, we knocked out more than fourteen miles.

Tough Love

Virginia's hot and humid weather in May helped loosen muscles but blossomed blisters. With little time to get her gear together, Sam chose boots based on a recommendation from an outfitter in Lynchburg. The outfitter sold her waterproof boots. They sound good in theory, but a waterproof boot sucks for long-distance hiking. They trap moisture in and create fertile conditions for blisters. Also, when it's hot and your feet sweat, there's no way for the wetness to dry. It leaves the skin soft and highly susceptible to blisters and infection. Sam rubbed her pinky toes raw. People pay little attention to their pinky toes when they walk. I certainly didn't until mine blistered. Then their presence becomes known at every step. I knew Sam hurt, but she toughed it out. Waterproof boots also breed trench foot. Ask a Vietnam vet. In Vietnam, they rarely had a chance to dry their feet out. With breathable footwear and good wool socks (I swear by Darn Tough – a shameless plug for which I am getting no endorsement money), the water squeezes out as you walk - a remarkable phenomenon to experience. I often took my shoes and socks off at breaks to keep my feet dry on the trail.

I sweated all day. Sweat soaked my pack; my gear was stowed in a trash compactor bag to keep moisture out. Thirsty, my throat parched, I caught up to the ladies who rested in a shady area. I whined about it being so hot. I checked my three bottles, no water.

"Sam, can I have some of your water?"

"Dad, we walked by at least five streams; you should have stopped and got your own water!"

Sam chastised me correctly. My lame excuse? Last, I didn't want to fall further behind in our formation. That is not a good reason for ignoring the basics. I sighed. Damn. Rock Steady listened to the whole dialogue. With her smile and distinct laugh, she cried,

"DAAAANNNG!"

Paradox picked up on the theme immediately. "Right Click, that's some tough love."

And that's how Sam got her trail name – Tough Love. I got no water from Tough Love. Several minutes down the trail, I quenched my thirst at the next water source at an intersection of two paved roads. We dropped our packs in the grassy area. Tough Love's pack sent a snake scurrying into the underbrush. Tough Love barely flinched; a dramatic improvement.

I noticed two lady day-hikers about my age emerge from the woods with a dog in tow.

"Good afternoon," I said in my most pleasant voice.

"Good afternoon. Are you thru-hiking?"

"I am!"

I told them about my thirst. They became very concerned and scrounged around in their packs and the car. They gave me water, a cold can of seltzer, an apple, and a couple of granola bars. As they did this, I talked to them about why I hiked the trail,

88

my recovery, and CCAR. One spoke of her daughter, now recovering after a long addiction struggle. I said goodbye and thanked them for their generosity. I walked back with my bounty. The three ladies doled out a rasher of crap.

"You're such a Yogi!"

They teased me with reference to the cartoon character Yogi Bear and his ability to charm vacationers out of picnic baskets.

"Right Click, they *liked* you!"

"Even the dog had a thing for you."

I drank and ate in silence as they needled me. I enjoyed their insults and the nourishment very much. I'm sure my smirk gave it away.

Next, a car pulled up, and a man wanted to know if anyone wanted a Coke and some M&M's. He offered a few sodas and one small bag of candy; unusual that he carried such a small amount of trail magic, but trail magic nevertheless. Several of us gathered, so we divvied everything evenly and equitably with no animosity - the thru-hiker way.

Later, we crossed a stream in the early evening, took off our packs, and the four of us agreed to eat dinner under the bridge near the water where cooler air resided. After eating, we crossed a road and arrived at a beautiful campsite. Dr. Pickles and Mockingbird tented there. We stopped to chat. They welcomed us warmly, very comfortable in their presence. The talk moved to setting up here. Sam wanted to keep going. I wanted her to rest and give her blisters a break. Plus, my sore left ankle gave an opinion about the miles. We decided together not to pass on a spot this beautiful. We set up, ready to prepare dinner, when the weather drove us inside. Grateful for an early evening, I jotted some notes and fell asleep while rain lightly pattered on the tent.

Dive Bombers

I eventually walked through the ankle damage. The heat and humidity didn't resolve Tough Love's blister problem. In addition, her left knee developed patellar tendinitis. She tied a bandanna around her knee to ease the discomfort. The bandanna added to her developing hippie persona. After nearly twenty miles, we arrived at a shelter full of Von Trapps. There weren't any good sites available, but we were tired and sore. I thought we agreed to set up in the less desirable spots.

I thought wrong.

I opened up my pack, got my Tarptent out, and unrolled it over a lumpy slanted site when the three ladies said they were moving on to another site about a mile more.

"Oh."

Well, another man might have been angry. Another man might have been hurt. But another man never would have let her go. I stashed the bill in my shirt."

Unexpectedly, I wasn't angry, and I wasn't hurt. I accepted the decision immediately. I repacked my stuff and followed them. I surprised the crew, too; they knew I could be pretty darn grouchy at times over stupid little stuff, but not this time. Maybe just too tired to argue.

We walked another mile and found a better place alongside a relatively tight, overgrown, but well-used stream. The hot, humid air made the Virginia woods tropical. As I perspired heavily while I set up my tent, I discovered I had left the top strut back where I prematurely unpacked. Going back to retrieve it never entered my mind; not a big deal as far as I was concerned. I just needed to develop a Plan B. Rock Steady noted my patience. A few days later, she'd bring it up again and thank me for not getting pissed off. She said a lot of other hikers would have.

Hmmm. Maybe my attitude and outlook changed. Could it be that my internal spring had unwound a tad?

Upstream a few yards from our site, a small pool with a two-foot rock ledge beckoned. I sat in the water, took my shirt off, and rinsed it. Ripe with hiker funk and grime, brown clouds of filth dispersed into the small pool. To my horror (amazement), crayfish began floating to the surface, shocked to death by the chemicals coming from my shirt.

No, they didn't.

I made that up, but I could picture it; my already active (and warped) imagination had reached new levels.

This campsite drew an abnormally large hoard of insects. Even with bugs buzzing around, I sat comfortably in the dirt and ate dinner. As darkness descended, biting mosquitoes emerged, and I submerged into the shelter of my tent. Well into the night, I got out to pee. I donned my headlamp, crawled out, forced my creaking, crying legs to stand, and moved away several steps. As I relieved myself, I got smacked in the head by a giant flying insect. Then I saw a glimmer of another one in the headlamp's beam, and "bam," it smacked me right into my forehead. Then I saw them come from all angles. Thinking they were divebombing the light, I clicked off the headlamp. I heard them buzz around me. I became alarmed as more of these

90

massive bugs whirred by. I finished my business and found my way back to the tent in the dark. Relieved to be back inside my shelter, I thought.

"Some things you anticipate out on the trail. Some things you don't."

Dismal Falls

I started the following day in pain. I took some more Vitamin I with breakfast. A recurring notion passed through my mind.

"Is eating ibuprofen for breakfast a good idea? Probably not."

But my left ankle, feet, and knees shrieked and creaked. I learned, like Tough Love, to walk through it. As we continued down the trail, my concern for Tough Love grew. Her knee throbbed. I could tell by her stride. As we went down a steep downhill, typically punishing on the knees but compounded with tendinitis, my daughter took a step with her right foot and then dragged her left leg. I watched this for a few miles. My heart ached. Far behind Paradox and Rock Steady, we came to a water source.

"Sam, sit down for a while. Put your foot up. Rest your knee. Take a couple of these." I offered her 2 Ibuprofen.

"I don't want those." But she took them. She must be in an incredible amount of pain.

"Dad, we have to keep going. I don't want to slow you down, and I want to keep up with Paradox and Rock Steady".

"Don't worry about that. You're not holding me up. And they'll understand. Please sit for a few minutes."

She reluctantly agreed. We took a long break, forty-five minutes, then moved on. Shortly after, I heard voices up ahead. I spotted an orange shirt. Paradox. She spotted us and smiled from ear to ear, Rock Steady behind her.

"What are you doing? You came SOUTH!" I exclaimed.

They violated the sacred thru-hiker decree, "Thou shalt not go south, no mattereth the reason."

"We thought you might be in trouble; you were far behind. Tough Love, let me take your pack." Paradox offered.

Stubbornly (like I knew she would), she said defiantly, "I'm good."

Tough Love carried her pack. We continued down the trail. Rock Steady, and Paradox joked and teased Tough Love about her pronounced limp. Tough Love genuinely appreciated their love and concern. After several minutes, we came to a shelter and their packs. We stopped and ate a light lunch together. They traveled a

91

fair distance to go to the aid of their trail sister. I quietly thanked God for putting these two women on my path. My soul, filled with gratitude, rendered me more quiet than usual.

I moved one step at a time, hot, hungry, and thirsty. We hit a road. Trent's Grocery called a half mile down the road. I faced a decision.

"Should I stay, or should I go? Should I stay, or should I go? If I stay, it could be trouble. If I go, it could be double."

I've discussed the unwritten decree that a thru-hiker does not venture more than two-tenths off the trail. We broke the rule. We went. Glad I did; Trent's Grocery offered cheeseburgers, pizza, hot dogs, fries, milkshakes, and the usual grocery stuff, along with roofing supplies, hardware, and fishing tackle. Not too many places in Connecticut offer that combination. I ordered a double bacon cheeseburger, fries, and a strawberry shake but passed on the fifty pounds of shingles and five hundred screw special. While waiting for my food, I downed a twenty-ounce ice-cold Coca-Cola.

Fueling my system, the half-mile back to the trailhead felt easy. Tough Love and Paradox soon outpaced Rock Steady and me. Tough Love either felt inspired, or maybe the Ibuprofen kicked in, or perhaps because the trail reverted to uphill, her gait returned to normal. I came to a side trail going down to Dismal Falls. A familiar bandanna hung on the sign.

"Hey, I think that's Tough Love's bandanna."

I said out loud to no one. The longer I stayed in the woods, the more I talked to myself. I pondered the bandanna until Rock Steady caught up.

"I'm assuming this is Tough Love's. I assume she left it here to say they went down to the falls. Is that how you interpret this?"

She searched my eyes and assessed my sincerity. She replied simply.

"It is."

We went on a second detour to Dismal Falls, a beautiful and popular swimming hole. Tough Love luxuriated in the water. Paradox soon followed. I got to the edge. I slid in. The cold water immediately stimulated a grimace. Gradually, the cold soothed my aching knees and feet. I lounged back in the refreshing water. After cooling off, we hung around and watched all the people. I overlooked the road above the falls until a truck drove by, explaining all the people. Invigorated, we shouldered our packs and headed up the trail in good spirits.

That evening, Tough Love and I camped on a flat area near the path to the Laurel Creek shelter, Rock Steady and Paradox several yards away. I woke suddenly to loud voices and flashlight beams swaying back and forth as a group of people trudged by on their way to the shelter. Startled, I tensed and listened. I looked at my phone for the time, just past midnight. I concluded that a youth group of some kind had ventured out, got lost, and now looked for a shelter to stay for the night. Ten minutes passed, and the noisy bunch with flashlights shining headed back the way they came. They walked a few inches from my tent. After they passed, Tough Love whispered.

"Dad, what was that? Where are they going at this time of night?"

"I don't know, Sam. I hope they'll be ok."

Pearisburg

After a long, sweltering walk of more than eighteen miles, we arrived in Pearisburg, VA. The last in line, or the caboose, I headed down a fairly steep hill where the three ladies stood on the pavement. Wooden steps led down, one more to go, but I missed it. Time slowed down; I pirouetted as I crashed. I lay in the dirt dazed, gazed at the blue sky above, and heard nothing but a few bird chirps. Finally, I spoke and raised one hand weakly.

"I'm okay."

The summer air burst with female laughter - hearty, gut-level, and deep. The three ladies took great delight in my misfortune.

One of them said, "I wish I had videoed that!"

They laughed long and hard. Their laughter was contagious; I giggled too. It took a long time for them to regain their senses. Delirious from the heat, I surmised. As I struggled to my feet, I retorted.

"It wasn't that funny."

That only renewed their reverie. They guffawed uncontrollably all over again.

We waded through an irregular patch of the AT to the next road, overgrown and muddy, to a picnic table. We called for a ride to check into the Holiday Motor Lodge. The four of us were in a very comfortable rhythm; we enjoyed each other's company. We had similar goals for the day and similar styles. I cherished our time together.

The next day, we walked far to get breakfast at Friends and Family. On our way to the restaurant, we stopped at the Post Office to mail some stuff home. We chatted with an amiable, warm woman. At the restaurant, we encountered strange looks from the regular weekend crowd. We didn't care at all. I wanted eggs, bacon, home fries, toast, coffee, and lots of it. As we paid for our food, a poster near the register garnered my attention. Rock Steady and Paradox joined me while I read and nodded their approval.

Don't Quit

When things go wrong, as they sometimes will,
When the road you're trudging seems all uphill,
When the funds are low, and the debts are high,
And you want to smile, but you have to sigh,
When care is pressing you down a bit,
Rest if you must, but don't you quit.

Life is queer with its twists and turns,
As every one of us sometimes learns,
And many a failure turns about,
When he might have one if he had stuck it out;
Don't give up though the pace seems slow,
You may succeed with another blow.

Success is failure turned inside out,
The silver tint of the clouds of doubt,
And you can never tell how close you are,
It may be near when it seems so far;
So stick to the fight when you're hardest hit,
It's when things seem worse, that you must not quit.

Message received, we ventured across the street to Walmart to resupply. In Walmart, Tough Love and I recognized the woman from the post office. She finished talking with another woman.

"Are you the mayor?" I asked. She smiled.

"No, but I know a lot of people here."

That led to a long conversation. We discovered she raised her three children from six, seven, and nine, all grown now. She told us about her husband, who worked at "the" factory. On the crew who originally built the factory, he accidentally touched a live wire. The high voltage charge charred his skin black. He dangled by his feet for hours from the scaffolding until rescue workers figured out how to reach him. When she entered the hospital to visit him, she received advice to pretend nothing happened, not to let him see the shock on her face. Still, it did not prepare her. Immediately and intensely horrified, she choked back tears and managed to mutter,

"Now, what have you gone and done to yourself?"

Soon, doctors amputated one arm and expressed genuine amazement at her husband's tenacity. He should be dead. Through it all, he remained lucid. They conversed deeply with significant meaning. They planned for life without him. Seven days after the accident, a heart attack mercifully ended his life. She testified about how God provided for her every need over all these years.

"The Lord is good."

Tough Love and I stood stunned. Spirit rushes ran up and down our skin. We quietly thanked her for sharing. She gracefully said goodbye and went about her business. I don't think we moved for a few minutes. We just looked at each other.

Did I think hiking the trail was difficult?

Tough Love and I sheepishly returned to our shopping. We finished our re-supply, repackaged our food outside Walmart, then headed to McDonald's for double cheeseburgers. On this journey, I discovered that McDonald's double cheeseburgers lasted indefinitely, even in the hottest weather. I stashed them in their wrappers and Ziplocked them in a quart freezer bag for consumption on the trail; I ate one four days after I purchased it. Delicious. Rock Steady ate one five days after discovering it flattened in the bottom of her food bag.

We enjoyed the Pearisburg McDonald's. With leather chairs, a flat-screen TV, and air-conditioning, we sat comfortably airdropping photos to each other. Before we knew it, a few hours had passed. We talked about a zero even though our packs were with us. The more we talked, the more we liked the idea. Ultimately, we decided to rest our aching limbs.

We successfully hitchhiked back to the hotel; the four of us crammed into the bed of a pickup. While the wind whipped, I reflected on the adventure of the trek, blessed to share it with my daughter, blessed to have the support of family. My heart swelled with gratitude.

Dude's Got a Gun

The next day, after ten miles or so out of town, we came to an exquisite view - a grassy meadow, flat ground, and high up. Three friendly locals chose this spot to stay the night. One guy, an Army veteran, carried a pistol, the first gun I'd seen on the trail. He seemed friendly enough. He chatted amicably while he set up his new hammock. I wondered about the weapon. The lady who accompanied him grew up in Pearisburg, now an international music judge/teacher. One of this lady's students moaned. On her very first hike, she ached. She could barely move.

Rock Steady, Paradox, Tough Love, and I stretched out. As we snacked, the deliberations began. Should we stay? Or should we move north? With a few hours of daylight left, we could go further. Or stay in a fantastic spot.

"But the dude's got a gun," I whispered so the dude with the gun couldn't hear.

Rock Steady replied with no hesitation. "So?"

So, we agreed that this spot was an incredible place to stay.

"Do you mind if we set up over there?" I asked the three locals. I pointed across the trail to the open field.

"No, not at all." The woman replied sincerely. "Please do."

We set up in the field several yards away.

Everyone was content with our decision to stay, so we looked forward to dinner together. Sandy sent some family-size pouches of macaroni and cheese in her care package that I picked up in Pearisburg. Macaroni and cheese, a trail favorite for many, took time to prepare. We poured hot water and let it steep. Family size translated into a prodigious amount that tasted a little…off. Together, Tough Love and I couldn't choke a full one down. Paradox cooked a complete package for herself. She groaned after a few spoonfuls. The rest of us settled back, and for amusement, we watched her struggle. She responded defiantly to our false encouragement. Astonishingly, that woman managed to eat most of it.

At this spot in Virginia, Tough Love took memorable sunset photos. I prayed as I drifted to sleep, contented, tired, and grateful. And again, God answered the prayer. I woke up with it light outside. The pistol guy had not murdered us. My attitude about guns budged slightly. We all slept well, except Paradox. The mac and cheese sat like a two-pound stone in her stomach. She groaned and wrapped her arms around her belly while she broke camp but maintained her humor.

We strode through the Virginia hills. After seventeen miles, we reached Wind Rock with a spectacular vista. As evening settled, we ate dinner with Blister Babe and Queen Bee and recapped our day. Tough Love jumped a foot in the air from a close encounter with a giant black snake. She helped me record a video to promote a golf tournament back home. I showed them on my phone; they got a kick out of it. I recalled first encountering Blister Babe and Queen Bee in the Smokies.

"You remember when we are all crammed into a shelter with thirty of our closest friends?"

They searched their memory banks. Nothing.

"I was with Flutter?" Everyone remembered Flutter.

"Oh yeah. It rained all that day."

"That was *every* day in the Smokies. You came later in the day, squeezed into the lower deck, and both wrote in your journals for a while. That impressed me. Are you writing a book?"

"I don't know. I'm a teacher and want to write things down, so I don't forget them."

We talked a while longer, then I quieted down, contemplating her comment about "not forgetting." I also thought I would never have guessed she taught for a living. All our outsides became similar – the same type of clothes, unkempt hair, unshaven, no makeup, strong body odor – but we hailed from vastly different experiences. I liked that. No, I loved that. I listened contentedly as the five women laughed and joked with each other. Once in a while, they tossed me a comment to see if I was paying attention.

"Hey, Right Click? It must be tough hiking with all these women. Aren't there any men on the trail?"

Night Fright

Ahead of everyone, I looked for a place to have lunch. We agreed that we'd all stop when I stopped for lunch. I felt the pressure to locate an ideal spot. Nothing materialized. After another hour, frustrated, marginally embarrassed, and extremely hungry, I plopped down, my feet on the path. After several minutes, the three ambled down the trail.

"It's about time! We're starved!"

"I couldn't find anything," I whined.

"You could have probably done better than this." They teased.

They sat down too. The second we pulled out our food, a single cloud moved overhead and burst open. It rained. Fiercely. Rock Steady dug out her poncho and huddled under it. I draped my rain jacket over my head. Paradox and Tough Love just sat there. We looked at each other in disbelief. What could we do? We waited. Soon we giggled. We got washed. As quickly as it started, it stopped.

"That was interesting."

As we drew closer to Route 42, we were all precariously low on water. We all needed food too, but the eight-mile resupply expedition down the road might prove difficult.

"Sam (I had a tough time calling her Tough Love), pray our resupply goes smoothly."

Right before the road, Dash Von Trapp stood by a beaver pond filtering water for his family. I was not too picky about the water I filtered and drank, but I would not choose beaver pond water. Rock Steady, Paradox, and I thought Dash harbored ulterior motives. Home-schooled, sixteen years old, superior athlete and hiker, Dash indicated all the signs of being smitten with eighteen-year-old Tough Love. Just maybe, he lagged to say hello. We all chatted for a while. Dash crossed the road with his heavy load of water. His family camped two miles further, a long way to carry all that water.

On the road, my attitude dialed into grouch mode. The four of us required a ride on a lonely country road to resupply eight miles away, a return ride, and then a hike to set up camp. Late in the day already, my optimism had eroded. With a positive attitude, Rock Steady stuck out her thumb. A couple of vehicles passed by. Everything hurt. I sat, and my butt thudded in the roadside dust. Dejected, I bowed my head between my knees and muttered to the ground.

"God help us."

Immediately, a car, headed in the wrong direction, stopped and dropped off two hikers. He turned to us and asked,

"You guys need a ride?"

"Yes!"

"All right. Let me turn around and bring you to the store."

Immediately, Homer brought us to the store eight miles away, waited for us to do our shopping, and then brought us back. We hustled and bought food quickly. When hurried, I didn't always make the best choices, but that did not matter now.

On the ride to and from the grocery, we learned a lot about Homer, a man in his seventies, his wife much younger. In 2002, he thru-hiked the AT with his wife and two kids. Encouraged to retire by his wife, he shuttled hikers and maintained a section of trail. His son ran track meets at Liberty University – two of my kids, Joshua and Sam, both attended Liberty. He gave his number to Sam in case she needed a ride to Roanoke Airport, where she'd catch her flight home back to Connecticut. As he dropped us back at the trailhead, he told us we would find an excellent stealth camp just a few tenths of a mile further. We thanked him profusely. After a leisurely climb up the hill through a grassy meadow, we found the site in the woods.

We found four friendly flat sites and set our tents. I thumped down in the dirt to eat, thinking how easily I adapted to sitting on the ground, though I still longed for a chair. The best trail magic crews provided camp chairs. They understood.

I looked forward to the meal immediately after resupplying – so much food to choose from, but Paradox helped me. I asked her,

"This might sound stupid, but how do you decide what to eat? You don't plan your meals like a lot of other hikers…."

"It's simple Right Click. I eat the best thing in my bag. That way, I always eat the best thing in my bag."

I agreed! I loved the simplicity of the concept, while I admired the depth. I wondered if it would work at home. What if we always ate the best thing in our refrigerator? Or our cupboard?

By this point in the adventure, I had learned one valuable lesson - the lighter my load, the further I went, and the more I enjoyed the journey. The food bag fluctuated in weight the most. Fully stuffed, my food bag weighed twelve pounds. After this resupply, it might have topped twelve pounds. I found it hard to pick the best thing in my bag. I decided on Frito's corn chips, onion dip, and two cherry pies. After "dinner', my mood significantly elevated by our good fortune, I crawled into the comfort of my tent. Before turning off my headlamp, I jotted down some notes and recorded others in the AT Guide. In the distance, a single dog barked. And barked. And barked. Where were the owners? Didn't they hear it? I drifted off to sleep with the dog barking.

Suddenly, I woke abruptly. Something yanked on my left foot. A creature had bitten through the tent, snatched my sleeping bag, and shook its head. My foot and leg jerked around. The tent jostled around. I tried to call for help. I tried to shout for Catie (Paradox). I tried to cry for Sami (Tough Love). I tried to summon Kristin (Rock Steady), but the words stuck in my throat. I panicked. The thing would not let go. A deep, mighty moan rumbled upward from my gut. I sat up. The groan morphed into a loud…….

"AAaarrrrgghhhhh… GET OUTTA HERE!"

I heard Sami ask. "What, Dad?"

I couldn't answer. Completely disoriented, my heart hammered. I frantically checked my sleeping bag for rips and the tent for tooth holes, everything still in order, untouched.

"What the hell…?"

It dawned on me that this might have been a dream. The sound of a dog bark drifted in. The dang dog still barked. I checked the time on my iPhone; just after midnight. I rechecked the tent, my sleeping bag, and my foot and ankle for blood. Everything intact. Quiet outside. No animals or monsters rustled through dry leaves.

I never answered Sam. She went back to sleep. I slowly concluded that I had experienced one of the most vivid nightmares of my life. Never before have I screamed because of a dream. At that moment, I could not separate the real and fantasy worlds. As I regained my senses, I wondered about the spiritual realm. Did something from the *dark* side attack? The dang dog barked all night without the owner doing anything. Why was it barking? Where exactly did we camp? On what kind of ground?

The following day, I woke up a little earlier than usual. I packed a little more quickly. I ate breakfast a little faster. I headed north at a slightly speedier pace, determined to put some distance between that site and me.

The Troll under the Bridge

"Hi, what's your trail name?"

"Nameless."

He dubbed himself "Nameless." A self-proclaimed section hiker, he left his brother at the Virginia border. He went north. His brother went south. He wore black leggings under tattered pants, an old army canvas backpack (cumbersome), a massive container of hand sanitizer that he'd offer to fill your little carry bottle with, and a gallon freezer bag of trail mix, a sleeping bag, and a tarp. He labored underneath his load with dark hair, beard, eyes, and broken glasses and rested frequently. I passed him a few times while he silently sat several yards from the trail. Was he in stalk mode? Could he be on the run from the law? He gave the ladies the creeps. Queen Bee and Blister Babe camped with him nearby one night. When it started to rain, he climbed into his sleeping bag and rolled himself in his tarp. From then on, the B's referred to him as Burrito.

The Nameless Burrito frightened Tough Love badly one day. And that pissed me off.

She had the lead in front of Rock Steady, Paradox, and me. We crossed a road and came to a stream. I noticed a familiar face, another Von Trapp, sitting on the stream bank. I didn't see Nameless until I crossed the bridge; he lay on his back in the dirt under the bridge.

"Weird, really weird," I whispered.

Another scorching day; maybe he sought the shade. But where was Tough Love? I asked Nameless.

"Have you seen Tough Love?"

She was here, but she moved on." No emotion in his voice. None.

I knew about the shelter a mile or so away. I knew she was headed there, and Simple Man (father of the von Trapps) would be there. The stream water looked refreshing. I took a bath and did my laundry. The water revived me a bit. I caught a few crayfish too. I dawdled too long, and Tough Love shook visibly when I got to the shelter. Agitated, she told me she encountered Nameless at the stream, no one else around. So uncomfortable, she just kept hiking. Miserable over the sight of my frightened daughter, I chastised myself. I should have hiked directly to the shelter. Grateful that Simple Man and other Von Trapps kept her company, we set up camp. I vowed to stay closer. We agreed she'd stop a few hundred yards before a road and wait for me.

Roads are where the worst things happen.

Dragon's Tooth

An impressive, imposing rock monolith, Dragon's Tooth, frightened me. I watched Tough Love, Paradox, and some Von Trapp's climb to the top of that thing. It gave me the heebie-jeebies. I climbed part way, far as my nerves allowed. I don't like places where one wrong step would lead to death. Dash climbed to the top, where he promptly froze with fear. He needed help down, one foot at a time. If a very athletic teenager loses his nerve, an older man like me stays away. After the crew played there for a bit, we moved on. The steepest descent of the trail lay ahead; we slowly picked our way down. Not particularly afraid and somewhat confident, I handled the scrambles reasonably well; it bordered on fun.

The rest of the crew gradually moved off, and I embraced my role as the caboose. A humid day, I wilted in the heat as I descended. Relieved, I spotted the end. A flat, soft dirt trail emerged and snaked through the woods. I needed to navigate this one last section. Two long rocks angled downward and away from me like children's slides. I placed my right foot on top of one stone, my left on the other. My left skidded and quickly slid down the incline, but my right foot stuck. As I fell, my right foot was pinned under my back. I felt and heard two distinct pops in my right knee. Searing pain ripped through my body. Flashes lit up my mind. I tumbled to the bottom. I lay on my side and sobbed in pain and fright for several seconds. After the initial shock subsided, my head cleared, and the crying dissipated, two thoughts rose,

"I can't believe my hike ended this way."

"How am I going to get off this mountain?"

I worked myself to a sitting position, no small feat. I brought my knees to my chest and cradled my legs with my arms. Tears streaked my cheeks as I fought back the pain, fear, and frustration. I rocked back and forth. Alone, I tried to comfort myself. Unexpectedly, I felt hands on both shoulders. A pleasant sensation spread across my back, soothing me. The intensity of the energy grew; warmth surged through my entire body. I heard a whisper in my left ear.

"You're OK."

Shock didn't allow me to register what happened. I simply stood. No pain. Nothing. I bounced on my feet a few times.

"I'm OK?" I questioned, then affirmed.

"I'm OK! I'm OK!"

Relieved, I grabbed my trekking poles and started walking. Down the trail a bit, it began to sink in. Doubt crept in. Did that just happen? Did I dream the whole thing? I looked at my legs. They had scratches. Blood trickled. I fell. I definitely fell. The more I processed the event, the more agitated I became. My anxiety elevated.

"Me? Why me? Did an angel or God just heal me? I'm not worthy. Yet… I must be."

After the emotions of doubt and unworthiness, anger reared its ugly head. I pointed my trekking poles to the sky and bellowed.

"You're not going to let me quit, no matter what, are You?"

I couldn't even break a leg to get out of this. Now deeply distressed, I caught up with Tough Love, Rock Steady, and Paradox. Tough Love looked straight into my tear-filled eyes.

"Dad, what happened?"

I told the story. She cried. I cried. Paradox affirmed my initial thought.

"Right Click, you might as well quit complaining and stop thinking about quitting. God's not going to let you quit. You're in it for the long haul." She affirmed kindly.

Did I hear the same whisper from my first day on the trail?

"Continue…"

I wanted to be alone. I let the three of them move ahead. We hit VA 624. We decided earlier to hike the four-tenths to the Catawba Grocery, violating the two-tenths rule. On the way down the hill on a paved road, I stepped off the pavement's edge and tumbled again. My yellow croc dislodged from the back of my pack and lay in the street, a bizarre but provocative image. It did not hurt, fortunately, but my confidence disintegrated a little more. Hot dogs and cold Coca-Cola helped a bit. We sat outside the store and watched people get gas. Tough Love remarked,

"I never thought I'd be sitting on concrete at a gas station.... And enjoying it so much."

I wondered if "enjoying" aptly described my experience to this point.

Options

After the delightful visit to the convenience store, we walked another two and a half hours in scorching, humid conditions. Even though I had just resupplied, I ran out of water. This caboose now traveled even more slowly. I felt skittish on descents now. I wanted my confidence back.

As I trudged alone, I thought about getting Tough Love back home. I had mapped a plan to get Sam to the Roanoke Airport for a 3:35 pm flight on Friday, two days away. Then Sandy texted me that the original flight filled up, so Tough Love was now booked on a 10:35 am flight. That five-hour difference completely screwed up the original plan. So, I considered another option; hike nearly fourteen miles, eat at Homeplace in Catawba, and stay in a shelter near the road. I checked the AT Guide and found out that Homeplace closed on Wednesday, effectively scrapping Plan B. It boiled down to two options. The first option, catch a ride into Daleville today, take a zero tomorrow and then bring Tough Love to the airport on Friday. Second option; hike all day Thursday into Daleville, a long, arduous trek of almost nineteen miles.

Options, you always had options…

I caught up to Tough Love, Rock Steady, and Paradox resting in a clearing fairly close to VA 311. Not seeing anyone for a few hours, I had considered all the options. I settled on the first option - get off the trail at VA 311, rest a night or two in the Daleville Super 8, then get Sam on her plane the following morning. When I am alone, I am often in bad company. Hot, irritated, sore, and tired, I informed Tough Love of the plan. She did not receive it well. She wanted to see McAfee Knob (part of the nineteen-mile leg) and hike into Daleville. Unnerved by the fall and subsequent "healing" experience, I told them I didn't think I could do eighteen-plus miles in my current condition, especially in the high heat. Irritated and upset, I got up, shouldered my pack, and headed for the road. Little did I know, Tough Love called home to talk to mom. She didn't want her AT adventure to end this way. Sandy prayed with her. Then Sandy called on the Valentine Battalion to pray for us too. They prayed for an intercession.

The road appeared much closer than I expected, just a few minutes down the hill. As I stepped into the parking lot, I spotted a pop-up tent.

103

"No! Really?" I mumbled. This must be a mirage. Trail magic!

I approached. Several warm greetings of "Hi, Right Click!" welcomed me. Little Von Trapps sat on the ground among tables filled with hot dogs, soda, chips, fruit, and more. I downed four cold sodas, hot dogs, chips, cakes, and fruit. When the three ladies arrived, my body and mind were restored. I cheerfully reversed my earlier decision. I willingly agreed to give the nineteen-mile stretch a go. Her prayer answered, Tough Love sighed in relief, and grinned in anticipation of McAfee Knob. They fueled up too. We walked another mile to John's Spring Shelter. Exhausted, I endeavored to get up early and get the miles done in a reasonable time. Tough Love, Rock Steady, and Paradox played Mafia with the Von Trapps and other hikers. I rested in the sanctuary and comfort of my tent. I scribbled some notes while I listened to the laughter of several hikers.

"I always have options. Always. You'll figure it out."

I quickly fell into a deep sleep, barely disturbed when the ladies returned well after dark.

Daleville

The climb to McAfee Knob looked steep on the AT Guide, but the excitement to reach the most photographed panorama on the Appalachian Trail motivated me. Paradox and Tough Love arrived a few minutes before me. Von Trapps already there; they took pictures while other hikers milled about. I stepped up onto a flat rock and gasped. Pictures did not capture my exhilaration at this magnificent, majestic view. But with the beautiful summer morning providing a perfect backdrop, I saw something that made my heart stop beating. I swore out loud; cardiac arrest loomed.

In cahoots with Paradox, Tough Love hatched a devious plot. Knowing they'd beat me to the Knob, my precious daughter scurried out to the famous overhang. She dangled her feet over the edge. Damn her. I looked at Paradox. She smiled as she photographed my daughter. Damn her too.

I fear heights. As I get older, it gets worse. At one point in my life, I relished being up high. I worked as a house painter, the high peaks and trim guy in my college summer days. I'd set up a thirty-foot ladder, climb near the top, put one foot on the rung, one foot on the house, and stretch as far as I could to paint. At fifty-five, those days passed long ago.

Tough Love knows about my fear. She does not share it. Obviously, and you might ask why I hiked up mountains all summer. Good question.

McAfee Knob stirred up an irrational fear in me to a record level; I disgraced myself with a crabwalk out to the lip. I sat trembling while I put my feet on the step where most people sit, all I could manage. Fighting back waves of terror, I posed for the picture. Once taken, I scooted back on my butt the same way I came. Self-aware, I knew one false step, one stumble, and I'd tumble to my death. My gravestone would read,

"Here lies Right Click. Dumbass fell off a mountain."

I gathered my composure away from the edge, but I couldn't watch the foolishness up there. It made my stomach hurt. What folly do you ask? Groot leaned back over the ledge while Dash held him with a rope. I fled. I sat with Chocolate and a few other Von Trapps and waited for the photo sessions to end. These nutty kids followed a dubious rallying cry.

"It's all about the Insta!"

Finally, the photo sessions ended, and we shouldered our packs. The AT, spectacular along this stretch of Virginia, wound along the edge of Tinker Cliffs. And I mean on the edge. If I stepped wrong and my left ankle rolled or gave way, I'd tumble to my death, one of the few places on the entire AT where one misstep meant death. I didn't like it. My crew moved confidently along the cliffs. I slowed way down, quite nervous. The rolled ankles and the fall at Dragon's Tooth messed with my mind. My confidence waned. Fear established a foothold in my soul. My faith eroded.

I caught up to the three ladies as they calmly sat on the edge of the cliff eating lunch with most of the Von Trapps. Tigger (ten years old) walked along the cliff like he was strolling down a country road. His mom, Chocolate, admonished him to move away from the edge. I could see she shared the same uneasiness and anxiety while we watched the kids. Parenting isn't easy on the trail. Even though I admired this most impressive picnic spot, I desired to leave quickly and move away from impending peril. I got up and followed the white blazes that continued along the cliff edge. I couldn't take it. I ventured inward a few yards and followed the blazes from the safety of the trees, following another worn path for those of us extremely uncomfortable on the edge.

Ultimately, the trail moved away from danger, but I encountered another problem along this stretch – lack of water. Between McAfee Knob and Tinker Cliffs, a distance of six miles, Campbell Shelter is touted as the only water source. We heard all other water sources from Campbell Shelter to Daleville had dried out, a distance of more than fifteen miles. The temperature, excessive physical exertion, and little water combined for a tough challenge. I filled everything I had, seventy-two ounces, knowing I'd have to ration it. Fifteen miles is a long way.

After a couple of hours, we descended into Lamberts Meadow Shelter to rest, the water source indeed dry. Looking at the AT Guide, the terrain seemed relatively flat for the nine miles into Daleville. We noticed lots of little jogs, but we did not expect the difficulty level we encountered. We hiked along the top of a ridgeline, with lots of short ups and downs and climbs up and over rock ledges, which were rugged and picturesque.

The four of us showed severe physical depletion for the last few miles. I looked straight down at the trail and willed my feet to move, the pain of fatigue intense. Altogether, we barely communicated, each of us absorbed in our world of suffering. Lack of water increased the agony. Paradox led. The sound of a lawnmower in the distance indicated we neared civilization. For me, it stirred up memories of home, a welcome option now. Suddenly, Paradox made a strange sound that snapped me out of my trance. I looked up. She made a very odd motion; it looked like a squirrel holding a nut.

"What?" I hissed.

Then she pointed. I looked in that direction. Bear! Holy crap! It meandered through the woods thirty yards away. It stopped. We took pictures and videos. It sat down, shot us a bored bear look, sighed, stood up, and wandered away.

"Paradox, what the hell was that?" I mimicked her signal.

"That's my bear signal, a standing bear."

"First, that bear was not standing. Second, you looked like a squirrel."

Through the pain, we appreciated the humor. Tough Love wanted to see a bear; one showed up less than a quarter mile from the end of her journey. When we stepped into civilization, relief and joy flooded over us. Immediately to our right stood Howard Johnson's. We checked in. In our first room, the shower didn't work, so I went back to the front desk, a very long walk after a very long day, and got another room. The shower worked, but we'd find out later that the air conditioner did not. On the trail, hotels often reserved rooms in disrepair for hikers. I know why. Often hikers piled many people into one room and deceived the hotel management. Their actions reflected poorly on the entire hiker community.

We celebrated Tough Love's nineteenth birthday the following day at the complimentary HoJo breakfast. Paradox and Rock Steady greeted her with balloons and chocolate. The restaurant patrons, primarily hikers, sang Happy Birthday to my daughter. Even though the women in charge of the buffet yelled at us, much to our amusement, this day boded quite sad for me. Tough Love had a plane to catch. We called Homer for a ride, he was not available, but he sent his son. We rode mostly in silence. I got Sam checked in and walked her to the security line.

"I love you, Sam. Because of you, I think I can do this. Thank you. I am going to miss you... more than you know."

"Thank you, Dad. This was an adventure of a lifetime. You're stronger than you think. I'll miss you too."

We hugged. I held on beyond the awkward point. Finally, I let her go and watched her navigate security. She looked back one last time. Her eyes blazed with gratitude and confidence. I waved and turned away quickly. As I walked back to the car, tears rolled down my cheeks.

Tough Love, a novice backpacker just twenty-three days earlier, hiked two hundred eighty miles of the Appalachian Trail and experienced magical, miraculous moments. She tested herself and succeeded. Pride swelled my heart and leaked out of my eyes. She arrived precisely at the right time and inspired me for three weeks. I'd definitely miss her. I envied her too. She'd have hot showers, endless cold water, flush toilets, electricity, a lavish food supply, and a comfortable bed.

As I rode away, I choked back the grief and tried to replace it with gratitude.

JUNE

Rock Steady

After Tough Love left, I shifted my mind away from the grief and focused on doing typical thru-hiker stuff. Luckily, I shared these chores with Rock Steady and Paradox. In the planning stage, I figured zeros (days where you do zero miles) would be a day of rest. Wrong. Going into town proved more demanding than hiking. Here's a list of typical tasks.

1. Find a way into town (hitch, shuttle, or, worst-case scenario, walk.)
2. Get a place to stay (hotel, motel, hostel, relative, friend, family, etc.)
3. Shower. Clean my body.
4. Do laundry. Clean my clothes.
5. Feed me.
6. Unpack, clean, and dry all my other gear (way harder if it had rained the previous few days).
7. Pick up packages (and process them) and mail stuff home.
8. Repair/replace gear.
9. Resupply – figure out how many days of food are needed until the next resupply, then find and buy it all.
10. Repackage the purchased food to reduce weight and protect it from the weather.
11. Sleep.
12. Re-pack everything in my pack.
13. Feed me again.
14. Find a ride (or walk) back to the trailhead.

I switched to a good room (my 3rd) near the lobby reserved for actual customers, not hikers. This time the shower flowed; the air conditioner worked (thank God – still steaming hot outside) with a television. I talked with Dr. Pickles and Mockingbird a bit, again impressed by their warmth, humor, and fantastic outlook.

The next morning, Paradox left the crew to spend a few days with her husband; she would slackpack some days so she wouldn't need to make up so much ground to catch Rock Steady and me. I hit the trail before Rock Steady. We planned to meet up later that day.

Most of the time, when you leave town on the AT, you're faced with a climb. Or, as I frequently heard, when in doubt which way the trail goes, look up, certainly the case coming out of Daleville. I lumbered into Fullhardt Knob Shelter for some water and a snack. On another beautiful summer day, I stretched out and rested. Paradox strolled into camp. I smiled; always wonderful to see the light in her eyes. Today she traveled light, slackpacking to meet her husband several miles down the trail.

Paradox and I talked several times about some AT rules I formulated. Here's one of Right Click's Rules.

"When you come across a privy in the woods, use it."

I used the privy at Fullhardt Knob. Preacher, seventy-three years old, a section hiker, used it right after me. When he came out, he addressed me.

"Hey, Right Click, didn't you see that huge black snake in the privy?"

"There was no huge black snake in the privy."

"Sure there was! It crawled out when I went in."

"There was NO huge black snake in the privy."

"I can show it to you; it's right over there." Preacher pointed toward the outhouse.

"You're delusional. Are you getting enough nutrition?"

He probed my eyes to see if I was serious. Understanding flashed across his face; he acquiesced.

"All right then."

Paradox knew me well enough to recognize my blatant denial in action immediately. She smirked at the whole exchange. It took Preacher a little longer to register but register it did. Paradox shook her head in disbelief; time for her to move on.

"See you in a few days." She said with affection.

She ambled off.

Rock Steady caught up. We chatted easily. We hiked the rest of the way into Wilson Creek Shelter. A guy named Maps greeted us.

"Hi, I'm Right Click."

"Is this Mrs. Click?" He asked.

Rock Steady quickly and vehemently corrected him. However, it would not be the only time people would make that assumption. Some people assumed Paradox was our daughter when she and I hiked with her. I was fifty-five, Rock Steady thirty-eight, and Paradox twenty-five; the math didn't quite work out. It pissed off Rock Steady but amused me. Other times, people assumed that Rock Steady and Paradox were a couple. People make many assumptions.

That night in camp Rock Steady and I met Cast Away, who looked eerily similar to the famous Tom Hanks character. He worked for the Appalachian Trail Conservancy and did incredible miles, between twenty and thirty daily. Cast Away, a fabulous storyteller, a vegan, and quite gregarious, told us about trips into restaurants with Wilson (he carried a pretty darn good replica of the famous volleyball too). He would order two meals. When Wilson didn't eat his, he scolded him loudly and then finished it for him. He loved the comments, looks, and whispers from the restaurant staff and patrons.

The following day, Cast Away was long gone; we went through our morning routines. As we packed our tents, a deer wandered into camp, and calmy strolled by just a few feet away. We set out and hiked back and forth across the Blue Ridge Parkway. We found Maps in one of the parking areas. He didn't feel good and didn't look good either, pale and sweating profusely. I wondered about his heart. He asked if he could hike with us for a while. Rock Steady was worried, she replied.

"Of course."

We made it thirty yards into the woods, and he couldn't go on. We suggested he get a ride into town from a man parked in the lot behind us. Wishing him well, we moved on. I'd run into Maps several hundred miles up the trail; he recovered nicely, something he ate, he said. Rock Steady, and I hiked seventeen miles as several thunderstorms skirted by but always missed us. Occasionally we'd separate for a bit, where I thought about what made a good hiking partner.

1. *True compatibility* (you like each other). Everyone liked Rock Steady; she listened actively and possessed a wonderful sense of humor.

2. *Same pace.* Rock Steady kept the same pace; that's how she earned her trail name. No matter the terrain, she was right on two miles per hour, rock steady. I could match her pace easily.

3. *Similar goals for each day.* When we first met, she and I agreed to start in single digits. We stuck to that game plan. Now that we were in better physical condition, we set higher daily mileage goals.

4. *Similar financial resources and beliefs.* We both had adequate resources. Many people who thru-hike are on a shoestring budget. We were not. We were willing to pay for hotel rooms (as opposed to the less expensive option of a hostel). We'd also call for rides through shuttle services instead of

110

hitchhiking.

5. *Similar philosophy about the Appalachian Trail.* I believed that I was responsible to the AT, an obligation to respect the trail. That meant cleaning up after myself (Leave No Trace). I picked up other people's trash when practical. Rock Steady appreciated the trail too.

6. *An attitude of gratitude.* Gratitude is vital, not only for my life but also for those I like to hang with. I believe gratitude is so precious a commodity that I heavily weigh the gratitude quotient when I hire employees. Gratitude makes for good employees and great companions. We were both extremely grateful to have the opportunity to hike the entire trail. Most of the people I grew close to on the trail were chock full of gratitude.

7. *Positive personality.* An optimistic perspective closely aligns with gratitude. At times my positive attitude waned or completely disappeared. I could get grouchy, sullen, and sad: not a fun person to hike with. I tried to keep my sense of humor and to take the adventure lightly, but the difficulty of the journey wore on me at times. Rock Steady never lost her positive perspective, even when physically ill.

8. *Comfortable in silence or conversation.* Sometimes I hiked with someone within earshot, but we did not talk. We just walked together. Comfortable with silence, I listened to many people fill the dead space with babble because of their uneasiness.

9. *Similar attitude about when to take zero days (or Nero days).* I probably wanted to rest more than necessary, especially in the beginning. For the first one hundred thirty-one days, I took eleven zeros every twelve days or so. For the last fifty-eight days, I took only one. As I got better at planning, I took more Neros (near zero), got into town midday, did all the chores, and left town the following day. That way, I hiked some miles each day.

10. *Flexibility.* I ran into people who believed being right very important, their way or the highway. Sure, I formulated my ideas about how far to hike, when to rest, and when to duck into town, but I also compromised. I listened to others and went along with an alternative plan. Sometimes I didn't. The

rooms of recovery reinforced this concept – flexible people don't get bent out of shape.

11. *Honesty.* Since 1987, when I began my recovery, I have based my life on honesty. I liked to hike with honest people. They openly reveal how they are feeling or what hurts. This helps the decision-making process and builds trust.

12. *Similar schedules.* Even though I'd wake up at first light, often I'd fall back asleep. Other hikers woke at first light, and less than an hour later, they'd be on the trail. Some were even up and out earlier than that. Not me. Or Rock Steady. Or Paradox. We took our time in the morning, but we would walk later in the day than most hikers.

Rock Steady made for an ideal hiking companion. She treated me gently with kindness during this time, knowing I missed Tough Love. I appreciated that. Gradually the pain lessened. Green, green, green Virginia soothed my spirit too. I've read that The Long Green Tunnel (Virginia) can be tedious and boring to some. I adored it. I found all the lush foliage healing and comforting. I loved Virginia, all five hundred fifty-four miles of it.

Then the rain came.

A Wet Grind

Perfect weather had blessed us for three weeks; we walked in the sunshine every day. When Tough Love left, the clouds set in. Rock Steady, and I rolled into a shelter where the Von Trapps resided. We set up camp, went to the shelter's picnic table, and ate dinner with them. I found the Von Trapps fun, exciting and endearing. They missed Tough Love too. Amid our reminiscing, thunder rumbled, lightning flashed, then dark clouds cruised in with a deafening rushing sound. Rain!

We bolted toward our tents. Rock Steady madly snatched the clothes she had laid out to dry and dove into her tent just as the deluge hit. She laughed loudly and delightedly before the thunder and the rain drowned out all noise. This torrential storm tested my tent like no other. And it failed. Miserably. As water dripped in from the seams, I mopped with bandannas and wrung them out in the vestibule. I kept my gear out of the puddles but didn't sleep very well in the moist conditions, concerned about another deluge.

Over the next day's hike, it rained off and on, and my gear never dried. I worried, which is unusual for me. I learned on the trail that once a tent started leaking, and stayed wet, the next time it rained, more water leeched in. Damn. The hike took us over Highcock Knob to Matt's Creek Shelter. Simple Man and some of the Von Trapps settled in the shelter. Rock Steady and I set up next to Matt's Creek – an attractive location. No precipitation fell, so I hoped to dry my tent. Rock Steady carried seam sealer, I planned some repair work, but the tent needed to dry completely.

As I waited, Dash, Tigger, and Groot (Von Trapps) came in with a small dead rattlesnake they killed on the trail. Another rainstorm moved in as we discussed the ambiguous merits of killing this creature over dinner. I went to check on my tent and found water pooled inside. Crap. Time to consider my options… Again.

Option 1: Sleep in a drippy tent for a long, wet night.

Option 2: Sleep in a crowded shelter with the Von Trapps, another long night with all those bodies in a crowded space.

Option 3: Sleep in Rock Steady's tent with her. Hah! Not happening; both crystal clear on that one.

Option 4: Fix the tent. Maybe I could drape my raincoat over the top?

Option 5 (presented out of the blue): Groot offered me the fly to his three-person tent. He planned to sleep in the shelter. I chose that option. It fit over my tent beautifully, and with some rigging from my trekking poles, I created a fully ventilated, dry, comfortable sleeping arrangement! Thank you, Groot. Hikers helped each other.

I lay comfortably and warm (my sleeping bag was slightly damp). I listened to the creek and the rain and thought about my response to this situation. My clothes stank (even to my high tolerance nose). All three of my bandannas stank. My shoes reeked. My grimy, muddy, soaked socks emanated a nasty odor distinctly their own. Despite being encased in extreme hiker funk, I felt grateful and a bit proud. Not mad or frustrated, I chose acceptance first, then engaged in some reflection. A solution beyond my comprehension presented itself. Could I be evolving out here on the trail? I prayed for a bright, sunny day; it would go a long way to cleaning up this mess. I drifted off to sleep.

I woke to people walking by – the Von Trapps. Up and on their way early, Groot would want his fly. But I didn't want to get up; outside rain dampened my motivation. Couldn't I just lay here? I looked for the positive. At least it was warm. I winced when I slid into wet clothes, groaned when I crawled outside, disassembled Groot's fly, and brought it to him. I thanked him profusely.

We hiked through misty rain all morning until we arrived at another Appalachian Trail landmark – the James River footbridge. As a rite of passage, some thru-hikers jumped off into the water. I considered it. As we crossed, the bridge felt pretty damn high. Quickly, I talked myself out of it. I listed several darn good reasons.

"It's not hot, so I don't need to cool off."

"I could get hurt; other hikers talked about people getting hurt."

"I'm older and frail; the likelihood of doing damage is greater."

"I could land wrong and drown."

"Right Click, the risk isn't worth the reward."

I didn't need any more justification; I convinced myself. Rock Steady decided to stay put too. We hung around for a few minutes and then moved through the mist. Later that day, we watched an iPhone video of Groot, Dash, and Ads all jumping. They survived.

Another slog, another night in the rain, another night, and Groot lent me his fly. Another morning with rain, another time to put on damp clothes and wet boots. Rock Steady, and I walked through the rain. She said her husband liked to say,

"You get to know a person's true character after five days of hiking in the rain."

It started to rain harder. Motivated to get to town, Rock Steady and I had eleven miles to cover to get to the road. We stopped at a shelter to rest a bit and eat something. Hikers filled the refuge, most extremely irritated with the days of rain. Ready to continue and excited to get to town, I stood and faced the shelter with my arms outspread and orated loudly.

"My hiking brethren, one must embrace the weather! One must become one with nature, like Treebeard in Lord of the Rings! With the proper attitude and channeling of energy from the precipitation, one can move effortlessly and gracefully through the forest!"

Blackout appeared from around the side of the shelter and growled.

"I'm going to MURDER you Right Click!" I officially received my first death threat.

Some people handle five days of rain better than others.

With no views to distract me and no desire to take breaks on wet ground, I covered miles quickly in the rain. Not much to do except keep moving. Rock Steady, and I made it to US 60 by 1:00 pm; time to get a ride. We called a shuttle driver from the AT Guide. He'd be there in less than half an hour; the cost was fifteen dollars. Rock Steady, and I elected to call (and pay) for a guaranteed ride straight to a hotel rather than the uncertainty of hitchhiking. As our ride pulled up, Blackout, Tick, and

Pocahontas emerged out of the woods. They acted like they were entitled to get in the truck.

I capitulated, but I asked them to split the cost, three dollars each. Blackout said he'd pay me back in cheeseburgers sometime down the trail. Tick didn't respond at all. Pocahontas handed me three dollars. Blackout and Tick got out at the first hotel; Pocahontas, a sweet young woman (I liked her spirit), stayed in the truck with Rock Steady and me. Her traveling companions? Not as nice. On the way to the post office, I gave Pocahontas her three dollars back. It didn't feel right to take her money when her two companions didn't pay. To her credit, she appreciated the gesture. I appreciated hers.

Rock Steady, and I got dropped off at the Budget Inn in Buena Vista. We began room negotiations with the owner; a single room cost eighty dollars, and a double room was the same price. After the briefest of hesitations and some unspoken communication with Rock Steady, I asked for two single rooms.

Once in the room, my work began. First, get the laundry done. I removed my socks and rinsed them in the sink to get some mud out. The Darn Toughs, darn tough and darn dirty, got wrung twenty-one times (I counted) and still generated nothing but *"old black water, keep on rollin', Mississippi moon won't you keep on shinin' on me."* Hands sore, I gave up. I piled all my wet, stinking clothes in a pile and hopped in the shower. Black water rolled off my shrinking body; a fantastic amount of black water pooled at my feet.

"I have never been this dirty. How is this even possible?" I wondered aloud.

I dressed in my town clothes - an extra pair of light gym shorts, a Marmot Precip raincoat, and yellow crocs. Sandy thinks I bought yellow crocs because they drew attention. That's not true. I purchased yellow crocs so I wouldn't lose them.

I called home while doing laundry. Sandy pondered a notion about me possibly coming home for Father's Day weekend. When she asked Matthew (our thirteen-year-old son), he said,

"Mom, to be honest, I don't think you should. I'd love to see Dad, but I think he'd probably stay home once he gets home and comfortable."

When Sandy relayed this conversation to Joshua (our twenty-year-old son), he laughed.

"Why are you laughing?" Sandy asked.

"Mom, I would have said the same thing Matthew did!"

Two of my daughters said the same thing too. They wanted me to finish, but I'd have to walk there to see home again.

Once in clean clothes, Rock Steady and I feasted in a local restaurant, then resupplied. The next priority, repair my tent. I applied seam sealant to my Tarptent Double Rainbow until 12:30 am. I went to bed with gear drying (hopefully) all around me.

I used every minute until checkout time the following day to completely dry my gear. Of particular concern were the seams of my tent. Ideally, they needed a total of twenty-four hours. I packed it last. I knocked on Rock Steady's door. We made our way to the fine dining establishment, Hardee's. I gorged myself on breakfast food, eating the last of their offerings before they switched to lunch. We weathered a rush of high school seniors who had just finished rehearsal for that evening's graduation. Several asked questions about the trail. Rock Steady answered politely but not with her usual enthusiasm. Plus, she didn't eat much. That concerned me. A thru-hiker without an appetite? Not good.

By late afternoon, we sauntered through sunshine up and over Bald Knob. After a peaceful hike of six miles, we entered a beautiful meadow just off the road and an adjacent parking lot. We talked about the magic of this place, factored in that Paradox traveled behind us, and decided to stay put. That evening I fell asleep somewhat enchanted, listening to mystical songbirds as the sunset.

Ahead, we faced a legendary climb – The Priest. I encountered legendary climbs earlier on the trail, for example, Blood Mountain and Jacob's Ladder. Each time, my mind concocted unwarranted anxiety. I managed them without an inordinate amount of difficulty. The Priest loomed immediately ahead, an ascent allegedly so difficult that people confessed their thru-hiking sins in the shelter's logbook. I resolved not to get anxious about it.

One of the seven most difficult hikes on the Appalachian Trail, the Priest proved not very difficult going northbound. At the top, we breezed through a nice flat area that sported some fantastic Stonehenge-like rocks just before a descent to the shelter. We checked out the shelter; plenty of camping on flat sites, but the bugs! Thick, thick, thick mosquitoes assailed me. While I got chewed up, Rock Steady read the entries in the shelter log. She laughed out loud. She shared some of the entries. People confessed to pooping in the woods and not digging a hole… stuff like that. I got grossed out when someone admitted to pooping in the middle of the trail.

"I'm going back up to get out of these bugs!" I insisted.

"OK, I'll meet you up there." She wanted to read the rest of the logbook.

I headed back up to Stonehenge. By now, I knew what I desired in a tent site - flat, high up (especially in the summer because of the cooler air), near water and pine needles. Rarely found, though, water challenging to find high up. I found a suitable spot, dropped my pack, and focused on removing gear when an orange flash jumped out from behind a rock and screamed at me! In response, I squealed like a terrified, small child. What the hell attacked me?

A smiling young lady with the trail name Paradox.

"You jerk! You scared the shit out of me! I gotta check my shorts."

"Good to see you too, Right Click!" She grinned, very proud of herself.

A hiking beast (said in utmost admiration), Paradox conquered massive miles to catch us, my awe of her accomplishment readily apparent. Rock Steady and Paradox reunited, chattered away deep into the night, truly soul sisters. I listened contentedly as I reclined in my tent out of the bugs. I drifted off.

Rock Steady's scream startled me awake. No longer dark, Rock Steady yelled again, this time in anger. Paradox laughed. A mouse ate through Rock Steady's costly Cuban fiber tent. Pissed off (rare for her), she patched the hole with high-quality duct tape. She remained angry for longer than usual but eventually laughed it off.

Despite waking to a Rock Steady holler, I drew on a good night's sleep. The other side of the Priest presented a brutal, vicious, steep descent; climbing up this way would have been nightmarish. Before this treacherous stretch, I had already concluded that hiking consisted of much more than just walking; I experimented with different steps. For instance, descending the Priest, I started using a sidestep, a move where you step sideways off a dirt bank, rock, or root. I learned later from Dr. Pickles, a Parkour enthusiast, that this particular move was labeled a "tack." I liked that. However, the tacks didn't prevent my knees from aching.

Next, we headed up Three Ridges Mountain; nobody warned us about this immense, challenging climb. By now, my body utilized a natural transmission, complete with downhill gears and uphill gears that targeted different muscles. When I switched gears, it took a few hundred yards before my body adjusted to the transition. Three Ridges, a long uphill slog in hot, humid conditions kept me in low gear; I poured sweat as I ground out one step at a time. After several hours, still, in my lowest gear, I collapsed at Maupin Field Shelter after a rugged fourteen miles. My two companions fell next to me; we lay in the dirt, packs still on, and said nothing; no need to say anything; we knew what we had just endured.

Rock Steady and Paradox made situations like this tolerable. At the time, I took them for granted. All through Virginia, I navigated through the green tunnel with no one in sight. Yet, I knew I walked ahead, behind them, or in the middle of the two. That reassured me, knowing we would meet soon. My spirit elevated when hungry, thirsty, sweaty, and tired; I spied Paradox's bright orange shirt through the foliage at either a water source or resting spot. Seeing their appreciation always inspired me.

Always. We shared about the trail, what we saw, and how we felt. We discussed our options without judgment, just with good humor, warmth, and friendship. I began to understand the "trail family" depiction.

The next evening, we stayed at the Paul C. Wolfe Shelter after sixteen miles. I found a spot up the hill a bit from Dr. Pickles and Mockingbird. While we ate dinner together, Finn (from Finland) strode into camp and set up four inches from Dr. Pickles, and Mockingbird's tent, similar to the move Chip made several weeks ago in the middle of the Three Wise Men. They shot us a look of disapproval but, to their credit, said nothing.

As night fell, I rested in my bungalow (tent) and succeeded in getting the US Women's National Soccer Team live on my iPhone in their first World Cup game; a small taste of technology out in the woods; not worried about using up battery power, we were headed into town the next day.

Walking with Wallet

Most thru-hikers are very open on the trail. What you see is what you get. I consistently felt welcomed and accepted. I tried to do the same. We shared the same quest, traveled the same ground, and built strong bonds. I met Wallet a few times. A young lad from Connecticut, he earned his trail name when he lost his wallet early on, then miraculously, the wallet made it's way back to him, all contents intact. He started the same day I did with a few other light-hearted, partying young guys, also from Connecticut – one of them, Cruise Control, who later underwent a name change to Little Giant.

I left the Wolfe shelter slightly before him. He caught up with me fairly quickly, and I stepped aside to let him go by. Young guys hiked much faster than me. He said he wanted to walk with me. Cool. We talked to the road. I told him about my recovery, knowing full well he smoked weed. He congratulated me on my twenty-seven years, clean and sober. I loved listening to his thoughts and his fresh perspective. Time flew by as we discussed a deep topic - evolution versus creation; he was an evolutionist, me a creationist. He did not try to sway me to his position, and I didn't try to persuade him to mine. He told me he felt comfortable with me; this topic usually became heated.

He laughed when I said, "Yeah, that's what happens when neither one is an asshole."

Before I knew it, we reached the road. A few of his friends waited. Rock Steady and Paradox weren't far behind me. We split up easily. Wallet went his way; I went mine. I'd run into Wallet from time to mine. I believe we mutually respected and admired each other.

Paradox's mom picked us up and drove us to Waynesboro, VA. I ate a huge breakfast. We resupplied, and I visited the barber. The dude had cut hair in the same little store for over forty years and did an excellent job trimming my goatee.

Flutter rolled into the motel the next morning; he hiked long days to catch us. To my surprise, I greeted him with some enthusiasm; little did I know what the future held in store. We caught up over the hotel-provided breakfast fare. We agreed to meet up the next day.

The two ladies and I headed into Shenandoah National Park.

The Tedious Trail

I pondered trivial things as I plodded into the Shenandoahs. At this moment, I contemplated pain.

"How many steps have I taken where something didn't hurt?"

It seemed like it was always something. I walked for days with blisters on my pinky toes. I had chronic knee pain. My shoulder ached. But I just kept walking. This stretch of Virginia became tedious, yet Shenandoah National Park provided perks, places called Waysides where I could buy food and cold Cokes. My passion for Coca-Cola intensified during my thru-hike - the elixir of the Gods! At the Waysides, I liked to talk with people; breaking the ice was usually relatively easy. People often gave thru-hikers celebrity status. They'd ask all kinds of questions. Sometimes I'd get a question about how much weight I lost. I'd say I started at two hundred fifty-four pounds, and to this point, I've dropped about "fill in the blank" pounds, usually around thirty. Then I'd point to Rock Steady and say,

"See her?"

"Ya."

"She started at three hundred twenty-seven pounds; look at her now!"

"No! Really? Are you kidding?"

"Yes, I am."

And we'd laugh. Rock Steady would shake her head and laugh too. She appreciated my idiocy. I did the same thing with Flutter.

"See that guy. He started at four hundred eleven pounds." Flutter didn't find it amusing.

We stopped on a ledge on Hightop Mountain with a thunderstorm in the distance. With a spectacular view, I set up the time-lapse feature on my iPhone. I had bought a bag of Skittles at the last Wayside, and I looked for them as the storm inched toward us. I dug through my food bag. Not there. I emptied my pack. No Skittles. I checked the pockets on my hip belt. Nothing. I did not notice Rock Steady and Paradox stifling their laughter. I tended to be a bit dramatic on the trail, so they pilfered my Skittles and thoroughly enjoyed my reaction. They waited until I emptied my entire pack and drove myself crazy before they held them up for me to see.

"Bastards! Give me those!" Fearing for their lives, Paradox threw them to me.

I tore open the bag as I feigned anger but secretly admired their ingenuity. We ducked into the trees just as the storm hit. Paradox and I laughed together when the deluge hit. It didn't last long, just enough to get us soaked. We continued to trudge along. As evening approached, we started looking for a stealth site. The AT Guide showed a spring at a former shelter site three-tenths of a mile off the trail, outside the go zone. But seeing no other viable options, we headed down a trail overgrown with high grass. We got soaked again, the tall grass still wet from the rain. We found the spring. Down the path, the old shelter had been converted into a locked shed for trail maintenance workers. The site sported picnic tables, a nice privy, and flattened tent sites with some of the area recently mowed. In the overgrowth, we spotted a bear pole. Flutter walked near one of the picnic tables and immediately started to howl. Wasps stung him as he ran off and yelped! A large nest hung under the table. I had walked by earlier, and they didn't bother me.

After things settled down, we decided to set up under a sign that prohibited camping. Flutter, the first to set up, first to finish eating, and the first to lie down, treated the process like a competition. The rest of us were still setting up when he asked,

"I have us doing sixteen point two miles; is that what you have? How far do you want to go tomorrow?"

Tired, wet, grouchy, I snapped back a testy reply.

"I haven't even got out of my wet clothes and haven't eaten yet, give me a break!"

He grumbled. I immediately regretted my response; I forgot he had been stung a few times. Later that evening, while lying in our respective tents, Paradox and I chatted about the AT Guide. We looked ahead to the end and commented on how intense New Hampshire and Maine looked. We wondered about the flatness of Maine on the last page or two until the climb up Katahdin. Flutter reacted angrily from his lair.

"Why the hell are you talking about the end when you won't plan tomorrow?"

He growled, his anger combined with mine, effectively putting a damper on the evening. As darkness fell, I lay in my tent, everything damp, hot, and humid, and stared through the mosquito netting. Floating lights caught my attention. They emerged from the grass, drifted for a while, moved vigorously for a bit, then settled back into drift mode. I've seen my share of fireflies, but these Shenandoans were the largest and brightest I had ever seen, like mini-lanterns. Was I on the set of Avatar? Hundreds upon hundreds of fireflies flashed and floated, flashed and floated. Genuinely mesmerized by nature's magic, my spirit lifted, and I quietly thanked God. I wondered if any of my companions noticed. It seemed that whenever my emotions rose, the trail addressed them.

The following day over breakfast, we reached an accord and set our sights on Big Meadows Campground. The trail passed near the entrance, and we found some food at the camp store. I watched the activity, hundreds of people and families on vacation, and my heart longed for home. I wondered what my kids were doing, what Sandy was doing. I wished they were with me. The four of us – Rock Steady, Paradox, Flutter, and I – hung out and talked with other hikers. We chatted with some of the vacationers. A few hikers met friends or relatives. Some got picked up and driven into the campground, where a site awaited them, with access to a hot shower.

We discussed our options and decided to get back on the trail to find a stealth campsite. The trail circled it's way back behind Big Meadows Campground. Almost immediately, Flutter looked up a hill and pointed.

"How about up there?"

Skeptically, he asked me to assess a site strewn with sharp rocks, fallen branches, and high grass. I told him I didn't want to camp there. He got angry and stormed off. He yelled.

"Every site has rocks; it's a goddamn mountain!"

Exhausted, a ball of despair burst deep within. I sat down on the side of the trail and let him go on as he cursed and ranted. Rock Steady and Paradox checked in with me. I told them I'd be fine; just go on. On they went. I pulled myself up after several minutes and trudged along, wondering why I had to feel everything so damn deeply. Why was I taking his reaction personally?

I walked by some excellent sites; they looked like actual campground sites that hadn't been used for a few seasons. Eventually, at dusk, we walked into the campground. After another good walk to where you pay for a site, we found very few available. After much discussion, Rock Steady and Paradox got a site together. Flutter and I opted out. We questioned how quiet this place would be with so many people

121

crammed in. We shuffled back down the road. We returned to the sites I had spotted earlier.

Another guy from Australia camped nearby. Flutter eventually offered me an apology, and I accepted, but I felt discouraged. Part of me appreciated the quiet away from the throng and felt abandoned and cast out. I listened to a thunderstorm approach and then drift away. I settled in and, as usual, fell into a deep sleep, aware I used to sleep to escape emotional pain.

The following day, we packed up and headed to the campground to avail ourselves of the facilities—nothing like a flush toilet and clean water to elevate a mood. We met up with the ladies. They relayed that though the hot showers were fabulous (with no towels), that sleep did not come easily due to all the noise. That might not have been entirely true; they may have trodden lightly around my emotional wounds.

Close Encounter

The four of us hiked closely together at the end of a long, humid hike. Flutter, positioned in front, suddenly shouted. With Paradox second, me third, and Rock Steady fourth, we quickly stacked up behind Flutter. He pointed to a bear and her two cubs. One of the cubs burst across the trail a few feet before him and immediately climbed a tree on the other side. That's when he shouted, startled by the little bear. Once he spotted the mother, he stood between mama and her two cubs, one of the most dangerous situations you could face on the trail (or so we had been indoctrinated).

Flutter calmly talked to Mama bear and backed up with his fist raised, the military man signaling for the patrol to stop. Mama stood on one side, the two cubs in a tree on the other. No way through. I could feel the anxiety rising in Flutter, his mind alerting him to perceived extreme danger. But I reacted differently. I watched mama bear. She stood calmly, looked at us, her cubs, and looked back at us. I felt peaceful, with no alarm bells going off in my mind. After several seconds of this, I became fascinated; not the experience we read about or heard stories about. Mama bear did not threaten us. What was she doing? I'm sure if we did something stupid, like try to pet one of her cubs, she may have reacted aggressively. But for now, we just stood still, together (as instructed), and observed – all senses on alert.

After a few more minutes, mama casually crossed the trail; motioned to her cubs by bouncing on her front paws; the cubs tumbled out of the tree. All three of them scampered off into the woods to our right. We all exhaled noticeably. We searched each other's eyes and knew we had just experienced something special. And Flutter now had a tremendous story to add to his arsenal. We heard it a dozen times in the next day or two, with a lot more drama than occurred. Rock Steady, Paradox, and I exchanged glances when he hinted that he saved us from a severe mauling.

Abandoned

The four of us formed an uneasy alliance. Three of us communicated nonverbally – one of us did not. We often hiked alone together. Yet at breaks, lunch, and night in camp, we talked cordially about getting to the unofficial halfway point – Harper's Ferry. Flutter wanted to make it for Father's Day weekend so he could be home with his Maryland family.

As we drew closer to Front Royal, we talked about going into town and possibly taking a zero. Rock Steady did not feel well; she was more tired than usual, her stomach bothering her, and she had no appetite. None. This worried Paradox and me. Flutter drifted away now when he called his wife. Typically, we overheard our conversations with loved ones. In the evening, I'd often talk with Sandy and the kids. I knew the others could hear me just as I could listen to them. Flutter did not want us to hear his.

Again, Sandy and I discussed the idea of me coming home to Connecticut for Father's Day weekend. It still appealed wildly to me – family, hot showers, flush toilets, food, my bed, flat screen TV – but I didn't dwell on the idea and certainly didn't push it. My kids' sentiments resonated. I'd stay put. So instead of feeling unwanted or rejected, I sincerely appreciated their love and commitment to me finishing this thing.

When our hiking crew approached Front Royal, we determined where we wanted to stay. The AT Guide served as an excellent resource for this. Before reaching the town, we discussed that the ladies would share one room and the men (Flutter and I) would share another. The day before, we hiked big miles (for us) in high heat and looked forward to the respite. Flutter broke camp early in the morning and headed out as per our routine. But we didn't see Flutter for the rest of the day – not at snack breaks or lunch. That was unusual. Usually, he'd wait for us. We came to the road, US 522. No Flutter. Now we have become a bit concerned. We looked for a note on the message board at the trailhead. Nothing. Where'd he go? As the ladies searched for a phone number for a shuttle, I stuck my thumb out, and a pickup truck stopped immediately. We clamored in the back and drove away into town. I called Flutter from the lobby of the Quality Inn. He said he booked a bed in a hostel near the trail. Quietly I responded.

"Oh."

I hung up. He abandoned the crew, and I didn't like how he did it; that pissed me off. I am such a baby sometimes. Flutter left, and Rock Steady grew sicker. Her appetite all but disappeared. Paradox and I convinced her to see a doctor. This stubborn, tough Pennsylvania farm girl called and went to a walk-in clinic, underscored how sick she felt. She told them about her lack of appetite and belly troubles. They gave her a kit to catch her poop – of course, we had great fun with that. They gave her an antibiotic and antiviral medication. They wanted her to stick around for a few days to get the test results. She felt listless. But I knew Rock Steady by now; one zero would be all she would consider – no more than one day off the trail - period.

Paradox accompanied Rock Steady to the clinic to drop off the bag o'poop while I wandered a bit through town. I found Spelunker's, Front Royal's famous burger place. The restaurant lived up to its reputation; the burger was so incredulously beautiful that I took a pic and posted it on Instagram. The ladies texted that they were on their way and would arrive shortly. I raved about the three burgers I ate, a massive mountain of fries, several Coca-Colas, and a milkshake. Paradox eyes burned with a hunger mania only fellow thru-hikers understand. She dug into her meal with controlled ferocity and, as I did, went back in line and ordered more food. Regular customers looked at us in awe. We got that a lot. Rock Steady ate a bite, and her whole being became dejected. She wanted to be hungry. The food smelled delicious, but she just couldn't eat it. She forced down a few morsels. Paradox and I, in our food-crazed states, could not relate to her condition. Our concern for our trail sister mounted.

We made our way back to the Quality Inn. I unlocked my door and realized the cleaning lady had thrown away my Aquafina bottle and two twenty-ounce Gatorade bottles. I had wanted to carry those three bottles the entire way. I concluded they looked like trash, but I still mourned their loss.

That evening, we stepped out and tried to feed Rock Steady, but unsuccessfully. At a local restaurant, several thru-hikers gathered. We listened to an aqua-blazing adventure at a table next to us; everyone at the table had just finished rafting, kayaking, and canoeing down the Shenandoah River. They skipped hiking many miles. I blatantly judged them (silently), no longer "purists" in my mind. But was I a purist? Though not intentionally, I missed a section back in Virginia on the Creeper

124

Trail! In my mind, I still reigned as superior. Again, I'm questioning my emotional intelligence.

Paradox and I ate well; we carried Rock Steady's leftovers back to the hotel; maybe she could eat them later. Once in my room, I remembered my missing bottles. Despair and grief overcame me; I cried myself to sleep.

I replaced my bottles the following day. The forecast called for temperatures in the upper nineties with high humidity. Not looking forward to our hike in the heat, we delayed our departure from Front Royal and hung out in air-conditioned rooms until a few minutes before the eleven am checkout time. We were on the trail by eleven thirty, in line with the hottest part of the day. Once on the trail, the heat slowed me down. I frequently stopped for water. I frequently stopped to rest. I stopped frequently. We managed eleven miles before we stopped for the night.

Rock Steady did not wait in Front Royal for her results. When they called, they found nothing conclusive. Rock Steady hiked through most of Virginia, West Virginia, Maryland, and Pennsylvania before she felt better. She regained her appetite and her strength in New Jersey. Walking with her for most of that time, I found her will and determination inspirational. She remained optimistic, enthusiastic, and friendly. I could not have done that. I believe men are proficient at whining, complaining, and making others miserable. I'm a typical male – I would have whined, complained, and done my best to share my misery. My heart went out to her for her struggle.

On the trail, a person's attitude is tested. Considering my reaction to Flutter's abandonment, the loss of my water bottles, and the judgment of other hikers, my attitude could use improvement. Rock Steady passed the test. Right Click, be like Rock Steady.

Foil Cap

We arrived at the infamous Virginia Appalachian Trail roller coaster, thirteen and a half miles featuring ten climbs and ten descents. In the early evening, we conquered the first peak, went down, and started to look for a stealth campsite. I passed a girl hiker struggling up the hill. I said hello. Usually, I would keep moving. But she shuffled, stumbled, and barely moved; I paused.

"Are you ok?"

"Please just leave me alone." She responded weakly.

"Are you sure?"

"Yes. Please."

I did. I reached the top of the second ascent and found some decent stealth sites. Low on water (not good), but higher up, I liked that the night would be slightly cooler. Thunder rumbled in the distance. As I set up, I felt raindrops on my back. I clamored in my tent, dug through my food bag, and plied my body with calories. The rain quickly stopped, and I got out to relieve myself. I looked over at Rock Steady's tent and did a double take. She had set up directly under a leaning dead tree that looked like it could fall and crush her at any moment; the tree was two feet above her tent.

"Rock Steady! Did you know you are set up under a dead tree?"

"Shut up, Right Click. Leave me alone."

"Seriously."

"Shut up!"

Instead of arguing with her, I went over and said,

"You may want to get out of your tent while I move this away." That motivated her; she got out. It also drew Paradox out of her tent.

"Oh my God! I can't believe I set up here. How did I not see this?"

"Why didn't any of us see this?"

I lifted the tree, swung it to the side, and let it fall gently to the ground. Paradox laughed and took pictures.

"Right Click, you saved my life! You're my hero!"

Rock Steady fawned mockingly, but she did seem appreciative. My good deed was done for the day; I crawled back into my tent. I heard the angry woman come up the hill. She and her companion set up near us as she grumbled and complained. That amused us too.

The following day, we continued up and down the roller coaster. Again, my mind conjured up the extreme difficulty, yet although strenuous, I managed the terrain quickly enough. Perhaps setting excessive expectations worked to my advantage.

The one-thousand-mile mark resided amid the Roller Coaster. I shared the milestone with Rock Steady and Paradox. Many days earlier, I impressed myself at the one-hundred-mile spot. I had never walked one hundred miles before, but one thousand miles? It seemed preposterous (and I still wasn't halfway). We took the obligatory photos. An Instagram post showed the number one thousand laid out in stones with me on my knees and arms lifted to heaven. As we moved away, I reflected on my adventure to this point. Tears of gratitude and wonder erased the grime on my cheeks.

The lack of water on the Roller Coaster presented a challenge. Spurred on by intense heat and humidity, sweat dispensed from my system profusely. I looked

126

forward to a water source late that afternoon. As we arrived, we spotted two familiar faces, Dr. Pickles and Mockingbird, who had also stopped for water. Polite, kind, and in good humor, we discussed the trail and options for the evening. The forecast called for a strong front with wicked thunderstorms. As we talked, it began to get darker. I went down to the water source, an icy, delicious, crystal clear spring. Dr. Pickles and Mockingbird joined me as I drank and filled all my bottles. They talked about calling it a day and camping with many inviting flat areas nearby. However, this spot rested in a valley near a stream and looked like it could flood, especially if we got significant rain that evening. Dr. Pickles and Mockingbird decided to stay; the three of us reluctantly started the next climb. Internally, I questioned our decision. As I climbed slowly, the sky grew ominous. Waves of thunder rolled in.

Uh oh.

Situated on a steep slope, with no viable places to pitch our tents and dive for cover, we climbed faster and harder. The sky got transformed into a diabolical purplish black. Thunder reverberated. Lightning flashed. The air filled with the scent of the storm and static electricity. We reached the top and, thankfully, a large flat area beckoned. Another single-person tent was already there. We quickly chose our resting sites. It wasn't an often-used area, so we were all situated on thick beds of leaves. Thankful I could pitch a tent quickly; I secured the last of my tent stakes while rain spattered in huge drops. I scurried in, zipped up, and braced for the deluge. I lay down to blow up my air mattress. The cool nylon felt good on my sweaty back. Suddenly, I felt something slither away underneath my shoulder blades. My heart leaped in my chest. I screamed, but no one could hear now. The vicious storm fell on me.

We camped at four thousand two hundred feet; the bottom of the storm cloud settled at four thousand two hundred ten. I recalled the storm back at Betty Creek Gap and gaged this one triple in intensity. Hard to imagine I would ever experience lightning so terrifyingly bright, thunder loud enough to damage eardrums and heavy rain that threatened to tear my shelter apart. My protection? A couple of millimeters of nylon braced by a single fiberglass pole. Despite the tempest, I managed to blow up my air mattress. I stretched out and shuddered. The storm raged; the intensity petrified me. I approached panic. Then I felt the first drip. That snapped me out of my paralysis.

"SHIT!"

More drips. The tent seams failed again, all of them at once. I sat up cross-legged on my air mattress. It soon became a pool float. I stuffed all my gear in the trash compactor plastic bag. I salvaged some empty plastic one-serving cereal containers from my garbage bag and placed them under the major leaks. Funny, the first time I brought them out with me, I watched the Sugar Pops tub fill faster than the Cocoa Crispies. I mopped water with my bandannas and wrung them out in the vestibule.

So, what would you do on top of a Virginia peak getting pummeled by an epic thunderstorm? I checked my phone. Astonished by a strong signal, I texted Rock Steady and Paradox. Paradox replied right away. We couldn't communicate any other way. I told them about my predicament. Paradox informed me her tent leaked too. Rock Steady's did not. I texted Sandy in Connecticut. She worried because she understood my situation. We texted about getting hold of Henry Shires, who owned Tarptent. I emailed him while I sat in the storm. He responded immediately! Talk about customer service. Even though my tent failed before this deluge, I am still a colossal fan of Tarptent. Henry and I would talk in a few days.

The storm subsided. I went outside and restaked all my lines. Could I cover the tent with my rain jacket or something? As I stood outside my tent, the rain picked up. I dove back inside. A second storm pushed in, built in intensity, and soon punished us worse than the first. Water trickled in steadily. I tried to position myself, so water didn't hit me directly in the face. The lightning and thunder struck simultaneously at levels so loud I clutched my ears. I reminded myself of an old recovery slogan, "This Too Shall Pass." I calmed myself as best I could. Being physically exhausted helped. I lay motionless, partly in a trance, and did my best to commune with God, who certainly made His presence known again.

I couldn't run to somewhere safer. I couldn't call anyone to get me. By now, I had turned my phone off, wrapped and stowed it away in a plastic Ziplock. I lay on my pad, clad only in hiking shorts. I started shivering; ironic, since only an hour earlier, I dripped with sweat and bordered near heat exhaustion. My sleeping bag, my sole source of warmth and comfort, was safely tucked away to stay dry. I did not want a wet sleeping bag. Ever. Taking it out now would only serve to soak it.

I lay still, slightly calmer, and listened to the sheer power and ferocity of the storm. Gradually, I noticed a slight time lag between a flash of lightning and a burst of thunder. The beast moved away to torment elsewhere. As I mopped up the best I could, I heard voices outside my tent, women's voices.

"Rock Steady? Paradox?"

"Yeah, Right Click. Are you OK?"

"Um, yeah, but a little bit cold."

"Stay in there; we have an idea."

With headlights on, they laid an emergency foil blanket (thanks to Paradox) over the top of my tent. The moisture helped it stick. They used two pieces of duct tape to secure the blanket, a cap for my Double Rainbow. They chuckled the whole time.

It might not seem like a big deal, but to me, it was. They came out of the comfort of their tents, in the dark, to take care of a fellow hiker, me. I thanked them over and over. They retreated to their tents. I pulled my sleeping bag out, still dry. I snuggled in. It felt wonderful! I ate cereal with water. I called and talked with Sandy. I assured her the storm had passed, but I shared my new concerns about my leaking tent. I didn't want another episode like this one. With the sound of water dripping off the trees and thunder off in the distance, I drifted off and slept well.

Father's Day

The day after the storm was Father's Day. I had a goal. I wanted to make it to the Appalachian Trail Conservancy in Harper's Ferry by four pm before it closed for the day. I fueled up on a Carnation Instant Breakfast packet mixed with a Via Starbucks instant coffee and water, some cereal, and a protein bar. I slid on wet shorts, a stinky shirt, a CCAR cap, and wet Darn Tough socks. It only felt gross for a few seconds.

By now, I engaged in a highly efficient morning packing routine; most of the ritual occurred within my tent's walls. First, I stuffed the sleeping bag into a separate garbage bag. Second, I stuffed that into a trash compactor bag that I used to line the inside of my back. Third, I got all my extra clothes and stowed them in their sack. Fourth, I put all my food in its sack. Fifth, I laid on the sleeping pad, let the air out, folded it, rolled it, and stored it in its bag. Sixth, all the miscellaneous gear (portable charger, cords, headlight, medical stuff, trail guide) I packed in its sack. Seventh, I slipped on my untied boots, unzipped the tent, threw my pack, sacks, and water bottles out onto the ground then crawled stiffly out. Eighth, I stretched a bit, unstaked the tent, took the ridgepole out, folded it, and made sure I put it immediately in my pack, extra careful not to leave that behind. Ninth, I folded the tent in thirds, rolled it up, and stuffed it in its sack. Tenth, I assembled the entire load.

Filling the pack became an art all in itself. Where and how I placed each item made a difference in how it felt on my back. I kept all the dry stuff in the big trash compactor bag and then folded that over. It worked well and saved me from needing a pack cover. The morning after the storm, I strapped the soaking-wet tent on top for easy access in case we came to a place where I could dry it out.

I did a few other things consistently: I kept my phone/camera in the left pocket of my pack's hip belt. This is one reason I loved the ULA pack; the practical, easy-to-reach pockets on the hip belt. In the right one, I kept my snacks for the day. A water bottle snapped into an elastic loop on either shoulder strap – also super convenient.

Once I packed up everything, I tied my boots, lifted my pack and swung it on my back, adjusted the straps, grabbed my trekking poles, double-checked the site, and took the first few steps that set the tone for the day. Off I went, northbound. The journey continued. And no matter how I felt in camp, walking always made me feel better.

This Father's Day, as I walked, I looked around. We survived quite a storm. Signs of heavy water runoff dispersed off the trail. Debris littered the muddy path. The woods dripped. Even though a formidable front had moved through, I could tell it would be hot. With fifteen miles to go, I looked forward to signing in at the Appalachian Trail Conservancy, then a hotel room with a flat-screen TV where I could watch US Open golf, eat some restaurant food and dry out my clothes. Happy Father's Day! Motivated, I pushed forward.

I didn't dwell on the fact that I wouldn't see my dad, one of my biggest fans. As I progressed, he and Dee (my other mom) placed pushpins on a large AT map. And any time my thoughts strayed toward Sandy and all my kids, I forcefully dismissed them. I didn't mind the emotion. I didn't mind that tears ran down my cheeks. I pushed them away because of their power; I didn't want emotion to drive me off the trail permanently.

We ran into Dr. Pickles and Mockingbird, who camped in the valley. Luckily, they survived but had a river running by their tent just six inches away. Dr. Pickles is a fantastic storyteller with body animations and facial expressions, thanked God they didn't get swept away by a raging torrent. We laughed heartily at his yarn.

Around three pm, we came into Harper's Ferry, climbed the stairs off the trail, and located the Appalachian Trail Conservancy. Air conditioning and cold cokes did much to revive me. I went outside and posed for the infamous Polaroid snapshot, the seven hundred seventy-first northbound thru-hiker photographed in 2015. We planned to stay one night at the Econolodge, but my tent needed repair. Paradox's tent needed repair too. And Rock Steady still had no appetite. For the second time in less than a week, the three of us decided to stay another full day, a zero.

I desired to rest in a comfortable air-conditioned room and watch TV, but no, necessary work beckoned. We got a ride to Walmart, where I bought silicon, paint thinner, and a small foam brush. In the heat of the day, Paradox and I set up our tents on the lawn of the Econolodge, where the sun quickly dried them out. I cleaned all the seams and applied the silicon/paint thinner mixture. I laid it on a lot thicker than the first time, following new instructions from Henry Shires. During my conversation with him, I posed a question to him.

"Why would a tentmaker sell tents without the seams sealed? I would expect a tent to be one hundred percent waterproof at the time of sale."

"I agree." He replied simply.

I liked that – an honest man. I sweated a few hours in the afternoon sun, took my time, and did my best to make my Double Rainbow watertight.

I'd find out soon enough.

The Amazing Paradox

Over the prior three months, Paradox and I occasionally talked about the Four-State Challenge. She wanted to give it a go. I thought it madness; she saw it as motivational. The challenge starts across the Virginia border, knocks off all of West Virginia and Maryland, and ends at the Mason-Dixon line when crossing into Pennsylvania – a total distance of forty-two point nine miles. The challenge requires the participant to complete it in less than twenty-four hours! In no way did this appeal to me.

But this extreme young hiker wanted to. I encouraged her. Rock Steady did too. We spent some time off that zero-day figuring out her game plan. Rock Steady, and I talked her into letting us carry some of her gear to lighten her load. She wanted to take her full load – nearly fifty pounds. We agreed that Rock Steady and I would head north the next day. Paradox would hang back, retrace her steps south a few miles, and camp that night at the border. She'd get up around four am and start hiking north, where she would catch us, pass us, and then wait for us.

I said goodbye and good luck to Paradox the following day. Rock Steady hung back a bit, so I started without her. Solo, I made my way through historic Harper's Ferry, watching groups of school-age kids taking tours. I crossed the railroad bridge and took the long walk along the river and canal; easy going for the AT, but the temperature hit the nineties. The trail took a hard left back into the hills.

By late afternoon, the trail made its way through Gathland State Park. I loved when the AT traversed through a state park. The maintenance crew in this Maryland park mowed pristine grass, adorned the area with inviting picnic tables, and served up deliciously cold well water. I drank liters, took off my shoes and socks, sprawled out on the grass under a big oak, and rested my head on my pack.

"Ahhhh."

131

I looked back down the trail frequently, expecting to see Rock Steady. Soon enough, a hiker appeared, but not Rock Steady. Nurse! I met him way back in North Carolina. To recap, we graduated from the same high school the same year and never met until the trail. He should be days and days ahead of me; he traveled super light, did big miles daily, and was a fantastically fit hiker. I expressed my surprise. It turned out that a metal plate in his elbow somehow got infected. He spent several days in the hospital. Anything can happen out on the trail. I felt so fortunate that nothing major happened to me. Yet.

Eventually, Rock Steady strode into the park and seemed agreeable to a rest. She didn't like to stop too often. For one, her feet would stiffen up and become difficult to loosen up again. Second, she wouldn't be Rock Steady. I introduced them and witnessed how Rock Steady interacted with him. Nurse was soon charmed by her smile, warmth, and sense of humor.

After several minutes, Nurse took off. Rock Steady, and I still rested. We heard the first thunder off in the distance. Are you kidding me? Again? We pointed at a pavilion; in the middle of the week, we probably could stay under the roof without anyone bothering us, but we wanted to cover more miles. We suited up and pressed on to the next shelter. By the time we got there, the sky had darkened. Others settled in to wait out the storm. I chatted with a young boy, about ten years old, hiking with his dad. A confident young lad, we found mutual ground around soccer. He talked about his play, and I recalled my coaching time. It also struck me deeply. It reminded me (again) how much I missed my family.

The storm skirted by and moved off. Rock Steady and I went back up the approach trail and chose two prime campsites spotted on the way in. Hundreds of lightly colored toads covered the ground, which was very weird. But out on the trail, strange became routine. I pitched my tent while tan toads hopped around. I lay down amid toads (they were outside, and I was safely zipped inside) and prayed for Paradox. She would set out to hike nearly forty-three miles in a few hours. Rock Steady, and I chatted a bit. I expressed my concern about my tent and another thunderstorm rolling through. Moisture fell off the trees, so far, so good – the tent held. A few drops weren't a test like hard rain, but I felt optimistic. Rock Steady called home and talked with her husband. I called home too. It helped my homesickness.

We broke camp early to do big miles to keep pace with Paradox. We estimated she'd pass us about midday. Around eight-thirty in the morning, I posted a previous picture of Paradox on social media. I asked people to pray for her as she attempted to do in one day what it would take me to do in three. Little did I know that at that

132

exact time, Paradox suffered from an intense sciatica attack, a severe pain that caused her knee to collapse. She questioned whether she could continue. Continue, she did. And just when people started to pray, the pain and weakness subsided and disappeared.

I didn't know any of this at the time. I took a break at an overlook, and much to my chagrin, who came walking briskly down the trail? Flutter. Sigh. Very happy to see me; I wished the feeling was mutual. He rambled about his trip home and how hard he had worked to catch us. He assumed he would jump right back in and continue with us. Miffed, I gave him the cold shoulder. I can sometimes be somewhat of a prickly pear, especially when I've been emotionally betrayed. My mood soured. Yet, he kept pace with me and talked, seemingly oblivious to my lack of enthusiasm.

I separated myself some when he stopped to pee. I cruised into a state park and stopped to eat lunch at the Mount Vernon shelter, not too far from the original Washington Monument. Flutter caught up and settled in. I plugged into the electrical outlets and took advantage of charging my cell phone. Rock Steady arrived. Being a better person than I, she treated Flutter with way more friendliness and courtesy. I said very little. I spoke only when spoken to, keeping my answers deliberately short. I acted like a jerk.

My interaction with Flutter took on importance (in my head) that would not have happened in the real world. I considered a theory I formulated back in North Carolina when So Way rattled me. Out in the woods, I had way more time to process information. I thought about conversations with other hikers for days. During life before the trail, I'd have a few minutes before the next thing hit me, forced to process information and interactions quickly. I believe all unprocessed information creates stress in me. Some I can let go. Other information often festers. On the trail, with fewer human interactions and way more time, I processed and then let it go. I let most things go. But I could not (or did not) with Flutter.

Flutter's behavior upset me. So, I dove internally; recovery is an inside job. I discovered that I didn't like to be judged. I didn't want to be hurried. I didn't like to feel incompetent or incapable. I wouldn't treat people the way he treated me. I held on to the resentment. It festered. I know from years of recovery that *"resentment only destroys the container in which it's contained."* I needed to let it go. But I did not. It must have served me somehow. Yet, I bore the consequences. My container began to corrode. I made myself miserable. These thoughts tumbled in my mind as I sat in the shade of the shelter.

I looked up and detected a blaze of orange moving down the path; Paradox was clad in her trademark bright orange shirt. My heart swelled. She walked with Rock

Steady and three other dudes who also attempted the four-state challenge. They all stopped to eat with us. Paradox's first story began in camp at four-twenty in the morning. She lit the way with her headlamp and became immediately frightened by eight blazing green eyes staring at her from just off the trail. Heart pounding, she told herself the creepy eyes belonged to timid, friendly deer and quickly moved on. Hiking in the dark required new skills I did not possess. I hadn't attempted a night hike since I tried to do the fifty miles in two days into Damascus; no plans to try again either.

Paradox looked good. Strong and athletic, she said she felt pretty good too. I learned about her back pain and crumpling knee. I barely responded, in awe of her determination. It wasn't until later that I remembered the prayer request. Rock Steady asked her about her load.

"How's the weight?"

"It's ok." She replied, but her look betrayed her.

"We can take some more." Rock Steady, and I offered simultaneously. Flutter flashed a look of astonishment that we carried some of Paradox's load already. Reluctantly he offered to help. Also reluctantly (but gratefully), Paradox gave up some more of her load. We said goodbye, wished her well and said we'd see her at the Maryland-Pennsylvania border, two days away for us.

I checked out the original Washington Monument and learned that a few months earlier, lightning struck the structure, fried some hikers inside, and was closed to the public. I understood how hikers might get severely injured, considering some of the storms I experienced.

The day transitioned into hot and humid; how unusual. After twenty-plus miles, Flutter, Rock Steady, and I made it to a shelter with a few flat, level campsites. A family, on an overnight, took up two of the best sites. I scoured the area. Rock Steady and Flutter set up, but I could find nothing I wanted to lay on all night. I opted for the shelter. Two other young section hikers shared it with me, one of them up on the loft, so with plenty of room, I spread out. Plus, I enjoyed being pretty far away from Flutter. Rock Steady did not get caught up in the emotional crap; she could deal with him. Being sensitive (and immature), I felt abandoned and very much alone. Again. I shook my head. I knew better. I resolved to get up early, get out of camp, and make it first to Penn-Mar Park with two things to look forward to – seeing Paradox and meeting my cousin Tommy.

I busted out of camp early and cruised along a meadow. I enjoyed the morning; things went better when I walked. Then I spotted some movement up ahead. Flutter strode out of a thicket, toilet paper in hand. Awkward.

134

But not as awkward as a moment back a few states ago. I had to poop so bad I dashed off the trail. Hikers call the urgent need to poop "turtling" because the poop head starts to poke its way out of its shell. Too much information? When I let the turtle free, Flutter cruised by and saw me. I didn't realize the trail switched back and left me fully exposed. A look of bewilderment flashed across his face. Embarrassment reddened mine. All I could muster was,

"I'm sorry you had to see that."

He shrugged it off. But he told *that* story whenever he could, the only times I felt genuinely embarrassed on the entire trail.

Here, we exchanged brief pleasantries, and I moved on. I stopped to get water. He strode down the trail and passed by without a word.

I got to Penn-Mar around lunchtime. Flutter regaled other hikers on the pavilion. I dropped down on the grass, took in the view, and made myself comfortable. My cousin Tommy arrived at about the same time. I greeted him with a big hug. He carried frozen lemonade. Much to my delight, Paradox moseyed in with a wry smile.

"Did you do it?"

"I did."

"Let the celebration begin!"

I offered her one of the frozen lemonades in honor of her extraordinary accomplishment. She loved lemonade. I introduced Tommy to Paradox and Flutter. We moved onto the pavilion when some light rain began falling, ate lunch, and waited for Rock Steady. I told Tommy all about the four-state challenge. Paradox completed it in seventeen hours and twenty minutes – remarkable! Very proud of her, like she was my daughter, I repeatedly expressed my jubilation.

My praise didn't seem to embarrass her… too much.

Silent Planner

While we talked with Paradox, I assessed Tommy's gear. He carried a little daypack stuffed with a blanket (no sleeping pad) and a new tent. I decided then we'd probably sleep in shelters.

Tommy quickly got a glimpse into life on the trail. A guy on the bench offered cold sodas for a dollar a can. I took him up on his offer. We followed him up the hill, where he opened the park museum, motioning us to follow him to a small cooler filled with ice-cold delights. He fished some out for us.

"Does stuff like this happen a lot?" Tommy asked as we walked back down the hill.

"It does. When you least expect it."

Rock Steady arrived. She embraced Paradox and congratulated her. After a brief rest, we all hit the trail. A short distance later, we came to the Mason-Dixon line and snapped several pictures. A few steps later, I crossed the invisible line into The North – a strange feeling, like I crossed a palpable boundary.

After the Mason-Dixon line, the crew spread out. I talked with Tommy. He helped me process some of my emotional muck, mostly around Flutter. My emotion outweighed the actual urgency and importance of the matter. I listened as Tommy shared some of his muck. With eight miles to the shelter, I remembered that the trail had not hardened Tommy like the rest of us. Eight miles, an easily managed distance for me even after several miles earlier in the day, could cause problems for a tenderfoot. We took our time. I checked in with him often. He handled the hike beautifully. Peace settled within him. He appreciated the woods, the quiet, and the physical exercise. Tommy and I talked a lot about the presence of God out there in the woods. Even though life circumstances might be difficult or downright disheartening, we discussed gratitude and our good fortune to be in the woods. He truly admired my quest and asked a lot of insightful questions.

"How have you made it this far?"

"I get up every day, suit up and show up… God has been with me every step of the way."

Tommy nodded in agreement. He shared the same faith.

It rained steadily by the time we reached the shelter. Tommy and I tucked into one of the two with Hot Pants and Crumbs; I met them earlier on the trail, good people who worked with kids in the Canadian outdoors. I thought they were far ahead of us, but Hot Pants developed a severe case of poison ivy (or poison something – he never did figure it out) in his genital area and landed in a hospital. The area became so swollen that his unit (penis) disappeared. Even I thought that was "too much information." Hikers share everything. But poison ivy that severe? It never occurred to me. Damn.

With a gentle rain falling, Tommy curled up in his blanket and slept on the hardwood floor. He seemed fine, but I harbored doubts. With not many options available for him, I fell asleep right away. I walked nearly thirty-nine miles in two days, not bad for an old guy. I'm sure that contributed to my fatigue.

The following day, Flutter stirred first, then bustled noisily about the camp. We planned a simple twelve-mile hike to Quarry Gap Shelters. He hovered close by as Tommy, and I ate a leisurely breakfast. His anxiety and what I interpreted as disapproval were palpable. I told him just to go on ahead,

136

"We'll catch you. "

He did not leave. Flutter lingered and talked and suggested and offered various opinions. Disguised through a veil of friendliness, his real intention was to see what he could get. He paid close attention to what came out of Tommy's pack and complimented my cousin on different items. Tommy did not take the bait.

Once on the trail, Tommy and I managed to separate from Flutter. Rock Steady and Paradox started later than us. We took our time and clamored over several random rock piles. Welcome to Pennsylvania. We stopped to rest; I took my pack off and noticed, to my horror, that one of my yellow Crocs, secured in the webbing of my pack, had jumped ship. Gone. I sighed, and my shoulders sagged.

"Oh no… Tommy, the question is, do I go back and look for it?"

"Whatever you want to do…."

Tommy replied, similar to Tough Love when we lost the AT in Virginia. My croc could have been one hundred yards down the trail or three miles. One of my beloved yellow Crocs lay on the track in distress; still, I could not bring myself to go south. I opted to continue northbound and hoped someone would find it and bring it to me.

"If you love something, set it free. If it comes back to you, it's yours forever. If it doesn't, it never was."

With sad thoughts of my Croc lingering, we sauntered into Caledonia State Park. The drizzly day kept park traffic minimal, but the grill was open. Joy coursed through my system. Tommy bought me a cheeseburger, a hot dog, large French fries, and a giant Mountain Dew. He grinned at my enthusiasm and gratitude over the heavenly feast. As a bonus, the young man running the concession charged my phone while we ate. Little acts of kindness meant the world to me and other thru-hikers.

From the park, the shelter loomed two uphill miles away. Tommy wished to stay the night, then walk back to the park the following day and catch his ride home. I thought setting a rendezvous with people on the trail would be straightforward. It's not. People often wanted to meet but couldn't make it happen. To select a specific time and place, one considered many factors – miles to the rendezvous, weather, physical condition, emotional state, and trail condition (to name a few).

On the way up to the shelter, we met a ridge runner hiking south in sandals. Ridge runners serve as "boots-on-the-trail" for the Appalachian Trail Conservancy. They provide information, educate about Leave No Trace (LNT) practices and help hikers have positive AT experiences for themselves and the trail. This ridge runner asked how we were doing. I told her about my yellow croc because she headed in that direction.

"I'll keep an eye out for it." She responded politely.

We admired the impeccably maintained trail to Quarry Gap Shelter and the meticulously placed rock steps. We met Jim Stauch, the Innkeeper, an AT legend who maintained and improved this section for forty years. During our conversation, I mentioned my missing Croc; he'd look for it. Tommy and I settled in one shelter. Afterward, I basked in warm sunshine and soaked my feet in a cold stream, and conversed with a hiker from Germany. Paradox and Rock Steady showed up. They joined me near the creek. We chatted warmly and kidded with each other. Tommy sat in the shelter and quietly observed the three of us comfortable with each other. Tommy shared with me later that the whole dynamic changed when Flutter wandered in. He said I shut down, and Paradox became reserved. Of course, Rock Steady didn't change.

The following morning, I said goodbye to Tommy, whom I dubbed Silent Planner. He liked that. After a hug, I decided to deal with the Flutter situation directly; time to put into action an adage one of my mentors had ingrained in me.

"Twenty minutes of intense discomfort is better than twenty years of prolonged pain."

I asked Flutter if we could speak in private.

"Look, Flutter, I think it's better if we don't hike together for a while. This is just about me; I need to separate from you."

"What? Why?"

I told him. I summarized my thoughts. I softened them. To his credit, he took it well and respected my decision. He appeared upset. My heartstrings tugged, but I did not lose my resolve. I believed my emotional well-being was at stake. He said goodbye to the ladies and headed north; Rock Steady and Paradox were unaware of our exchange. They lingered in camp as I set out alone. The rain intensified.

Of course it did.

Halfway

I took no breaks to keep warm in the steady, soaking rain and moved at a good pace. I hit a shelter about lunchtime. Flutter sat and ate his lunch. Awkward. I stripped off a wet layer and ate. I did not talk much. Soon the ladies showed up. When The Twins arrived, they spoke of staying. Already wet and not wanting to spend an entire afternoon and evening with Flutter (beyond my tolerance level), I suited up and headed out. They all stayed behind.

As the shelter receded, I said, "OK, Right Click, embrace the suck."

I did. The rain became biblical; hard to comprehend how it could rain so hard for so long. The trail turned into a stream. With water running over my boots and ankles, I ran into a pack of young women headed south. They planned to stay at the shelter I had just left. I counted fourteen of them. I smiled at the thought of all of them crowded into that shelter. My decision to move on in the downpour might prove fortuitous.

At the next road crossing, I quickly scanned the bulletin board and discovered a note from Jim Stauch. He had no luck finding my Croc. Impressed with Jim's kindness and thoughtfulness, I pressed on.

I reached the official halfway point in epic rain and felt like the Priest in Caddyshack. Wet fingers don't work well on a smartphone, but I managed to take a short video. I turned the phone off, packed it away in a plastic bag, and let go of the idea of taking pictures; it was just too wet.

My body temperature dropped, so for the last few miles, I put my head down, picked up my pace, and finished a thirteen-mile hike by four-thirty. A group of kids gathered under a pavilion, but no one dwelled in the Tom's Run Shelter. Nervously and quickly, I stripped naked, fished out my one set of dry clothes, and thanked God again for the trash compactor bag system. I blew up my air mattress and nestled in my dry sleeping bag. I relaxed as the shivering subsided.

Pretty soon, I heard footsteps splashing. U-Haul from Germany showed up.

"Do you mind?" He pointed to the far side of the shelter.

"Of course not. Make yourself at home."

I sat up and rummaged through my food bag. I ate while I watched U-Haul set up.

Two more hikers arrived, Blackout and Chief Two Sticks. They threw their packs between U-Haul and me.

"Hey, Right Click. Pretty wild out there, huh?"

I nodded. I scooted to the end of the shelter next to Blackout. I wanted more water, plus I needed to pee. I dropped one wet boot and my one croc to the ground. Blackout looked down at my mismatched footwear, reached back for his pack, stuck his hand in, pulled out my other Croc, and dropped it on the ground.

"Here ya go." He didn't even smile. Too miserable because of the weather, I guess.

I sat motionless, stunned.

"Oh my God! Thank you, Blackout!" He acknowledged my enthusiasm with a satisfied nod like mission accomplished. Remember, Blackout was the guy who jumped into a ride Rock Steady and I had paid for. I told him,

139

"I erase your cheeseburger debt."

He had no clue. I let it go. I slipped both yellow Crocs on and headed to the stream. While I walked, the Crocs chattered about their separate adventures. I lovingly scolded the one who leaped off my pack and pleaded with it not to do it again.

I returned to the shelter and longed for my JetBoil, a hot cup of anything just what the doctor ordered after the day's long, wet slog. But I sent my stove home several weeks ago. I figured a JetBoil cooked water, only water. I tired of dehydrated meals, oatmeal, or coffee. I liked the cold food just fine, but this night, as I ate Pop-Tarts, the other three guys pulled out stoves and cooked up some big feeds. Quite the production, dinner occurred as the highlight of their day. It smelled wonderful. Dinner conversation flowed easily. Four men, probably never to meet again, shared an unforgettable day of challenging hiking and close quarters. We slept in the shelter that night, comfortable and grateful.

Pine Grove Furnace State Park loomed three miles up the trail, the home of the half-gallon ice cream challenge. On the path early in anticipation of food, I took time to notice the landscape and how the previous storm had left its mark. Curious about how water moved on, off, and through the trail, I studied the patterns formed by the many streamlets. Soon, I looked up and noticed a road. After a few more steps, I strolled into the park and found the general store. Thru-hikers milled about; by now, I knew most of them. Tinkerbell winked (like she usually did), and instantly I felt welcome. I smiled, said hello, and dropped my pack. I walked into the store, not even remotely interested in ice cream. I ordered two bacon, egg, and cheese sandwiches... to start. I took my feast outside and sat down.

Flutter arrived; we barely acknowledged each other's presence. He immediately held court and told a tale from the previous night. Few people hung out at that shelter when I left them yesterday. Flutter described how people kept piling in. All those girls showed up and immediately stripped off all their wet clothes. Flutter said the guys were embarrassed by their immodesty. More hikers showed up. More hikers squeezed in. People slept on the floor and under bunks. My heart swelled a bit; my decision to move on was good.

Paradox quietly tried to sneak in. I saw her, though, and caught her eye.

"Hey, Right Click."

"Congratulations on making it halfway."

"Thank you. You too!"

"How was your night?" I asked with a smirk.

Paradox shot me a look that said,

"Don't ask. Besides, you already know." And the last glance might have meant, "Asshole."

But she communicated lovingly. She disappeared into the camp store; Rock Steady not far behind. She caught my eye, smiled, and nodded. Rock Steady talked and laughed with them, very popular among our bubble of hikers. I finished my massive breakfast with the last swallow of orange juice. As I ate, my phone recharged along with many others; I appreciated places that made outlets available to hikers.

An Appalachian Trail museum resides at Pine Grove Furnace State Park. I didn't go in. I walked down the hill where the Potomac Appalachian Trail Club hosted a trail magic buffet at the park's pavilion. With a vast spread of hot dogs, hamburgers, fresh fruit, salads, and hot and cold drinks, I took my pack off and decided to hang out here for a while. I waited for the ladies who toured the museum before I started eating again. Rock Steady still had no appetite. She ate what she could. She forced food down to give her some fuel for hiking. Paradox and I had no such problem. I ate a lot, even after just consuming a large breakfast.

Hanging out in the Pennsylvania state park and consuming pounds of food made it quite challenging to suit up and move on. I delayed. The ladies lingered with me. Seven miles lay between us and the next shelter. Eventually, we shouldered our packs and trudged out of there. I carried extra weight, but not in my pack. The previous day's storm left the trail particularly muddy, with several trees down across the track. We navigated blowdowns and took silly videos slogging through several inches of mud and water, a typical enjoyable day on the AT.

Boiling Springs

Over the last few days, Rock Steady had talked with her family about a rendezvous in Boiling Springs, PA. She cheerfully invited Paradox and me. However, I knew we'd probably run into Flutter in town, and he would maneuver for an invitation and put Rock Steady in an awkward spot. I quietly told her I'd be ok with her decision. I meant it. She appreciated that.

We cruised easily into Boiling Springs, about twelve miles. The AT runs through the middle of this quaint little town and traverses a beautiful pond. We walked along the water in warm sunlight, the picturesque setting surreal. We relaxed on a freshly cut lawn at the Appalachian Trail Conservancy office. Rock Steady's mom and aunt arrived.

Before the trail, I feared my body odor. I read in disbelief about thru-hikers strutting into restaurants unshowered and offensively odiferous. I couldn't imagine

I'd ever walk into a restaurant in full hiker stench mode. By Boiling Springs, I had become accustomed to my body odor and couldn't detect it on other hikers. If I walked behind Rock Steady, her ripe pack made my nose twitch, but that was about it. However, I sniffed out a dayhiker immediately. As they passed, I asked myself,

"What was that strange smell? Soap? Ewww. Lavender? Ewww. Lilac? Yuk."

We jammed our packs in the back of her mom's small SUV, stuffed ourselves in the back seat, and drove a short distance when Rock Steady's aunt started gagging. Rock Steady said,

"We smell pretty bad, don't we?"

"You have no idea. I think I'm going to throw up!"

Rock Steady's mom exclaimed, "Don't throw up in here! Let me know if I have to pull over!"

Instead of being mortified, I giggled. So did the ladies. We wore our stench like a badge of honor. Not amused, her aunt covered her nose with her hands.

"It's not funny! You smell horrible!"

We laughed harder.

"We're sorry!" But not really.

With great relief, they dropped us off at the Allenberry Resort, a beautiful historic vacation destination known for theater. They agreed to retrieve us for dinner, but only if we cleaned up. The Allenberry Resort proprietors are big fans of thru-hikers and offer a considerable discount. I usually would have shared a double room with Flutter, but he was gone, so I prepared to pay the full price, but Rock Steady paid for my room. To this day, I still don't know why. I found my room, peeled off putrid clothes, and luxuriously showered off layers of grime. The water ran blackish-brown between my toes for several minutes.

After the shower, I talked with my cousin Tommy (Silent Planner) on his way to bring me new Merrell Moab Ventilators. I desperately needed new boots. My boots broke again; the soles gave way, my feet hurt immediately, and my toes blistered. The boots looked serviceable on the outside, but they didn't function properly. On this journey, I'd wear out six pairs. With Merrells, I anticipated a perfect fit right out of the box. Silent Planner met me in the Allenberry Resort parking lot. Incredibly grateful, I took pictures of my old Merrells next to my new ones, the contrast startling. Tommy couldn't stay long. I hugged him goodbye in disbelief at his act of kindness.

Hungry, I knocked on my hiking partners' door to get them to hurry up. Paradox opened it, and my eyes widened. Paradox kept her hair bound in a buff on the trail,

142

so you never saw her beautiful, wavy, luxurious brown locks. Again, I got caught off guard. She knew it.

"Hi, Right Click. What?"

"Nothin'. Hurry up, will ya?"

Rock Steady's parents waited in the lobby talking with… Flutter. Of course. I sighed. Among his many trail stories, he subtly fished for an invitation. I stood by quietly. Rock Steady deftly communicated that there was no room in the vehicle. I said goodbye and good luck to Flutter. That would be the last time I'd see him.

Rock Steady's family did not disappoint. Treated like hiker royalty, we feasted on rib-eye steaks, fresh vegetables, fruit, casseroles, and desserts. Rock Steady grew up on a Pennsylvania farm with two brothers and said these feasts were commonplace among family. If I had to rank my meals on the trail, this spread took the top spot. Wonderful to be in someone's home; gratitude oozed out of my pores. Paradox and I opened some eyes with the amount we ate and quickly grew sleepy. Rock Steady offered to bring us back to our rooms; she wanted to stay and visit with family. We hopped in a car. Rock Steady settled in the driver's seat. I had walked with this woman for one-thousand miles and had never seen her drive. She drove fast, too fast!

"Rock Steady, what the hell? Slow down!"

She laughed.

"What's the matter Right Click, too fast for you?"

"Yes!"

I gripped the handrest tightly. The speed of the car jolted my senses. My top speed on the trail topped out at three mph. Fifty? Rock Steady drove faster, eyes focused on the road, grinning widely, thoroughly enjoying the drive.

"You're such a jerk!"

She smiled, focused on the road, and stepped on the accelerator.

Duncannon Sucks

As much as I didn't want to leave the Allenberry Resort, I knew I must. If I stayed put, I wouldn't get too far. The funny thing about thru-hiking, the only way to get from one place to another was to walk there. Unless you didn't, some hikers found other ways to go north. Yellow blazers took rides in cars, trucks, vans, or anything with a motor and wheels. Other thru-hikers generally disdained yellow blazers. I never considered yellow blazing. I previously mentioned the Aqua blaze – travel by water. Other hikers would ride to a northern point, slackpack south, retrieve their pack, then get another ride back north. I didn't do that either. I never went south

143

(except by accident). I held a firm conviction to *walk* the entire Appalachian Trail northbound, and that's what I did.

We hitched a ride back to the Boiling Springs Appalachian Trail Conservancy and picked up where we left off. Happy in new footwear, I trudged along roads and through farmland with the terrain friendly but the weather not. Hot and humid. Rock Steady, Paradox, and I traveled effortlessly. We communicated frequently and stopped to look at views or something Paradox pointed out. Often in the lead, Paradox had the eyes of a bird of prey. She'd spot anything from a bear to a butterfly to a budding flower, in tune perfectly with her surroundings. I admired her. Paradox enjoyed every second; her enthusiasm was contagious.

Hot, sweaty, and thirsty, we arrived at a rustic, whitewashed barn with an old-fashioned well, the Scott Farm Trail ATC Crew headquarters. The three of us stretched out on the grass. We took off our shoes and socks. We dug around in our food bags. Any time Rock Steady took off her shoes, I knew we'd stay more than a few minutes. Six Twelve was there; more on him in a bit. Just Doug was there too.

"Mind if I ask you a question?"

"Sure. How'd you get your trail name?"

"People asked me my trail name, and I'd say just Doug. It stuck."

We shared stories about the weather, the trail, our feet, and food. The groomed, manicured, flat lawn around the barn appealed to our camping instinct, but the many signs posted said no. After sitting for too long, we pushed through our stiffened muscles, and after fourteen miles in the heat, dusk welcomed us to the Darlington Shelter, home of the Taj Mahal privy, an oversized, very clean privy. Just Doug bunked in the shelter. Six Twelve set up his hammock just outside. Known on the trail for his loud radio and questionable choice of music, Six Twelve got dubbed by another hiker who thought he must be six feet twelve inches tall. He strung Christmas tree lights in the hammock's rigging. I'm not sure how he got it to light up. Did he carry a battery? Word on the trail was that Six Twelve skipped large sections of the trail after some unusually enthusiastic partying episodes, but who knew?

The night darkness engulfed us when we finished our evening meal. The ladies went out into the woods to hang their food bags. Their laughter made me know they struggled to get the rope over a suitable tree limb. I didn't bother. By now, I mostly slept with my food. I believed what Pretzel told me.

"The surest way to lure a bear into camp is to hang your food in a tree and let them smell it from miles away."

Possession is nine-tenths of the law, even in the woods. If a bear wanted my food, he'd have to go through me. I banked that a bear didn't want to do that. It proved true. A bear never bothered me. But I could have just been lucky. You decide.

At night, I made notes in my AT Guide. I tried to record a few other thoughts too, but my notes got fewer and fewer as the hike progressed. Once I had the Thermarest pad blown up, and the sleeping bag laid out, I relaxed. Completely. But not this night. I fiddled with my iPhone and watched most of the United States Women's National Team World Cup semi-finals game against Germany. The LTE signal drifted in and out. I waited while the video buffered. Off in the distance, the ladies still laughed.

Finally, they returned to their tents. I gave Paradox an update; the score tied nil-nil (they eventually won two-nil). Then Paradox screamed, but not an imminent death scream or even one of mortal danger. Frightened? Yes. And that was unusual. An enormous spider, probably a wolf spider, dared her to a battle.

"This is my tent!" Paradox defied the spider.

Up to the challenge, the spider reared its ugly head. Paradox screamed again. The spider disappeared and freaked her out - a dangerous spider somewhere in or near her tent. Rock Steady laughed robustly.

"Please be quiet. I'm trying to watch the game."

"Shut up, Right Click!"

They replied in perfect two-part harmony with no respect. No respect at all.

I set out the following day in a positive frame of mind. I expected to see Sandy and three of our kids in a few days over the July fourth weekend. That motivated me and lifted my spirit. On my way to Duncannon, I got a preview of the famous Pennsylvania rocks to come.

Again, sweat poured off my body in the sweltering conditions. I drank liters of water. By the time I descended to the streets, the high sun had steamed the sidewalks. Rock Steady, Paradox, and I traipsed our way through town and came to the legendary, historic Doyle Hotel. From the outside, it looked like a complete dump. The owners didn't maintain the place. Hikers slept in their sleeping bags on top of the beds because the bed linens were so dirty. If a hiker says something is dirty… beware. I appreciated the nostalgia and the history, but standing in front of it, I didn't see the attraction. I took one picture of the Doyle sign and walked on. So did the ladies. None of us were fans of the bar scene, and we heard drunkenness as the norm at The Doyle.

We found a pizza place a few doors down the street and stepped inside. Just Doug came in, stood beside us, and scanned the menu behind the counter. Not

145

impressed, he walked out. We should have followed his lead. They managed to screw up a meatball sub and pizza for famished hikers. Rock Steady ate a couple of bites of a large pizza and immediately lost any remaining appetite. I drank several Cokes, my drug, I mean, drink of choice. Just Doug told us later that he thoroughly enjoyed his cheeseburger at The Doyle. In hindsight, maybe we should have dropped in.

Now late in the afternoon, the ladies craved ice cream. I did not. The questionable Italian food gurgled in my belly.

"Do you mind if I go ahead? I think I need to walk this off." I held my stomach.

"Sure, Right Click. We'll see you at the shelter."

I walked through the rest of town, starting a four-mile trek. My upset gut, combined with an amplified feeling of uneasiness, heightened my anxiety. Always hyper-sensitive to negative, dark energy, Duncannon felt full of it. I quickened my pace while keenly scanning ahead to look for the next white blaze.

To escape Duncannon, the Appalachian Trail crosses the Susquehanna River. Hikers use a highway bridge. I found walking near cars and trucks moving that fast disconcerting and disorienting. Looking ahead, I spotted the hill I knew I'd eventually climb.

"When in doubt which way the AT goes, look up."

The steep climb out of Duncannon settled my stomach, and as I climbed, I felt the energy lighten. I left the town behind. A beautiful giant beetle meandered across a stone in the path. Refocused on nature, I grabbed my phone and took a video. Mentally back on track, I carefully picked my way up and along the ridge. I heard laughter and two women chatting behind me. No way! Rock Steady and Paradox caught me. How could that be? I felt old and slow.

"How'd you like that walk along the highway, Right Click?"

"Um, I didn't."

They laughed and went on by, the shelter not too far away. I arrived near dusk. As I set up, I recapped my day – visited Duncannon, ingested terrible Italian food, wrestled evil energy, walked sixteen miles – another typical day on the Appalachian Trail.

JULY

Valentines in Lickdale

Wake up, get up, eat up, pack up, suit up, hike.

Repeat.

Nearly eighteen miles later, the sun sat low in the sky as the two ladies, and I pushed ourselves to a stealth camp near a stream. I pitched my tent at Rattling Run practically under a rhododendron bush adjacent to a stream - a spooky site. I imagined an enormous alligator easing up the bank, using the rhododendron as cover, violently snatching me out of my tent, dragging me into the water, drowning me in a Jurassic death roll, and feasting on me for a few days. Too far north for alligators, my imagination conjured up other monsters that could slide up the bank and get me. I wondered about my nutrition level. Too damn tired to dwell on the matter, the ladies jabbered away as I fell into a deep sleep. If a monster got me, I'd just be deadweight. I probably wouldn't even wake up.

A monster didn't get me that evening. I woke up energized. Only twelve miles to go, I would reach the intersection of PA 72 and PA 443, where the AT Guide showed a parking lot. Not just another parking lot, this promised a reunion with my family! At this very moment, Sandy headed south with Sami (Tough Love), Matthew (13), and Mary (10). Eager (and nervous) for Sandy to meet the ladies, I started the day's hike. I remembered Sandy's words,

"Aren't there any male hikers on the trail?"

The miles ticked by. I stumbled upon my first and only porcupine of the entire trip. Was that symbolic of anything? No idea, but a very cool-looking creature nonetheless.

We arrived at the parking lot and sat in the grass. I texted with Tough Love; my family is close. The beige Suburban soon appeared, and emotion deluged my soul the moment I spotted it. It rose from deep within, a type of primitive response. I connected with the sets of eyes in the truck. Samantha. Matthew. Mary. And Sandy! One hundred ten days since I had seen my wife was one hundred five days longer than any period in our lives. Love poured out of me. I burst into tears of gratitude.

The family got out of the car. Sandy wore a royal blue t-shirt with "Where's Phil?" in big, bold white letters. Similarly, the kids donned matching t-shirts that boldly asked, "Where's Dad?" My heart swelled even more. I tentatively held out my arms,

147

aware I smelled pretty bad (stunk). She overcame her obvious disgust, hugged me, and kissed me. Quickly.

"Oh. Wow. That's a distinct funk." She wrinkled her nose.

"Yes, it is!"

I grinned from ear to ear. My kids didn't want to hug me either. OK, by me, incredibly happy, borderline ecstatic.

Sandy looked at my hiking partners. Without hesitation, she said.

"You must be Rock Steady, and you must be Paradox."

They connected immediately. Tough Love positively beamed, thrilled to be reunited with the trail ladies. Sandy, known for her party preparations, prepared a thru-hiker banquet. First, I spotted the big Igloo cooler packed with ice and beverages. Coca-Cola for me, iced tea for Rock Steady, lemonade for Paradox, and bottles and different colored Gatorades for all of us. I admired her attention to detail. Sandwiches, fruit, and chips were all served to us while we sat in the greatest of thru-hiker luxuries, bag chairs. Toes (another thru-hiker) wandered through, accepted our invitation, joined the feast, and agreed to a photo. Sitting in the shade with my friends and family felt like true bliss, a priceless moment in time, one to cherish forever.

We piled in our old Suburban and headed to the Lickdale Best Western. The air conditioner blasted in her face as Sandy drove to protect her from the extreme hiker funk. I couldn't blame her. We dropped Paradox and Rock Steady off at the Days Inn and said we'd pick them up for dinner. I showered and changed into some Loudmouth Golf shorts that had never come close to fitting, always way too small around the middle. Sandy also brought other clothes for me. It felt odd to choose between so many items. I relaxed on the bed, mindlessly watching something on the flat screen while I iced my battered and bruised feet. Surrounded by family, life was good.

But in the back of my mind, I knew they'd leave again. How would I handle that? I pushed the thought aside.

Over a wonderfully tasty dinner at Harper's Tavern, Sandy got to know Rock Steady and Paradox even more. Warmed by the laughter, the stories, and the good humor, Matthew and Mary listened to our yarns with eyes wide open. Tough Love glowed with pride and happiness that she had walked two hundred eighty miles with these women, more than friends, trail sisters. After dinner, we drove back to the hotels and ventured across the street to get ice cream at a camp store where I investigated a bait (for fishing) vending machine, a first for me.

The following day, we took Rock Steady back to the trail in the rain. Still not feeling well, Paradox, Tough Love, and I all pleaded with her to stay one more day

148

with us. But Rock Steady refused to yield, using a scheduled visit with her family in a few days as the determining factor. As we drove to the trailhead, the rain came down steadily, people primarily silent as the windshield wipers filled the void. At the trailhead, Rock Steady lingered. I wondered if she'd change her mind. She did not. We promised we'd catch her in a few days. In the back of my mind, I knew that Paradox could catch her. Me? Not so sure. Rock Steady disappeared down the trail. The lump of disappointment in my throat surprised me. I swallowed it and helped the rest consider our options for the day. Paradox needed new shoes, time to go shopping.

As a continuation of yesterday's trail feast, Sandy planned to provide trail magic for other hikers at this parking lot, but the weather did not cooperate. Matty and Mary weren't thrilled at the prospect of sitting in the rain. Instead, we left food and drink in the parking lot with a note and drove away to shop for shoes for Paradox. Her current shoes approached uselessness, ripped to shreds by the trail.

She tried on many. She needed good ones. Early on, her feet became badly blistered in a pair of boots, so she switched to running shoes. Ultimately, she *settled* on a pair.

Next, we ventured to a theater and saw an Avenger movie in 3D. I relished the air-conditioning and munched popcorn, and slurped Coca-Cola. After we climbed in our old Suburban, Sandy asked me to drive. Well over one hundred days since I had been behind the wheel, I pulled up to the road to a right turn-only sign. We wanted to go left back to the hotel. Sandy looked around and said,

"Just go left; there's no one around."

I did. Police lights lit up behind me. I got pulled over. Paradox snickered in the back while she took pictures and video. Luckily, the police officer, in a good mood, just wrote me a warning.

I relaxed for the rest of the day. I dreaded the next day, the day when my family dropped me off at the trailhead and drove away. I didn't think I could do it.

As I put on my clean hiking clothes the following day, everything felt… heavy; my heart was burdened. Was this hike worth it? Why don't I just drive home with them? I swung my backpack on my shoulders. The weight threatened to bury me in the ground, my boots made of lead. I shuffled slowly out to the Suburban. We picked up Paradox, the ride to the trail eerily quiet. I fought back the tears. We pulled into the parking lot. I helped load up the leftover trail magic.

Time to part ways, Paradox said goodbye to everyone and took off down the trail. A compassionate, emotional woman, this proved hard for her too. I became numb; the shock of the situation overpowered me. I hugged and held everyone until the awkward phase. I tried to smile and wave as they drove away. I looked up the trail, and my feet started to move mechanically.

I worked on my thought process. Maybe I could use my emotional pain to my advantage. I could be home in Connecticut in a few weeks if I kept up a good pace. I decided to focus on that. And as usual, once I started walking, my spirits lifted some. I caught Paradox, who waited for me. She didn't say much because she knew how much I hurt. We quietly passed the one thousand miles left marker. Time to count down the miles. From this point forward. Only one thousand miles left. Only. Felt like forever.

The trail became rockier. Brutal on the footwear, Paradox immediately tore her new shoes.

In the afternoon, I used my Fox Sports app and LTE power to listen to the World Cup final as Paradox, and I strolled through the Pennsylvania woods. The US Women's National Team played Japan. I listened to the audio when Carli Lloyd scored in the third minute. I pulled the iPhone from my pocket and watched with Paradox. We couldn't believe it! Then she scored in the fifth minute. Holiday scored in the fourteenth minute, and then Lloyd scored from midfield. Are you kidding? The five-two Unites State's victory diminished some of the gloom from the day. By the time we settled for the evening, we had covered more than eighteen miles. Another way to ward off emotional distress? Walk long and hard.

Port Clinton Pukes

The following day Paradox got up and out of camp before me, eager to pick up a package in Port Clinton, almost nineteen miles away over Pennsylvania rocks. The post office closed at four-thirty, so she needed to hike aggressively. I'd meet her there. I wandered through the woods solo and encountered a long black snake and a fearsome box turtle. The box turtle stood smack dab in the middle of the trail and bellowed.

"Thou shall not pass!"

I ignored him and walked by. About three miles outside Clinton, I found a nice flat campsite with a pine needle floor and took a breather. I took my shoes and socks off, put my feet on a tree, and alleviated my foot stress. I took a picture of my beat-up feet and legs. It looked like a good Instagram pic to me; I posted it. Then I texted Paradox. I said I was still three miles out. She sat at the Pavilion in Port Clinton happily with her package. I considered camping right here a perfect spot, but I did not. I booted up, suited up, and headed on into town, the descent crazy steep and

150

treacherous. I slid down the hill for the last half-mile or so. When I hit the town, dead tired, I got turned around. I called Paradox to guide me to the Pavilion.

Casually perched on a picnic table, Paradox chatted easily with Dr. Pickles and Mockingbird. Our eyes met. She smiled. I said hello to them all. To Paradox,

"You are a beast! Wow!"

"Sit down, old man." She replied.

I shrugged off my pack and sat heavily on one of the benches. Hiker tents filled the pavilion. I needed something to eat. Dr. Pickles and Mockingbird had dinner plans at the Port Clinton Fire Company. They served food and alcohol at meager prices, appealing to frugal thru-hikers. Technically, patrons required membership. However, the AT Guide says they allow "guests." Hot food appealed to me, yet the Fire Company required walking. No. I ate cold food from my pack.

Across the street, I considered the expansive lawn next to the Little Schuykill River; it looked better than this pavilion. I set up near the moving water. Some light rain fell. I wondered if my tent would keep the water out. Paradox set up nearby too. She didn't like the idea of all those people in the pavilion either. I tried to sleep over the roar of trucks on nearby Route 61, but they proved too loud. As the traffic subsided, my naps became longer until the first train thundered by. I hadn't noticed the tracks right across the river.

After the first train, I heard other rowdiness coming from across the street. Hikers returned from the bar after a few too many. I patted myself on the back for my decision to set up near the river. At about one in the morning, three very drunk people made their way to a small pavilion near me. They talked loudly. Intoxicated people think their companions must be deaf. They shouted. My patience, already tested, boiled over. I shouted.

"Hey! There are people out here trying to sleep! Shut the hell up and go to bed!"

One guy mockingly said, "That's hilarious…."

My comment made no impact. He continued to yell with the other two. Quietly furious, I resisted the urge to unzip my tent and engage in battle. I projected my voice and issued one last threat.

"Don't make me come out there. Leave. Now!"

Pretty intimidating from a fifty-five-year-old man, wouldn't you say?

Some more snide remarks followed, including another "That's hilarious." But I could tell they weren't up for an altercation either. They got the message and wandered away. It sounded like two of them had set up tents near me. The other guy got in a car (Oh My God!), started it, and turned on the headlights. Oh shit, I hadn't thought of that. What if he went on an alcohol-induced rampage and ran over my

151

tent? And other tents? On full alert, I watched the headlights. The car turned around and drove up the road.

Relieved, I settled back in but slept the rest of the night fitfully; trucks and trains still rolled by. Compared to the peace out in the woods, Port Clinton proved utterly chaotic. I welcomed the grayness of the dawn. Get me out of here. Up very early, too, Paradox agreed. As we packed up, we noticed Dr. Pickles and Mockingbird stirred. Paradox and I wandered over.

"How was your night?" I asked.

In whispered tones, mindful of all the other hikers who still slept (passed out), they relayed a nightmare story; a drunk dude threw up outside their tent. The stream of puke flowed by and narrowly missed them. It didn't smell too good either. Many other hikers partied late into the night, loud and rowdy, making sleep impossible. Up the road, opposite the AT, 3 C's Restaurant, beckoned to Paradox and me. I asked if they wanted to join us. They politely declined. They wanted to get out of there.

We gathered our stuff and headed out. In the field, a young girl sprawled half in, half out of her tent. It had rained during the night; she and her gear were soaked— another young man in another tent in a similar condition. We left them alone.

"What did you think of all that, Paradox?"

"I'm glad you said something. I was about ready to go out and kick some ass."

"You were?"

"Yeah, Right Click. I had your back."

"I would have needed it. I'm not much of a fighter."

She laughed. At 3 C's, we sat down and sincerely appreciated the breakfast menu. I ordered "bacons and egg" and lots of it. Paradox bought breakfast. Touched by her generosity, I felt much better as we moved back through town and headed back to the trail.

I'd later learn some other stories about Port Clinton. I heard the people who lived next to the pavilion were once hiker-friendly and opened their pool. One morning, a hiker went to the Fire Company, got ridiculously intoxicated, and puked and crapped himself. Still mostly drunk from the previous night, he jumped in the neighbor's pool to clean up. That ended that.

Paradox and I wondered who shouldered the responsibility of cleaning the pavilion. We learned that a volunteer from the local church maintained the property. Would he have to clean up all that puke? We knew the hikers wouldn't do it. Shameful. I believed it would be a matter of time before the church said no more hikers. Other places reject hikers now. Like other aspects of life, a few ruin it for all the others.

As I walked away from Port Clinton, I slowly shed my embarrassment as a member of the thru-hiker community, remembering that most hikers are polite, respectful, and well-behaved. I meditated on a slogan from Alcoholics Anonymous.

"But for the grace of God go I."

What would I be like if I still drank? Gratefully sober, hiking the trail was hard enough. I couldn't imagine backpacking several miles with a horrific hangover.

But what if I was still in my twenties? I could imagine being the kid lying out in the grass and laughing it off. I used to drink until I passed out, threw up, fought, or ended up in handcuffs. Alcoholics, when drinking, cause many problems. Many people who attempt a thru-hike struggle with addiction. I witnessed it first-hand. In that sense, the AT mirrored life off the trail, exactly. I'm not sure why Port Clinton allowed such easy access to alcohol for hikers. It sure got messy and ugly for all involved.

Bake Oven Knob Breakdown

Paradox and I broke camp the following day; Rock Steady was still in front of us. The AT Guide indicated little elevation change over the next several miles; I thought our chances were good to catch up with her. Paradox tolerated my slower pace for a bit, but I told her to go on ahead. She soon distanced herself from me.

I negotiated the rocks fairly well, happy hiking through the Pennsylvania woods alone. I knew Paradox would handle the rough trail way faster than me. I started to feel lonely. I looked ahead for a glimpse of her bright orange jersey, hopeful she'd wait for me, but the bright color never materialized.

I reached Pennsylvania's Knife's Edge (not nearly as infamous in AT lore as Katahdin's Knife's Edge). I managed the climb up well enough and soaked in the expansive view. At the summit, I looked to the left and spied a smooth trail running along the forest floor around the Knife's Edge. Why did the AT route us up this pile of rocks? Picture a stone Mohawk haircut; the AT ran along the spikes. It pissed me off. Angry, I started down the north side and encountered downright treachery.

Completely alone, my anger joined forces with escalating fear. Late in the afternoon and fatigued, the severe terrain eroded my confidence. I'd spend the night on the rocks if I fell and got seriously hurt. I hadn't seen anyone for hours. I doubted that anyone was walking behind me. My self-assurance frayed; navigating a short stretch took a long time.

153

Finally, I stepped off the Knife's Edge onto what could be called a trail for humans, not mountain goats. I sat down and checked the AT guide. Bake Oven Knob Shelter, my destination, beckoned just two and a half miles away. The terrain looked reasonably flat. I trudged slowly along, body aching, emotionally hurting – every step agonizing. I reached Bake Oven Knob, very tired. I looked at the trail ahead, shook my head at another stupid pile of rocks, and decided to encourage myself.

"I'm close now. You can do it, Phillip. Just climb this last pile. You successfully conquered many piles bigger than this. You can do this one. Paradox will be at the shelter."

I mustered up some energy. I focused on the task at hand; I took one step at a time. I kept myself calm. I reached the top, but… I gasped when I gazed down the other side. Uncontrollable emotion swept through my body. Sobs of anger, frustration, and despair emanated from the bottomless well of my soul.

Through tear-filled eyes, I stared, horrified, at an enormous boulder field. I sat down while my body released all the pent-up emotion. My body heaved with my head in my hands, and tears fell and dotted my dusty Merrells. After several minutes, I asked the question.

"What choice do I have?"

I stood up and composed myself as best I could. On wobbly legs, I began to take on one obstacle at a time. I navigated several boulder scrambles where I needed my hands. The trail taunted and frightened me. I rested often. It took me more than an hour to go a few hundred yards. I felt my age when I dropped back onto a dirt trail.

Hot, sweaty, angry, and with muscles screaming, the foliage from the overgrown trail tore at my skin. Fueled by infuriation, I hacked at the leaves and vines with my trekking poles. In the middle of a few f-bombs with foliage flying, the sign for the shelter appeared. The rage left, and relief flooded in.

"I made it."

I turned right and made my way down. Far from inviting, the lean-to was wildly overgrown too. Parquet welcomed me.

"Hi, Parquet. Hey, have you seen Paradox?"

"Yeah, she was here and told me to tell you she was going on to the next shelter."

I felt my heart drop in my chest. The next shelter? Really? No chance I could do another six point eight miles. I'd already gone seventeen, a massive day over rugged terrain. Part of me admired Paradox. How did she hike that far over all those rocks and have the stamina to go on?

But mostly, I felt abandoned. Again. My eyes moistened with despair.

Quickly and respectfully, I thanked Parquet. He didn't need to see me like this. The shelter was utterly unappealing; I returned to the trail where I had noted a friendly stealth site. I shrugged off my pack, dug out my stuff, and muttered to myself while I pitched my tent. I blew up my air mattress, dropped to my knees, and started to crawl in to stretch out, relax and eat. I looked up. I positioned the tent directly under a huge dead branch – a classic widow maker. If it fell, it would be lights out. Permanently.

I didn't care. Irritated, I swore.

"Go ahead, God! Let it fall on me. I don't give a shit."

In my tent, my tortured body protested while I lay with intense emotion. I muttered some more.

"It's too big. It's too big. I can't do it. It's too big. I want to go home. It's too big…",

I came to a stunning realization.

"I'm done," I said out loud.

The immensity of the trail overwhelmed me. The AT won. No, it more than won; the Appalachian Trail crushed me. I gave up. With my decision solidified, I calmed down. Relieved that the ordeal was over, I called Sandy.

I told her I needed to come home. She lovingly agreed to pick me up. I'd call her from the road (seven point three miles away) the following day. Resigned, I opened the orange Sea to Summit food sack to eat my last meal on the trail.

But I didn't have any water. Damn. I can't eat without water since radiation treatments left me with only half a salivary gland. The water source was down past the shelter, a long walk after a devastating day. I dragged myself out, glanced at the dead branch above my tent, gave it the finger, and headed down the trail. At the shelter, I saw a familiar face. I said hi to Just Doug. But when our eyes met, I instantly perceived the same look of resignation. He looked exactly like how I felt. I told him of my recent plight. He did not judge or try to convince me otherwise. Just Doug concurred.

"Hey, you want to hike to the road together?" I asked.

"Sure. I'd like that."

"Great. I'll see you in the morning. Ummm… Thanks." I felt something shift slightly in my attitude.

"No. Thank you." He replied sincerely.

I shuffled slowly up the hill to the AT and my tent. After I ate, I lay in my tent alone and thought.

"Do I really want to quit?"

155

I pushed that notion aside; I wanted nothing to do with this freaking hike. I just wanted to go home. I resolved to stick to the plan. Just Doug and I would hike out, get to the road, get to a hotel, wait for Sandy and get my butt home. Exhausted, I went to sleep quickly.

But before I did, I muttered one quick prayer.

"God, please keep that huge dead branch on the tree for just one more night."

Just Doug

I woke up unsmooshed, the branch still on the tree. Still resolved to make this my last stretch on the AT, I ate four Pop Tarts, a Cliff bar, and drank a Carnation Instant/Starbucks Via combo. Adequately fueled, I found Just Doug at the shelter, waiting patiently. We started down the trail. We got to know each other a bit. Just Doug, a recently retired cop from Cleveland, considered his Appalachian Trail thru-hike a gratifying reward for his thirty-six years of service.

Since I decided to part company, the AT chose to leave me one parting gift, pain. My right foot ached, then throbbed. After five miles, I could only hobble. Did I break my foot?

I limped into Young Gun, Rainbow, and Wannabe at a trail magic station. Former thru-hiker Starman had filled sizeable plastic storage tubs with goodies. A chocolate frosted chocolate donut (or two or three or four) did heavenly things to adjust my poor attitude. Even with a painful foot, I began to reconsider my decision.

Just Doug and I could see the road when we came across a pair of blue suede high-heel shoes in the middle of the trail. We came up with many theories. I'm sure he'd seen weirder things in his years on the force. I hobbled down the hill to the road; my foot was excruciatingly painful; I called for a taxi and sat heavily on the ground. I waited. I wondered if a hospital visit rested in my immediate future.

Our ride came. First, we went into Lehighton and checked into a room. Feeling better after our showers, Just Doug and I went for a short walk to a local restaurant. I wore my yellow Crocs. Strangely, my foot felt a lot better. Before the waitress came to take our food order, Just Doug downed two beers, either very thirsty or he needed a dose of alcohol to deal with me. After all, we barely knew each other and shared a hotel room. Over dinner, Doug and I discussed our experience. We shared similar attitudes and beliefs about hiking. We made a gentlemen's pact; we agreed to finish one more state, Pennsylvania, together, then reassess at the border. I was relieved and grateful.

I called Sandy. She understood and unconditionally accepted my decision to continue.

What about my foot? Since putting on my Crocs, my foot felt fine. I thought. "There's a clue in there somewhere, Phillip. Figure it out."

But I'm not too quick sometimes. That evening, Just Doug did laundry and offered to do mine with kindness and sincerity; the act of generosity pointed to his integrity.

We got up the next day, dressed in our clean hiking gear, and grabbed a taxi out to the trailhead. The first task, climb the "cliff" out of Palmerton into the Superfund section of the trail. I knew nothing about a Superfund site, although I surmised it wasn't good. I found this on Wikipedia:

> Superfund or Comprehensive Environmental Response, Compensation, and Liability Act of 1980 (CERCLA) is a United States federal law designed to clean up sites contaminated with hazardous substances and pollutants.

Palmerton, the site of a toxic zinc smelting operation, declared a priority for Superfund in 1983, posts warnings not to drink the water. Wonderful.

On the brink of another brutally hot day, I started up the copper-colored cliff. Steep, full of shale and slag, the climb forced me to use both hands to get up the rock faces. With Just Doug's blessing, I moved on ahead. High up, I could see for miles, but I looked at a highway, a couple of bridges, a few other roads, building roofs, and rocky, ugly scenery. Near the top, I took a selfie with an American flag painted on a rock. The stars in the flag looked more like circles. Even the flag was ugly.

The wind blew hard as I continued. Up ahead, I watched Mockingbird pose for a pic. I called to her, but the wind drowned me out. I tried to catch her and Dr. Pickles but never did; the rocks slowed me down. Twice, I thought the trail ventured upwards, but after slowing down and scanning for the next white blaze, I saw that it traversed the mountainside. Paying close attention, I made my way out of the rocks and followed the trail as it wound through underbrush onto a ridge. I stopped at a flat spot, took in the view, opened up my food bag, and waited for Just Doug, the usual operating procedure when I hiked with someone.

I ate a snack. I ate another. I drank a bottle of water. I waited some more. I started to think.

"Should I violate the code and travel southbound?"

After forty-five minutes, no sign of him. After an hour, still no Just Doug. I headed back on the trail, concerned that he might have fallen. Maybe he got lost.

157

After ten minutes or so, I heard a voice up ahead, Just Doug, as he talked to himself. Pleasantly surprised when he saw me, he asked,

"Did you come back for me?" I could feel the respect in his query.

"I did."

Just Doug relayed how he got lost; he went straight up instead of swinging left along the ridge side. Day hikers forged multiple pathways making it very easy to get lost. If I had not been hyper-vigilant about locating white blazes, I would have ended up top too.

He bled from several scratches. I noticed the blood.

"Are you OK?" I asked.

"Yeah, just some scratches. I had to bushwhack."

Just Doug thrashed his way through a lot of brush, some of it quite thorny. He relocated the trail when I caught up with him. He didn't whine or complain. He laughed it off. However, he did seem relieved to be back on track. Quietly impressed that he found the humor in it all, my respect for him grew.

My foot felt better and didn't cause me much grief on the climb, but the pain began to build once the trail flattened out. This unnerving, ugly section disturbed me. I could tell something wrong happened here. I detected no old growth, and all the new foliage appeared… off. We passed a life-size cut-out of the *"most interesting man in the world"* advertising Dos Equis beer. I asked the Dos Equis man.

"Hey, can you do something for my aching foot?"

No reply. Just Doug shot me an amused look. We pulled into a campsite and ate lunch. Out of desperation, I pulled my Superfeet insoles out of my shoes. I thought they'd protect my feet against all the sharp, jagged rocks. Within a few hundred yards of leaving, my foot stopped aching. Problem solved.

Lesson learned. When my foot, ankle, knee, or leg starts hurting, change the footwear. For me, discomfort always started with the shoes.

Sometimes on the trail, you shoot for a spot on the map to settle down for the night, but you fall short. About three miles from where Just Doug and I targeted, we crossed a road and immediately heard from the woods,

"Hey, Right Click, come on over!"

Young Gun, and several of his friends, laid out another feast – hot dogs, chips, drinks, and fruit. They invited us into their circle, a friendly fire with camp chairs. Just Doug and I looked at each other, and without a spoken word, we nodded in agreement. Thanking them all, we found two spots nearby and set our tents. We joined the party. I had the option of getting high as a bowl of marijuana meandered over to me, but I passed it on; still not the time to sabotage twenty-seven years of

158

sustained recovery. Everyone seemed cool with it. Just Doug didn't get high either. Everyone else did. The marijuana smokers often hung out together, while those who disapproved of ganja use avoided them and often besmirched them. I liked them very much. Mellow folks, they enjoyed the woods, the adventure, and yes, their wampum. Stoners didn't get drunk and do idiotic stuff, as I had witnessed. As I feasted, I enjoyed the camaraderie with several fellow hikers who smoked pot, got high, ate a lot, laughed, listened to music, gazed at the campfire, and then ventured to their places to sleep. No trouble, only warmth, and friendship.

The next day Just Doug and I hiked seventeen miles in July heat over jagged Pennsylvania rocks. We encountered a mother black bear and her two cubs, passive as they meandered through the woods. Later, we ran across a big male bear. He looked at us over the top of some undergrowth, got bored, sat down under a tree, then eventually laid down, not too worried about us. We weren't concerned about him either.

During the day's hike, Just Doug and I stopped to rest. As we sat there, two older gentlemen (older than us) passed. They barely acknowledged us, too angry. White Wolf and Hardware marched in big heavy hiking boots, matched each other stride for stride, and garnished fierce grimaces. They stomped, odd and somewhat ridiculous, considering the terrain. I'm not an expert hiker, but the Pennsylvania rocks in this section required some strategy. You either walked on top of them or between them. Would you rather have the bottoms or the sides of your feet shredded? In any case, it called for a hiker to tread lightly. These two guys chose option three; smash the rocks and pound them into the ground with each step. The recovery coach in me wanted to ask,

"How's that working for you?"

But even I felt intimidated by their growling as they tramped by. But after they passed, Just Doug and I enjoyed a good chuckle. I got miserable too. However, I didn't stay miserable. Eventually, I worked my way through it. These two old codgers, miserable all the time, made me wonder why they were out there. In recovery, I have often heard and said,

"I didn't get sober to be miserable."

I pondered this often in Pennsylvania. The rocks took their toll. Once, a few yards ahead of Just Doug, I rounded a corner, looked ahead, and for the hundredth time that day, I saw nothing but sharp white rocks embedded in brown dirt for as far as the eye could see. I laughed at the ridiculousness.

"What's so funny Right Click?" Just Doug asked with curiosity.

I pointed up the trail.

"She's not gonna let us out."

I don't think he picked up on The Perfect Storm reference. He looked up. He thought for a moment. He smiled. He didn't utter a sound. He walked on, not just tough, Doug Tough.

Continually adjusting my attitude, Pennsylvania wore me down, frustrated by the rocks. We'd be in Delaware Water Gap on the Pennsylvania/New Jersey border a few more miles the next day.

We arrived in the morning, made our way through town, decided on an overnight stay at the Pocono Inn, and sweet-talked the manager into giving us a room early. Paradox texted me, who was already in town to spend a long weekend with her husband, Dan. Thoughtfully, she offered to take us to Walmart to resupply. Part of me wondered if some guilt of leaving me behind triggered her generosity. But all my ill feelings dissipated when we met in the parking lot. I gave her an affectionate hiker fist bump. She introduced us to Dan. I liked him immediately.

"So, did you catch Rock Steady?' I asked.

"I did. She left this morning."

"Did you do twenty-four miles that day?" Paradox nodded yes.

"Over all those rocks?" Again, she nodded, and she beamed.

"You're amazing!"

A fine, sunny Sunday drew the crowds to Walmart. I shopped very quickly. Loud, busy, and chaotic, I felt my anxiety heighten around all those people. So different from the trail's rhythm, the noise disturbed me deeply. It bothered Paradox too. She didn't even shop. She just waited patiently for us to finish getting out of there. I wondered what it would be like to return to civilization again. Yet a more significant question loomed in the shadows that I didn't even want to acknowledge.

Could I return at all?

After a night and a few good meals in Delaware Water Gap, Just Doug and I strolled out of town with our enthusiasm renewed. Paradox stayed behind with Dan. She'd catch up. We paused at the border, marked on a sidewalk on the long bridge across the Delaware River, to take a few obligatory photos. Just Doug and I had honored our contract; we hiked through Pennsylvania together. As we stepped into New Jersey, I asked him if he wanted to do another state with me. He replied.

"Why not?"

High Point Park

Magical. Magical describes our first day in New Jersey. Early in the day, I videoed an impressive rat snake gliding across the trail. As I strode up the path with Just Doug a few minutes behind me, I looked up and stopped dead in my tracks. A black bear crouched on the trail about fifty yards away. After the initial gasp of disbelief, I responded calmly.

"Hey, bear."

She heard me and stood up on four paws to reveal two cubs. While she looked at me, I took the opportunity to turn my back to her and take the coveted, elusive three-bear selfie. I faced her again and talked calmly. She watched me nonthreateningly. Then she bounced on her front paws; the two cubs scurried up a nearby tree. We both watched them climb. She looked at me again. She bounced again, and the cubs clamored down the tree, hit the ground running, and all three scurried into the woods to my right.

"That was very cool," I said to no one.

One time was fabulous, but when she met me twice more and repeated the drill, I realized we had established a nonverbal agreement. I was no threat, so she used me to train her little ones. My mind was boggled.

Just Doug caught up with me, and we shared recent wildlife encounters; his concern was a rattlesnake that challenged him on the trail. Luckily, I missed the snake; I wanted nothing to do with rattlers. Later, we watched a mama bear and her two cubs climb a very tall tree, astonished at how quickly they moved. I wondered if these were the same bears from earlier in the day. We passed the thirteen-hundred-mile mark, then ate lunch next to a picturesque lake. After thirteen miles, we found an attractive campsite for the night on top of a ridge. Just Doug hung his food expertly. I felt encouraged, a far distance from the emotional low a few days ago.

Only one-hundred-fifty miles from Connecticut and home, Just Doug and I fell into an easy trail partnership. We accumulated miles quickly and experienced incredible fortune with wildlife. The day after we saw a mother bear and two cubs; we saw another set. Never once did I feel threatened or alarmed. New Jersey bears seemed comfortable sharing the trail with thru-hikers; I cherished every sighting.

Earlier in the day, I reached the Sunrise Mountain pavilion. I stopped and prayed. In Jennifer Pharr Davis' book, Becoming Odyssa, about her first thru-hike, she discovered a young man hanging in the rafters – he committed suicide. She also wrote about her reaction to returning to this location on her record-breaking hike coming south a few years later. I sensed the uncomfortable energy here and decided to sit and talk with God for a bit. It helped me.

A quick radar check on a cloudy, hot, humid afternoon indicated a huge thunderstorm nearby. Luckily, we approached High Point State Park Headquarters as the skies darkened. We checked in; thru-hikers received a free soda, which tasted wonderful like usual. Afterward, we sat outside with fresh water and a snack; it started to spit rain. The rangers let us drop our packs inside, and we hung out as the downpour pounded outside. I watched a video on black bears and learned what they ate and in what season. I learned something new; black bears feasted on acorns in the fall. Unlike brown bears (grizzlies), people are not part of their diet.

The rangers let us know that they'd be closing at four.

"You're not going to kick us out in that, are you?" I mustered my most pitiful voice.

Not new to hiker drama, they politely responded, "Yes, we are."

However, they called ahead to the concession stand in the park and asked if they'd stay open for us. The concession stand agreed to wait for us.

"Wow! Thank you." I replied sincerely, especially considering there were no other patrons in the park.

With no choice, we stepped out into the deluge. Instantly soaked, I reached the trailhead and ran into Young Gun and Rainbow a hundred yards away.

"Dang, Young Gun, the headquarters just closed."

"Figures."

We briefly discussed their thoughts about possible night campsites, then off they went. Young Gun, a phenomenal hiker, light on his feet, traveled super-light. I tried to keep pace. As we descended a hill, he stepped onto some wet grass, and his feet flew out from under him. He sailed into the air. If he were competing in a high jump competition, he would have cleared the bar at a respectable height. He landed on his back with a loud splat and a thud. And just lay there in a grassy puddle. Rainbow bustled up to him.

"Are you OK?"

Between grunts and moans, he managed.

"Ya, I guess so."

Then he cursed his treadless trail runners, too many miles on them. Just Doug and I stood in awe. With maybe too much enthusiasm, I voiced,

"Dude! That was the most spectacular fall EVER!"

"Glad you liked it, Right Click."

162

He muttered sarcastically from the prone position. Young Gun failed to see the humor. He slowly got up, and off the two went, mumbling about the rain, crappy shoes, and lack of food. But they went fast. Just Doug and I couldn't keep up.

The rain stopped. We reached the side trail down to the concession stand, further than we usually would. We debated for a bit and decided to march down there anyway. Dr. Pickles and Mockingbird had already used their considerable charms to convince the concession stand workers that two more hikers were on the way. Just Doug, mesmerized by one of the ladies, placed his order. I asked for two cheeseburgers, an order of fries, and three cokes. As we ate, Just Doug told me the older woman looked and acted exactly like his deceased mother-in-law, for whom he held great affection. He believed this meeting not to be a coincidence.

"Guys, where should we camp? This place looks pretty nice, right here on the water."

"Let me ask."

Dr. Pickles worked more of his magic. With Mockingbird, the two proved irresistible. Eventually, one of the two lifeguards remained in an otherwise empty park called the "boss." Granted permission to camp at a picnic pavilion a few hundred yards away, we walked past open bathrooms with running water and flush toilets, luxuries for us. Incredibly blessed, we appreciated our good fortune. My two-person Tarptent Double Rainbow, Just Doug's tiny one-person tent, and Dr. Pickles and Mockingbird's two-person tent made up our mini-caravan.

We walked back to the concession stand early to eat breakfast on the deck and dry some of our stuff in the sun, the crisp, cool morning unusual for July. The four of us proceeded together on the Appalachian Trail through New Jersey. Impressed with the beauty and relief (the sharp rock segments absent), I enjoyed the walks on dirt, grass and the occasional boardwalk over boggy land. At one point, I soaked my aching feet in a crystal-clear cold stream and made a mental note to acquire another pair of boots. By now, we routinely hiked miles in the teens, not hurrying and not lagging.

After a long, flat walk along three sides of an extensive square wetland to our final destination, the Pochuck Mountain shelter, the AT Guide pointed us to an unoccupied house to use the spigot in the back for water. We fully hydrated, filled every bottle, and went to the campsite. As we set up, two familiar voices followed by two friendly smiles filled me with elation. Paradox! Rock Steady! But it couldn't be; they were in front of me, weren't they? Paradox shot me a wry smile. I knew instinctively she worked some magic to get us all together. I loved that girl.

163

We sat together, consumed our evening meal, and shared stories. The profound depth of our relationship reminded me of childhood friendships, picking up right where we left off. With every thought filtered through gratitude, my motivation to finish elevated to a high-water mark.

From the Pochuck Shelter, I coordinated a rendezvous with some guys from my church in Connecticut. The pastor, Frank Riley, and a dear friend, Nate Shippee, planned to meet me bearing the best barbeque in the whole world from Bears Smokehouse. I used all the technology – email, Facebook, text messages – and settled on a meeting place, Wawayanda State Park. Excited for the whole crew – Just Doug, Dr. Pickles, Mockingbird, Rock Steady, and Paradox – to meet my friends and feast, I strode enthusiastically northward.

BBQ and Jurassic World

Specifically, we were scheduled to meet at the *top* of the Stairway to Heaven, an intimidating name for a section of trail. After crossing flat terrain and a road, with the ridge up ahead, the trail turned right and straight up. I started to climb. Focused on my footwork, I recognized a couple of faces but couldn't immediately place them. Not in my current frame of reference; it took me a few seconds to realize Pastor Frank and Nate! My heart swelled. The presence of the first people from home besides Sandy and my kids visibly moved me. They took the time to support me and hike with me. As we climbed, I got caught up with events back home. An avid outdoorsman, a few years older than me, in tremendous physical shape, and a dedicated family man, I deeply respect Nate. Like a younger brother, I felt affirmed when he talked about getting a taste of the trail and acknowledged the overall difficulty. I detected a trace of admiration, colossal praise from this humble, confident man.

At Wawayanda State Park, we took a short side trail to the parking lot, where we accessed their load of incredible trail magic. Coca-Cola, lemonade, iced tea, chips, other snacks, and, most importantly, a massive quantity of Bear's Smokehouse BBQ. Nate agreed to drive Just Doug to the post office to pick up a new pair of shoes. Just Doug's shoes fell apart. I don't know how he walked in them without falling. Rock Steady and Paradox walked in, but Dr. Pickles and Mockingbird went into town to resupply.

We relaxed in a grassy area just off the parking lot and enjoyed ice-cold drinks. I expressed my appreciation for ice, much to Pastor Frank's amusement. When Just Doug and Nate returned, Pastor Frank fired up the grill and heated the barbecue in a

164

cast iron skillet. As we reveled in the gastronomic deliciousness, we discussed where to stay. I heard a rumor that the Warwick Drive-In allowed thru-hikers to camp and watch movies for free. Frank and Nate agreed to take us to resupply, then the drive-in. It's hard to explain how meaningful these acts of kindness are to hikers. My thought process went something like this,

"You'll give us a ride? And you want to? Aren't you inconvenienced? I don't want to be a bother. It looks like you want to. Oh my. Thank you. I'm deeply grateful."

Nate accompanied us, fascinated with our approach to resupplying. I expertly picked out food with the highest calorie per ounce – sugary things most common. Wolf Pine used to carry buttercream frosting in a one-pound Ziplock. Yuck. However, Fritos have one of the highest calorie per ounce ratios; corn chips also sport an alternative use as a premium fire starter. Finding protein for the trail proved a challenge. I could only eat so many protein bars. Usual suspects in the protein category included bags of tuna, bags of salmon, pepperoni, cheese, peanut butter, summer sausage, salami, etc. Side note: I'll never eat summer sausage again.

Dr. Pickles and Mockingbird hung outside and removed all excess packaging from their groceries while they finished eating. Hikers congregated outside a trail grocery store, filled their bellies, and commenced an art form – the repackaging of their supplies. No need to carry extra weight, right? Hikers became proficient at maximizing space in their backpacks, food included. I informed the couple about our plans to stay behind the grocery store at the drive-in.

Nate and Frank drove us up the hill to the Warwick Drive-In. Rock Steady took charge.

"Let me do my thing." She quietly commanded.

"Yeah, go do your thing." I encouraged; Nate and Pastor Frank to be thoroughly engrossed.

Rock Steady charmed the living daylights out of the person in charge with her friendly, genuine smile. She and Paradox returned with the owner's permission to camp on the hill for the night. She said the guy loved hikers and gave us free admission and AM radios to tune into the shows.

Seeing our place for the night secure, Nate and Frank huddled us together while Pastor Frank prayed for us. Beautifully. I basked in God's presence amongst our traveling band as the words of love washed over us. As I hugged Frank goodbye, I couldn't hold back the emotion, and some sobs escaped. I might have left a few tears on his shoulder, too, so grateful for their love and support. Their tender care inspired me and touched me deeply.

"Right Click, you have some great friends." Dr. Pickles commented as they drove away. The others concurred.

"I do, don't I?" I responded more to myself than anyone else.

Now to the business of setting up camp. Five tents and six people lined up afforded quite the spectacle for hundreds and hundreds of people as they drove in. Friday night at the drive-in drew a vast crowd. With plenty of food from our resupply and leftovers from the barbecue feast, we, again, appreciated our good fortune. This night would not be a quiet one in the woods, but it would be one to remember. From our vantage point, three movie screens with double features offered options. I tried to watch Minions, but it lost me, so I jumped back and forth to the others. Talk about sensory overload. I watched most of Jurassic World, just an updated version of Jurassic Park (1997), but it entertained me. I grew sleepier and sleepier. On the trail, nightfall indicates "hiker midnight." Far past my bedtime, when the movie finally ended, I crawled into my bag and tried to sleep but could not. Vehicles on the gravel road just thirty feet away rendered slumber impossible.

The following day, we discovered that no one slept well. Groggy, we took our time. My usual morning brew - a combination of Carnation Instant Breakfast and Starbucks VIA - kickstarted my metabolism. I ate a couple of Pop-Tarts, some Frosted Mini-Wheats, a protein bar, and copious amounts of water. Next, we figured out how to get back to the trailhead. With little traffic on the road this Saturday morning and six of us to transport, the odds of hitching a ride were slim.

We called two cabs.

Agony Grind

I estimated I'd reach Connecticut in a week. With great people, I hiked in a much better mood. Yet we suffered. Summer arrived in full force – hazy, hot, and humid, with temperatures in the mid-nineties. I thought back to my preparation. I constantly fretted about cold temperatures. Now I worried about boiling to death.

The heat made the basics difficult, breathing and hiking with thirty pounds on my back. But what bugged me? Trying to sleep at night while hot and filthy with salty legs pasted together. I found it supremely annoying. I took a bandanna bath whenever possible. Gold Bond Medicated Powder helped soothe skin abrasions, cuts, welts, and rashes but did not wholly alleviate stickiness. On uncomfortably hot nights, the surface of the sleeping bag took on new importance. I liked slippery nylon. Sticky nylon drove me crazy, particularly on warm nights that perpetuated perspiration. I found my nine-degree bag better in hot weather because the outer cover is more slippery. My thirty-five-degree bag, with a different outer material, stuck to me like a light, cheap bag I tried. Usually, by early morning as the atmosphere cooled, I'd settle into deep restorative sleep. For me, the colder the temperature, the better I slept. Give me freezing temperatures any night. Thankfully, I found an ally in physical exhaustion, facilitating deep sleep despite my discomfort.

We hiked up to a ridge the first day after the night at the drive-in. The morning sun blistered. Our party of six stopped at the New Jersey/New York border. The white letters painted on the rock floor served as the background for our group selfie; this photo is one of my favorites. Most of the water sources had dried up. The sun roasted me, so I rested in the shade. An annotation in the AT Guide worthy of the rare exclamation point got my attention.

"Despite the unimposing profile, rocks, abrupt ups and downs make this section challenging."

I climbed an aluminum ladder up one of the "abrupt ups." That's abrupt. The guide didn't say how long to expect these ups and downs, so I stuck to my strategy; take one step at a time. Thank goodness, near the end of the day's hike, I came to a road with trail magic. Nothing like the feeling of lifting a lid off a Styrofoam cooler and seeing red Coco-Cola cans submerged in ice.

"Thank you, Jesus!"

Young Gun's mom set up magic with fresh fruit, other food, and more liquids a few yards away from the Coca-Cola cooler. Young Gun joyfully showed off his new shoes, loving the new tread.

In New York, kind and thoughtful people, well aware of the scorching heat and low water supply, consistently assisted thru-hikers. Some left food and beverages and returned later to resupply and clean up. Sometimes, you'd lift the lid and find nothing but thru-hiker garbage. Now that's disappointing! Others set up a trail magic café with comfortable bag chairs and a pop-up tent for shade. I *always* appreciated trail magic, but in New York, it became essential. Just too dry and hot, heat exhaustion and heat stroke loomed as a viable possibilities.

The six of us – me, Rock Steady, Paradox, Just Doug, Dr. Pickles, and Mockingbird – camped together at Wildcat Shelter – hot and tired. We looked ahead. The forecast for the next few days promised no relief.

I made a decision this day about my ingestion of pain relievers. By this point in my f journey, I had resorted to alleviating pain with ibuprofen and acetaminophen. I took it daily. I noticed that at about 2:00 pm, my legs started to ache, no, cry for relief. Once I took the medication and waited for twenty minutes, I could miraculously hike several more miles, pain-free, loose, enthusiastically, and energized. I intuitively knew that I had developed a habit. Not good. Today, I denied the craving, which was not easy to do. My knees throbbed, my ankles rebelled, and my feet asked questions. But I did not cave in. I didn't for the next four days. By the sixth day, my body stopped screaming for relief. It said this guy is not giving an inch; time for Plan B. I did not take another dose for the rest of the trip. My body dealt with the strain and the pain naturally. Overall, I felt much better.

The oppressive conditions sapped my energy and affected the crew similarly. We talked about the upcoming stretch of trail. Although not indicated in the AT Guide, the section near Arden Mountain known as Agony Grind, an intimidating moniker for a stretch of trail, threatened to test us severely. We decided to go about fifteen miles, but very few "water drops" appeared in the AT Guide (drops are used to show water sources). We prepared mentally for a scorching day with very little water.

The hiking, as we expected, became brutal; climbs up and scrambles down although the elevation changes; not long, but frequent and steep. On the way up Arden Mountain, I found a tent on the trail's side. It looked like Dr. Pickle's tent. Two bodies lay motionless inside. Pretty sure they were asleep and not dead; I guessed they decided to get out of the heat and rest. I couldn't afford to. Finding water remained my top priority. With no water and on the verge of dehydration, I came to a steep descent and slid to the bottom toward NY 17. To my delight, I found fifty plastic gallon jugs filled with water. I drank my fill. Paradox slid down next, then Rock Steady. We lay in the cool dirt and shade, exhausted. We waited for Just Doug. After a few minutes, he skidded down the hill, red-faced, soaked in sweat (like all of us). We pointed to the water.

"I am so hot and so tired. Maybe we could duck into a hotel or something." I suggested.

After some debate, we attained a ride into Harriman and checked into the Days Inn. Showers, laundry, air-conditioning, and food revived us some. I texted Dr. Pickles and Mockingbird, and they decided to stay on the trail. We'd try to catch up tomorrow. That evening I lay practically motionless on the bed in an air-conditioned room. I only moved my fingers on the remote. I killed several thousand cable channels that evening.

The following day, I walked across the street to Dunkin' Donuts. I ate a breakfast sandwich, twenty-five munchkins, orange juice, and a large coffee. I could have eaten more. We resupplied at Walmart. As we sat outside and repackaged our purchases, Paradox zealously scraped out and ate the remainder of her old container of Reese's Peanut Butter Chocolate Spread. Not to worry, she replaced it with a new one. This woman's passion for the stuff startled me.

Just Doug and I struggled through the Lemon Squeezer back on the trail. We laughed about it. If not for the heat, I would have enjoyed the route here. Although still chock full of ups and downs, the woods opened up with ample ferns and grassy areas. At times, the beauty of the trail inspired and motivated me. After a few hours, I went down to Tiorati Circle in Harriman State Park. The vending machines took credit cards! I had a Coca-Cola. Then I ate a Creamsicle. Then I ate two more Creamsicles. Rock Steady, Paradox, and I went to the beach, took off our shoes, and went swimming – incredibly refreshing. Just Doug took a nap under a tree. I sat on the beach. I found it very hard to get motivated to hike again. As I begrudgingly prepared to get on the move, I repeated to myself.

"The funny thing about thru-hiking, if I don't hike, I won't get anywhere."

Internal Combustion

Water still posed a problem even after filling all our bottles at the park. We carried all we could, but I soon ran low with extreme exertion and no water sources. After ten miles, we arrived at the William Brien Memorial Shelter. I scouted around a bit and found the "unreliable" source; the water at the bottom of a reasonably deep well, but it stank severely. I filtered all my water from streams, ponds, and wells like this, but dead creatures floated here. As the four of us scooped and filtered, we looked at each other skeptically. The following water source rested beyond several obstacles, more than two miles over rugged terrain, an additional four-tenths down the Palisades Parkway to a small visitor center in the median. Much work for late in the day, so I tried a teeny sip of the skanky water, filtered but still skanky.

"Damn!" I gagged.

Everyone laughed. Just Doug drank a little. With only a few ounces of clean water left, I carried two full bottles of skanky water for emergency purposes.

Dusk fell as we reached Black Mountain's top and stumbled upon an excellent site. With the New York City skyline in view, we pitched tents. We ate dinner as it got dark. I crawled into bed, but I awoke at three in the morning with bulging eyes.

"OH MY GOD!"

My gut felt awful, and I needed to poop. Immediately! Not fun when it happens at home, but out here on a mountaintop, many other issues made this situation nightmarish. First, I had to get out of my bag and tent. I groped for my headlight and wipes. I tried to allay the panic, but I only had a few seconds before my body would decide without me.

Damn!

I extricated myself from the tent; where do I go? In a tight area, Just Doug very close, girls to my right, steep ledges, and cliffs to my left, one wrong step…

"Oh, God! Oh, God! "

I waded out through bushes, legs scratched and battered. Three steps. Four steps. Five…, no time left. I yanked down my shorts, squatted, and a bomb went off. Have you heard of projectile vomiting? This was projectile diarrhea. I sprayed coffee, Coca-Cola, Munchkins, creamsicles, and skanky water over a fifty-foot area. The force behind the explosion alarmed me greatly; I didn't know my body capable of such power. I cleaned myself up the best I could. My gut groaned. My legs wobbled; I struggled to straighten up.

"Uh oh, where's the tent?"

I gathered my composure and found my bearings. I stumbled to the tent, collapsed at the entrance, and rolled myself back in.

"Oh, man. Oooohhhh."

I tried to sleep. My belly hurt. I didn't want to explode again. Thirsty, I tentatively unscrewed the top to one of the skanky water bottles. The water smelled even worse than before. I immediately gagged. I could not drink any of that. I lay around until dawn. I slowly packed up my stuff. I told Just Doug what happened: I needed water, and I'd meet them at the Visitor Center.

After I carefully descended the mountain, I hit the road, the Visitor Center four-tenths to my left. I didn't hesitate. I arrived at seven-fifteen; the place opened at eight. The rain started to spit from the sullen gray sky. It matched my mood. I checked the outside spigot; it worked. I rinsed out my water bottles (two twenty-ounce Gatorade and one thirty-two-ounce Aquafina) and drank my fill. I ate some breakfast. I wedged under an information sign to get out of the rain. I watched cars drive by. I mused about all the people with everyday lives; a piece of me was envious.

"Did these people even realize how good they have it?" I mumbled to no one.

Another part of me was saddened that most of them would probably never experience a thru-hike.

Just Doug wandered down the side of the road with his distinct stride. Concerned, he asked.

"How are you feeling, Right Click?"

"A little better."

I showed him the spigot. He quickly filled his bottle and drank a copious quantity. Rock Steady and Paradox came down several minutes later. Water and food revived me. I felt better but still eager for eight o'clock to arrive so I could visit the porcelain throne inside. I worried my upset stomach might be more than just overeating crap food; Just Doug survived a Norovirus episode on the trail that rendered him incapacitated for three days. The store opened up. We used the facilities. The rain stopped. Bear Mountain (New York) loomed ahead.

Up and over Bear Mountain, I went. I expected a grueling hike especially given the state of my stomach. As I settled into a rhythm, my body recovered, and the day brightened. In Harriman State Park, the magnificently maintained trail made the hike agreeable. Thousands and thousands of person-hours built an incredible staircase up and over Bear Mountain. Fascinated, Dr. Pickles and Mockingbird told me they used this area as a training ground for their thru-hike.

In the park, I walked among many visitors from New York City. Vending machines that accepted credit cards caught my eye, but I learned my lesson. No creamsicles today. Alongside a picturesque lake, I shook off my pack with Just Doug, Rock Steady, and Paradox, then made my way to the concession stand. With my stomach settled and hungry again, I dove into a cheeseburger and fries. We sat at a picnic table. Rock Steady ordered chicken tenders and fries but couldn't eat them; still not feeling good. Finn strolled in and won the thru-hiker food lottery, the lucky recipient of her chicken tenders. He wore authentic shoes.

"Hey, what happened to the sandals?" I asked.

"They fooking sucked. My feet got all fooked up."

He mumbled between mouthfuls of chicken. Finn usually said something prickly. He complained frequently and seemed disgusted a lot of the time, but he spoke with a smile. I could never figure out if he liked hiking; maybe a love/hate relationship?

I sat by the lake and watched two guys fish. One displayed a practiced, graceful casting motion. The other guy? Not so much. I used to love fishing, becoming obsessed with surf casting, then kayak fishing. The craving to fish left me long ago; perhaps it may return. I reflected on cycles or phases. As my kids grew, Sandy and I often explained away some kid behaviors as "it's just a phase." Recovery says, "this too shall pass".." Had fishing passed for me? Seemed so.

Along with golf, although I still play the occasional round. When I'm on the beach, I still carry a few fishing rods – just in case. My thoughts drifted to family vacations on Cape Cod beaches. This summer, Sandy scheduled a week on Cape Cod. That sounded appealing. But Matthew might want to hike with his dad instead of going. I could only hope.

Just Doug slept under a tree. He liked his midday naps. I attributed it to his age; he was older than me, sixty, me fifty-five. I kept too much caffeine coursing through my system to nap well, so I hoisted my pack and meandered off down the trail, which at Bear Mountain Park meant a sidewalk through a zoo. Because I wasn't interested in exploring the zoo, I got ahead of the crew. I crossed the Hudson solo in brilliant sunshine. I wanted to do some miles. Home beckoned.

At my destination for the night, the Graymoor Spiritual Life Center, my AA sponsor, often led retreats. I felt a connection, eager to see it for the first time. About a mile before Graymoor stood the Appalachian Market, a well-known deli, smack dab on the trail. I wanted dinner from that place. On my way, I called Sandy. We talked about my estimated time of arrival in Connecticut and that I thought it still looked good. Sandy prepared for five other hikers to inhabit our home in Manchester, about ninety minutes from the trail.

"I'm thinking about inviting two more, what do you think? They can set up in the yard, no big deal."

No response.

"Hello?"

"Dad, what did you just ask mom?"

Matthew asked; Sandy just handed him the phone. I detected irritation and a touch of anger in his voice.

"I asked her if two more hikers could stay at the house."

"No!"

He replied firmly.

"OK."

"Did he ask them already?"

I heard Sandy's voice in the background. Fair question; I'm known to beg for forgiveness, not ask for permission. I told Matty that I had not.

"Are you sure?"

"Yes."

No big deal, I said goodbye and that I'd call again when I got settled. I wanted to invite Hot Pants and Crumbs to join us. I bumped into them several times and liked them. They fit in well with the crew.

As I got closer to the Appalachian Market, the sky darkened. The black cloud let loose when I got to the parking lot. Dr. Pickles and Mockingbird giggled in the deluge. I tucked my pack under an overhang before I scurried inside. I ordered a cooked salami grinder and bought other deliciousness. After the rain subsided, packs loaded with a fabulous meal, Dr. Pickles, Mockingbird, and I walked the short distance to the Graymoor Spiritual Life Center while dripping foliage soaked us. The crew assembled on the ball field. We ate dinner together at the picnic table, speaking easily and cracking jokes in a spirit of love and kindness. With a large, wooden cross nearby, we paused our banter to admire a spectacular sunset – purples, blues, reds,

172

oranges, yellows painted on the passing storm cloud. At that moment, we connected with nature and each other. Later, alone in my tent and in the middle of my trail family, I anticipated reaching home in a few days. I reflected on how far I'd come. Gratitude overwhelmed me. I wept.

Probably just exhaustion from a sixteen-mile hike in the heat.

Attack of the Zombie Pigs

On the trail, I cherished the privacy of a privy porta-john or bathroom. After breakfast, I used the porta-john and counted my blessings. I had become quite regular. One morning constitutional and done for the day.

As I packed my gear, I watched my fellow hikers. They moved efficiently, gracefully, silently, each with an individual rhythm that whispered of mastery. I moved the same way. After fourteen hundred miles, I finally felt competent on the trail.

I hiked with Just Doug in the afternoon when we approached Clarence Fahnestock State Park, just two-tenths off the trail, with a concession stand/camp store, showers, bathroom facilities, and picnic tables. What more could a hiker ask for? I ordered food from two college kids (I know this because their tip jar said, "Tips for College") and chatted with them. As we talked, thoughts of my kids flooded in.

"I'll be home soon," I told myself and pushed back the emotion, surprised by its power.

The rest of the crew trickled into the park. After fourteen miles in the summer heat, drenched in sweat, hiker funk odor at peak level, I hit the shower fully dressed. I stripped and rinsed out my clothes in the ice-cold shower several times. When I turned the water off, my teeth chattered behind blue lips. With no towel available, I put my wet clothes back on and stood in a sunny spot by the concession stand, closed for the day. As I stood there, a young woman strolled up.

"Hi, big fellaaaaaa:"

Her intent was obvious; she wore very short shorts and a button-down shirt tied above her belly button.

"Are you hikers?"

She asked as Dr. Pickles joined me in the sun.

"No, we're homeless people by choice, and this is what we do every day."

I joked. She didn't buy it. She asked many questions. I told her I hiked the trail for recovery. She responded.

173

"Oh, I just left a treatment center a few days ago. I don't need that."

That explained a lot; she must be high to be interested in an old hiker like me. Mockingbird sat down at a picnic table as Dr. Pickles visibly squirmed, much to her entertainment. I admit it, Dr. Pickle's discomfort amused me too.

The young woman's friend wandered over. I could not tell if this person was a woman or a man, not that it mattered.

"Would you two guys like to visit our campsite tonight?"

The person said in a deep voice that sounded masculine and feminine simultaneously.

"We have a big can of beans. We could share everything."

The young woman (younger than my oldest daughter) said with a wink. I thought to myself.

"Wait. Did she just wink? Really? What? A big can of beans?"

I choked the laughter back. Dr. Pickles wriggled away, mumbling some excuse, leaving me to fend for myself. Not happy and somewhat distressed, he joined his wife at the table.

"A big can of beans sounds… tempting."

I said with sarcasm dripping off every syllable. They didn't pick up on it.

"Our campsite is number 151. Come on by."

"Um, thanks for the offer, but we're moving on. I'm not staying here tonight."

Drawing from my media experience, I spun off to another topic. I talked to them more about my recovery and what I do for a living. Now they started to squirm. I used my recovery coaching skills – actively listened, asked good questions, and managed my stuff. They needed cash and implied their willingness to do anything to get it. Seeing that the young woman was crying for help, I tried to encourage them back toward recovery but seeing I was a dead end; she moved on. I walked over to the crew, who, of course, took their shots.

"Dang, Right Click, they wanted YOU!"

"You still got *it*."

I listened to this all the way to the Shenandoah Tenting Area, a well-maintained site with a hand pump well. An unusual place, freshly mowed lawn featured a good-sized building, all boarded up and locked. What was that for? We wondered.

"That's where the zombies are imprisoned."

As it got dark, the bugs came out. Hungry and tired, I retired to my screened-in tent to eat while the rest sat at a picnic table. I listened to their easy sharing, their laughter, enamored by their care for one another. Once in a while, someone would

174

throw a barb my way to keep me in the circle. Without getting too corny, love was in the air.

OK. That was corny.

I thought to myself.

"This is special. This is rare. Where else do people get along like this? "

The trail knocked down personal barriers. We lived soul to soul. What you saw is what you got. And what you got was true, good, and beautiful – the essence of being human. For me, no other dynamic supersedes a relationship. Nothing takes on greater importance. Love God. Love others. Simple, really, but not shallow. Not easy. The trail allowed me to experience relationships at a profound level.

I lay down surrounded by kind, playful whispers from the crew and drifted off to sleep. Not long after falling deeply asleep, I woke to weird sounds. I thought.

"Am I dreaming again? What is that? Pigs? What are pigs doing out here in the New York woods? I think they're pigs… Not much I can do about it…."

So, I did what I always did when "threatened" while in my tent; I turned my back to the sound, curled up in the fetal position, and went back to sleep. Instantly. But I woke up again to the pigs. This time I heard Rock Steady and Paradox laughing.

"Haha, very funny."

I said, not knowing what they were up to, too groggy. They laughed even harder.

"I'm going back to sleep."

I said heavily and slowly. And I did.

The following day, I heard the story while we packed up and ate breakfast. They hatched an elaborate plan to make me believe a zombie attack was imminent. When I heard them whispering and laughing, they listened to zombie ringtones on their phones. Rock Steady snuck over to my tent, put her phone just outside near my head, then Paradox called it. While they plotted, Rock Steady's husband Aaron called, and she hissed.

"I'll call you back; I'm in the middle of something!"

Credit to Aaron, if not an understanding and trusting man, that exchange could be interpreted in various ways. After all, it was ten at night.

"Right Click, weren't you scared? What were you thinking?"

"No, I thought it was pigs. I couldn't figure out why wild pigs were in the woods of New York."

That sent everyone into fits of laughter. They played the ringtone again. They heard it too. It did sound like pigs, but with more of a groan than a squeal. We laughed even harder.

"I told you we should have used this one."

They played another with more zombie-like sounds and creepy music.

"That *might* have done it."

I hit the trail feeling light. I knew my trail family loved me because they wanted to terrify me. I'd be home in two days, my brothers and sisters from the trail accompanying me, eager for my family to get to know these wonder-filled people.

Just Doug and the Lumberjack

With forty miles left until Connecticut, energy coursing through my system, I planned with the crew to try for a pair of eighteen-mile days, setting us up for a short hike on day three to the extraction point. As we tended to do, distances gradually opened up between us. No one in our crew felt the need to be in a pack all day long. I saw other groups that walked together the entire hike, staying within a few feet of each other. Not us. Up ahead, I spotted an impressive tree with a blaze of orange up in it. Yep, Paradox. She loved climbing trees. Envious of her twenty-five-year-old energy, she perched on a lower branch; after a late night, she was still fresh enough to climb trees in ninety-degree heat.

"Hey, Right Click." She said with that beautiful, wry smile.

"Nice spot, Paradox." I smiled back. I couldn't help it.

"I couldn't resist. There's room up here."

"I'm good. I can see it now; fifty-five-year-old dumbass thru-hiker breaks neck falling out of a tree."

She laughed. A lot cooler in the shade, another broiling day; I decided I'd cool down a bit and then keep going. In a good rhythm, I didn't want to kill my momentum. As I rested a bit, Rock Steady walked into the shade, and without saying a word, removing her pack or dropping her trekking poles, she fell on her side and closed her eyes. Without opening them, she said,

"I stayed up too late."

"That's what you get for trying to scare the crap out of me."

She responded with a long groan. I snapped a pic of Paradox in the tree and Rock Steady on her side. I laughed and left them to their tree, a long trek ahead of me. When I reached the Telephone Pioneers Shelter, the heat and the eighteen miles took their toll. The AT Guide indicated no tenting at this shelter, but there were usually areas to set up. True to my experience, several tents dotted the landscape around the shelter, none of them on level ground. With the flattest sites already occupied, the crew spread out. I found a less slanted place near a big oak tree. I used my pack,

176

yellow crocs, and clothes to prop up one side of my sleeping pad to level it out and make the most out of the situation.

The crowded area illustrated a "bubble" of hikers traveling together. I discovered the pluses and minuses of being in a bubble. Pluses? You meet a lot of different people, many people to hike with and talk with. Minuses? Overcrowded campsites and sloping ground. Sometimes all these people were a bit loud. I liked outside the bubble more.

The slanted sleeping spot woke me occasionally to resituate myself. Regardless, I awoke refreshed and excited to cross into Connecticut, just ten miles away. On County Road 20, I hugged the Dover Oak, the largest tree on the Appalachian Trail. I was out of water. The AT Guide directed us to a house nearby to use their spigot. However, the house, now unoccupied, had the water turned off. Dang. Thirsty, I walked a couple more miles with Just Doug, over more boardwalks, and across railroad tracks to the Appalachian Trail RR Station. A few steps further, I stood on NY22; to my left, a thru-hiker-friendly landscaping business. I bought food and drink, filled my water bottles, and sat down. Other hikers mingled about. We learned a great little deli served breakfast sandwiches a half-mile down the road. Just Doug, Rock Steady, Paradox, and I agreed to bend our two-tenths rule, and venture five-tenths one way, a total of one mile off-trail hiking! The food craze left us all marginally delirious.

The ten-minute trek up the road felt like an eternity. However, the heavenly offerings justified the inconvenience. Beverage coolers filled, sparkly and colorful, racks loaded with sweet treats, an extraordinary over-the-counter menu... thru-hiker paradise. The Lumberjack Sandwich appealed to me strongly - three eggs, bacon, sausage, ham, cheese, and home fries stuffed into a foot-long grinder roll. Just Doug and I ordered one each.

I sat outside on the deck, unwrapped the foil, and gasped in awe at the fantastic culinary creation. I took a picture and a huge bite. The Lumberjack garnered my full attention, and I relished each bite when a guy in a pickup truck pulled up and disturbed my reverie.

"You guys going back to the trailhead?"

"We are."

"Hop in. I'll give you all a ride."

He offered. Not one to turn down transportation, especially a half-mile in scorching heat, I wrapped the Lumberjack up and jammed it in the top of my pack; good for later. We clambered aboard.

177

Back at the garden shop, Detox informed us that hikers were once allowed to tent in the back until a week ago. But no longer. An out-of-control hiker (again) warranted a call to the cops. The owners endured enough from unruly hikers who disrespected their generosity and shut down their offer. I treated thru-hiking, an opportunity of a lifetime, with the utmost respect and sincere appreciation. Why did others act like such jerks? I came across my share of hikers who believed they were entitled to free food, water, and places to stay. It sickened me. These same hikers proclaimed that "donations accepted" while staying in a hostel meant "free."

Detox wanted to camp behind the garden shop, but when he heard it was no longer available, he hiked across the road and found a place a few hundred yards up the trail. He packed his gear as we hiked by. Detox earned his trail name when he quit drinking alcohol the day he started; the first few days were not enjoyable. As far as I know, he's still sober. I admired his pathway of recovery.

In the middle of another sweltering day, I was resting in the shade of a maple tree when Just Doug shuffled up. He didn't look too good.

"What's the matter?"

"Oh man, my stomach is killing me." Just Doug never complained. Ever.

"That Lumberjack... I ate the whole thing, and it's sitting in my gut like a lead balloon."

He groaned. I queried, stifling back laughter.

"You ate the whole thing?"

"Yeah. I can't believe I ate the whole thing."

Both of us are old enough to remember the old Alka Seltzer tagline.

"You did? I couldn't do it. I'm impressed!"

I glanced toward my pack, where half my Lumberjack resided, wrapped in tin foil. He took off his pack, sat down, then lay down. I watched, concerned and amused. Just Doug took on the Lumberjack in one sitting and won the initial battle. Forging a dramatic comeback, the Lumberjack retaliated and knocked down Just Doug, the toughest sixty-year-old on the trail. But Just Doug was not done. He rose to his feet, hiked for two more hours, and ultimately claimed victory.

Doug Tough.

Don't You Cry No More

Most of the time, I didn't have music in my ears; I preferred listening to my surroundings. When I did, I sometimes clicked on my Praise Trail Mix. When I heard the opening riff of Lifesong by Casting Crowns, my spirit lifted. The words hold profound meaning; they clarified the purpose of my hike and my life. I'd label it as the theme song of my thru-hike. I often had tears streaming down my cheeks when the song finished.

Empty hands held high
Such small sacrifice
Not joined with my life
I sing in vain tonight

May the words I say
And the things I do
Make my lifesong sing
Bring a smile to you
Let my lifesong sing to you

Let my lifesong sing to you
I want to sign your name
To the end of this day
Lord led my heart was true
Let my lifesong sing to you

Lord, I give my life
A living sacrifice
To reach a world in need
To be your hands and feet

And the words repeat. All I wanted, and want, is for my lifesong to sing to the one who rescued me. Paradox caught up and noticed the tears.

"Listening to a good tune, Right Click?" she asked without judgment.

Choked with emotion, I managed, "What gave it away?" She saw it in my eyes, I saw it in hers. We said nothing else. And continued north.

The Appalachian Trail crosses the New York/Connecticut border three times. At the second crossing, positioned ahead of the crew, I crossed a road and came across trail magic in the form of a few coolers full of ice-cold drinks. Beautiful! I grabbed a can of Coke and sat down. Young Gun showed up with Wild Turkey and a young woman with incredible dreadlocks, Fiddlehead.

"Hey, Young Gun. Some nice trail magic here."

"Looks good Right Click."

Young Gun responded without any enthusiasm; he looked visibly shaken. As I sat quietly with them, I sensed a deep sadness emanating from Young Gun. Were those streaks on his cheeks? Then it occurred to me.

"Where's Rainbow?"

The other two winced. I hit the nerve.

"She's on her way back to the Shenandoahs to hike the part of the trail we aqua-blazed."

He responded matter-of-factly. It seemed the romance of the century ended bitterly. More to the story, but I didn't inquire. They got up to leave.

"Well, gotta hit it, Right Click. See you down the trail."

We gave each other the hiker fist bump. Hikers didn't shake hands in an attempt to stop the spread of bacteria-born illness - a bit futile to me. Knowing his love for music, all I could say was…

"Carry on, my wayward son. There'll be peace when you are done."

He walked away. But after several seconds, without looking back, he strummed his air guitar and responded ferociously.

"Don't you cry no more!"

I smiled, the last I saw of Young Gun.

Dr. Pickles Lonely Hearts Club Band

Enthusiasm and promise marked the final crossing into Connecticut. After another eighteen miles through the summer heat, I arrived at Schaghticoke Mountain Campsite (yeah, I can't say that either). One twist, where was it? Dr. Pickles and Mockingbird got here before me (I thought); I barked loudly to signal them. They knew my bark. I heard a reply above me. I noticed a sketchy, unmarked trail leading up a steep face. Up there? I climbed, and there they sat, tent set on a nice flat patch with ample room for the crew. We ate dinner, banter warm and loving, eager to meet the Valentines in the morning. As darkness fell, the bugs got thick, so we retreated into the sanctuaries of our tents, yet the chatter continued. Other hikers camped nearby, all bonded together through appearance and quest. We looked similar – trail-hardened, hairy, and dirty. We stunk. Our eyes sparkled, fully alive, fully bathed in nature. We shared everyday trials and difficulties with the same destination: Katahdin. Fortunate - best describes my attitude.

I drifted off to sleep, content and excited. I woke early and, for a change, didn't curl back up and get more shuteye. I sat up, found a Carnation packet, a Starbucks

180

VIA, and some water, and consumed my first dose of nutrient-laden caffeine. I ate a protein bar, some cereal, strawberry Pop-Tarts with strawberry frosting, and another Carnation-VIA combo. I listened to music through my earbuds, a habit adopted from Rock Steady, who listened to tunes every morning. With great music, my already elevated mood, and the caffeine surging, I decided my companions might welcome a little music too. I unplugged the earphones and played some songs. They started to sing along. I found songs for them. Rock Steady got "Rock Steady" (Whispers version), and Mockingbird got "Mockingbird." I found a Ram Tough commercial, and the whole crew chimed in with Doug Tough – funny! For Dr. Pickles, I found the Beatles tune, Sgt. Pepper's Lonely Hearts Club Band. The music began, and everyone revved up. We sang.

"It was twenty years ago today,
Dr. Pickles taught the band to play,
They've been going in and out of style,
But they're guaranteed to raise a smile,
So may I introduce to you,
The act you've known for all these years,
Dr. Pickles Lonely Hearts Club Band."

With my heart on fire, I broke camp, scrambled down the hill, and anxiously hit the trail. Sandy would be on Schaghticoke Road, just three point two miles away. I flew down the path. I glanced down through the trees and spotted a familiar face with an athletic gait, baseball cap on backward, climbing the hill towards me – my son Joshua! Close behind him, my other son Matthew. I bellowed.

"HELLO, MY SONS!"

I imagined myself as some mythical wilderness creature. I rushed down the hill to greet them. I choked back tears as I hugged them both. They beamed. I introduced them to my trail brothers and sisters.

"Where's Sam?

"She's not feeling well, Dad, but behind us."

We soon found her sitting on a log, really sick from a summer cold, but making an effort to meet us in the woods. Talk about being grateful.

A half-hour later, we found the road. As we stepped out, hikers surrounded our old Suburban. Sandy, my daughter Mary, and dear family friends Al and Chris Boudreau attended a breakfast trail magic station. I strode toward Sandy. Slightly aromatic, Sandy gave me a quick kiss and held me at arms-length; our interaction entertained the other hikers. Delighted, I sat in a comfortable camp chair and savored a fresh sausage, egg, cheese sandwich, and orange juice.

With an AT shelter just a few tenths of a mile from this road, Sandy and her crew fed a wave of hikers. A second wave came from our campsite; they feasted too. And then, finally, the late rising Dr. Pickles Lonely Hearts Club Band cascaded down the hill onto the road. They served us like royalty. Sandy, Joshua, Samantha, Matthew, Mary, Al, and Chris immediately connected with the hiker community.

After the last of the other hikers moved on, including Hot Pants and Crumbs, Sandy mused about their gratitude, politeness, and respect. Sandy, the consummate hostess, loved the sincere appreciation more than she expected. Al and Chris, impressed with the character of the thru-hikers, became engrossed and fascinated by their stories. After packing the trail magic gear, Sandy asked me to drive home. I settled into the driver's seat of my old Suburban. It felt comfortably recognizable but still not used to the speed.

Home Sweet Home

After a relaxing ride, I drove into our neighborhood, rounded the corner onto our street, and laid eyes on my home for the first time in four months. I pulled into the driveway in disbelief. After helping all our guests settle (Sandy managed the process), I stripped and showered in my bathroom, the shower foreign and familiar at the same time. As I washed layers of grime off, I reflected on the long walk back and sifted through many emotional experiences. After the shower, I went to my bureau and admired the many choices within drawers full of clothes, most all too big for me now.

We arrived early on Saturday afternoon; everyone agreed to take Sunday off the trail. The conversations enthralled Sandy and our kids, with the crew relaxed and grateful. They loved Dr. Pickles' amazing unique stories. One of his favorites was when he and Mockingbird encountered a bear in the Smokies.

"We pitched our tent just off the trail. There was no one else around. I woke up in the middle of the night and heard footsteps circling the tent. At first, I thought it was a guy, and I wondered what somebody was doing walking around the tent. Then I realized it wasn't human. It was an animal. And it must be a bear. I froze. I didn't know what to do. So, I stayed really quiet and hoped it would go away. Eventually, it did. I tried to go back to sleep, but I couldn't. Mockingbird had no idea."

Mockingbird confirms with a nod. Dr. Pickles continues.

"I didn't hear a thing. A few hours later, I'm lying on my back trying to sleep when I hear the footsteps again. I start nudging Mockingbird, so she wakes up. She says, "What?" I say, "Shhh. Listen." She hears it too. We both sit up. We don't know what to do. I thought if I yelled, it would get scared and angry and attack us. I know now you're supposed to calmly talk to a bear and let it know that humans occupy the tent. But we didn't. We held each other and remained perfectly still, but we were shaking and completely silent. The steps got closer. Then the bear put his nose into the vestibule of the tent. It was all we could do not to scream. The bear was out there for what seemed a long time. Finally, it went away. Mockingbird and I did not sleep or get out of the tent until morning."

The crew joined us in church on Sunday. Pastor Frank pulled me up in front of the congregation and asked about my journey. I got all choked up, mentioning my family and trail companions. With the entire community in support, he led a prayer for me, Dr. Pickles, Mockingbird, Just Doug, Paradox, and Rock Steady.

See Ya

On Monday morning, our little tribe broke up. Rock Steady and Paradox returned to the trail. Just Doug, Dr. Pickles, Mockingbird, and me (especially me) desired one more day off-trail. We agreed to return on Tuesday. Rock Steady resolutely stuck to her game plan of only one zero at a time; Paradox was unsure what to do. She knew we welcomed her company, but ultimately, Paradox decided to accompany Rock Steady. Before I drove them back to the trail, I took an opportunity at our kitchen sink to talk with Paradox. I started.

"First of all, thank you for all you did for Tough Love. I will always deeply appreciate how you welcomed her."

"That was nothing, my pleasure."

I could see Paradox get a bit uneasy with the emotion in my voice, but I pressed on.

"Well, thank you. You helped give her a gift of a lifetime. Paradox, I believe you have an incredible gift. You have a tremendous capacity to love deeply. Don't be afraid of that; embrace it."

She looked at me, finished her task in the sink, and left quickly to cry outside the Paradox way. I let her be. I drove Rock Steady and Paradox back to the trailhead; the ride was quieter than usual. I hugged them goodbye with a promise that we'd catch them. With my heart heavy, I steered the Suburban back home. Those two ladies helped me get to Connecticut. They embraced Tough Love with huge hearts and open arms. They worked their way into my heart. I already missed them. Alone, I allowed the tears to trickle down my cheek.

On the way back, I visited my place of employment – the Connecticut Community for Addiction Recovery (CCAR). What a welcome! Embraced with enthusiasm, hugs, laughter, remarks, and questions, I felt deeply encouraged and validated. The staff truly believed in me. I concluded by doing three interviews - two for television and one for a newspaper.

That evening, we feasted on barbecue from Bear's Smokehouse. Jamie "Bear" McDonald, the owner, supported my adventure and provided free meals. One last sleep at home, and the next day I'd hit the trail again. I knew from the moment I accepted The Call that leaving home and heading north would be my most challenging time; one thing to walk home, another to walk away. I considered driving to Maine and walking south to Connecticut, but that didn't sit well. I aspired to finish on Katahdin.

We packed on Tuesday morning, then we posed for pictures in the front yard. After a quick hug and kiss from Sandy, we piled into the Suburban. As I drove the ninety minutes to the trailhead, I felt an odd numbness creep over me, a personal coping mechanism to disregard all emotion. I used to numb myself with alcohol and drugs, but no longer. I quietly contemplated my feelings, lifting the lid on some internal containers without letting the contents out. My conclusion: fierce love and desire to be with my family dominated. I wanted to stay home. I forcibly pushed the notion aside.

We arrived at the trailhead on Schaghticoke Road. Tough Love said goodbye to Dr. Pickles, Mockingbird, and Just Doug. Then, my turn. Like me, we stared deeply into each other's eyes, perceived each other's thoughts, and said goodbye. We tried to hold back tears, but neither of us could.

"I love you. You can do it, Dad."

She hopped in the driver's seat, started the engine, turned around, and headed down the road.

"Let's go," I said to Dr. Pickles, Mockingbird, and Just Doug.

Funkytime

With seven hundred and forty miles left, I struggled with each step away from home. My companions knew. I became quiet; my soul was heavy. They left me to my thoughts and took the lead. As I hiked those first few miles, I pushed the image of my daughter driving down the road out of my head; determination and resolve slowly settled in. I muttered to myself bitterly.

"Let's do this."

The weather didn't help my mood; hazy, hot, and humid. Again. The four of us stuck close (me, Just Doug, Dr. Pickles, and Mockingbird). Given their full-day head start, I felt our quest to catch Rock Steady and Paradox futile. I walked down a paved road near Falls Village, CT. I sat down in the shade near a bridge construction site. Good to get out of the sun and rest for a bit; Just Doug sat down too.

"Pretty hot down that road, huh?" He looked for an affirmation.

"It sure was." I paused. "I'm having a hard time, Doug. You probably figured that out…."

"Uh-huh."

Just Doug didn't say much. But he knew when to sit down next to someone, and at that moment, the best thing he could have done for me. Dr. Pickles cruised in with our feet in the street and our butts on the lawn of a lovely home.

"Nice spot, guys!"

He dropped his pack and decided to venture just a bit further. He always ventured north at least fifty yards to scout out a better place to rest, a better view, or a better campsite. He disappeared down the trail while Mockingbird used a portable toilet for construction workers; sure he wouldn't find anything this time; a reflection of my pessimistic attitude, he shouted with enthusiasm a few seconds later. He found a cooler laden with Gatorades on ice and other snacks. An angel left some trail magic. Just Doug and I ventured down. I grabbed a twenty-ouncer and returned to the shady spot.

"Thank you, Dr. Pickles. That was a great find." I said with a smile (an infrequent occurrence today).

"It was, wasn't it?"

Damn his enthusiasm. Refreshed and encouraged by the trail magic, I hiked the next few miles in a slightly better frame of mind.

AUGUST

If I Die, It's All Right

The following day, my feet trod familiar territory on Bear Mountain in Connecticut for the first (and only) time. Just Doug and I crossed Route 41 in Salisbury, and we took a picture together at the fifteen-hundred-mile mark a few hundred yards up the trail.

"Congratulations, Just Doug!"

"You too, Right Click."

"Not bad for two old guys."

"Not bad at all!" He beamed.

I climbed Bear Mountain three times before the thru-hike, the only miles of the AT my feet had ever walked on. When I hit the Riga Junction side trail, I recalled standing in the same spot with Rick McCracken (a dear friend), Tough Love, and people from CCAR and the Multiple Pathways Hiking Club. I took a moment at the junction to express some gratitude.

Aware that a summer thunderstorm approached, I picked up my pace and headed up the trail. It soon became apparent that I would not dodge this storm. Lightning blazed, and thunder reached epic noise levels. I still climbed. Amid the tempest, I found Just Doug squatting underneath a little tree. His backpack perched on the ground.

"What are you doing?"

"I came down from the tree line to let this pass." He talked loudly so I could hear him.

"I think I'm going to keep going," I replied uncertainly.

"I just saw Finn. He's up ahead. He didn't want to stop either. You know what he said?"

"No. What?" I leaned in.

"He held both his trekking poles up to the sky and yelled, if I die, it's all right! And he kept going. Not me. I'm staying here!"

Just Doug beamed, alive with adventure. Crazy friggin' Finn! I loved his morbid sense of humor. Yet, part of me believed what he said rang true. So crazy friggin' Right Click decided to keep going, too, and the thunderstorm moved away. I reached the summit and bounded up the rockpile observation tower. I recalled my previous hikes here and that this seemed a formidable obstacle. Not today; amazing how fifteen hundred miles on the AT whipped a guy into shape. Just Doug followed shortly. I threw him my phone and asked him to take a pic. I posed dripping wet, rain coming down, with trekking poles pointed upwards to a dark and stormy sky and yelled.

"If I die, it's all right!"

Even in the wet, slick conditions, I handled the steep descent on the north side of Bear Mountain. I picked my way down on previous descents very slowly. The way I took it this time, I thought it was spectacular. When the Undermountain Trail veered off to the right, I headed down into Sage's Ravine for the first time, promising to be on virgin ground again; two day-hikers merged in from the left, unusual considering the wet conditions. The woman talked much more than the guy, so talkative I thought she might be high. Just Doug and I let them go on ahead.

Dr. Pickles and Mockingbird caught up. We stopped and took some photos and videos, enamored by the beauty of Sage's Ravine. We cruised along the boulder-strewn stream. I rounded a curve along a ledge and glanced left into a deep pool; the talkative lady stood naked in a swimming hole, obviously not shy or modest; her chubbiness elevated the surprise factor. The guy stood nervously, teeth chattering, in knee-deep water, clad only in dark blue boxer briefs. She cheerfully extended an invitation for us to join them.

"Come on in! The water's great!" She encouraged enthusiastically. The guy shot us a look.

"Ethel? Is that you Ethel? What do you think you're doin'? You git your clothes on!"

"Um, no, thank you. We have to keep moving." I replied. The woman answered.

"OK, enjoy your hike." No big deal to her, but her friend seemed relieved.

"Ethel! Where you goin'? Ethel, you shameless hussy! Say it isn't so, Ethel!"

We tried to act like this always happened, but you could cut the awkwardness with a knife. We continued. I was hiking between Dr. Pickles and Just Doug when out of the blue, Dr. Pickles remarked.

"I would have stopped to take a picture. That was an incredible spot, but the view was ruined."

We crossed the brook and another state line, out of Connecticut and into Massachusetts. I quietly vowed not to return to Connecticut until I summited Katahdin, but part of me knew failure still to be a distinct possibility. I enjoyed days where I hit milestones, so with some sense of accomplishment, we had set a goal for a big day, but the ascent up Mount Race proved much more demanding than the elevation profile indicated. We decided to stop short and set up camp at Race Brook Falls.

The Joy of Slackpacking

The steep but short climb up Mount Everett offered appealing views. After a few miles on the ridge, we descended back onto the valley floor, followed by several miles of relatively flat walking; long flat stretches now infrequent. I crossed several roads as I made my way from ridge to ridge. After a good day of more than sixteen miles, we camped a mile short of Lake Buel Road, where Sandy said she'd meet us. We planned to slackpack the next day.

Even though I had left home just a few days prior, I stepped out on the road filled with anticipation. Five minutes later, I spotted our Suburban with Sandy and Mary, my ten-year-old daughter, in the passenger seat. Sandy packed the vehicle like a seasoned Trail Angel. We feasted on a variety of breakfast foods and beverages. We gratefully piled our packs into the back, and she promised to meet us at the next road crossing, less than a trail mile away. Just Doug hesitated to leave his pack, but we ultimately convinced him; the allure of shedding the weight and walking through the forest unburdened irresistible.

I talked Mary into hiking with me. We stepped into the woods; an incredible blessing to share a piece of the AT with my youngest. Pleased to become a section hiker officially, she adapted quickly to the soft, easy trail. Sandy, as promised, waited at the road crossing. The path crossed another road in another mile. Mary decided, on her own, to walk this too. As we climbed a hill, Mary's pace slowed. We rested so she could catch her breath. This time, when we reached Sandy, Mary climbed into the passenger seat and strapped on her seat belt.

"Mary, do you want to keep going?"

"I'm good." The answer was obvious.

She settled into her seat. Total for Little Click? Two miles and one-tenth.

We agreed to meet six more miles up the trail on Beartown Mountain Road. Those six miles felt wonderful. Without a pack, I felt free, almost like I could fly. I floated up and over rocks and handled ascents with ease. The four of us stepped onto a dirt road two hours later. We traveled quickly without weight on our backs, but no Sandy. Just Doug shot me a glance I interpreted it.

"This was what I was afraid of." But he didn't say a word.

"She'll be here," I assured.

I called her. I detected panic in her voice. "Your phone says I'm miles from the AT."

We swapped phones so mine could recharge in the truck.

"Hold on. It's ok. Settle down. I didn't update the Guthook app to the next map. It has different ones; you're reading the last map. We're probably fine. Let me get our exact coordinates."

Dr. Pickles, who had already researched on his phone, relayed them. She plugged them into the GPS.

"Oh my God! You're only two-tenths of a mile away!"

She responded with great relief. Sure enough, we hooked up within minutes and happily reunited. Sandy was glad to see us, yet much more shaken than us. Sandy drove up and down Beartown Mountain Road (a dirt road) for miles wondering if she missed us. I offered to hug her, but she declined, too stinky for her liking.

*Footnote: I purchased the Guthook app (name changed since my hike to FarOut) for iPhone in Northern Virginia after seeing Rock Steady and Cindy Loppers use it effectively. The GPS feature tracks your exact location on the trail. Combined with the AT Guide, I became pretty comfortable navigating the AT. This is from the Guthook website. "Our Guthook Guides apps feature world-class hikes, wilderness regions, and trails from all over the world. Feel secure in your adventure by following our easy-to-use hiking guides, whether you are headed for a backcountry wilderness thru-hike or a countryside cultural walk."

Sandy again met us later in the day after fourteen more stress-free miles. We discussed options. Should we continue and try to slackpack more miles with Sandy available? Should we resupply? Do we stay in town at a hotel somewhere? Should we get dinner somewhere? Many options, and with a group of four, differences sometimes arose. I wanted to go for the elusive twenty-mile mark. However, my crew convinced me that we needed to resupply. If we resupplied, camping on the trail became problematic; Upper Goose Cabin, the next available spot, was more than seven miles away. We piled into the Suburban and looked for a hotel room. The idea of having more time with family appealed to me greatly. However, getting a room in the Berkshires on a summer weekend proved difficult and pricey. We tried a place where another hiker had stayed a few days earlier for seventy-nine dollars. The Saturday price? One hundred eighty-nine dollars.

Everywhere else displayed "No Vacancy" signs. Damn. The AT Guide specified another option, a field near a community center. We drove to it and checked it out. Seemed a bit sketchy, close to the road and adjacent to a parking lot. Just Doug seemed OK with the idea. Dr. Pickles and Mockingbird acquiesced too. Sandy and

189

Mary wouldn't stay with us in the field. I wanted another evening and another day with the two of them. Another day of slackpacking sounded great too. Putting off the inevitable, I suggested we go resupply and see if we could come up with something else. With things not going my way, my attitude soured. I finished shopping way before the other three as they did their usual hiker thing; taking their time in a grocery store, making thoughtful choices, and enjoying the atmosphere. Not me. I pouted. I retreated into myself. I became non-communicative and surly. I sat down on the curb with Mary, and we unpackaged and repackaged my purchases. She didn't mind my sour disposition.

"Mary, what do I do? Maybe I should just go home with you, give this thing up."

"Dad, you can't do that." She encouraged.

"I know, I know. But I don't want to sleep in that field. I don't want you to leave."

Somehow, through the emotional smoke, I recalled one other option. At first, I dismissed it; I don't like to impose on people, and I don't want to ask for help, a pride thing with me. So, I swallowed my pride and called a friend and colleague who owned a home in the Berkshires. He encouraged me to call when we arrived in the area. He frequently *liked* my recent posts on social media, so I hoped my call wouldn't come as a complete surprise. He answered his cell immediately.

"Hi, Phil."

He replied calmly, in alignment with his personality.

"Bill, I'm in the area, and my friends and I are kinda stuck."

I described my situation.

"Say no more. I'm at a concert at Tanglewood, but we will meet you outside the Red Lion Inn in Stockbridge. You can follow us home and stay with us for the night. We'll give you a ride to the trailhead the following morning."

"Are you kidding me, Bill? You don't have to leave the concert."

"Think nothing of it. We'll see you soon."

"Bill, thank you! I am so grateful. We are so grateful!"

"Sure, no problem."

We met them and followed them to their beautiful, custom, contemporary home. Sandy and Mary said goodbye. I choked back a torrent of emotion and watched them drive away. I showered and felt better. The other three ate big meals from the grocery store out on the porch. I didn't know they bought dinner for the evening; I drove through McDonald's before meeting Bill. While they ate, I sat and chatted with our hosts.

The trail continued to generate unexpected twists for me. I lounged in a beautiful, clean, comfortable home with giving, loving people. Yet my heart still hurt. My friends, amazed at our good fortune, sincerely expressed their gratitude and appreciation.

Opposing Desires

After serving us an excellent pancake breakfast with strong coffee, our hosts drove us in two cars back to the trailhead. I thanked them and reluctantly headed north, further away from home. Self-aware of my toxicity and not good company for the crew, I separated and moved out ahead—no need to spread my discontent. The journey had worn me down. The daily grind away from Sandy, away from comforts, dominated my thoughts. I needed to shift my internal narrative; I pulled out a tool discovered in recovery; I drafted a mental gratitude list.

1. I am blessed. How many people get a chance to try this?
2. The agency I work for, the Connecticut Community for Addiction Recovery, supports me. I know of no other hikers whose employer agreed to cover their salary.
3. I got to see my wife just yesterday.
4. I've maintained my health – no Norovirus, Giardia, or broken bones.
5. I'm in the best physical shape of my life.
6. I've got wonderful companions.
7. God loves me and cares for me.
8. Look at how beautiful my surroundings are.
9. I stayed in an incredible home last night.
10. Look how far I've come…

Nice list, but yeah, it didn't work. The vile bitterness festered deep in my gut– not a pleasant emotion. It eroded my enjoyment and my spirit of adventure. Ahead of the pack, I came to Goose Pond. On the bank in a deep grove of pine trees. I sat down, pulled off my shoes and socks, and grabbed my food bag – time for lunch. Paradox came to mind as I rummaged through my food.

"What's the best thing in my bag? I asked, with no one nearby in this idyllic setting. I settled on some Port Wine cheese spread, pepperoni, and Ritz crackers. The others eventually came by and sat down. Dr. Pickles never lost his optimism and gratitude.

"Nice spot, Right Click!"

"It is, isn't it?" I agreed.

"How are you doing?" He inquired.

"OK, I guess. I wish I were better…"

I responded despondently. He sensed my tone and left me to stew in my juices. I stewed. I thought about the people in the boat fishing just offshore, cooler stocked with assorted beverages. I looked at my water. I wondered if they were a family. If so, did they realize how lucky they were? Bastards. After I ate and moved on, the bitterness subsided some. Crossing Mass Pike (I-90), I looked east down the road home and contemplated hitching a ride. I put my head down and kept going.

For the next few days, I isolated myself more. I preferred to be alone. I still camped with the crew. We chatted now and then. We covered good ground, usually fifteen to eighteen miles per day. Even in a funk, moments of good humor and enthusiasm surfaced. For example, as we approached a shelter, caffeine from an energy powdered drink kicked in. With earbuds in, Golden Earring's "Twilight Zone" popped up on my Steeps Trail Mix, and my speed picked up. I put the song on repeat. I flew along the trail, energized by the music, caffeine, and a dose of frustration. I passed Dr. Pickles and Mockingbird, who gave me an odd look as I streaked by. Dr. Pickles did not like to be passed. He wanted to race with me, but he hung back with Mockingbird.

"Go for it!" He encouraged.

The song drove me faster and faster, close to a full-out run. Feeling proud of myself and my athletic prowess, my left foot landed slightly wrong on a stone, and I rolled my ankle. Not too badly. Just enough to slow me down and bring me back to earth.

Later, I retreated into my tent at night and ate dinner. The others hung their food. I slept with mine. I heard Dr. Pickles and Mockingbird quietly get up in the morning, pack up their sleeping bags and tent, sit down and boil water for breakfast, coffee and oatmeal. Just Doug, quiet too, sometimes got up earlier, drank his coffee, and ate breakfast. In no hurry, he didn't talk a lot. Sometimes I'd get up and have breakfast outside with them. But I usually sat in my tent, drank cold coffee and Carnation, ate breakfast, and got dressed in aromatic, damp hiking shorts and shirt. I mainly packed all my gear while sitting inside. Eventually, I crawled out.

"Good morning, Right Click!"

Dr. Pickles said with a huge smile, his damn good humor infectious.

"Good morning," I responded, but not nearly with the same energy level.

"How'd you sleep?"

And the day started. Mockingbird, masterful in planning days, studied the AT Guide the night prior and usually suggested a destination for the day. We trusted her implicitly. She researched the towns ahead and found things that appealed to us. Just Doug carried the entire ATC Guidebook, different from our guides, and we'd compare notes. I used Guthook, so as a team, we covered navigation well.

I walked through Dalton, MA, where I found the crew eating and drinking in a little bar and grill. After a cheeseburger, French fries, and several Cokes, we debated if we should stay in town or not. When in doubt, we kept moving. We walked another few miles out of town and bedded down.

Rock Me Gently

Every time I resupplied, I looked for powdered drink mixes. I drank liters of water daily; flavored water was a real treat. I loved the hard-to-find, individual orange Gatorade pouches. I craved Gatorade so much that I once carried a full pound of Gatorade powder in a plastic screw-top container. Difficult to stow in my pack, I tried putting the powder in a one-pound Ziplock bag. That got pretty messy. However, a scoop (or two) of Gatorade powder elevated twenty ounces of water into a delightful concoction. I preferred the twenty-ounce Gatorade bottles because of the wider opening; I carried two. I used a thirty-two-ounce Aquafina bottle with a Sawyer Squeeze to filter water to complete my "hydration system."

Some stores stocked cheap powdered energy drinks. In my feed bag (food bag), one Ziplock contained only powders, my apothecary. At various times, I carried pouches of coffee (Starbucks VIA, Folgers), Carnation Instant (Strawberry flavor the rarest and most valuable), Swiss Miss Instant Cocoa, Gatorade, Starbucks strawberry lemonade, energy drinks, Hi-C, Grape and Orange Crush packets and others. Purchasing drink powders evolved into an art form. I thoroughly enjoyed scanning the selection.

After my midday meal at the Mark Noepel Shelter, I refueled with an energy drink and not my usual Carnation/Starbucks VIA concoction. The steep ascent immediately out of the shelter up to the summit of Mount Greylock required caffeine. Being a recovering alcoholic and cocaine addict, I wondered about this craving... but not for long.

With three miles to the top, I plugged my earbuds in, cued my Steeps Trail Mix, and set out. As the caffeine kicked in, I caught up with Dr. Pickles. We settled into a rhythm. Golden Earring's "Radar Love" emanated into my head. I kept pace with the good doctor. He moved a little faster. Usually, he'd lose me. With the beat pulsing, I

193

matched his steps. After several minutes, he glanced behind and saw me still there. Surprised, he smiled. Game on. He picked up the pace slightly. I hung with him. He glanced back again. I sensed his response.

"Nice, Right Click. Nice. Let's see what you have, Grasshopper."

He picked it up again. The terrain steepened. Andy Kim's "Rock Me Gently" pulsated. Another surge of energy. I took a second or two to click on Repeat, one song to the top. We were moving, probably the fastest I had ever hiked. I kept pace, but he held the lead. No way would he let me pass. I pushed. We crossed a road, the trail wider here. This often happened at popular landmarks. Steep and rocky, Dr. Pickles flew, his pride at stake. He couldn't let a fifty-five-year-old dude keep pace. In my head, I heard,

"...ain't it right that you are with me here tonight. Rock me gently. Rock me slowly. Take it easy. Don't you know that I have never been loved like this before?"

I bounced from stone to stone, my body fully fit and wanting to show off. I sweated freely and vigorously; my eyes and mind calculated each step quickly. I felt glorious, like a thru-hiker deity. Up ahead, a left foot tack could be tricky, a stone ridge just an inch wide. No problem, I hit a few of them already.

I missed.

My left foot went over the top; no chance to save myself. I crashed loudly, and my trekking poles clattered. The fall knocked the breath out of me. I groaned and looked up. Dr. Pickles disappeared up and around a bend. I stayed still for a second. I pushed myself up to my feet; pride hurt more than my body, just a slight knock. Dr. Pickles showed up. I pulled an earbud out as he started to talk.

"You all right? I thought I heard something."

"I am. Keep going." I smiled.

He smiled. Unspoken words passed - mutual respect and admiration. He kept going but not at the same pace. I lost the desire (and the capability) to try to match him. We still hiked quickly. Dr. Pickles made it to the picturesque Greylock summit first. No surprise.

Lots of people. Lots of activity. Dr. Pickles and I waited for our companions. After I dropped my gear, I strolled to the concession stand and got some food and two cold Cokes. We hung out on the summit for a couple of hours. We basked in the sun and answered questions from people who drove to the top.

I remembered Chip, who said this was his final destination for the hike. I wondered what had happened to him. I felt connected with Dr. Pickles, a remarkable moment racing up Greylock. I admired that he hiked with his wife. Mockingbird, herself, a fierce hiker; I also held great respect for her. Very few had Pickles

194

capability, except maybe Paradox. The two of them chose to hike with mere mortals. I witnessed him near his best, graceful, powerful, and fast. I wondered what he would be like unleashed, at full power. How fast and how far could he go?

Just Doug left the Greylock summit first. He sweated heavily and cooled down quickly. He preferred to keep moving. When we started to get chilly, we headed down to the Wilbur Clearing shelter, three miles away.

To Tell the Truth

The next morning, I woke to another big day for milestones. A short time out of camp, we passed the six-hundred-miles left mark. After a long descent to MA 2 near North Adams, followed by another long climb, we passed into Vermont. Several people rested at the state line; only three states left!

After a little break, it took me a while to get going. I struggled along the southern end of the Vermont Long Trail; the Appalachian Trail and Long Trail run concurrently for one hundred and five miles. I ultimately hit my stride. I quietly cruised along behind Dr. Pickles. I enjoyed the solitude and the pace. Suddenly, he stopped at a side trail down to a shelter. What? Why?

"What's up?"

"I'm going to wait here for Mockingbird. See what she wants to do."

I sat down hard. A wave of feeling hit me from the blind side. I felt angry, frustrated, and exhausted. I felt like giving up – at least for the day. I whined.

"Why don't we just stop here and stay for the night?"

Quite the sarcastic remark, considering it was very early in the afternoon, Dr. Pickles didn't take kindly to it. I didn't blame him. To his credit, he calmly said,

"I'm going to wait here for Mockingbird. Feel free to keep going. We'll catch you."

I heard the disapproval. I struggled to my feet, fought back the emotion, and without saying a word, headed north. I knew we wanted to top seventeen miles and end up at the Congdon Shelter, so I stuck to myself. Later in the day, the crew passed me while I rested. We didn't say much. By early evening I hit the shelter, all the nearby tent sites occupied. I found Just Doug; his little one-person tent tucked near the stream. Dr. Pickles and Mockingbird found a nice flat area but packed in with other hikers. I checked in with them and received an icy reception from Dr. Pickles, his anger directed at me.

"What's the matter?"

"I don't want to talk about it."

"Why not?" I pushed.

"You don't want me to talk about it right now, Right Click."

There was a strong emphasis on "Right Click." Mockingbird sat next to her husband, her face difficult to read.

"I'd like to talk. I'm not going anywhere."

I sat down. He sighed.

"OK, Right Click. You've been pretty negative since we left Connecticut. And I'm getting tired of it. I'm not sure I want to hike with you any longer."

He referred to his father, and that stung. Dr. Pickles and Mockingbird started this hike with Dr. Pickles' dad, and it didn't end well. They grew increasingly frustrated with each other and parted ways. No longer on speaking terms, Dr. Pickle's dad was the same age as me. Pickles and I had talked frequently about that situation. Bound and determined not to let history repeat itself, I did not interrupt his thoughts. Also tired of my jokes, he informed me.

"The first ten times I heard you yell "Taxi!" when we hit a road, it was funny. It's not anymore!"

I had pushed Dr. Pickles to his breaking point, and I knew from my experience with Flutter how frustrated he must be. I took a deep breath and replied.

"You are right. I have been negative. I am so sorry. Please give me another chance. I will work on being more positive, a lot more. I thoroughly enjoy hiking with you two. I don't want to split up, but I will if it's what you want."

On the verge of tears, the words stuck in my throat.

"And thank you for telling me. I appreciate the courage and how much you must care just to tell me the truth."

I paused. I asked a question.

"Do you think we can move on from here? Do you think we can continue? Together?"

I watched him consider many factors. After a long time, he looked directly into my eyes. He sincerely replied.

"I do."

I exhaled. I thanked him, and then I asked.

"Have I really been that bad?"

"You have."

"What about yesterday when we were racing up Greylock?"

He smiled. "That was fun."

"I thought so too. I will head back down the trail, check out a flat spot I saw, and set up."

196

"We saw that site too. Someone pooped in the fire ring. We dropped some rocks on it but decided not to stay."

Glad the conversation returned to normal (hiker normal), I said goodnight, went back, and decided I could deal with rock-covered poo. With not many options and tired, very tired, I ate in my tent and processed all that happened. Dr. Pickles was right. I had become negative and toxic to others. That attitude harbored the potential to kill my hike. Not proud of my behavior, I took some time that evening to dive into the deep dark water of righteous indignation, blame, resentment, humiliation, and shame, then finally surface into the clarifying light of gratitude. Conflict precedes clarity.

Resolved to do better, I drifted off to sleep.

Bennington

I set out the next day, determined to keep a more positive attitude. With only four miles to Bennington, I felt confident I could keep my promise. Mark, a dear friend, and colleague of mine, promised some support; I looked forward to it. Dr. Pickles and Mockingbird booked a night in the Bennington Hampton Inn; I'm sure they liked the thought of not dealing with me. We descended to Route 9, where Rock N Roll Sue picked us up (thanks to Mark) and brought us into town. Sue worked at the Turning Point Recovery Community Center in downtown Bennington, Rock N Roll Sue, her Alcoholics Anonymous moniker (not a trail name).

After introductions, four hikers with gear crammed into her little red Toyota Matrix. She marveled, then gasped, at the aromas filling her vehicle and fogging her mind. She gratefully dropped us off at the Blue Bonn Diner for breakfast. She'd pick us up after we feasted. And feast we did; our little table piled high with pancakes, eggs, bacon, sausage, juices, waffles, pastries, and coffee.

Rock N Roll Sue picked us up after breakfast and drove us to our respective hotels. After cleaning up, I left Just Doug behind and went to be interviewed by the Bennington Banner at the recovery community center. While waiting for the reporter, I talked with staff and some volunteers. One of the volunteers, excited about my visit, ran out to buy candy. When he came back, he announced.

"I thought to myself, what would I like after a long time on the trail? So, I bought some peanut butter and chocolate!"

He gave me the bag and beamed.

Oh no. Not peanut butter and chocolate. I lived on Hershey chocolate bars and scoops of peanut butter. I kept my smile and thanked him profusely. I promptly ate a piece even though I preferred a banana or some cherries. I recalled my worst trail magic experience. Back in Maryland, someone left individual paper lunch bags with a bottle of water, granola bar, and peanut butter and jelly sandwich. How disappointing! A note to trail angels: bring food that hikers cannot carry on the trail.

My interview went well. Afterward, Mark took me to dinner and partially satisfied my craving for beef after I consumed a massive rib-eye. After dinner, we sat outside my motel room and talked. Mark, an avid outdoorsman, and I share decades of recovery in common. The beautiful summer evening lent itself to introspection. His pathway to recovery, established in the seventies, had Bennington roots. His "marijuana operation" rented a room here at this hotel where we now sat. They rented the room for a year at a time just in case they needed to lay low. Through recovery, Mark helped thousands of others in their recovery process. I knew about Mark's inspirational legacy but hadn't heard much of the back story. His history proved to be particularly dramatic and wild. Riveted as he shared yarns about airplanes, FBI, and bales of marijuana, I found it remarkable that he survived.

Eventually, I said good night to my brother in recovery. Just Doug showed up shortly after; he enjoyed a nice dinner and explored the town. In the morning, I scheduled Pastor Frank and a few guys from church to help us. We looked forward to slackpacking again; we planned an ambitious day, over twenty miles; pretty far even without packs.

True to his word, Pastor Frank arrived the following day and brought us to the trailhead. The AT crossed a gravel road more than twenty miles out; they planned to park the car there, then hike south until we met up, then we'd all hike north together.

We set out for the big day with a light load. We proved that the lighter the load, the further you traveled and the more enjoyable the journey. Dr. Pickles and I revitalized our friendship thanks to his loving confrontation two days earlier. We talked openly. My close friend Art Woodard, with a unique talent for creating words, doesn't like the word confrontation. He called it a care-frontation, precisely what Dr. Pickles did. He care-fronted me. And it saved our relationship.

The weather cooperated on our big climbs out of Bennington. We trekked to the Glastenbury Mountain lookout tower. We climbed up and took the obligatory lookout tower photos. We stumbled upon Warren Doyle, a trail legend, when we came down. On this day, he served as a guide for several hikers. We met him as he headed back south to the support vehicles. He agreed to take a picture with us. This guy walked the Appalachian Trail more than any other man, seventeen times by 2015, and accumulated more than thirty-six thousand trail miles. Jennifer Pharr Davis talks about how Warren influenced her thru-hikes, one a record-setter. He shares his

198

profound hiking wisdom through his book, website, and classes. As I prepared for the journey, I took some of his words to heart. Warren Doyle carried an enormous gut; he certainly didn't look like an accomplished thru-hiker, but his massive calves told a different story.

Soon after, Pastor Frank marched up the trail in combat fatigues and boots. Pastor Frank served as a chaplain in the U.S. Navy. A cheerful, enthusiastic man, he greeted us with warm hellos. Johnny Golemba, a young guy, followed close behind, about the same age as my daughter Tough Love. When I met his eyes, I saw he had contracted hiker fever. Lit up, his love for the woods, the hike, and the adventure emanated from his eyes.

"Like this, Johnny?" I asked.

"Oh yeah."

"Think you have a thru-hike in you?"

"I do."

I asked Frank about Brian Richards and his son Seth; they waited a few miles down the trail at the Kid Gore Shelter. A short time later, we reached the shelter. Brian shared cookies with us; hard to describe the ecstasy of a home-baked treat eaten in the middle of the woods. Brian expressed sincere disbelief that I had walked so far, the six miles out to the shelter a lot harder than he anticipated. Now, he dreaded the six difficult miles back to the car.

Brian moved like a man in pain. However, he never complained. I admired that. Pastor Frank took off and moved quickly. I kept my usual pace, by now, well-tuned to my body. My legs felt the last fourteen miles but were still primed for another six, thanks to several months on the trail. I just needed to pace myself and keep putting fuel in regularly. My right knee hurt a bit, but something hurt every day. I walked through the pain.

I came to a shelter that marked one point six miles to our final destination. It looked gradually downhill, so I picked up the pace to see if I could get there in half an hour. I did. I found Pastor Frank napping in the car. His military training got him to the gravel roadway before anyone else. He opened the trunk, reached into a cooler, and offered me a Coca-Cola. Delicious. The others gradually arrived, and we moved down the road to a flat, cleared area with grass (on the long side) and considerable underbrush. Just off the grass, in the bushes, I found a discarded sleeping bag and various articles of clothing. Odd, but we stayed in places weirder than this one. Profound fatigue simmered, and no one wanted to scout out a new site. As we set up our tents, Pastor Frank fired up a stove and quickly got burgers sizzling. He knelt in the grass and took to the task with determination and efficiency. Baked beans went on too. The other men watched with keen interest as we pitched our tents efficiently. Soon I wolfed down hot cheeseburgers with lettuce, tomato, onion, baked beans, potato chips, cherry pies, cokes, and lemonades. I filled my belly.

It quickly got dark. My concern rose for Brian, who didn't move from the car, his pain restricting his movements. He got out when we circled up. Pastor Frank prayed for us. I embraced him and sobbed, awkward for Frank, I'm sure. Again. I became a mushy mess and cried at a moment's notice, my emotion raw and pure, grateful for their support. After prayer, they left us with more food and beverages, piled into the car, and drove off quickly. They had two hours back home to Manchester, CT; I watched them go away with my heart and belly full. As we settled into our makeshift campsite next to a gravel road, Dr. Pickles, Mockingbird, and Just Doug expressed their sincere appreciation to me.

Riptide

I fell asleep physically tired, yet emotionally high because my 13-year-old son Matthew gave up a whole week on Cape Cod to hike with me. I planned to meet him the following day. A novice backpacker, Tough Love helped prepare him, but the rendezvous could prove difficult. To be exact, I gave my dear friend, Arno, some coordinates on a gravel road – the Stratton-Arlington/Kelly Stand Road – at the base of Stratton Mountain. I prayed for a safe reunion.

We strode onto the road at the designated time. To our right, cars parked in a dirt lot with an Appalachian Trail kiosk. We hung around and waited for Arno. A day hiker carried a large watermelon, about to bring the heavy gift four miles up to the Stratton Mountain caretakers, quite the workout. After a few more minutes, Arno's truck appeared. When my eyes met Matthew's, my soul lit up; my love for my children can best be described as divine. I opened my arms wide and welcomed Matthew; I held him for a long time. I did the same with Arno and the Turtle Man.

They packed treats from home, which we gratefully consumed. I thanked Arno for safely delivering my boy and said a long goodbye. We started up Stratton Mountain. Super excited to share the trail with my son, Matthew displayed some nervousness, unusual for him, an athletic, intelligent, outgoing and confident kid, always self-assured, even at two years old. I recalled driving the Suburban oversand to Race Point in Provincetown, MA - the tip of Cape Cod. Specifically, we parked at Hatches Harbor, a tidal estuary, a great place for kids to enjoy acres of sand, shallow water, and a variety of sea critters. We dragged our stuff out of the truck. As we set up, our toddler Matthew disappeared. After looking frantically for a few seconds, we found him perched on the tailgate of another family's pickup truck with a peanut butter and jelly sandwich in one hand and a juice box in the other.

Matthew had grown tall and strong in the last two years, getting accustomed to his new body. He lost a lot of baby fat. At first, he worried that he'd hold me up, and just like Tough Love, it soon became apparent that I'd have difficulty keeping up with him.

At the top of Stratton Mountain, we scaled the fire tower; the view was impressive. We gazed upon the evergreen trees and bright blue sky while cumulous puff clouds scudded along, sharing this with Matthew, an unforeseen, unplanned bonus.

"In and around the lake, mountains come out of the sky, and they stand there."

He would also spend time with amazing people and meet many other hikers, a breed all our own. Our pace over the last several days drew us closer to Rock Steady and Paradox; the possibility that we could all hike together again motivated me.

That changed with one text.

My friend Peter owns condos on Stratton, so on a whim, I texted him. He offered one. The gondola ran only on weekends (this was a Saturday) with no charge to thru-hikers. We decided to go. We rode down to the base and ate an incredible lunch in Stratton Village. Some other thru-hikers milled about, but primarily vacationers bustled about with the intent of playing golf or tennis; their crisp, clean shirts with Vineyard Vines and Polo labels contrasting sharply with our beat-up, dirty gear. But for some reason, Dr. Pickles always looked fresh. So did Mockingbird. They fit in. How did they manage that?

We made our way to Peter's condo, which gave us access to the sports center, where we swam in the pool, sat in the hot tub, and took long luxurious hot showers. We chilled out and watched the Desolation of Smaug on HBO while we ate pizza. Life was good. But Matthew wondered about this thru-hiking thing. We hiked until lunchtime, then took the afternoon off.

"Dad, is this what you do all day?"

"No Matty. This is highly unusual."

He nodded, but he seemed disappointed. While I lounged around on a luxurious sectional couch, I texted the ladies ahead of us. Paradox responded. They hung back a bit and camped less than ten miles from us. If we had hiked that afternoon, we might have caught them, but the offer of a beautiful condo in Stratton Village was too enticing. She responded that they would not wait for us. One chance to catch them, and we opted for the condo, the way of the trail. Choices and consequences. Choices and consequences. Dr. Pickles offered his perspective.

"Right Click, it's all about the smiles, not the miles, right?"

"Sure, sure. I just have to let it go."

Deep down, I hoped we'd catch them. I loved their company. But I accepted we might not hike together again.

The next morning, we left the condo cleaner than when we found it. However, I made a mental note to let Peter know we cooked and ate three frozen pizzas from their supply. We wove our way through the village, hopped on the gondola, walked back to the fire tower, and reconnected with the Appalachian Trail. Matthew asked if he could go on ahead.

"Sure, just stop and wait for us at Stratton Pond."

Off he went with the enthusiasm of a thirteen-year-old. An hour later, I found him on shore eating peanut butter.

"How are you doing, Matty?"

"I'm good. I got some water over there and talked with other hikers. They gave me a trail name, but I don't like it." He said sheepishly.

"What is it?"

"Fraidy Snake."

"Fraidy Snake?" I held back my laughter. "How'd you get that?"

When Matthew reached the pond shore, he found a nice rock, took off his pack, and set it down on top of a snake. The snake didn't like that too much; it raced off and startled him. Matthew jumped. Unfortunately, the other hikers noticed this and didn't waste any time telling him about it. Matthew was quick to say they were very kind. They asked him his trail name when he said he didn't have one…

Dr. Pickles joined us and thought, now the time to give Matthew a trail name before Fraidy Snake took hold. He knew Matthew loved the water because of my countless stories about Matthew's swimming prowess. Dr. Pickles threw out many names, but when he hit Riptide, that resonated. Riptide was born. A good day for Riptide to settle in: nice weather, beautiful scenic trail, and even with a late start, we managed thirteen point seven miles.

We landed at the intersection of Vermont 11 and 30, where Rock N Roll Sue would slackpack us the next day. Hikers often get picked up or dropped off near roads and set up camp nearby for several reasons. Partying young people use these spots to get wasted and then sleep it off, a spin on "camping." The party crowd loved Friday and Saturday nights, so we tried to avoid roadside campsites then. We crossed the road, entered a good-sized parking lot, walked through it, took a left onto a path over yet another road, crossed a stream, and found a lovely area with fire rings. We'd be packed in a little closer than we preferred, but workable. I helped Riptide set up,

202

and he absorbed it once he went through the process. He didn't like his zipperless tent, the openings secured by hooks and Velcro.

"Can anything get in here, Dad?"

"No Matty. You'll be fine. Do you want to switch tents with me?"

"I'm good." But his face gave him away; he didn't fully believe me. I'd find out long after I finished that he genuinely feared bears coming into camp and his tent. He also knew I slept with my food and the others hung theirs. He didn't sleep too well that first night. The rest of us did, however.

Poor kid.

The Red Matrix

Rock N Roll Sue's beautiful red Toyota Matrix rolled into the parking lot the following day. We greeted her with enthusiasm. She brought us coffee, baked goods, fresh fruit, and other snacks with foresight and kindness. Grateful, we filled our bellies and talked about what to bring on our slackpack. I decided to use my ULA Catalyst pack without most of my stuff. I put my tent, sleeping bag, sleeping pad, and extra clothes into the back of the car. I kept my water filter, water bottles, a rain jacket, and food. I thought long and hard about trekking poles. Taking into consideration my lack of grace, I took mine along. We kidded Just Doug because his pack looked just as heavy.

"What do you have in there?"

"You never know. I have things just in case." Just Doug smiled somewhat defiantly. The trail name "Justin Case" might have better suited him.

We said goodbye to Rock N Roll Sue in good spirits and headed north. We planned just under eighteen miles over four Vermont peaks – Bromley Mountain, Styles Peak, Peru Peak, and Baker Peak – then down to Danby-Landgrove Road, where hopefully the red Matrix would be waiting. Rock N Roll Sue said she'd bring dinner as an added incentive. That's the thing about slackpacking; you have no choice but to meet your benefactor at the appointed place and time. That's a bit disconcerting; options are suddenly severely limited, and even if we came upon a perfect spot, we couldn't stop for the night. However, being unburdened outweighed the inconvenience. The lighter load made a huge difference. I traveled more quickly and didn't need to rest as often.

Riptide impressed me during this long, physical day. Sure-footed and determined, he handled the hike well, his transition into the crew seamless. After a grueling day, true to her word, Rock N Roll Sue rolled into the designated parking lot with Subway

203

sandwiches. We wolfed those down in record time; Rock N Roll Sue was immensely amused at our hunger's voracity. Before she arrived, we scouted around for campsites near the parking lot. The exception to prove the rule, there seemed to be no good campsites anywhere. Sketchy, quite sketchy. We learned from a fellow hiker that Warren Doyle's crew used the area immediately behind the parking lot, but the hilly, rocky area seemed unsuitable. We recognized fresh tent impressions and wondered how they slept on the steep slope. Not sure of our next move, we explored our options. We could set up in the lot itself, although I couldn't get any stakes in the ground. The thought of getting run over by a vehicle did not appeal to me either. I'd rather take my chances with bears in the woods than humans and cars.

During our chat with Rock N Roll Sue, she agreed to meet us the next morning for another day of slackpacking. We thanked her intensely as she prepared to drive away.

"Goodbye, red Matrix. See you tomorrow."

Forced to find a place to sleep, we spread out in all directions and combed the surrounding area for tent sites. The location right next to a "permanent" privy held promise, but only for one, maybe two, tents. No luck on the AT north or south; we didn't want to hike too far away from the parking lot. I was headed up Danby-Landgrove Road when Just Doug appeared from a side road.

"We can camp up there. It's a good spot. A guy will be leaving in a few minutes. He's packing up his stuff now." Just Doug reported.

"Wait. What?"

"There's a guy up there. He's packing up his stuff. He'd rather camp alone; if we came up there, he wouldn't be alone. He's a little…off." Just Doug explained matter-of-factly. Yet, when a 36-year veteran of the Cleveland police force says someone's a little off, probably time to pay attention.

"But he's OK. I talked with him." He assured us. A few minutes later, a guy in a white Ford 150 pickup came down the road and drove by.

"Think he'll come back?" I inquired nervously.

"I don't think so, but you never know. I talked with him."

I scanned the area. "Why didn't he want to share this site? It's huge, flat, lots of room."

"I think he likes to do his own thing, which means not having other people around."

"What's his own thing?"

"I don't know."

204

I suspected he did know but wasn't going to say. I dropped the subject. We got to the task of setting up as it started to spit rain. That's the way of the trail – you think one option is probably the best, then another appears. On the brink of setting up on crooked, ridiculous, uncomfortable spots, we comfortably camped on ideal ground. I prepared for a good night's sleep.

Unless the guy came back. I pushed the notion out of my mind and relaxed. As I did, I wondered how Riptide felt.

"Matty?" No answer.

"Matty?" I heard him rustle and take his earphones out.

"Yeah?"

"You OK?"

"Yeah."

"OK, good night. Love you. Great job today."

"Yeah."

After the profound father/son exchange, I turned on my side, curled up, and fell asleep.

Demonic Dancers

The "off" dude did not return. Or maybe he did and just didn't wake us. We started stirring simultaneously in the low light of early morning, a little damp and cooler, much to my relief. After getting some fuel into my system, I packed up and headed back down the side road with Riptide to the parking lot.

The red Matrix soon made its way into the parking lot to our cheers. Mockingbird planned an "easy" slackpacking day of fifteen miles culminating in a descent into Clarendon gorge adjacent to VT 103, where we'd meet Rock N Roll Sue for a pizza dinner.

Motivated and unburdened, we cruised easily. I relished Riptide's company as we ventured through the Vermont woods. The AT Guide showed a sharp descent into the gorge that concerned me a little. However, we discovered a pine-needle-covered hill and surveyed the steep incline. It looked simple to navigate. Without stress, I reached the floor, a spacious flat area in the evergreen woods ideal for camping, but with No Camping signs posted on several trees.

"What's up with that?" I asked no one in particular.

Another level down, next to the stream, were campsites with No Camping signs posted. Yet, the tents already there confused me.

We crossed the gorge, the VT 103 parking lot just a few yards further. We climbed to the lot, and sure enough, like a vision from heaven, a red Matrix appeared. Rock n Roll Sue emerged delighted to deliver fresh pizza. While we chowed down, we debated our options. Do we hike north another mile to the Clarendon Shelter? It looked like a pretty good climb. Then we'd have to come back south to this spot because Rock N Roll Sue offered her services for yet another slackpacking day. I hated to hike south. We all did. Or do we go a few hundred yards across the gorge and camp along the river on a picturesque, comfortable, "illegal" site?

We chose to live on the wild side and camp near the gorge. After getting on our knees and worshipping Rock N Roll Sue, she drove off with a promise to meet us in the morning. We faced an unusual choice for us, many sites to choose from. We thought going up the river a bit might be best, a little more concealed from the road. We set up in the pine trees next to the stream. Riptide and I set up close to each other, Dr. Pickles and Mockingbird found a flat area nearby, and Just Doug tucked in several yards away.

No one seemed to occupy the few other tents nearby when a couple came walking by from further upstream. They carried a basket of laundry. They muttered a greeting of some sort, definitely not friendly. We watched them disappear over the bridge to the parking lot.

"What was that all about?" Dr. Pickles asked.

"Maybe people live here?" I offered.

"Hadn't thought of that, but that would explain these tents."

Due to the shorter mileage day, Dr. Pickles and Mockingbird took the opportunity to bathe in the stream. I followed and laundered my clothes. In other words, I lay in the water with my clothes on. Riptide soaked his feet. He developed a nasty rash under his arms and groin area. He tried to cool those off. I gave him some Gold Bond medicated powder. To his credit, he did not complain. I would have.

Near my tent, I stripped off my wet clothes, wrung them out, and dove inside, aware of my growing immodesty. I pulled on my camp clothes. Just Doug tied his paracord between two trees, and we hung our clothes to dry. Our bellies were full of pizza, and we sat and chatted, repaired some of our gear, and enjoyed our peaceful time together until nightfall.

On a cooler evening, I looked forward to deep sleep. I'd need it; we planned to go up and over Killington the next day, Vermont's second highest peak.

But I woke in the early morning hours to loud cracks. What was that? Gunshots? Then I heard shouting. A bright light flickered and bounced off my tent. Completely disoriented, the shouting continued. I clicked on my phone at 2:07 am. I heard my fellow hikers mutter.

My first concern was for my son. "Matty, you OK?"

"Yeah." The reply from his tent was one of annoyance, awake a lot longer than me.

"What's going on?" I asked groggily.

"People up the hill…." He replied, already resigned to the noise.

I unzipped my tent and stuck my head out. An enormous bonfire on the hill illuminated a man dragging a giant branch. He snapped it between two trees, the loud cracks precisely the same as those that woke me. People yelled too (or maybe they sang); I couldn't tell; the ruckus was very loud. Surely alcohol, large quantities of alcohol must be involved. With no people there when we arrived or bedded down, I deduced they lived there temporarily and either worked late or drank until the bars closed, then made their way "home."

So what do I do? What were the options?

1. Go up there and give them a piece of my mind. That would entail a high risk of personal injury.

2. Call the cops. I don't think so. We were not supposed to camp here. And what would they do?

3. Join them. Too tired. And this didn't seem like the best time to throw away twenty-seven years of sobriety. And I didn't feel like making new friends at two in the morning.

4. Ask Just Doug to tell them to shut up. After all, he's a cop. I gave it a try.

"Hey. Just Doug, go tell them to shut up." I whispered loudly.

"No way." He replied from his tent. Dr. Pickles and Mockingbird laughed. Dr. Pickles chimed in.

"Come on, Just Doug; you're Doug Tough; go kick their asses."

"No way." Said the man of few words. Our one final option?

5. Lay low, wait it out, and try to get back to sleep. That seemed like the safest one. I let the others in on my innovative thinking.

"I'm going back to sleep." I notified everyone.

"Good luck."

I gazed up at the colossal fire one last time. I could see dancing silhouettes framed by the blaze. Damn. Was I witnessing some kind of demonic ritual in front of Hell's fire? Or was it just some drunken dudes dancing? I zipped the tent back up. I watched the firelight bounce off the ceiling of my tent. I listened to the madness.

207

After lying awake for God knows how long, either their idiocy diminished or my fatigue kicked in, I fell asleep.

Killington

My eyes opened to morning light, no more shouting but a hint of smoke in the air. I heard the others rustle. I didn't want to move. I wasn't sure if I could move. Snug and warm and groggy from the fitful sleep, I wanted to close my eyes, make the world disappear, and sleep late into the morning.

But I couldn't. Rock N Roll Sue would be in the parking lot soon.

I reached back, found the nozzle to my Thermarest, and gave it a quick twist. The air hissed out. I put my mind and body into automatic. Soon I stood with damp clothes, pack on my back, and ready to go. So did the others. I looked up the hill. I could detect no sign of the previous night's mayhem from where I stood.

Silently, we shuffled off. We sat in the parking lot and watched the red Matrix slowly turn into the lot. Grateful, we dug through Rock N Roll Sue's supply of goodies as we relayed the previous night's story. She didn't know what to say. I wanted to linger awhile, but we had a long, difficult day ahead. The AT Guide indicated seventeen point four miles from here to US 4 with a long steady uphill slog of more than eleven miles to reach the peak of Killington. Even without packs, a strenuous hike.

The trail to Killington did not disappoint; rugged and beautiful. We passed a marker showing five hundred miles to go to Katahdin. Riptide and I posed for a pic. The map portrayed a long gradual ascent. The trail proved rough; lots of roots and rocks made it slow going. Over a stretch of several miles, the path traversed the mountain, my left foot consistently above my right; both feet ached because of the angle.

"Right Click, something always hurts. Continue."

Thank God for Dr. Pickles' enthusiasm and fitness. He loved this. I mean, he *loved* it; his gratitude was contagious. I found myself inspired by his remarkable way of lifting people's spirits. After one of Dr. Pickle's engaging joyous outbursts about the majestic surroundings, Riptide confided in me.

"Dad, I love them."

"Cool. I do too." I confirmed.

"No, dad. I mean, I really love them. Dr. Pickles and Mockingbird. I love them."

He put a heavy emphasis on "love." I nodded my head, a serious admission for him. I thought about what this experience must be like for him. Tough Love grew to

208

love Paradox and Rock Steady. Even though the ladies still hiked a day ahead of us, the trail arranged for Dr. Pickles and Mockingbird to impact Matthew positively. I hiked up Killington, full of gratitude and pride for my son.

Mid-afternoon, we reached the side trail to the summit of Killington. Even without packs, we only managed eleven miles, a tribute to the difficulty of the terrain. To summit Killington required an additional two-tenths, straight up. Then we'd have to come back down. Remembering my promise to Dr. Pickles, I gave my best effort to remain positive.

"Guys, we still have more than six miles to go; maybe we should skip this," I said.

Without hesitation, all four of them replied in unison, "No. I'm going up there."

They dropped their daypacks and poles and started the scramble up the rocks. I followed reluctantly, becoming less and less a fan of the steeps. More precisely, I still liked to climb; the views always inspired me. I craved spiritual nourishment. But when you go up, you must come back down. I scrambled up the rocks, used both hands and feet, and knew I'd have to deal with this on the way down. That scared me, but I was thankful this climb was short.

We emerged out of the trees straight up onto the bare rock. Riptide's eyes blazed with hiker fire. As he looked over the mountains, I took photos of him standing on a rock; distant rain showers framed the shot. The light, the setting, and my young son discovering himself made this one of my favorite memories; the panorama was stunning.

Until age eleven, Riptide carried much more weight, not as lean and athletic. I coached his soccer team for a few years; Riptide played a lot in goal; he didn't like to run. A massive growth spurt gained him nearly a foot in eighteen months. He stretched out. He lost all his baby fat. He started eighth grade in a few weeks and looked forward to playing soccer, basketball, and track. He'd run a lot. He identified his time in the woods as a way to get in shape and test himself. The stories relayed by Tough Love fueled his need to prove that whatever she could do, he could do better. Sometimes sibling competition can be healthy.

Other people milled about the summit. Killington, a popular winter skiing destination, drew many tourists during the different seasons. Sightseers poured out of the gondola at regular intervals and admired the view. The weather cooled down. With forty-five pounds of body fat gone, I noticed I chilled quickly. I checked my phone battery; in the red zone, below ten percent. We had another seven miles to go; we needed to contact Rock N Roll Sue and give her a time to meet us. I checked with the crew on their power levels; Mockingbird's phone had enough juice.

I picked my way carefully and descended the steep side trail without incident. The crew waited for me at the bottom. We gathered our gear and followed the white blazes north. Two miles later, we saw a dad with his young boys looking for the Mount Pico summit. We consulted our AT Guide and shared some information. They wore shorts and t-shirts without any other gear. They seemed lost. Late in the afternoon, daylight fading, the temperature dropping, an internal warning flag waved; something bad could happen here.

"We have about four miles left to the road. Do you want to hike with us?" I offered them an option. The dad hesitated.

"No, we'll keep going this way."

"Are you sure?" I asked. The boys looked at us, their faces hard to read.

"No, thank you. We're good."

"OK. Good luck." I meant it. Off they went. I didn't hear any stories about someone getting rescued, so I believed they made it to their destination, hopefully unscathed.

Dr. Pickles and Riptide moved out and walked far in front of us. Dr. Pickles wanted to stretch it out; Riptide joined him. Mockingbird and I had similar paces, so we ambled through the woods near each other. We didn't talk much, comforted that she traveled a few hundred yards behind me (or sometimes in front of me). Just Doug brought up the rear. He loved to stop and take pictures.

I met Dr. Pickles and Riptide on the side of US 4. Since they arrived thirty minutes earlier, Dr. Pickles scouted for campsites. He reported that a drunken man occupied the only suitable site that could handle all four of our tents. Dr. Pickles didn't think we'd want to deal with that, especially after last night's antics. So, as usual, we discussed our options. At Mockingbird's suggestion, we called a nearby hotel and got a reservation.

Soon, the red Matrix appeared, slowed, and turned in the parking lot to a resounding ovation. When Rock N Roll Sue emerged from her car with sacks full of McDonald's cheeseburgers, double cheeseburgers, chicken sandwiches, and apple pies, joy and anticipation tore through my body. It got hushed very quickly. The only sounds were sandwiches being unwrapped and moans of appreciation. Rock N Roll Sue watched in wonder. While we ate, the drunken guy came out of the woods, unceremoniously unzipped his shorts in the parking lot, and stared at us as he peed. He zipped up and staggered back into the underbrush. We looked at each other.

"Um, Sue? We don't think we want to stay here tonight. Think you could bring us up to the Inn on Long Trail?"

"Why? Don't you like your new neighbor?" She teased.

210

"Sure, I can give you a ride." But before she did, she produced another small surprise. She printed a little sign that read,

8/12/15
Passed
1700 miles
WOOHOO

We took turns holding the sign while she took a photo. I noodled on walking seventeen hundred miles for a bit. Impossible. Really? I impressed myself, but more impressed with my Higher Power. He led me to recovery twenty-seven years prior, walked with me through Stage 4 cancer, and now carried me along the Appalachian Trail. I asked him silently,

"Dude, are your arms getting tired carrying me?"

I felt God smile.

"Continue."

I beamed as I got in the front seat of the red Matrix while the other four crammed in the back; being tall had its advantages. Rock N Roll Sue brought us to the inn. We said goodbye; now permanently out of her range, this would be our last slackpack with her. We all watched the red Matrix drive off into the setting sun. I don't know about the others, but emotion tugged at my soul. After resolving a slight misunderstanding with the Inn, we settled into two rooms and hit the showers. Riptide showed me the angry rash on his feet and under his arms. I tried not to show it, but the nasty outbreak concerned me. I took pics and texted them to Sandy; it concerned her too. After his shower, we applied a liberal coating of Gold Bond; that seemed to cool it down. He mentioned it hardly at all. I admired his toughness, unusual for any thirteen-year-old.

Fearsome Footsteps

The Inn at Long Trail includes breakfast for all guests. Thinking we might get coffee, pastry, cereal, waffles, and a piece of fruit or two, Riptide and I ventured downstairs, Just Doug was already there, up early and exploring as usual. He informed us.

"The restaurant doesn't open for another thirty minutes or so."

We killed some time and sat in the restaurant shortly after it opened, genuinely surprised at the full-service menu. I ordered an omelet, and so did Riptide. The food was excellent; we texted Dr. Pickles and Mockingbird to tell them about the wonderful surprise awaiting them downstairs. After we feasted and revved up on multiple cups of coffee, time to hit the trail.

Hikers usually walked the eight-tenths of a mile to the trailhead. That seemed far to me (coming from a guy who had already walked seventeen hundred miles). The five of us stood outside the inn and debated the merits of hitchhiking or not. Just Doug did not hesitate.

"I'm walking down."

Off he went. He never minded the "extra" steps; to him, they were all part of the adventure. The rest of us didn't like extraneous mileage. Our burdensome packs factored into our decision-making. Who'd want to pick up four hikers with packs? Dr. Pickles and Mockingbird agreed to start down the road and try to hitchhike as a couple. Riptide and I would do the same after we gave them some space.

Sometimes you get a ride right out of the parking lot. Sometimes not. Riptide and I did not. With very little traffic, we started down the road, Dr. Pickles and Mockingbird far down the hill. After resigning ourselves to the walk to the trailhead, a man stopped in his SUV and asked if we needed a ride.

"Yes, please!"

We excitedly replied. We squeezed in with our packs on our laps. We passed Dr. Pickles and Mockingbird on the right, Just Doug farther down on the left. They didn't see us. We got dropped off and headed into the woods. Riptide asked.

"Think we should wait for the others?"

"I don't know. What do you think?"

"I think they'll catch us; let's go."

"Me too. OK, let's go."

Just a mile into our hike, the Long Trail and the Appalachian Trail split, with the AT veering to the right and east, the fork clearly marked and well-traveled.

"Think we should wait here for the others?" Riptide asked again.

"No, they'll be all right. This shouldn't be a problem for them. It's pretty straightforward."

We continued. After four miles, the trail dumped into Gifford Woods State Park among legitimate campsites, complete with tents, pop-up trailers, RV's, cars, trucks, and people. Riptide and I sat at a picnic table to wait for the others to snack. When Dr. Pickles came out of the woods and spotted us, confusion flashed across his face, then relief. He questioned.

"How'd you guys get in front of us?"

"We got a ride to the trailhead," Riptide replied.

"Oh! We waited for you there."

Genuinely sorry, I acquiesced. "Hopefully not too long. We thought you might have seen us get dropped off?"

"We didn't. We waited for a while." Dr. Pickles informed, not upset but more concerned.

"I'm sorry. Here we are."

Mockingbird and Just Doug expressed similar reactions. Finn stepped out of the woods and joined us as we sat at the unoccupied site. We listened to his stories. Finn caught a stomach bug that hit him with such ferocity that he pooped his pants while hiking. The bug kept him off the trail for five days. Then he contracted Lyme disease and took medicine for several weeks; that left him weakened too. Through severe trials, but here, in Vermont, still moving along. He told us this adventure was still much better than his job as a Correctional Officer in Finland.

We decided to stop at Stony Brook Shelter, a day of just ten miles. On the way, we climbed up Quimby Mountain; it hurt more than usual with full packs. We got to the shelter in the early evening. Finn was lying there with a liter of Mountain Dew and a big bag of potato chips. Finn stayed at the Inn at Long Trail with a lady friend; they looked like they loved each other. I refrained from asking about it earlier in the day.

"How's the romance of the century going?" I teased.

"She headed up the Long Trail. It's over." He said with a heavy Finnish accent. I detected a trace of sadness. I'd find out later that she broke his heart.

"So now you are drowning your sorrows in Mountain Dew and potato chips?"

Without saying a word or sitting up, he put down the soda and gave me the finger with both hands. He responded to my chuckle with a wry smile. He continued to drink his Mountain Dew and eat his potato chips. Riptide witnessed the exchange and shook his head.

I sat in front of the shelter, near a small campfire, working on a dilemma - no phone service, and I needed to talk with Arno. He agreed to drive my friend Rick McCracken the next day and meet us, but I had to tell him our location. Finally, as the sun dropped near the horizon, I decided to head north on the trail and see if I could get cell service. I walked about half a mile to a rock outcropping near an aluminum ladder (actually part of the AT) and found service as long as I stood in a specific position. Able to speak with Sandy, I informed her that we would be on Chateauguay Road, four and a half miles away. She looked it up on her Appalachian Trail Guide and said she'd let Arno know. The road looked sketchy, just gravel, and the terrain looked rough. Knowing Arno loved a challenge, and that Rick knew the area, I felt confident they'd find us. Sandy and I chatted longer, concerned about

Matthew and his rash. The powder seemed to help some. I enjoyed talking with my wife, always a highlight of my day, so I lingered and disregarded the darkness enveloping me. I ended the call.

"I love you, honey."

I looked around. Damn. When did it get this dark? And I left my headlamp back at camp. Dumbass. You didn't prepare too well for your little excursion, did you? But wait, I had light; I used the flashlight on my iPhone and lit up the trail immediately in front of me. I headed back south towards the shelter. My senses were on high alert but not frightened or nervous; I knew the way back, the trail well-worn and well-marked. I walked for a short distance.

Then I heard footsteps in the woods to my left. I stopped. I listened intently to a few more steps, then they stopped. I walked. Whatever was in the woods next to me started walking too. My system immediately shifted to hyper-alert. By the footsteps, the creature next to me sounded massive. I tried to deduce immediately. "Deer? No. Bigger than a deer. Bear? Maybe, but not shuffling the leaves like a bear. Moose? Oh no. God? Really? What do I do?"

I continued. I continued to walk, and the animal walked alongside me. I decided I'd make my presence known. Calmly I spoke.

"Hello there. I am here and a human, just in case you were wondering."

The animal still walked calmly next to me. Do I shine my light to see what it is? Part of me did not want to know. Part of me was intensely curious. Could I see my first moose? The inquisitive part won out. I shone my iPhone flashlight into the woods. I expected to see a great wall of moose. Nothing. I could feel the animal's presence, but the damn iPhone flashlight revealed nothing. The footsteps stopped. I expected to see a pair of eyes blazing back at me. Nothing. I walked. The footsteps started.

Shit.

I shone the light again. Nothing. Shit.

"Hey, there, critter. I mean no harm. Just headed back to the shelter. Going to get a good night's sleep. Thank you for keeping me company."

No response to my monologue, just the leaves rustling as the animal moved along with me. I drew near a stream I crossed earlier, close to the shelter. I navigated over and around some large rocks. The footsteps stopped. I moved quickly, adrenaline coursing through my system. Finally, I reached the side trail to the shelter and home. I could see the fire flicker. I made my way to our little encampment and dove into my tent.

214

"Dad, you were gone for a long time. Did you get to talk with mom?" Riptide asked.

"Huh? What? Oh yeah, I did. We're all set. Meeting them tomorrow at 10:00."

"You OK?" He heard the adrenaline in my response.

"You won't believe what happened…." I told him. The others listened closely. As I talked and answered their questions, I calmed down. I wondered if we'd have a visitor that evening; I think the others may have speculated about that possibility too. I prayed for Matthew that my story didn't frighten him too much and that he could rest. I bid him good night, curled up, and soon fell asleep.

McPackin

The first to step onto Chateauguay Road, I thought. "Uh oh, this isn't much of a road."

Washed out in places not used often, I wondered about the chances of a vehicle navigating it. I stepped across into a parking area big enough for two cars. I shrugged off my pack. The others filed out of the woods. No sign of Arno. Intangibly connected, we sat down simultaneously and settled in to wait. We knew each other's thoughts without speaking. I stood and paced.

"I have no idea what direction they'll come from," I said to no one in particular. Off in the distance, we heard a car horn.

"There they are. You guys wait here. I'll go find them."

They nodded in agreement. I walked up the road as the horn signaled regularly. I replied with my signature loud bark, but no reply. After fifteen minutes, I walked into a large open area with a pond and immediately saw Arno's truck. The Turtle Man first spotted me. I strode confidently to greet them. They were happy to see me. Especially Arno, shaking when I hugged him. The GPS took them over terrain that could hardly be classified as a road. But continue, he did.

Rick McCracken (whom I would soon dub McPackin) chattered away excitedly, telling me all about the road. Rick and his wife Sharon are Mary's (Little Click) godparents. He grew up in rural Pennsylvania and fostered a deep love for the outdoors. He told entertaining stories of how he took his two young boys on wilderness adventures. One time, a bear got their food in the Adirondacks, and they hiked many miles to a hut where they bought twenty dollars worth of Snickers bars to survive the remaining time in the woods. Rick also ventured out on bushwhacking (no trail) solo hikes. I consider Rick an older "brother," having engaged in many intense, deeply spiritual conversations that brought us closer to God. The previous

215

Christmas, Rick lost his younger brother Jimmy to alcoholism. Rick found him dead on the floor and gave me one of Jimmy's Alcoholics Anonymous 24-hour coins to carry (which I embarrassingly lost somewhere on the trail). I talked with Jimmy several times about recovery, but alcoholism won this battle and killed another talented, kind, intelligent man. It often does.

During the four years I prepared for this hike, I learned much from Rick, a much more experienced hiker than me. He hiked Bear Mountain (CT) with me back when I was still pretty weak from cancer treatment, causing him to wait for me often; the six miles we covered were near the peak of my capability then.

I led them down the "road" to where the trail crossed. Arno parked the truck in the middle of the road, not concerned about other traffic. After introductions all around, Arno revealed the magic in the back, and cans of Coca-Cola won me over. A rude SOBO (short for Southbounder) with a snotty entitlement attitude appeared; he attempted to pilfer stuff my friends brought for us. Worn down and pretty mellow, thru-hikers don't usually confront, but this guy annoyed us. Finally, McPackin still revved up from everyday life, chastised him.

"No! Stop taking that. You can't have those. They are for my friends."

"Oh. Oh. I'm sorry." The SOBO replied meekly but insincerely. Meanwhile, he videoed the whole interaction. We didn't know why.

Rick showed me his external frame pack, more than twenty years old. I'd seen a few other hikers with these, most notably Boots and Wannabe, who purposefully went old school. Back in 1974 (or so), I went on my only other backpacking trip through the Adirondacks. I sported an orange Kelty external frame backpack. Rick liked his and started asking me about gear and things to leave behind. I couldn't focus on his questions, too many distractions. I watched the weird SOBO guy eat our pretzel sticks, drink our soda, and anything else he could grab. Arno wanted to tell me about the ridiculous road they had just driven. Turtle Man asked Riptide questions about the hike and talked with the crew. I wanted to hear what Riptide said. What I would consider normal in the real world seemed chaotic out here in the woods, all this commotion too much for my slow biorhythm.

Finally, we got Rick sorted. We posed for a picture sitting on the tailgate of Arno's truck. Arno and Turtle Man headed down the road and hoped for a much smoother ride home. We set off hiking.

I noticed Rick's shoes. Uh oh. Previously, Rick proudly talked of his leather hiking books that served him well for many years. He called them "old friends." Leather hiking boots, definitely old school, possess many advantages when broken in properly. They are amazingly tough, supportive and protect the feet and ankles well.

216

Disadvantages include breathability, dry-ability, and weight. Curious to see how they'd play out on the trail, I asked. "Dude, where are your leather boots?"

"I left those at home and bought these! They're waterproof!"

I didn't respond immediately; he sensed a warning in my hesitation. As previously discussed, waterproof boots suck for a thru-hike. This ran through my mind, and he felt my "disapproval."

He pushed. "Why? What's wrong with these? They're comfortable."

"Let's see what happens." I tried to redirect the conversation. He didn't let it go. He pushed for more information. I told him my theories and what happened with Tough Love. He listened but didn't respond. He went into process mode.

I loved hiking with this crew, my son, an older "brother," and three dear members of my trail family. Soon we came to a side trail that led to The Lookout. Within our side trail limit (one-tenth of a mile), we dropped our packs and headed up the hill to a house with a steep ladder up the side to the roof-viewing platform. I voiced my disapproval.

"How ironic would it be if I fell to my death climbing a ladder?"

I didn't like Riptide climbing up that thing either; the view from the platform was okay but not worth the risk. I descended very slowly and carefully, the others back on the trail. I reached for my pack, threw it on, and reached into my front left pocket for my earbuds, but they were not there. Crap. I left them on the bench on the viewing platform. I decided to hike back up the hill and climb that stupid ladder again. I reached the house, not sure my earbuds were even there. Shakily, slowly, I climbed. I reached the top and found them exactly where I had left them. I made my way down the ladder even more carefully. My knuckles turned white from my death grip on the ladder. My legs wobbled.

"One rung at a time," I said to no one. I stepped on firm ground and breathed a sigh of relief, went back down the hill, shouldered my pack, and continued far behind everyone else. Eventually, I caught up after a few hours. They wondered what happened to me, definitely not impressed with my reason.

Rick, in his glory, talked a lot about backpacking and consistently asked about my lessons learned. Late in the afternoon, we reached VT 12. The AT Guide described a general store close to the trail. We found it. I bought smoked chicken, fresh tomatoes, and onions, among other things. The AT Guide didn't have the hiker-friendly resident that opened up his barn or let you set up in his yard. We heard about Dan through other hikers. Dr. Pickles and Mockingbird knocked on his door and conversed with him. Dan welcomed us, thanks in part to their charm and genuine likability. He pointed to a nice mowed lawn near a stream and access to fresh water

217

from the outside spigot, plush accommodations for a thru-hiker. After we picked our spots and got our tents up, we gathered for dinner, Rick's tent smaller than Just Doug's. I didn't know they made them that small.

I looked forward to dinner; fresh food is always a treat. I dug out my package of large tortillas and my small Leatherman knife and started dicing up smoked chicken, tomatoes, and onions. The store owner gave me a small container of mayo too. I wrapped them up and gave one to Riptide. He devoured it, barely speaking.

"Good? Right?"

With a mouthful of food, he just nodded. I chuckled and took a bite. I moaned in approval. As Rick boiled water to add to a packet of dehydrated food, he stared in disbelief, his mouth open and his jaw almost touching his chest. Between mouthfuls, I asked.

"Dude, what's wrong?"

"I can't believe you're eating this way."

"What way?"

"Fresh chicken, vegetables, dessert…."

He packed nine days' worth of dried food; his load was heavy. Outside his experience, he never purchased food on his trips (except for Snickers Bars). His first night with us, we camped next to a road in a guy's yard and ate freshly bought food, a little miffed that our meal appealed much more to the senses than his dehydrated crap. The others also enjoyed fresh stuff from the store. We all chomped away happily, thoroughly amused by Rick's ramblings. I chided.

"Hey, you're carrying a lot of stuff, especially food, aren't you? I have a possible trail name for you. How's McPackin sound? See what I did there. McCracken. McPackin?"

"Yeah, I got it." The others laughed.

"I like it." He said good-naturedly; The conversation remained friendly, and again I silently thanked my crew for their acceptance of yet another guest. Gentle rain drifted in, and we sought shelter in our tents.

We packed wet tents in the morning. Dr. Pickles and Mockingbird led the way and soon outdistanced us. We found them on a sunlit hill not too far away. We always took the opportunity to dry gear out when it presented itself. We laid our wet tents on the grass and waited for the sun to do her thing, not long before our equipment dried nice and toasty.

Over the rugged terrain and several miles, McPackin's feet started to trouble him. As anticipated, the waterproof boots kept his feet moist and the skin blistered. I identified with his pain; I walked hundreds of miles with blisters, not enjoyable. We

218

managed almost thirteen miles when clouds and darkness forced us to settle in under some pine trees near VT 14 without Just Doug ahead of us somewhere. I walked into town to see if I could find him and scope out any better tenting sites, but no luck with either.

We ate in our tents as the rain came down and thunder rumbled in the distance. I heard McPackin boiling water outside in the rain for another foil pouch of dehydrated food. He couldn't do anything in his tent except lie down and sleep. He handled it with good humor. I called over to Riptide.

"Matty (I couldn't call him Riptide), you ok?"

No answer. That probably meant he adapted by slapping in his earbuds, listening to music, and shutting out the rest of the world. I let him be, his response to undesirable conditions similar to mine. I'd find out later that Riptide did not like this site; he slept very little, very nervous about a possible bear visit.

Sometime in the night, two other hikers came into camp and set up nearby; all I heard until morning.

New Hampshire

Scheduled to meet Sandy and Little Click in Hanover, New Hampshire, we headed out before Dr. Pickles and Mockingbird, another exciting, motivating day. My wife and daughter, driving from Cape Cod, would arrive later in the day; no need to hurry. Somewhat of a culture shock to step out onto a road and follow the AT through the middle of a town; it felt good to see people, cars, homes, and shops in West Hartford, VT. Again, McPackin shook his head; he didn't realize we'd walk along real roads.

We crossed a few more roads on the way into Norwich. With my mood elevated by Sandy's pending visit and an energy drink, I put in my earbuds, found the Steeps Trail Mix, and stepped out. Quiet Riot's "Bang Your Head" quickened my pace. My energy surged. I could see Riptide up ahead. I turned the volume to max and clicked repeat. Bang Your Head banged in my head. I flew past him. That startled him. Once the shock of seeing his old man pass by wore off, his competitive nature kicked in. He surged by me. He thought he had made his point. I passed him again. We seesawed back and forth a few more times over a few miles. He finally drew ahead, and as we neared the road, I resigned myself to defeat. I watched him fly through the forest. But then he stepped on a long, flat, wet rock, lost his footing, and fell spectacularly. He went down hard. I could have stepped over him and raced by. I thought about it. Victory would be mine! Ha ha ha ha.

But I did not. I stopped. I yanked my earbuds out. "Matty, are you OK?"

"I am." He got up slowly, slightly embarrassed. We walked together to Elm Street.

"You know I could have beat you to the road, right?" I said.

"No, Dad. I would have got up and passed you again."

"No way." I lied. He spoke the truth.

We walked together for a mile through town, gazing at the well-kept homes and manicured lawns, way ahead of the others because of our furious pace over the last few miles. At Main Street, we took a left, still on the Appalachian Trail, and located an excellent deli. We bought lunch and headed to the gazebo in the center of Norwich. We charged our phones, ate, and lounged around. Riptide got a little bored, so he headed to a nearby basketball court, found a basketball in a bin, and started shooting. You wouldn't find a basketball lying around a public court in Manchester, CT, where we live. I recognized Dr. Pickles's distinguished gate as he cruised down Elm Street towards us, Mockingbird close behind. Soon came McPackin. He hobbled determinedly on sore feet. They dropped their gear at the gazebo and went to the deli.

We texted Just Doug. In Hanover, he would wait for us. After lunch, we cruised down Main Street and paused for pictures at the Vermont/New Hampshire border on the bridge over the Connecticut River. The Appalachian Trail Conservancy ranks all the states according to difficulty on a scale of one to ten, with ten being the most difficult. New Hampshire rates an eight earning the second toughest state, the fabled White Mountains ahead of us. After that, the most brutal state – Maine. That's why most people go north; the first twelve states serve as training for the last two.

We entered Hanover, a college town famous for Dartmouth, an Ivy League school, the amount of activity indicative of a school about to start. We reunited with Just Doug at the town green; he felt good yesterday and decided to keep hiking. Together, we worked our way through the busy streets of Hanover. McPackin limped along, blisters worse. He never complained, aware he needed different footwear.

I ran into Baltimore Jack (his trail name taken from a Bruce Springsteen song), who I first met at Neels Gap, then Boiling Springs (where he eye-balled Rock Steady), and now he sat outside a little coffee shop in Hanover. Somewhat of a trail icon, he hiked the AT eight times. He died a few months later from heart failure; the "Baltimore Jack" obituaries and stories on the internet fascinated me.

With twenty backpacks outside, we quickly found Ramunto's Brick & Brew Pizzeria, famous for giving a slice of pizza to a thru-hiker. Pretty full from lunch, so I didn't mind when I missed my pizza slice. I sat outside in a trance. I nursed a coke and reveled in how wonderful it felt to sit on a chair at a table. My phone barked;

Sandy was nearby. The old beige Suburban appeared; it once again carried the people I loved most. Sandy and Mary stepped out, and bliss filled me. I hugged them for as long as they could take it. Sandy carried camping and Cape Cod gear, so we dealt with a significant logistical problem. Six thru-hikers with packs, Sandy and Little Click to transport. Solving problems became a fine art on the trail; we quickly threw the packs up on the roof and strapped them down; Dr. Pickles worried they'd fall off, so he secured them personally. We wedged ourselves in. Well, the others wedged themselves in; I stretched out in the front passenger seat while Sandy drove, windows down and air conditioning on high to combat the odor.

Jacobs Brook Campground would serve as a base camp for the next few days with electricity, running water, hot showers, and a swimming pool, the stability unsettling yet completely welcome. No camp store, though, so we "roughed" it and bought food elsewhere. We drove onto a wonderfully flat, open area. Sandy brought our biggest tent; a ten-person behemoth dubbed the Taj Mahal. With a swinging door, it felt like a small house. How weird to stand up and change clothes. I blew up an air mattress and laid it next to Sandy's. It looked inviting. They lugged in their duffels stuffed with clothes. My pack sufficed for me. By this time, I didn't need or want anything else.

I relaxed in the peaceful atmosphere of Jacobs Brook Campground. Being with these people generated an air of love, and their camaraderie warmed me. Recovery taught me to live in the moment, one day at a time, yet I could not fully live in this moment. A notion that "this too shall pass" nagged me. My wife and kids would soon be gone, leaving me to conquer the rest of the trail without them. The thought hurt. I had been gone long enough. I'd miss the first day of school and some of Matthew's middle school soccer games. Joshua and Samantha were already in Lynchburg at Liberty University; Colleen was married. I longed for my role as husband and father. I felt accountable and responsible, and I grew weary of the trail. Even though in fantastic physical condition, after losing nearly fifty pounds, I experienced fatigue to the bone. As I sat extravagantly in a camp chair, thoughts tumbled around in my head while I listened to warm conversations. I did my best to push the anticipated grief aside and joined in.

The same peaceful atmosphere permeated the camp the following day. As usual, Just Doug got up early to make coffee, soon joined by McPackin. I think those guys got up early because of their tiny little tents. They also slept on thin foam pads. I'm amazed Just Doug slept that way the entire hike. They sat and whispered under a popup tent. Very snug with my wife sleeping next to me, I listened to Riptide and Little Click breathe on the other end of the Taj Mahal, sound asleep. Sandy soon

221

stirred. During the night, our mattresses slowly deflated; I remedied my situation by blowing up my Thermarest, and the flattened mattress served as a ground cover. Sandy did not sleep well.

Scheduled to do a radio interview with Vermont Public Radio, we drove back across the border, where Sandy dropped me off at King Arthur Flour. I met Mark Ames, Rock N Roll Sue, and the host. Again, the thru-hike provided an opportunity to carry the message of recovery. I shared openly during the session.

"The only way I walked to Vermont was because I haven't picked up a drink or a drug for the last twenty-eight years. "

As always, God worked His way into the conversation. I owed my life to His grace. Hopefully, my gratitude showed.

I hit the trail late morning for a relatively simple, slackpacked fourteen-mile day. Riptide took the day off, problems with that nasty rash and sore feet. McPackin kept him company. His badly blistered feet kept him in camp where he hoped they'd heal quickly with liberal applications of Bag Balm.

The trail weaved around Dartmouth College, and as we gradually ascended away from town, we came across an odd sight; next to the path lay a foam mat, an empty beer bottle, a pair of pants, a t-shirt, and a button-down shirt. No person. We didn't know the story, so we made stuff up. Just Doug didn't say much. Being a retired cop, he'd probably seen too much of this, most of it beyond my imagination. Without packs, we hit our extraction point in good time. Sandy and Riptide met us on the road; Sandy told me about the new air mattress she had purchased. We arrived back in camp by 6:00 pm.

Trail Family Reunion

Over dinner, we contemplated the next day's plan with only two road crossings available for extraction, one under six miles out, the next one just under twenty. We agreed to go big. Sandy said later that she wished I had taken a zero day to rest, heal, and, more importantly, spend the day with her and our children. It didn't even occur to me.

Dumbass.

I realized (again) how selfish I can be. I placed my ambition above the needs of my wife and children. I could have suggested a zero-day to the crew. Even if they didn't want to, I had the option to catch up. I justified my decision to ease the guilt. I thought that maybe, just maybe, if we could catch Rock Steady and Paradox, we could all finish together. Only a day or so ahead, one big day on our part, and we'd

222

gain significantly. I texted Paradox, about ten miles in front of us, and arranged to have Sandy pick them up, then pick us up, and we'd all stay at Jacobs Brook Campground together.

We left early the next morning. McPackin wanted one more day to Bag Balm blisters and look for new footwear, so understandably, he bagged out. Riptide loved challenges, and this would be one. It was also my other son's birthday; Joshua turned twenty-one, a significant number. In Lynchburg, VA starting his senior year at Liberty University for athletic training, I crafted a "Happy Birthday" sign and planned to take a picture or two holding it. Sandy harbored sadness about her baby boy turning twenty-one without his family to celebrate. Frankly, I did too.

The rugged day's trek commenced with a steep climb to Holt's Ledge; the climb up Smarts Mountain was grueling. I slipped, banged my right shin against a rock, and opened a good gash. Blood flowed down my leg into my sock. It looked savagely cool, so I took a picture and posted it on social media. Even though it hurt, I took pride in my "shinjury." It validated the mythical thru-hiker persona I conjured up for myself.

The trail gradually turned rougher. One place featured rebar hammered into the rock to serve as stairs. I climbed an enormous, smooth granite slab with Mockingbird on another stretch. We stopped and admired the view. I was tired when we reached the top of Mount Cube. We posed on top, holding Joshua's "Happy Birthday" sign. Late in the afternoon, we still had more than three miles to reach the road.

Down the mountain we went. I descended slowly; Matthew hung back with me. I knew he and Tough Love responded similarly to a few miles left late in the day; go as fast as you can and get it over with.

"Go ahead, Matthew; I'll see you at the road." I nodded and smiled.

"Thanks, Dad!"

He went off with two of the crew still near; Mockingbird just a few hundred yards behind and Just Doug a little further back. I checked in with my body, weary but still strong enough. I settled into the zone, took one step at a time, absorbed entirely in the moment, and focused on picking my way down the trail. I loved when I could sense the road below. I listened for passing vehicles. As I drew close, the route became broader and more manageable. More people tread on the AT near the roads.

I stepped onto the road. I immediately noticed the soccer field across the street. Memories of coaching my kids flooded back. I loved soccer fields. But Riptide paced frantically up and down the road. He waved his hands around his head. Mosquitoes! Millions and millions of mosquitoes. Dr. Pickles handled the thick swarm a little better. The two battled the bugs for thirty minutes while waiting for Sandy. I looked down the road, and the Suburban headed our way; timing is everything in life. I grinned from ear to ear.

Plus, Sandy had Rock Steady and Paradox! So incredibly happy, I tried to contain my emotion and played it cool, but the delight in my eyes gave me away. I said calmly.

"Paradox. Rock Steady. Good to see you."

"Good to see you too, Right Click."

One glance from Paradox, I knew she was thrilled to be with us again. Riptide dove into the sanctuary of the truck. He listened to our animated and lively conversation as we waited a few minutes for Mockingbird and Just Doug. Soon we all crammed in and drove back to the campground.

McPackin and Mary were excited to see all of us too. He stayed behind with Mary while Sandy rounded up the entire crew. Earlier, he bought some new shoes, Merrell's like mine but low cut. His feet could breathe. Speaking rapidly, he happily babbled away.

"I was in the store with Mary, going back and forth between two pairs. One felt like slippers, and one felt they'd give me more support. Then Mary asked if I would rather walk in slippers or with more support. And I said, well… slippers, of course. Man, I tell you, these are comfortable! She was right. She made it so simple. Of course, I'd rather walk in slippers."

"I know. That's why I wear them. Great grip too. Comfortable right out of the box. They might not last as long as you'd like, but they have been good to me. How are your blisters?"

"They're better. I think I'll be able to go tomorrow. I can't wait to get back out there."

"Well, thank you for spending time with Mary. I'm sure she appreciated it. You're a good man."

With experienced eyes, Paradox and Rock Steady looked around the site and nodded their approval. This place worked beautifully. We sat around the picnic table. We feasted. We talked a lot. Once in a while, someone would break away and head to the showers; the atmosphere was relaxed and straightforward. We lived momentarily in perfect harmony, buoyed by our shared adventure. Sandy got caught up in it too. I was so thankful she could experience this with me.

Paradox and Rock Steady had just hiked our upcoming ten miles and talked about it. They said we would have an easy day. I could sure use it; my legs ached. Then a thought occurred to me.

"You know, if you stayed in camp for a day, we could catch up…."

224

I watched Paradox; she liked the idea. Then I looked at Rock Steady. She did not. Like before, I knew she had a plan with no chance of altering it. She confirmed the thought.

"Well, you could catch us if you do another big day."

She was due to meet her husband in the next few days; he had just returned from active duty in Korea. I didn't blame her. They would finish the hike together.

We openly discussed our options. We had just done nineteen point seven miles, and if we were to join them and finish the thru-hike together, we'd have to do another nineteen. Possible, except for one thing. Moosilauke. The ladies had hiked to the base of Moosilauke on the NH 25 trailhead. We had nearly ten miles from the mosquito-filled soccer field to that trailhead, and then we'd have to go up and over Moosilauke. I understood why a day in camp did not appeal to them, excitement about checking off another milestone, the first mountain in White Mountain National Park. The climb and descent in the AT Guide looked daunting. Rock Steady and Paradox assured us that the hike to NH 25 wasn't too hard, but Moosilauke worried us. McPackin, who had hiked it previously, affirmed the AT Guide, indeed a rugged trek.

Well past hiker midnight (dark), I felt my body shutting down. I wanted desperately to stay awake and extend my time with everyone, but I could not. The next day planned to have the ladies drop us off; then they'd drive to NH 25 and leave the Suburban there. We'd hike to NH 25, jump in the Suburban, go to Kinsman Notch, wait for them, and come back to Jacobs Brook for one more night.

That's what we did. Riptide sat this one out and stayed behind with Sandy and Mary. They wouldn't have a vehicle but seemed comfortable with a day of lounging by the pool, swimming, and reading. Sounded good to me too. Why didn't I stay? McPackin, back in the mix, received some attention from our trail family expert on blisters, Paradox. She reinforced the use of bag balm and gave him some tips on taping. Thru-hikers, through necessity, learn methods to handle hot spots and blisters.

The ladies' assessment proved correct; we cruised over those nine point eight miles. We got pretty good at knowing how little to carry for a day hike. McPackin loved his new Merrells, excited to be back with us, and I, too, thoroughly enjoyed his company. He talked about how the trail family had bonded, about how we loved and supported each other. I appreciated his insight. He expressed gratitude for having the opportunity to accompany us for eight days. We reached NH 25 by 2:30 in the afternoon and drove to Kinsman Notch to wait for the ladies. The drive on NH 112 frankly frightened me a bit. It's one thing to be on the trail dealing with one step at a

225

time; it's a different story to see the peaks from a road. Kinsman Notch, surrounded by steep, rocky cliffs, intimidated me. We pulled into the parking lot and collectively whispered.

"Damn."

I exhaled and calmed myself. I practiced some positive self-talk. I could do this. Maybe. We didn't wait long. The ladies popped out of the woods into the parking lot to our hugs and greetings. One glance at Paradox, eyes lit up, and I knew she loved the hike.

"How was it?"

"Hard. Beautiful, but hard."

For Paradox to say it was hard stoked my anxiety. Looking at the mountains around me, I swallowed. Paradox knew my thoughts and pushed me.

"Get in the car and drive. Let's go."

They were officially in the Whites. I would be the next day. It took nearly an hour to drive back to Jacobs Brook. We gathered around the table and laughed, told stories, and kidded each other well into the night. Tomorrow we would say goodbye, so we lingered and languished in the moment, making it stretch as long as possible.

In the morning, we assembled for a trail family picture, the last one together. We did not look our best, but to this day, I can look at each face and feel a deep connection with each one. My experience with my trail family taught me that love and relationship amplified when we gather as a community; a remarkable phenomenon.

Our old Suburban could only carry so many, so Riptide and Mary stayed behind while Sandy drove us to the two different trailheads. At the NH 25 trailhead, I said farewell to the ladies. In pain, Paradox embraced me and caught my eye. She whispered,

"Catch us. Please."

"Wait for us."

Reading her mind and both of us knowing that wouldn't happen, I promised.

"We'll try."

She jumped back in the truck, so I wouldn't see her cry. I loved that about her. Rock Steady encouraged us to catch them. We said we'd give it our best shot, but that was the last time we'd see each other. I didn't know that at the time. They drove away.

Time to tackle the task at hand. We had Moosilauke to conquer. I disregarded my self-doubt and the lingering notion that the Appalachian Trail was too big for me. Rock Steady and Paradox verified the AT Guide; Moosilauke had challenged them.

226

For the last five months, I heard stories about the legendary, notorious White Mountains. Commonly regarded as the most demanding section of the AT, we anticipated slow-going and difficult camping. Huts were a pain in the ass. And Mount Washington, the king of the Appalachian Trail, presided over the Presidential Range. Although higher in elevation, Clingman's Dome did not come close to the mystique of Mount Washington. No other mountain on the AT keeps a tally of people who have died. Doubts dominated my imagination. Could I physically (and mentally) do it?

But first, I needed to deal with the doubts about the mountain in front of me, Moosilauke. McPackin and I settled into the climb. The others spread out ahead and behind us. McPackin recognized my fear and helped alleviate them. I pushed them aside, and as recovery taught me, I focused on the present. I focused on the next step. The climb was not as rigorous as I anticipated; we reached the Moosilauke summit shrouded in clouds (zero visibility), high winds, and chilly temperatures. We posed for photos at the summit sign, then cowered behind some rocks to eat. Just Doug cooled down quickly, so he hustled off the mountain and headed down the trail to Kinsman Notch. The descent down Moosilauke scared the crap out of me. McPackin and I took time and picked our way down slick, smooth rocks. Exhausted, my legs shook from the strain. After a long slow descent, we hit the flat area at the bottom. I checked the Guthook app. McPackin asked how far. Much to my relief, I replied.

"Point four."

"Oh crap, OK."

"No. Point four (emphasis on point)." He didn't hear "point."

"Oh. Oh wow! I can do that!"

"Yes! We can!" I chuckled with relief. With a last burst of energy, we bustled down the flat trail into the Kinsman Notch parking lot. Sandy arrived several minutes later, her cheeks wet.

"What's the matter, honey?"

"This. This place. It's disorienting. I can't believe that (she waved her hand at the mountain) is what you're doing. Are you crazy?"

"I know. Right?" I wept a bit with her. We took the long drive back to Jacob's Brook. Quieter than usual, I knew our time together was ending—one last night in our temporary homestead. One last night in the Taj Mahal. One last night with Sandy, Matthew, and Mary. One last night with the family. I basked in their love and companionship. I soaked it all in. It would be the spiritual fuel I craved. I'd need it to finish this thing.

227

The following day, I said goodbye to Riptide and Little Click. I wouldn't see them again until I returned home to Manchester. So proud of Matthew, I told him he impressed me with his athleticism and attitude. Then I held Mary for a long time and openly cried. I knew I would miss them deeply. I also knew they were my biggest fans. They wanted me to finish. They told me this too. Mary's last words were,

"You can do this, Dad."

Matthew nodded in agreement.

We didn't have enough room in the Suburban with all of us and our full gear, so my two youngest children packed up camp while Sandy dropped us off. Sandy's cheeks glistened with tears as we approached the Kinsman Notch parking lot. I fought to keep my emotion in check. Hard for her, she took pictures in the parking lot. I heaved my heavy pack onto my back and found the weight oppressive. Combined with the burden of departure from my family, I could barely stand. Sandy and I hugged and kissed lightly in the cold misty rain. To top off the grim separation, the forecast called for steady rain.

"Goodbye, Sandy. I'll see you in Maine. It won't be too long."

With a long drive to Jacobs Brook, then longer drive home, she did not linger. She jumped in the driver's seat. I watched the Suburban drive away for the second time in a month. I stood in the rain, shivered a bit, and choked on emotion.

"Why am I doing this? Somebody tell me." It wasn't the first time I asked. I muttered bitterly. I faintly discerned an answer.

"Continue."

The craggy trail north of Kinsman Notch taxed my will. Although much lighter than when I started in Georgia, the heavy pack sapped my strength. The weather dampened my spirit too. The last couple of views of NH 112 heightened the homesickness that seethed inside me. Thank God McPackin walked with me. His chatter and enthusiasm distracted and engaged me. We made poor time along the rough trail. We were all spent when we reached the Eliza Brook Shelter, just seven and a half miles from the road. Stunned by how difficult that last stretch had been, I sat in the shelter out of the rain eating and looked at the AT guide; only four miles to the next shelter, but it included a climb over Kinsman Mountain. If we moved on, we'd do it in the rain. The longer we sat, the more noticeable we would not hike anymore this day. I sighed.

"No chance of catching the ladies now."

It didn't make any sense to continue in this weather. I settled in the shelter. I got out of wet clothes, put on dry ones, blew up my Thermarest, and nestled in my sleeping bag to warm up. I might set up my tent, but I wasn't sure if my new seam seal job would keep steady rain out, so I reluctantly decided on the shelter.

Later that evening, Queen Bee and Blister Babe arrived with a few other hikers, exhausted, wet, cold, and hungry after an impressive eighteen-mile hike. The most cheerful people I knew on the trail were not cheerful now; they were miserable, desperate to get out of wet clothes and put something warm in their bellies. The trail does that to people. Glimmers of good humor still surfaced through their considerable discomfort, to their credit.

The following day, the weather broke. We basked in warm sunshine on the challenging climb up Kinsman. On top, I texted the Boudreau's. We hoped to meet them in Franconia Notch, just nine miles away. But now I understood why everyone said you slow down in the Whites. These were long miles. It took an extraordinarily long time to go just one mile, sometimes more than an hour. The trail, ridiculously steep and rugged, offered stunning views. The rocks, the forest, the ponds, and the marshes demanded reverence. All the incredible photo opportunities contributed to the slow pace. Difficult going.

But magical.

Over the Guardrail

We stretched out in the Flume parking lot when the Boudreaus found us. Dear friends of ours, they shepherded the Valentines through some difficult times, most notably my bout with cancer in 2010. Al and Chris allowed us to load our stinky packs and smelly bodies in their van with grace and kindness. They took us to resupply and to a laundry. While we washed our clothes, we repackaged our food. Al helped me with genuine curiosity. Impressed with what I considered routine, Al saw mastery. He found grace and expertise in the economy of motion and something as simple as resupply. I agreed with him; I had become quite efficient.

Over dinner, we described our adventure. Fascinated and enthusiastic, they asked many questions. We eagerly answered them all, enthralled that anybody took such keen interest and delight in our trek. We started to look at places to stay for the evening. On a Saturday night, hotel rooms were scarce and expensive, we decided on a campground far from the trailhead. That presented a logistical problem of returning to the trailhead. Al and Chris said they'd get us the following day, but their little Bed and Breakfast was more than an hour away. As we drove up I-93, I opened the Guthook app and saw the road passed right over the trail. True enough, we had hiked under I-93 earlier in the day. I remembered seeing friendly stealth sites close to the road. As we drove further from the trail to head to a campground many miles away, I suggested that Al drop us off.

"Really? It's pitch dark outside."

"We know. We'll be fine. We know exactly where we are, and there's good camping close by."

"Are you sure? It's no problem. We'll come back and get you in the morning." Chris chimed in with care and concern in her voice.

"We know. And we appreciate it, but this will be easier for us too."

Al took the next exit and turned around. We monitored our position with Guthook. At the overpass, he slowed down, pulled over, and switched on the emergency flashers. Dr. Pickles and I jumped out, fished through our packs to find our headlamps, and went over the guardrail, down the embankment to the path by the stream.

We determined that, indeed, we passed this way earlier. Confident, Dr. Pickles strode down the trail a bit. We clamored back up the slope and let Mockingbird and Just Doug know we were good to go. Surprisingly, Just Doug was a bit hesitant. I cajoled him with a mischievous grin.

"What, jumping over a guardrail in the middle of the night isn't a good idea?"

"Um, not sure."

I could see the concern in Al and Chris. They felt like they shirked their duty by just dumping us on the side of a highway. McPackin, hitching a ride back to Connecticut with them, sealed the deal.

"They'll be OK. Trust me. They know what they're doing."

After hugs all around, I embraced McPackin and thanked him. He helped me through a tough stretch. His companionship stabilized me, supported me, and strengthened me. I'd draw on it for the stretch to come. Al lifted one eyebrow in doubt; then an admiring smile flashed across his face.

"Good luck, you Putz. I'm proud of you."

"I love you too. And thank you. Bye Chris, we'll be OK. I promise. I'll text you when we're settled."

He scooted into the van and drove away. Down to the final four, the crew stayed close as we navigated in the darkness. We found the trail, the road we had hiked earlier, and the site we remembered, a good place - flat on pine needles- next to a stream. Our tents went up quickly, even in the dark, a testament to our proficiency. Comfortable in my dwelling, I texted Chris to let them know we were settled, only twenty minutes after they "dumped" us. They were greatly relieved.

As I lay on my well-worn Thermarest pad, I thought about my friends and family who had helped along the way. Three more of them would be on their way back to Connecticut the next day. With no other support lined up, it would just be me, Dr. Pickles, Mockingbird, and Just Doug. My most valuable resources now would be my legs, attitude, wits, and debit card (as long as Sandy deposited funds in the account). Part of me mourned. Part of me harbored bitterness. Part of me spouted enthusiasm. Part of me curious to see how I would handle the challenge offered by New Hampshire and Maine. Part of me desperately wanted to finish. Part of me was thoroughly immersed in the adventure.

I missed McPackin and wondered what he thought of his time with us. I'd find out in an email message sent a few days later. Here it is, unedited.

Dear Right Click, Mockingbird, Dr. Pickles and Just Doug,

Thank you for so graciously admitting me into the "pack" for 10 days. I felt welcomed and included from the time Arno dropped me off until we hugged goodbye at the guardrail. I enjoyed every minute with the possible exception of the blister incident.

I learned a number of things (that will come later) but the #1 thing is that when anyone ever asks me what walking the AT is like I will unequivocally answer -

IT IS FREAKIN' HARD!

And I'm not just talking physically but emotionally, logistically, relationally, ethically. When a person is continually "red lining" on 3 or more of those categories for 1/2 year it builds and it demonstrates a strength that is not usual.

I just reread what I wrote and don't want to give other people who may read this the wrong idea that it is all bad and no rewards - the big pay off comes when a new day dawns and you climb out of your tent and pull on the same smelly wet clothes that you pulled off the night before, and the night before, and the night before. Man, it doesn't get any better.

I'm just joking. It is just that I'm not articulate enough to describe the loving bonds, thrill of accomplishment, laughs, shared hurts, vistas, friendships that last even when you don't see the person for several months and 1,000 miles.

It has probably occurred to you guys how the demands of the AT has sifted through hundreds of candidates to a unit of 4 whose strengths, abilities and personalities complement each other so precisely. If it hasn't, think about it.

A dozen things I learned as a 10-day thru-hiker:

- How much fun you have is inversely proportional to the weight of your pack.
- There are many really cool people thruhiking the AT.
- Walking sticks are good.
- Plans, strategies, tactics, no matter how good, are not as valuable as a highly functional team.
- Shoes are the most important piece of equipment.
- There are quite a few AT-holes.
- Backpacking technology has improved over the last 25 years.
- Socks are also important.
- It is better to risk being a little hungry for a day or so than to carry too much food.
- "Smiles not miles".
- It is possible for downhill to be harder than uphill.
- Loving and supportive family and friends are worth $1 million.

When you catch up with Paradox and Rock Steady say "hey" for me. They are really cool also.

Heaven knows I can't give you guys any advice but I leave you with this -

1. Pick 'em up and put 'em down . . .repeat . . .
2. Set 'em up and take 'em down . . . repeat . . .
3. Walk - replenish - walk . . . repeat . . .

And remember the repeats are finite and then this adventure is over. Have fun - there are people living vicariously through you.

Love,

McPackin

PS - Good news of great joy! When I was lifting my pack out of Boudreau's car it broke! And Christmas is coming.

The Whites

When we descended into Franconia Notch, I didn't realize I'd be on Franconia Ridge the next day. Why? I don't know. Maybe the formidable challenge of Mount Washington distracted me. Having lived in Connecticut my whole life, I learned about Franconia Ridge, only a few hours away, but had never ventured there. I knew from the AT Guide that eleven miles of trail rested above timberline, but I didn't prepare mentally. I'm glad I didn't.

232

I focused on one step at a time, hiking up the rough, rocky trail with Mockingbird. Suddenly, we magically stepped out from under the tree cover and stood above the timberline. I gasped audibly. The panorama blew my mind!

"Shut up, God! Are You serious right now!".

Mockingbird replied with awe.

"Oh my! This is amazing!"

"It is. We made it Mockingbird. We are officially in the Whites… Wow. Do you believe it? Is this even real?"

We fist bumped. Our pace slowed as we took in the view. Dr. Pickles perched up ahead on a rock, gazed at the three-hundred-sixty-degree view, almost delirious, definitively intoxicated with grandeur. Blessed with a beautiful, bright day, cumulus clouds flowed by at eye level, the setting mystical. The reliable iPhone got a workout. We took our time along the ridge. We rested at the Mount Lincoln and Mount Lafayette peaks. We sat for long periods and let nature wash over us, fill our souls and lighten our spirits. Yet, our mission called.

Continue, we must.

After scaling one more mountain, I arrived at the Garfield Ridge Shelter/Campsite. I checked in with the guy who oversaw the place and paid my eight bucks to stay. He took my debit card and wrote down the numbers. I found that weird. I worked through my anxiety. I listened to countless tales about camping in the Whites; most people described it as a pain in the ass. With no stealth sites available, designated shelters and campsites were the only options. I assessed the opportunities in the shelter, which was already a bit crowded. I found Dr. Pickles and Mockingbird setting up their free-standing tent on a large wooden platform. My tent needed to be staked, so the platform was not convenient for me, but I could make it work. After some deliberation, I returned to the shelter and staked my claim under the stairs to the loft. I blew up my Thermarest and laid out my sleeping bag, spot secured. I grabbed my food and went back up to the tent platforms. I joined my friends.

"Oh my!" I exclaimed when I rounded the corner.

Two wooden platforms lay adjacent to each other, and both were full. Dr. Pickles and Mockingbird claimed one corner. Just Doug wedged in behind them. Next to them, a section hiker with two young boys set up, all three tents on a platform designed for one. The section hiker hailed from Connecticut, a professor at a university (I forget which one). His boys didn't respond well to his parenting. A colossal tarp hung over the adjacent platform and housed twenty college students on a first-year orientation. Seriously?

233

We ate quietly together. Knowing each other so well, we sensed each other's feelings and discerned each other's thoughts. After bidding them good night, I dropped my food into the bear box. Usually, I slept with my food, but in a shelter stuffed with people, I thought this the prudent choice. I made my way back to the shelter, tiptoed through the sprawled bodies, slid into my slot, and tried to make myself small and invisible. One thing about shelters, though, is that peeing in the middle of the night sucks. I drank much water to fight off dehydration and keep myself lubed. To climb through all these bodies went against my habit of not disturbing anyone. I hated to do that. I discovered another advantage of sleeping in my tent away from everyone when it came to peeing at night: if too groggy or sore to climb out and find a tree, I unzipped my tent, rolled on my side, and peed out the door. I learned the hard way to position my tent, so the pee flowed away from the tent, not under it.

Don't think about it too long.

I shut out the fact that I was amidst a sea of bodies by reading Andre Agassi's book "Open" on my iPhone. Previously, I read "The Boys in the Boat." I focused my attention on his fascinating story. As darkness developed, the shelter grew quiet. I fell asleep to the tune of deep breathing and the occasional snore. Sure enough, I woke up in the wee morning hours with an urgent need to pee. Rolling on my side and peeing was not an option here; I found my headlamp, switched on the red light, struggled to my feet, and found my cold, wet boots (my yellow Crocs went home with Sandy), and made my way outside. Chilled by the night air, I hurried back inside, repeated the whole procedure in reverse, and snuggled in my bag, credulous at the incredible comfort. I quickly fell back asleep and was thankful I didn't seem to disturb anyone too badly.

When I met my trail family for breakfast, I sensed their anger. Uh oh. The two boys ran around on the platform until eleven without their father's correction. My friends, unfortunately, discovered that a wood platform transfers every movement from other people. This includes rolling over in a sleeping bag. My friends bounced in their bags when the kids ran on the platform. Then the boys chattered even longer into the night. Even after the kids went to sleep, the boys tossed and turned all night and jiggled them mercilessly. They told me this over breakfast. They looked haggard and irritated. Grateful for my shelter experience, I wondered about the dad. Why didn't he do anything?

We tackled the first section in cool, damp conditions. Coming down Garfield, super steep and slippery, I confronted long, flat wet rocks angled precipitously downwards, and my anxiety rose. Dr. Pickles sang. He loved this stuff. Soon he and

234

Mockingbird disappeared out of site. With Just Doug out in front of them, I dealt with my fear alone. I slid and skidded and swore my way down. The Garfield descent eroded any acquired confidence. One slip on this dangerous section, and I'd be seriously injured. I battled my anxiety. My mantra?

"One step at a time."

The crew waited for me at the bottom. They called up and encouraged me. I made it. We gave each other fist bumps as we congratulated each other for still being alive and unharmed. We learned later that three hikers fell badly on this stretch this morning; all three tore up a knee. One of the hikers, a German fellow named Hulk, because of his strength and power, could not continue. A terrible place to get hurt seriously, these three limped on damaged knees to the Galehead Hut a few miles away and faced an even longer hobble to the road.

The Galehead hut, an Appalachian Mountain Club (AMC) hut, allows thru-hikers to stay a night but with a requirement to work and usually only two thru-hikers per night. AMC huts charge one hundred and seventy-nine dollars a night for a bunk, including dinner and breakfast. Thru-hikers sleep on the floor in the dining room only after they have completed their kitchen work. In my opinion, the "work for stay" concept is a bad idea. Some of the AMC hut workers, usually young college students, treated the thru-hikers disrespectfully, like "hiker trash," with utter contempt and disrespect. Perhaps, the rare hiker earned this through an attitude of entitlement or arrogance, but the vast majority did not. The three injured hikers stayed in the Galehead Hut on the dining room floor, but still, the workers forced them to work. One woman peeled potatoes. Another washed dishes as he stood on a wrapped up, swollen, severely damaged knee.

Seemed cruel and heartless to me.

As I traveled through the Whites, my stress level peaked; many factors elevated my anxiety.

- Uncertainty about the hut system.
- The crowds at the shelter/campgrounds.
- The most rugged terrain on the trail so far.
- The potential for serious injury.
- The notorious weather on and around Mount Washington.
- Walking further and further away from home.
- Missing my family.

Yet, with the increased stress, I noticed other things had improved.

235

- My balance (I didn't know that was a thing you could improve).
- My stamina (amazing, especially uphill).
- My ability to confidently set up camp almost anywhere.
- The awareness of my surroundings.
- The bond with my fellow hikers. They'd always help me. I would always help them. No questions asked.

The trail toughened me physically, mentally, and spiritually. Yet, emotionally I was not tough; I'd use the word raw. Two primal emotions, love and fear, raged within. Every response on the trail to every situation emanated from either love or fear.

For example, when I climbed, I loved how my body responded. I loved the exertion, the challenge, and the reward. On the other extreme, I feared a debilitating fall when I descended. My body locked up, and I slowed way down.

"Uphill exert. Downhill hurt."

Dr. Pickles and Mockingbird danced along before me when we came upon the short side trail to the Galehead Hut. We veered off the AT with no spoken word between us. Other hikers milled about. We stepped inside, and an AMC hut worker offered up some leftover oatmeal, very kind and generous. Or maybe they needed to dispose of it? As we ate, we wondered why Just Doug didn't join us. Once he didn't show, we thought he must have gone by, so we set out determined to catch him. The rough trail hampered our effort, but we figured we'd find him sitting on a rock waiting. We never did. Maybe Just Doug believed we were in front of him, so he hiked furiously without any breaks.

After nine taxing miles, my conditioned body rebelled. In the early evening, we decided to look for a stealth site. Dr. Pickles, way faster and fitter than Mockingbird and I, surged ahead and looked for a campsite. We spotted his pack in the middle of the AT next to a stream. As we looked around, he materialized from the woods.

"Up here! I think you'll like this one!"

He found a beautiful rock and tree-lined clearing upstream a few hundred yards. A series of natural terraces formed beautiful pools. The site was tucked in on the opposite side, a fantastic find by Dr. Pickles.

"Wow, Pickles. How'd you find this? This is your best one yet."

"I know. Right? Mockingbird and I will go down here, and you can have this one near the water."

"Beautiful. Thank you! Are you sure?"

He smiled and nodded. We set up. The two went upstream a few pools and bathed in their own private pool. I left them alone. I washed up in the pool near me.

When they returned, I told them I ordered room service and would eat in my tent. They chuckled. Without cell service here, we couldn't get a message to Just Doug. We missed his company but knew he'd be okay, reasonably sure he'd eventually wait for us.

The following day we reached Crawford Notch around lunchtime in dismal weather – chilly, wet, foggy. The AT Guide indicated a rugged climb out of Crawford Notch, with the next available tent site still six miles away. We doubted there would be many opportunities to stealth camp in this terrain. We ran into Detox again in the parking lot, and camped directly under a "No Camping" sign. Detox told us he could not get not phone signal, even on the road. We couldn't either.

We sifted through our options. We considered where Just Doug might be. We decided to hitch down the road. Detox succeeded first and promised to send someone back for us. Yeah, OK.

We thumbed for an hour but got colder and wetter with very little traffic. Stuck. We thought about continuing to hike north when a shuttle from the AMC Highland Center showed up. I talked with the driver.

"Can you give us a ride?" I pleaded.

"I'm not allowed to pick up thru-hikers unless you pay."

"I understand. We'll pay." I agreed. I'd pay for all of us. I didn't care. Just please get us out of this weather. Then he looked at the three of us shivering.

"Ahhh. Get in. I'm not going to charge you. I thru-hiked once too."

He brought us to the AMC Highland Center. In the lobby, we eyed other hikers and Detox.

"I was working on getting you a ride." Detox responded guiltily.

"Uh-huh."

We inquired about a room. Wildly expensive. And for once, I felt really out of place. Most people milling about wore high-end logos on fresh, crisp clothing. We hung around, absorbed disapproving glances, got warm, and discussed options. A young woman working on a laptop overheard our conversation.

"I'll give you a ride down to the Lodge at Bretton Woods in a few minutes."

With cell service, Mockingbird plied her magic and found a room at the Lodge. On the way over, our kind driver told us about the injuries coming down Garfield (mentioned previously); she worked at one of the AMC huts. Situated directly across the road from the Omni at Mount Washington, we checked in and shared a room, no longer awkward. We cleaned up, walked over to a nearby restaurant, and devoured a mountain of nachos and then our meals; the waitress was partly in awe, somewhat

237

horrified. The three of us smiled as we exchanged knowing looks; we could have consumed much more.

Just a few miles away from the notch, the weather improved. We walked over to the Omni and roamed through the lobby and shops. I looked out over the golf course. I didn't think I'd be hitting a golf ball soon. This place reminded me of The Shining; old, huge and beautifully maintained. I took some fantastic photos of Mount Washington shrouded in clouds. I visibly shook off an ominous feeling as I gazed at it, fear lurking just below the surface. We left messages for Just Doug with no response. We were not alarmed.

After we took full advantage of the Lodge's complimentary breakfast, we finagled a ride back to Crawford Notch. A much better day; we enjoyed the views on the challenging climb out. As evening approached (and evening arrived earlier each day), we arrived at a side trail to a campground where we could pay eight dollars to sleep on a crowded platform. Nope. We continued north and looked for a stealth site. We approached the tree line, and our options quickly diminished. We ended up (after some serious scouting) on the rocky, lumpy ground covered in this mossy, sponge-like material. Blister Babe called it "nature's memory foam." Technically, I don't think we were supposed to camp on it, but we staked our tents with limited options. Dr. Pickles even went north for several tenths and didn't find anything but rocks. After hiking most of the day and managing only eight miles, we ate dinner overlooking a spectacular view of the Omni. The hiking lived up to the Whites hype, hard.

Wicked Washington

My tent, set up on a crack between moss-covered rocks, boasted an outrageously lumpy floor. I managed to wedge my skinny butt into a somewhat comfortable position to get some rest. When I stuck my head out of the tent in the morning, I gasped. We were above the clouds, and the freshening breeze moved the clouds up and over mountain ridges on both sides. On the west side, the sun rose behind and lit up the tops of the clouds. They shone brilliantly white as they drifted up the ridge toward the warmth and light.

"Oh my God! Pickles. Mockingbird. You've got to see this!"

Unlike me to wake someone, they mumbled something. As I took photos and videos, they crawled out. They did not sleep well. They kept sliding onto each other on the slanted surface. But when they saw what nature created, the poor night's sleep retreated from their thoughts. We took our time as we packed and ate. Every so often, one of us would proclaim.

238

"Wow. This is so beautiful. Can you believe we are here?"

With nothing else to say, we looked at each other, smiled, and shook our heads.

But today, my emotional quotient consisted mainly of anticipation and anxiety. Today I headed over the top of Mount Washington, home to the world's worst weather. The early morning trail wandered above the tree line along a ridge. Fairly windy, I hiked in two shirts, one short sleeve, and one long sleeve. The clouds raced up the mountain from my left. I kept a good pace to keep myself warm. Far down the mountain, I noticed the Cog railway fire up with a plume of thick, dark smoke as it chugged along slowly. Soon, we reached the famous Lake of the Clouds hut, stepped inside, used the facilities, and ate a little snack. On our way out, I stopped at the infamous sign and took a picture.

<u>STOP</u>
THE AREA AHEAD HAS THE WORST WEATHER IN AMERICA. MANY HAVE DIED THERE FROM EXPOSURE, EVEN IN THE SUMMER. TURN BACK NOW IF THE WEATHER IS BAD. **WHITE MOUNTAIN NATIONAL FOREST.**

Was the weather bad? I asked myself. Windy, the sun shone; I thought the temperature suitable to attempt a summit. But what did I know? As we climbed away from the Lake of the Clouds hut, we looked back and took a few pics of it bathed in sunshine. Low clouds scuttled a few feet above the hut. I looked up the trail; we headed into a mist. I didn't fully understand the significance. Just over a mile to the summit, Dr. Pickles took the lead. Again, Mockingbird and I paced at a similar rate. The visibility decreased. We could barely see thirty yards, so she and I stuck close to each other and focused on the trail. Before long, we came to a building adorned with satellite dishes.

"We're here already? That wasn't so hard." She affirmed with excitement.

"Right?" We walked onto the pavement but still couldn't see very far. After we scouted around a bit, we finally found Dr. Pickles near the Tip-Top House; that didn't look like where we wanted to go. We found the Sherman Adams Visitor Center through the thick fog and went inside. We discovered a room downstairs for thru-hikers to separate the stinky from the clean. We shrugged off our packs, left our trekking poles, and explored the cafeteria. I devoured two hot dogs, a bowl of chili, and a coke. I watched tourists from the Cog railway flow in and out. Others drove up presumably to justify their "THIS CAR CLIMBED MOUNT WASHINGTON" bumper sticker. I thought about the irony; I had hiked more than one thousand eight hundred and fifty miles, and they hopped in their car, paid twenty-eight dollars a person, and arrived at the same destination. No one could see anything but gray out the windows; Mount Washington was completely socked in, as it is most days of the year.

After I ate, we made our way back to the hiker room. Queen Bee, Blister Babe, and three other women thru-hikers clamored in from the trail. They talked about emerging lousy weather. Again, that didn't completely register with me for some reason, thinking about what we just traveled through. I took obligatory pics at the Mount Washington summit sign, elevation six thousand two hundred and eighty-eight feet, and we headed off the mountain.

Shortly, we heard the Cog railway go by only about ten yards away but couldn't see through the thick fog. The "tradition" of thru-hikers mooning the people on the train wouldn't happen from anyone in our crew; too modest, too cold, and foggy. The wind and cloud drizzle chilled me. I fished my Marmot Precip jacket out, put that on, and tied down the hood. We crossed the Cog railway and continued. I paid careful attention to the trail now marked by cairns (piles of rocks). Several side trails ran through this area. Cairns, too, distinguished them.

The wind gradually picked up even more; the visibility was still bad. The temperature dropped. We neared Mount Jefferson and the trail toughened. The deep spaces between rocks, slick with moisture, beckoned menacingly. One slip, I could easily break a leg, blow out a knee, or worse. The going became painstakingly slow. It took more than two hours to go two miles, with more than three miles between the Madison Hut and us. We came to a crossroads, and a sign, secured by piling rocks around it, didn't map out our path too well, the fog cloaking the next cairn from our vision. We chose to go to the left directly into the teeth of the wind.

We chose wrong.

I noticed the smaller cairns but didn't think much of them at the time. We tried to navigate on what proved to be a hostile moonscape. A cold rain smacked directly into our faces about three-tenths after we made the turn. After four-tenths, we realized we might be headed in the wrong direction. We encountered a middle-aged male day-hiker descending Mount Jefferson, visibly rattled, cold, and eager to get down. He wore nothing but shorts and a tank top.

"It was sunny and warm down at the bottom when I started."

"Yeah, we know. Hey, do you know if this is the AT?"

"The what?"

"AT. Appalachian Trail?"

"I'm not sure, but I don't think so. Good luck. I *have* to get back to my car."

240

He headed off down the trail. Dr. Pickles and Mockingbird sheltered me while I pulled out my iPhone and tried to get my wet, frozen fingers to work. The Otter Box protection made it nearly impossible for the touch screen to function correctly. After much swearing and praying, I got the Guthook app open, and indeed we were about four-tenths of a mile off the trail. The trail beckoned back in the direction we had come. We briefly discussed the option of finding a "shortcut" but dismissed that and correctly decided to go back to the crossroad and continue from there. The severe wind and ice-cold rain tested our resolve and ravished our morale. With our heads down, we climbed back up. Looking desperately for a silver lining, at least the wind now pushed us along.

Going the wrong way over a rugged terrain under challenging conditions discouraged me. When we finally arrived back at the point of our mistake, we theorized the sign must have spun in the wind. The fog was not quite as thick, so we detected the next AT cairn, a large one, and I wondered how we missed that. Was the fog that thick? Our calculations showed we still had three miles to the Madison Hut.

The wind now severely hampered us. I've been in some high wind before, which was well over fifty miles per hour with gusts much higher. Seventy? Eighty? Or more? Let's put it this way. When I lifted my foot, the wind caught my boot, and I'd misstep. I frequently fell, unusual for me. I usually moved too slowly to fall. My legs got scraped and banged up. The wind blew my trekking poles too. Placing them correctly became tedious.

The wind chilled me more and threatened hypothermia. I ducked behind a rock, took off my pack, and pulled everything out to get my down puff coat. I got that on; no more clothing left. Unfortunately, with no pants of any kind, I hiked in shorts, a short sleeve t-shirt, a long sleeve shirt, a down puff coat, and a hooded rain jacket. As I shouldered my pack and watched Dr. Pickles and Mockingbird combat the wind up ahead, I thought about my next option. I still had shelter. Whether my tent would hold up in this wind, I did not know. How would I get stakes in this ground? But I did have my down sleeping bag, so I still had survival options. My best option was to forge ahead.

So I did. I fought the wind, wet and cold. I picked my way across the rocks. Things got highly disconcerting to me when my eyesight failed. Severe double vision kicked in and made walking more than problematic. I fell more often. At the time, I thought the low light, the anxiety, the stress, the exertion, and maybe some dehydration exacerbated the double vision. However, I would experience this from time to time for the rest of the trip. Even as I spent the following five years writing this account, I've had bouts of double vision. Doctors still haven't figured out what causes it. On Mount Washington, my eyesight hindered my ability to navigate safely.

On one fall, my feet skidded down an angled, slick rock; I fell on my back cushioned by my pack, but my shin banged hard into another rock. I lay there stunned. I closed my eyes to try to shake the double vision.

"Right Click? Right Click? Are you all right?"

I opened my eyes, and Dr. Pickles stood over me, concerned. Actually, two Pickles. I covered one eye with my hand.

"You know Pickles. It occurs to me that if I don't get up and keep going, I could die right here."

Said with a wry smile; my morbid sense of humor kicked in. Pickles saw my smile and smiled back.

"Very funny."

But I could tell he didn't think it was all that funny, yet he agreed with my assessment. He offered me his hand, helped me up, and we kept on. We inched our way toward the Madison Hut shelter. I hiked with one eye closed. That helped a little. Other hikers passed us. Detox, determined to get to the hut to be one of the "work for stay" hikers, flew by us. Given my current condition, the "work-for-stay" option appealed to me, but I didn't have any chance of beating other hikers to the hut, another reason I'm not a fan of the system.

Eventually, I noticed the rocks formed a much more level path. Indeed, humans had placed them, an encouraging sign. The trail became easier to navigate. Eventually, the Madison Hut came into view. It took me more than six hours to go five AT miles (plus an additional eight-tenths). Oddly, I felt nothing. No emotion. Nothing. I took my pack off outside, propped my trekking poles up on the side of the building, walked into the warmth, and sat down on a bench at a table. I barely noticed the other people around. Pickles and Mockingbird sat down.

"Right Click? Right Click? Are you OK?"

I couldn't speak. Or I didn't want to. I couldn't tell the difference. I just nodded my head yes. Mockingbird looked very worried. She thought I might be in shock. I felt catatonic, not knowing what that feels like; it might have been shock. Mockingbird advised.

"Eat something."

I nodded again. I stood up and went to the coffee table. I got some hot water and instant coffee and mixed a thick, very thick brew. I ate a couple of Pop-Tarts. I felt parts of me revive. It occurred to me that I needed to get out of my wet clothes, warm up and lie down. I approached the girl behind the counter.

242

"Are there any work-for-stay options?"

"No!" She barked.

"How much is a bunk?"

"Are you a member?" She responded snottily.

I thought, "Are you giving me an attitude now? Today? Really?" Instead, I replied calmly. "Um no.".

"One hundred and seventy-nine dollars."

I thought the price reasonable given the intense fatigue I felt. Ready to dig out my credit card, Pickles and Mockingbird stepped in. "Where is the nearest campsite?"

Again, with attitude, she responded. "Half a mile."

"Right Click, come on. We can make it. You don't want to spend that much money for one night."

"I do. And it comes with dinner and breakfast." I replied meekly, still strangely unemotional, even about the uber rude employee. They talked me into putting my pack back on. We headed down a side trail to the campsite. Our wonderful host at the AMC Madison Hut neglected to tell us the camp was a half-mile straight down a cliff. As we dove below the tree line, the temperature rose, and the cloud cover dissipated. Even in much better conditions, it took me forty-five minutes to go half a mile and find the designated camping area.

We scoured the area, but no unoccupied sites were left.

My friends squeezed into one remaining space. I intruded on a guy in a hammock and asked if he minded if I shared a corner of his site. To his credit, he warmly welcomed me. Robotically, I went through my setup routine and told him briefly about my day. I crawled in, blew up my air mattress, stripped off my wet things, slid on my camp clothes, and nestled in my bag. I ordered room service again. No getting out and socializing. After I ate a few selected things from my food bag, I called Sandy, grateful for the cell service here.

Her voice, her love revived me, precisely what I needed. I soft sold the dangerous crossing; no need for her to worry more than usual. Dr. Pickles and Mockingbird checked in with me one last time. Exhausted, too, they wanted to sleep, but they made sure I was OK before they did. Moved by their concern, tears streamed down my cheeks. After they left, I made some small talk with my kind neighbor through my tent walls. He tried to get a smoky alcohol stove going with the wrong fuel. While he relayed his struggles, I welcomed the smoky smell, with people again and off that damn mountain. I reflected on how conditions changed so quickly and dramatically on the trail.

"This too shall pass," I whispered loudly, drawing comfort from the well-worn recovery slogan. Soon, darkness came. Soon, I slept; safe, secure, snug, and warm. What a difference a few hours made.

The following day, the weather improved. Under bright blue skies and no wind, I climbed that damn cliff up to the Madison Hut and the AT. When I started walking, I offered a prayer of gratitude. I thanked Him for another day. I thanked Him for being alive. I talked with Dr. Pickles

"What a difference a day makes." He replied with his usual enthusiasm. He encouraged me.

"It sure does. It's beautiful today!"

"Pickles?"

"What?" My eyes teared up; the words croaked forth.

"Thank you." He searched my eyes. He understood.

"You're welcome." He replied with genuine compassion. We moved on. I tried my best not to dwell on yesterday. I thought.

"Focus on this day, Right Click. One day at a time."

I pulled out recovery slogans all through the Whites. Our plan for this day was to hike to Pinkham Notch, catch a ride into Gorham, NH and meet up with Just Doug. Motivated, I climbed for another half mile. Then I assessed the next section of the trail.

A dreadful trail, my anxiety rose as I surveyed a long, rocky, steep descent. My courage wafted away like a balloon. I stopped and took pictures, biding some time before I tackled this treachery. Clouds no longer covered the summit of Mount Washington; she taunted me. I looked for gratitude; Mother Nature provided a picture-perfect day to get out of this place.

Dr. Pickles and Mockingbird loved the challenge of this intimidating descent and took off, leaving me to deal with my anxiety alone. I watched them move from rock to rock effortlessly and gracefully. Dr. Pickles bounced like Tigger all the way down. I related to Eeyore.

Yesterday shook my confidence. Fear ran rampant and crippled me. Long steps I previously made confidently, I now took with hesitation. I didn't want to fall. I slowed way down. I sat down on my butt more than ever and slid down rocks. I picked my route carefully. My strong legs trembled. My acute balance wavered. The previous day's trauma debilitated me. I crept along. Dr. Pickles and Mockingbird moved way ahead, but I could still see them. I could see for miles, and the path went down the ridge. Other hikers passed me. Gradually, my nerves settled. I didn't worry

244

about keeping up. It would take what it would take. I whispered another damn recovery slogan.

"Easy does it… But do it."

As I relaxed, my movements became less rigid and more confident. I began to enjoy the stunning views. I took some more pics and moved at my own pace. And that was key – to move at my own pace. I looked over at Mount Washington and took pics of the auto road and the clear summit. I took several pics of the ridge I just descended.

Once my descent finished, I settled into "normal" hiking. This section hosted a lot of other people, mostly day hikers. I crossed the auto road and glanced to my right after a few hundred yards. A peaceful, magnificent moose stood motionless. She chewed on some leaves and branches. Mesmerized, more movement drew my attention. Her calf! No one else came by; I was the only one to see them.

"Thank you, God, for blessing me."

I took a short video of the calf. My spirits lifted. When I emerged from the woods into the Pinkham Notch Visitor Center and saw many hikers stretched out in the sun, I felt relief, reprieve, and gratitude. My friends were there, shoes off, glad to see me, and appropriately envious when I told them of my moose encounter. The place bustled with activity. Cars, trucks, and buses flooded into the lot. People streamed into the buildings. Thru-hikers held court with tourists and day hikers who celebrated our hike.

"You came from where? How far is that? How long did that take you? Did you start by yourself?"

I quietly went inside. I didn't feel much like talking. I bought myself a Coke, looked at the scale model of the mountains, and traced the Appalachian Trail with my fingertip. I impressed myself. I did that. Look at that. I found a restroom, washed my hands, and splashed water on my face. I savored that small luxury. Outside, we talked about getting into Gorham and finding Just Doug, where he reserved a room for us. We hitched a ride and disembarked at the Northern Peaks Motor Inn. Just Doug waited. He arrived yesterday, so he would take a zero to be with us.

We quickly figured out what happened and where he missed us. He hiked some significant miles on his own. He also had two nights in two AMC huts as a work-for-stay guy. He cleaned dishes once and an oven another time but got to sleep on the floor. He enjoyed it. After showers, we ate in a restaurant. I loved restaurants. Sitting at a table and having someone bring you food and drink was a remarkable and incredible event—all in exchange for a little plastic rectangle with numbers. Or give them a few pieces of inked paper with numbers. Miraculous!

Later, Dr. Pickles did our laundry. He consistently helped in this way, a lot more gracious than I. We also resupplied. Dr. Pickles and Mockingbird slept in one double bed, I slept in another, and Just Doug slept on the floor.

He preferred it that way.

Wildcat Meltdown

After a huge breakfast, we rode back to Pinkham Notch. With full packs, we tackled the beastly climb out. The last couple of days left me in a fragile emotional state. Tentative and unsure about my hiking ability, I poured over the AT Guide and fretted over the elevation changes that looked like an EKG– up and down, up and down. The ups didn't worry me; the downs did, some of them viciously steep.

After a grueling climb, I reached the first Wildcat Mountain summit, grateful I didn't have to go down what I just came up, but I knew I'd have to go down something similar. I could feel myself losing my nerve. Fear forced its way in. I was walking along the ridge for a few minutes when small buildings and an open area came into view. Signs told me I reached the gondola up Wildcat D. The first of our crew to arrive; I checked out Mount Washington; another perfect, cloudless day for the folks on top of it. I shook my head. I watched some people walk off the gondola and admire the view. A great spot to rest, I unshouldered my pack, found my phone, and checked for a signal, four bars. I called my mom on August 29th, her eighty-first birthday. She answered, and I heard my sister Shelly in the background. Before I knew what happened, my pent-up emotion bubbled out. I described the rugged terrain and that maybe the trail was too big for me. The steeps were too steep, the downhills too treacherous. With only three hundred and twenty miles left, a severe dose of fear and doubt riddled my soul. Mom just listened, but I knew she was worried. Finally, I said I'd be okay. I wished her a happy birthday. I ended the call.

Happy birthday, mom, while your fifty-five-year-old son freaks out on a mountain in New Hampshire.

I stood on Wildcat, holding the phone when the solution became glaringly apparent. Unprepared for a powerful onslaught of emotion, I rode the wave without thinking.

Home!

Yes! That was the answer. From where I stood, I could see the bottom of Wildcat, the parking lot, and the road home. The teeming emotional flood produced sobs, not just a few tears trickling down my cheeks, but full-out bawls emanating deep within, physically and spiritually. I dropped to my knees to stem the tide. People glanced my way, concerned. But I didn't care; I couldn't do this any longer.

I needed a ride. I called Sandy.

"Hello, honey." She heard nothing but sobs.

"What's wrong?"

"I'm done. Please come get me."

"Are you hurt?"

"No."

"Umm… I'm in line at BJ's. Can I call you back? In ten minutes?" The phone went dead.

Wait. What? The shock of it snapped me out of my hissy fit. The sobs subsided, but tears stained my cheeks. Meanwhile, more families rode up the gondola and stepped off with trays of food - hot dogs, hamburgers, and French fries. Damn. The crew gathered at a picnic table, but I couldn't talk with them now. I retreated to a shady spot. Sensing the gravity of my despair, they gave me space. Soon, they suited up and prepared to leave. Before they left, they stopped to check-in.

"I'm pretty sure I'm done."

They didn't know what to say. I started to cry again. I didn't want them to see me like this. I told them just to go. They hoped they would see me again. I stifled back more sobs as I watched them head north. I put them in an impossible situation. They wanted to see me continue, yet if they thought they were the reason I reluctantly decided to keep hiking and then I fell down a steep, they'd feel responsible.

Feeling awful, I rummaged through my food bag and found the best thing. I grabbed a strawberry Carnation Instant, usually reserved for special occasions. I poured in some water and started dropping in strawberry Frosted Mini-Wheats, suitable for my last meal on this damn trail. I waited for Sandy to call. She did. I cried harder as soon as I heard her voice.

"Come pick me up. I'll take the gondola down and wait for you in the parking lot. Please?"

"How do you think you'll feel a few months later? Won't you feel bad about quitting so close?"

"No. 1,869 miles sounds pretty damn good to me. It's a lot further than anyone thought I'd go."

"OK." Then she asked me a question that only someone who truly loved me would ask.

"Do you think God is calling you to leave the trail now?" That took my breath away. Damn. I searched inside for that intuitive recognition I relied on. I could not lie. "I don't."

"As much as I want you to be home, I don't feel it's your time either."

I searched again for God's whisper, still discernible; I sensed it more than heard it.

"Continue." Offered gently, kindly, lovingly. I felt God's encouragement. "Trust me."

I lost emotional control again. But this time, I started to cry for another reason. Sandy cried too. We came up with a short-term strategy. I thought I could walk for a few more hours. I'd check in with her later. There would always be another road where I could quit. I put Sandy on official standby status. Exhausted yet somewhat emotionally stable, I ended our call.

Resolved to my fate, I lifted my pack on my shoulders and cinched tight the waistband. Before I set out, though, I sought more motivation. I fished out my earbuds, plugged into my iPhone, clicked on my Praise Trail Mix, and hit shuffle, more than six hundred songs of praise music. The very first song I heard was? Matt Redman's "Never Once." These lyrics thundered in my spirit as I set off down the trail.

Standing on this mountaintop,
Looking just how far we've come.
Knowing that for every step
You were with us.

"Seriously God? Seriously?" I am now talking to no one.

Kneeling on this battleground
Seeing just how much You've done.
Knowing every victory
Your power in us.
Scars and struggles on the way, but with joy, our hearts can say...Yes, our hearts can say...
Never once did we ever walk alone,
Never once did You ever leave us on our own.
You are faithful.
God, You are faithful.

I felt His presence. Powerfully. I started to relax as a peace that surpassed

248

understanding began alleviating my fear. As the song subsided, I spoke aloud.

"OK, God. That was pretty cool." The next song (out of more than six hundred) started; "Abide With Me" by Matt Redman. Here are the words.

I have a home, eternal home, but for now I walk this broken world.

"Why yes. Yes, I do."

You walked it first.
You know our pain, but You show hope can rise again from the grave.
Abide with me.
Abide with me.

This is where it got real...

Don't let me fall.
And don't let go.
Walk with me and never leave.
God, abide with me.

I listened, dumbstruck. Don't let me fall? Don't let go? I pointed my trekking poles at the sky and bellowed.

"YOU'RE BEING RIDICULOUS RIGHT NOW!"

I'm not saying whether or not I threw an F-bomb at God right then and there, but I might have. I don't recall. But now I cried. I smiled. I laughed all at the same time; too good, too wonderful for me to fully comprehend. I willingly accepted His love and His grace. But fear still lingered. Fear lost a lot of its grip, but it still held on by a fingertip; only a matter of time before I had to come down off Wildcat. I knew it would be stupidly steep. I'd have to face my fear right away.

I saw it coming; the light ahead was blue through the trees. Once there, I looked down at a fifty-foot cliff masquerading as a trail, but with no panic or fear. I shrugged with resignation. I looked up and challenged Him.

"OK, God, now what?"

He responded. "Turn around."

249

I vocalized loudly. "What? Screw that. I'm not turning around. I'm NOT going south!"

The calm, loving voice persisted. "Turn around."

"NO!" One more time with divine patience.

"Turn around." I paused. I contemplated. "Oh… Ohhhhhhhhhhh!"

I understood. I chucked my trekking poles down to the bottom. Then I *turned around* and faced the rock face. I used both hands and feet and went down using the same scramble technique I used to go up. I have long legs for a reason. It worked. I felt more solid, more secure. Screw style points. From that point forward, I would negotiate severe steeps the same way. I gathered my trekking poles and negotiated the rest of that descent with no anxiety.

At the very bottom, I rested and meditated at a beautiful pond with sheer rock walls on one side. The late afternoon light danced on the water and drew my attention. The surface was a perfect mirror to see clouds reflected on the pond. I felt some blessed assurance sitting there. After several minutes, I checked the AT Guide. I faced a mile climb up Carter Dome. I didn't know where my friends had stopped, but I knew I liked to camp in high places, so I decided to take the long trudge up. After an hour of climbing, I reached the top just below the tree line and stepped into a clearing. Just Doug sat there next to his tent. He fiddled with his stove as he prepared dinner.

"Hey, Right Click. I heard someone coming up the trail. I hoped it was you. Glad you could make it." His voice was calm, the sentiment genuine.

"Me too." He said Dr. Pickles and Mockingbird set up fifty yards down the trail.

"Dr. Pickles found you a place. Through there." He pointed.

"Really? Wow. Thank you."

My favorite trail couple came down and greeted me warmly. "I'm sorry. I just…" And the emotion welled up again; I couldn't speak and only cried.

"Go set up. Good to see you. We wondered if we would."

Hidden off the trail, this spot neared perfection, nestled in scrub pines, flat, soft, and cozy. It fit my tent perfectly. How did he find this? After setting up, I joined Just Doug to have some food. Comforted by his presence, we didn't need to talk much. We communicated in other ways that are hard to explain. I bid him good night and settled into my luxury suite. My phone vibrated with a text from my son Joshua (who obviously talked with Sandy).

If your own strength is failing you that is when you need to rely on God to carry you through the rest.

250

"Joshua, I think I'll need Him the rest of the way… big time."

On a crisp night, a fresh pine scent enveloped me. I listened to the sounds of the forest. After this physically grueling and emotionally exhausting seven-mile day, I would sleep well. I called Sandy. I thanked her for coaching me through the crisis. Even though I missed her desperately, I let her know I could continue for one more day. We cried together.

I was so tired.

Over the next few days, the crew never mentioned my meltdown on Wildcat. We covered many brilliant miles over rugged New Hampshire terrain. The classic New England hiking transported me along mystical forests, precipitous climbs, bogs covered by artificial boardwalks, and treacherous descents. We often stopped because of all the photo opportunities at astounding scenic overlooks.

Accustomed to trail life, the days flowed by. I loved the simplicity. I felt connected to nature and, therefore, to God. Surrounded by unfathomable beauty, I moved confidently up and over mountains. The deep woods healed my soul; maybe healed isn't the right word. If I think of the soul as energy, my soul recharged, reenergized. Like an iPhone battery, I started the trail with my internal battery down to ten percent (in the red). My battery surged into the green zone in the New Hampshire woods, above the ninety-percentile line. At peace, the fear subsided. Confidence resurrected. I lived in the moment.

Until I thought of my family, my soul wanted to be there too; but the love motivated me to finish.

On one of the peaks, I turned on my phone. A message from my AA sponsor Rick P. awaited. He did not coddle me (that may be putting it mildly). I listened.

"Hey. I hear you may be having some difficulty, thinking about quitting. My wife saw it on Facebook. Listen. You have two noble options left. Finish this thing or die trying."

The message ended. No good-bye. No nothing.

Another man might have been angry. Another man might have been hurt. Another man never would have let her go. I stuffed the bill in my shirt.

Not me. I smiled, encouraged. Rick lovingly kicked me in the ass when I needed it. As I hiked over the last few miles in New Hampshire, I agreed with him.

"I'm going to finish this thing. Or I am going to die trying."

The only two *noble* options.

SEPTEMBER

Maine

On September 1st, I crossed the New Hampshire/Maine state line. The milestone exhilarated me; thirteen states down, one to go. The night before the state crossing, we staged at Full Goose Shelter. Several other thru-hikers, including Blister Babe, Queen Bee, and a crew of women, overnighted there. The talk focused on Mahoosuc Notch – the trail's toughest (or most fun) mile loomed ahead.

I read about the Notch for the last few years. I held a vision of it in my head. I imagined a climb up and through huge boulders. I wondered about my capability. I harbored some concern about getting hurt, but mostly, eager to see it, hike it, put it behind me, and keep on. I wanted fiercely to finish this hike; Mahoosuc Notch was just a major obstacle in my way.

When I saw the beginning, it was nothing like I imagined. Cliffs on either side formed the notch, the bottom filled with massive boulders. The trail wormed its way through. I must admit I enjoyed crawling through holes and tiptoeing along some edges. Some of the deeper places held snow from previous winters. I embraced the opportunity and enjoyed the challenge. I hiked with Dr. Pickles, lit up like a Christmas tree. He likened this section to a wonderful obstacle course. He loved it! But instead of flying through it, he stayed back and helped the rest of us through. We rested at the end of the Notch. The trail veered left and severely upward.

"I'd like to go back and do that again." Dr. Pickles said.

"Seriously?"

"Yeah. I want to see how fast I can do it."

"What? Not me; I'm glad to have it behind me."

I admired his athleticism and his adventuresome spirit. He didn't go back, however. We still faced a rigorous hike. We headed up Mahoosuc Arm. I knew nothing about Mahoosuc Arm. Indeed, no one talked about it. They should have. We climbed straight up the notch, a crazy challenging mile-long ascent. I got to the top first, wholly gassed, and waited for the others. As I greeted each one, the looks exchanged brimmed with satisfaction and confidence. We understood each other.

We finished our day's hike at Grafton Notch, ME 26; our goal for the day just under ten miles, but a punishing ten miles. The AT Guide told us that cell phone reception did not exist here. We wanted to get into town. Bethel looked good. How

252

would we get a ride? Dr. Pickles talked a young college student into helping us out. More than glad to bring us, he ended a few-day expedition into the mountains of Maine and arrived at the parking lot at the same time we did. We piled into his old car. I trusted his youth and confidence while he handled a splashy suspension and loose steering. He dropped us off at the Chapman Inn and continued down the road.

Just Doug and I checked into one room; Dr. Pickles and Mockingbird another. We took a zero the next day as a line of thunderstorms moved through. It would be our last zero. It would be my only zero in the final fifty-eight days after leaving Connecticut. We did all our usual chores (laundry, resupply) and waited for a shuttle the following day.

The guy who picked us up worked for a campground. He drove the shuttle to pay for a slot for his camper. Retired, he and his wife lived year-round in their RV. They moved from site to site across the country. At times he picked up odd jobs to defray costs and keep himself busy. Intrigued by his lifestyle, I asked him many questions on our way back to the trailhead.

Beast Mode

Finally, I felt and looked like the consummate thru-hiker. My Merrell boots, nearly worn out again, fit my feet perfectly. I wore high Darn Tough full cushions socks. I prevented debris from getting in my boots with Dirty Girl gaiters (Urban Struggle blue camo). Hiking shorts with a mesh inside eliminated the need for underwear. A blue Under Armour dry-fit t-shirt showed permanent stains. My once jet-black CCAR Nike golf hat had faded to light gray. I threw on a long sleeve black Nike dry-fit shirt in chilly conditions. My ULA pack was super-light because I sent home everything I could; I missed my yellow Crocs. I cinched the waistband almost all the way. Now rail thin, I pondered getting another waistband. The pouches on both sides used to ride on the outside of my hips, which was inconvenient to reach. Now both pouches rested just left and right of the center in easy reach. The left held my iPhone and the right had my snacks for the day (protein bars and candy). On sunny days, Maui Jim sunglasses rode on top of my hat. Most of the paint wore or chipped off the Black Diamond trekking poles. Beaten up and bent, they saved me from many bad falls. I did my best to straighten my trusty companions but never quite succeeded.

My body transformed. Down about sixty pounds, I felt light, agile. My legs were super strong, calves as big as my thighs. I chuckled at Rock Steady's observation back in Virginia every time I thought of that. I didn't believe her then. I could see it now;

my calves were massive. My feet splayed out. I started in size ten and a half boots and now wore twelves. My balance improved dramatically. The arthritic pain in my left shoulder disappeared. I could walk quickly and efficiently and not lose my breath. Internally, my furnace fired at an all-time high and burned hot; anything would incinerate promptly and efficiently. I ate high-calorie junk food and still lost weight. I poured gallons of water into my system daily and flushed it consistently. My metabolism cleaned me out every day. I pooped once a day at the same time every morning. I slept deeply every night, rarely remembering any dreams.

Here's an example of my athletic prowess developed over the previous five months. Walking along a ridge in Maine, alone at the time, the path consisted of smooth dirt. Up ahead, a rock ledge about four feet high straddled the trail. Previously, I would have slowed down, probably stopped, and figured a way over or around the obstacle. I kept my pace and strode confidently toward the ledge. In one smooth motion, I transferred the trekking pole in my right hand to my left, wrapped two fingers on my right hand around a small tree trunk on the right side, and my left foot rose to the top of the rock. I pulled myself up effortlessly without missing a stride. I continued on the path above. I switched one of the poles back to my right hand. After a few more paces, I looked back and said out loud.

"Whoa. Pretty cool! How'd I do that? Not bad for fifty-five!"

My body had transformed. I experienced another transformation. As part of my preparation for this hike, I read over twenty-five books written by thru-hikers; very few described the finish. Some briefly narrated the time in New Hampshire and Maine, but the ones I read were heavily front-loaded. I wondered why. I have an inkling now. My soul resided in a new dimension, hard to identify and portray accurately. My internal spring was completely unwound; I lived unfettered. My daily tasks were simplified; wake up, fuel up, pack up, walk, set up, sleep and repeat. The outdoor life, the simple routine, and the physical exercise connected me to my surroundings. I became utterly aware.

Like me, the people I traveled with thrived. Other thru-hikers displayed the same elevated spirit. We sensed each other's presence and confirmed it in each other's sparkling eyes. Eyes are windows to the soul.

"The eye is the lamp of the body. If your eyes are healthy, your whole body will be full of light." ~Matthew 6:22

Our bodies were light-filled, while the outside was usually dirty, stinky, and hairy. The inside underwent an unplanned spiritual purification. Away from a life that cranked my spring tighter and tighter, I adapted to life in the woods, with far less stress than in society.

Sometimes our conversations would drift. "I wonder what it will be like to return to the *real* world?"

"Is *this* the real world?" No one ever responded.

In Maine, I hiked with confidence in my ability but balanced with humility. Nature pulled me to her bosom. God spoke to me continually. In divine presence, I walked through magnificent settings. I lived in a perpetual state of awe and wonder, absorbing the dramatic beauty of creation in a spectacular vista or a solitary mushroom. Was I just more aware? Or was I delirious with fatigue? For me, the journey reached a mystical level in Maine. Wonder and determination replaced the fear that plagued me.

Victory Lap

After the zero in Bethel, we returned to Grafton Notch in blue sky and sunshine. No more zeros; the finish beckoned strongly. My friend Wanderbus, who hiked the trail the year before, described Maine as a victory lap.

"It's easy."

Right. And it's flat. Common lies heard on the trail. But I liked the idea of a victory lap. I wanted to enjoy this, but how would I deal with my intense longing for home?

A rugged climb up Baldpate faced me.

"Come on, AT, what you got?"

I was not prone to openly challenge the trail, but on this day, I summited with a fit, rested body and an excellent attitude. At the top, I soaked in the sunshine. The surrounding mountains framed a panoramic view. The trail led along a ridge above the tree line. I stopped. I could see the path ahead and behind me, carving through pine trees along a granite surface. Hiking did not feel like a chore in this beautiful section. I felt privileged. I felt blessed. Gratitude surged its way to the forefront.

"Dr. Pickles, think about it. How many people will ever see anything like this?"

"I don't know, Right Click, but I'm sure grateful to have this chance. Look at this." He made a sweeping gesture. We all loved the trail, but Dr. Pickles expressed his love more fervently than anyone.

Our conversations had become shorter; not because we were tired of each other or ran out of topics; we communicated intangibly. Entirely immersed in a new dimension, we connected in different ways. A natural spirit flowed between us and linked us, a bond that was not fleeting or temporary. Incredible and rare, the bond was welded together by mutual respect, admiration, and love.

After twelve miles, we settled in at Surplus Pond next to a seldom-used woods road. An abandoned cabin on the shore fascinated me. I wondered who built it and why they left it. We camped in a nice flat area nearby. The sunset brought an evening chill, puff jackets, the garb of choice as we ate dinner.

The following day, Pickles whispered outside my tent. "Come on. There's a moose down the road."

Not too much motivated me to vacate my snug, warm sleeping quarters, but that did. I scrambled out and shook off the morning chill. We followed him down the road and past the spring. As we went by the abandoned cabin, he slowed and got his phone camera ready. I followed his lead. In the perfect morning stillness, I heard something in the pond to our left. I heard rustling in the woods to the right too. I clicked on video, took a few steps, and turned left; a young moose stood in the water on the edge of a mountain pond. I kept my emotion in check. The four of us stacked up and took pictures. The moose glanced back and kept doing what young moose do. This one nonchalantly chewed on some plant life. I whispered, "Hello, little guy."

We took more pictures but did not linger. We left him alone, munching breakfast, and retreated to the campsite. Momma moose remained close by, probably the noise on the other side of the road. No need to press our luck and irritate her. Back in camp, we chattered away, amazed at our good fortune. Dr. Pickles shared.

"I went to the spring to get some water for breakfast, and I looked up and saw him (maybe her) walking down the road. I returned to get my phone and decided to wake you up."

"Thank you! I'm so glad you did."

I posted one of the pics on Instagram – the silhouette of a young moose in the early morning light. The pond behind perfectly calm mirrored a sunlit hillside impeccably on the surface; charming moments seemingly became more frequent in Maine.

Or was I seeing the world through transformed eyes?

We hiked over Wyman Mountain, Moody Mountain, and Old Blue Mountain. Three mountains in one day seemed routine now, although Old Blue proved formidable, conquered in the usual manner, one step at a time. I no longer whined or complained. What was the point? Not practical, and not much to whine or complain about. My attitude renovated, and now in this to the finish. I willingly adopted the enthusiasm and appreciation of my companions.

I realized the trail epitomized my spiritual journey of recovery. I now existed in another domain, connected to nature. I peacefully lived and enjoyed each day and

256

each moment. If a steep climb loomed ahead, so be it. If a steep descent challenged me, so be it. I clung to gratitude and thrived in a fantastic place in His amazing grace.

But not one hundred percent of the time.

Just two afternoons later, the four of us arrived at the Sabbath Day Pond Lean-to at about 4:30. They wanted to stay for the evening, and why wouldn't they? The lean-to sat on the shore of another crystal clear, picturesque Maine pond. With caffeine coursing through my system from an energy drink, I wanted to continue my favorite time of hiking in the late afternoon. But I didn't want to venture out solo. We discussed it. They stayed. I continued. No hard feelings, just one thing that happens on the trail. Separately, we made decisions, and all parties respected them. As I took my first few steps, serious doubt occupied my thoughts, then a little frustration and anger. The petulant child in me didn't get his way; they should have joined me. Gradually, the anger subsided. The frustration drifted away. My adventuresome spirit kicked in. As I walked, my attitude improved. It always happened. Always. I was walking, always the panacea for a poor attitude.

"OK, Right Click. What do you have? How much do I trust God? Let's go see what happens."

After forty-five minutes, I arrived at a fantastic stealth site just off the AT. High up, nestled in some evergreens, a bed of soft pine needles beckoned my Double Rainbow. As darkness settled, I ate another cold dinner in my tent. Intensely aware of my feelings, they surprised me. As far as I knew, the nearest human existed two miles away, perhaps the only time I was so isolated in my life. Deep in the Maine woods, I rested, perfectly at peace, not afraid.

I drew confidence from the energy that coursed a few feet away through my lifeline, the AT. After I ate, I lay back, pulled out my iPhone, and scrolled through pics from the day. I queued up a few for Instagram. I turned off the phone and listened. Not only was I not afraid, but I also enjoyed the sounds. I felt self-sufficient, confident, proud, and comfortable. Obvious to me that my best option, right then and there, was to wholly and willingly put my situation into God's hands. I did, and He held me. I prayed for my crew and hoped they'd catch up to me early tomorrow; odds were they would. They'd get a much earlier start without me delaying them. Plus, we had plans to go into Rangeley and resupply.

The following day, I broke camp early. As I completed the usual morning chores, I frequently glanced south down the trail and hoped to see Dr. Pickles surging up the course (except during my morning poop). He didn't.

After double-checking the site, I left no trace. My rested legs warmed to the day's task spurred on by Starbucks VIA instant coffees. After heading north for an hour, I

257

hit the Little Swift River Pond campsite and chatted with another hiker. I found the spring that fed the pond and filled my water bottles. I took pictures of the canoes on the shore in the bright morning; Dr. Pickles showed up.

"Hey, Right Click! How was your night?"

"Pickles! There you are. Good to see you! My night was excellent. I'm sorry that I didn't want to stay. I just felt like I needed to keep moving. And you know what? I think I needed to test myself. "

"Hey, no problem. We had a good night. The others aren't too far behind. I'm looking forward to getting into town. I'm low on food. I only have one protein bar left!"

"I'm low too. Oh. And Happy Labor Day."

"It's Labor Day?"

"Yeah."

Soon Mockingbird strode down the trail, followed by Just Doug. Friendly greetings filled the air. We didn't natter long; time to keep moving. We wanted to get to ME 4 and get somewhere to resupply.

On the road, we hitched rides separately to a local IGA grocery store right on ME 4. By now, we loved grocery stores; our affection was immense! We rested our packs against the front of the building and dug out our money. I never carried much; I used a debit card and driver's license for identification. A small Ziplock bag that I repaired with red, white, and blue stars and striped duct tape served as my wallet.

Along with any paper money, I kept a couple of other trinkets. I experienced a mild form of culture shock this late into the thru-hike when I entered a food store. Rail thin, unwashed, odorous, scraggly long beard, sweaty, I scoured the shelves for the highest caloric foods with the lowest weight. I also calculated how much food to carry until the next resupply. Once inside, the four of us scattered and set upon our missions. Least finicky; I usually finished first. At this IGA, I purchased some food for lunch.

Outside, I sat at a picnic table and dug in. Pickles bought a pile of fried chicken with macaroni and cheese. Mockingbird purchased a bag of salad. She craved fresh vegetables. With mouths full of food, we compared purchases, nodded approval, or expressed surprise. Someone usually bought new Ziplocs and doled them out. We unpackaged and repackaged, shedding weight, and ensured our precious food remained dry.

Dr. Pickles and I worked on our clogged Sawyer Squeezes; they filtered water painfully slowly, no matter how often we back-flushed them. Another hiker cleansed his with a bit of bleach, and it worked much better. I bought the smallest bleach

258

container; we cut plastic bottles from the trash and made a mild bleach solution. We filled our Sawyers, let them sit, and then flushed water through. We repeated the process several times, another life-on-the-trail task I did not foresee. It worked! Our filters worked much better.

I watched people pull up and operate gas pumps; a long time since I pumped gas. We lingered for a couple of hours. I returned to the store and purchased hotdogs and rolls for a Labor Day cookout dinner. I stretched out in the sun as my phone charged with a full belly. Slowly, we began to move, our food bags stuffed and our packs heavy.

In the IGA parking lot, a busy place, I turned on my considerable charm (haha) and negotiated a ride back to the trailhead in the back of a pickup truck. We thanked our ride for their generosity and shouldered our heavy burdens. We moaned and groaned dramatically. My body rebelled against the load but soon acquiesced, and I settled into a rhythm. Before too long, we arrived at the Piazza Rock lean-to. With many places to camp, I found a nice flat spot down below the shelter and quickly set up. Dr. Pickles and Mockingbird set up quickly too. But where did Just Doug go?

Some other hikers stoked a small fire near the shelter. Perfect. I provided hot dogs and rolls; Dr. Pickles contributed sausages too. As we roasted our Labor Day feast, Just Doug showed up.

"I went up the side trail to Piazza Rock."

"What was it?"

"It looked like a spaceship, a flying saucer, maybe."

"Really. Was it worth the trip?"

"Not really. But what the heck? I probably won't be back this way again."

We listened to stories from other hikers while we shared our bounty. They appreciated the hot food, especially fire-roasted meat. I put a can of baked beans in the fire. I'd have to carry the empty can until I could properly dispose of it, but worth it. Dr. Pickles brought a can of beer to celebrate the holiday. A couple of SOBOs stopped at the shelter for the night. They talked about the trail; not too bad, but what they said did not align with the AT Guide. The following section appeared difficult, even by our standards. The elevation changes looked like another EKG strip over three peaks - Saddleback Mountain, The Horn, and Saddleback Junior. I examined the AT guide without fear, armed with a strategy to get down steep descents safely.

I went to sleep in a reasonable frame of mind. I woke to overcast skies and mist. The crew set out together. We hiked for ten minutes when a frightening sound stopped us dead in our tracks. Something huge crashed through the underbrush. Instinctively, we huddled together.

259

"What the hell is that?"

"Moose?"

"A bear?"

"T-Rex?" I suggested.

We chortled nervously. We couldn't see it. The thick woods shielded the creature from our vision. No trees snapped or branches waved as the animal moved noisily away from us. What a ruckus! I guessed a moose - they have a magical ability to become part of the landscape and virtually invisible. But not silent, far from it.

"I'm definitely awake now."

We moved again. As I climbed Saddleback, I reached the tree line, and the wind whipped the mist sideways across the exposed ground, another wild weather morning. The wind gradually blew the clouds up and away. The afternoon became dry and mostly sunny, with every step another photo opportunity. The rugged panorama took my breath away.

I looked up the trail; the next peak to conquer loomed ahead. But before I climbed that, I descended four times; all four were ridiculously difficult. Along this stretch, the AT dove off cliffs and disappeared straight into holes. I took each descent one step at a time. The hole always turned into a path through the trees. At the exceedingly steep parts, I practiced the command whispered to me back on Wildcat.

"Turn around."

I faced the rock and crab-walked down the steep parts. I used my long legs to my advantage; I probed downward with one foot to find the next stable foothold. On one steep, I chucked my beat-up trekking poles forty feet and started down. Near the bottom, I latched onto a small tree for balance. I put too much faith in that skinny tree and leaned back for the next step, and the tree snapped. I didn't fall far, about five feet; I landed squarely on my back on flat dirt.

"Ooooooooooohhhh."

I groaned, more startled than hurt. Mockingbird heard the tree snap and my groan. Concerned, she asked.

"Are you OK?"

"Yeah… I'm fine." I was. My backpack cushioned the fall perfectly, my Pop-Tarts a little worse for wear. I mumbled.

"Well, that was one way to get down." I picked up my trekking poles and continued. As I walked, I thought. "Wow. That didn't even bother me."

My fear had transformed into respect, no longer afraid of descending or falling. I didn't *want* to fall but didn't fear it any longer. I trusted my ability now. I navigated

260

hundreds and hundreds of miles of rugged trail, my balance at a high-water mark. Even though I fell, my confidence remained. The foundation for my faith rested in God. He had my back. He just caught me.

Again.

Inchworm

We stopped briefly at the Poplar Ridge Lean-to, made infamous as the last known sighting of Geraldine Largay, Inchworm. Posters about her at the previous few road crossings instructed anyone to contact local authorities if we found any clues. Familiar with her story since she disappeared two years earlier, she still had not been found. Hikers speculated about many theories of murder, kidnapping, animal attack, alien abduction, etc. Thoughts of what happened to this sixty-six-year-old woman intrigued me.

A logging company surveyor found her remains just five weeks after we stopped at the Poplar Ridge Lean-to. Inchworm lived for at least an additional twenty-six days and kept a journal. Inchworm lost the trail after a bathroom break and died in her tent tucked into her sleeping bag. Her camp was neat; she waited for a rescue that never came, the cause of death listed as exposure and starvation. I believe she responded appropriately for the first few days. She stayed put. But when rescue did not come, why didn't she move?

Inchworm's tragedy raised other questions.

- News accounts mention her anxiety and fear of being alone. Was this a factor?
- Out of desperation, why didn't she set a signal fire? She had matches. They found some burn marks on trees.
- Located under a canopy of hemlocks, why did she camp in such a concealed area?
- She tried to send a text message, but none went through. Why didn't she climb to the highest point near her and try to get one out?
- How did she survive for nearly a month?
- What was it like for her to be completely alone, isolated, and frightened?
- What was the end like for her? Did she just curl up, fall asleep and die?

The one that disturbs me the most is…

- With a massive search initiated and carried out, why wasn't she found while still alive?

After our rest at Poplar Ridge, we continued for a couple more hours and camped near a stream on an old logging road. Pickles and I explored a dilapidated bridge. Just Doug went down the road and scouted for more of a clearing with no luck. The couple set up in the middle of the road in a nice flat spot. Their freestanding tent did not need stakes. Just Doug and I pitched our tents off the side of the road in some grass. Out one side of my tent, the road. I heard water flowing on the other side, tucked into the underbrush on the edge of a ditch.

We camped within a mile of where Inchworm lay.

There Arose Such a Clatter

I covered fourteen miles over rough Maine terrain and fell asleep quickly. I awoke to a voice. The voice shouted. Groggy, I opened my eyes. I heard Pickles shout loudly and clearly.

"GET. OUT. OF. HERE."

At the sound of the shout, hooves pounded down the road and headed toward Just Doug and me. Instantly terrified, I instinctively wrapped my arms around my head and curled into the fetal position for protection. The ground vibrated as hooves pummeled the ground inches from my head. At full gallop, the animal roared past, and the clamor rapidly receded down the road. Just Doug asked.

"What the hell was that?"

"A moose. Probably." I responded, surprised at my calm. The surge of adrenalin passed quickly. Deep grogginess returned. I heard the others talk. I could not stay awake. I returned to slumber immediately. The following day, I got the whole story.

Mockingbird first heard the footsteps; she instantly knew a large animal was approaching. She kept calm, but she thought her husband should know. So, she whispered. "Brian. Brian. Wake up." He heard his real name and woke up quickly, but not entirely.

"There's an animal outside." He heard the first step. Not wanting to have a recurrence of the bear incident, he remembered to speak with authority. That's when I heard him shout.

"GET OUT OF HERE!"

That startled the moose (we think), and it galloped away; I'm delighted it missed my tent's guidelines; it could have dragged me and my tent away. We talked about it all day, another day of rugged hiking.

Even though trail-hardened and somewhat serene, I still got angry. The tricky descent down the north side of Stratton fired me up. Anger was better than fear,

262

however. Anger did not cripple me. I used it to make my way down, throwing expletives at no one in particular. By mid-afternoon, I made it to the top of South Crocker Mountain and waited for the others. While I rested, I noticed some weather might move in.

Still unsure whether my tent was fully waterproof, I wanted to find a suitable site, especially in a downpour. The AT Guide indicated no campsites within reach, so another night of stealth camping appeared likely. I volunteered.

"How about I go ahead and scope out a site?"

"Sounds good Right Click."

Solitude

I set off down South Crocker and up North Crocker. On this section of the trail, I walked through mounds of moose poop. My senses were on full alert; I anticipated seeing a bull moose around every bend. But I did not. On the other side of North Crocker, I stopped at a spring-fed stream, drank my fill, and scouted the area. The AT Guide showed no water for several miles. In Maine, though, many water sources crossed the trail and were not denoted in the book. Directly across the trail, I detected where others had camped. Pine needles covered the lumpy forest floor with a lot of dead wood above, not ideal for tenting; a borderline choice, even for seasoned campers, but I had camped in worse.

I had not walked by any other possible campsites in harsh terrain over the last few miles. I decided I'd hang out and wait for the crew. Thunder rumbled as the temperature gradually dropped, with the sky overcast and the air thick with moisture. I slipped into my puff coat and waited some more. After an hour, I grew irritated and concerned.

"Where are they?" I wondered if someone had injured themselves.

"Should I go back?" I contemplated—more thunder in the distance. The clouds started to spit rain.

"Should I set up? Should I wait and see if they approve of this spot? Where are they?"

"Should I keep going and hope to find a better spot?"

Finally, with growing frustration, I decided to stay put and set up. I left the best location for Pickles and Mockingbird. Just Doug could sleep just about anywhere. As I filled all my water bottles for the night, Dr. Pickles bounded down the trail a couple of hours later than expected.

"Hey, Right Click."

263

"Hey, Pickles. I waited for a long time. Not sure about this site. But I made a decision." I barely hid my frustration.

"We had LTE up on the mountain, so we decided to hang out."

"Oh. I decided to set up here."

The other two ambled in and scouted the area. They would not stay; the site was too sketchy. My heart sank. I made the wrong decision. Rested, with not much light left and rain imminent, Just Doug said with some sadness.

"We're going to keep going. We'll see you in Stratton to resupply."

"Yeah. Sure. OK." I said sullenly. Dr. Pickles offered an alternative.

"You could come with us."

I could, but I didn't want to pack everything up, hike for an uncertain distance to another rocky spot and set up all over again. I settled. I heard the words of Art Woodard in my head.

What you have is good enough.

"No. I'm good." They left me and headed down the trail. Bitterly, I second-guessed myself. I should have moved on. I should not have set up here. I wondered.

"Have I irritated them so much they now want to avoid me? I allowed myself time to wallow in self-pity, hurt, and resentment. I grumbled into the quiet woods.

"I hope it pours on them."

"No, I don't." I recapitulated.

Gradually, I accepted my situation. I examined my role. I held myself accountable for my actions. I embraced the solitude. I ate my food and drank water inside my shelter, comfortable, warm, and dry. The rain moved out. A bonus, LTE reception! I called Sandy as darkness settled. After the call, I scrolled through social media, turned off the phone, and used my headlamp to look at the AT Guide. In the last two days, I covered more than twenty-six miles over eight summits; five of those peaks over four thousand feet. No wonder I was bushed. I encouraged myself.

"Not too bad for an old man."

I wrote some notes, stowed the AT Guide back in its bag, flipped the light off, turned comfortably on my side in my forest nest, and listened to the sounds of the deep Maine woods. I awoke to the gently growing light of dawn and the task of hiking three miles to ME 27, getting a ride into Stratton, ME (not VT), meeting the crew (hopefully), resupplying, and getting back on the trail. On the way to the road, I would pass the two-thousand-mile mark, a mammoth milestone in my mind. The crew and I discussed this milestone many times, a considerable number for thru-hikers.

264

Refreshed and invigorated, I headed downhill to the road. I came across a reasonably nice stealth campsite where the others probably stopped. Shortly, I reached the two-thousand-mile mark, signified by an artistic sticks-and-stones marker. I hoped to meet the crew here, but I was alone even though I started early. I took a selfie. I fought off a feeling of abandonment. I didn't like this about me. I've worked hard on my recovery process and myself. I've learned to set reasonable expectations for others and myself. However, I still justified my negative feelings.

"In a similar circumstance, I would have waited," I mumbled as the forest listened. I whined some more.

"They must not care for me as much as I care for them."

But that wasn't correct either. With too much emotion to process, I sat down and posted a pic on Instagram. In it, I have a big smile; my eyes lit up. I thank God in the caption. All true, but not full disclosure; my face did not belie the pain from the emotional blow of not sharing the moment with my trail family. Rock Steady and Paradox passed here two days earlier. Just Doug, Mockingbird, and Pickles passed this way, maybe a few minutes earlier. I felt left behind.

I stood up slowly and continued down the trail. Just Doug waited for me at the road, grateful to see me. The couple had already hitched into town. I didn't share much of my churning emotion with him. Instead, I said. "It would have been nice to see everyone at the 2,000-mile mark."

He replied simply. "We must have just missed you."

We got a ride into Stratton, a tiny Maine town, Dr. Pickles and Mockingbird not hard to find. I ordered a breakfast sandwich at a little store and ate with Just Doug. We resupplied at the grocery store and repackaged our stuff. I sat on a bench, pretty quiet as raw emotion rummaged through my gut. Ready to go back to the trail, I asked.

"Hey, we have a big climb up to Horns Pond. I'd like to get going."

Pickles pointed. "There's a hostel across the street. How about we stay for a bit and have a shower?"

Mockingbird and Just Doug affirmed that idea. I did not.

"OK, I think I'm going to head back. Good-bye. I'll see you on up the trail."

"See you Right Click."

Frustrated, no longer on the same page with my crew, I shouldered my pack, headed down the road, stuck out my thumb, and got a ride immediately from a pickup truck. The young man, a forester, told me about his work on the way to the trailhead.

Once on the trail, I cruised to the Cranberry Stream campsite. Late in the afternoon, I decided I could do the three-mile climb to Horns Pond before dark. I did. I enjoyed setting my own pace and relying on my own experience. The trail overlooked Horns Pond, and the view impressed me even in the gray, drizzly weather. I made my way down to the lean-to; only one other guy there. I set up on a beautiful flat site. The rain intensified. Once inside, I inspected my tent seams. Much to my relief, they held.

I fueled up inside my tent in the morning as the rain pattered against the nylon roof. Highly motivated to finish, I decided not to wait for the others. One absolute sure thing about hiking, you did not get anywhere unless you moved. I packed all my gear while inside the tent, put on my rain jacket, and stepped out into the gray, wet morning. The cool air on my bare legs invigorated me. I pulled the stakes and removed the arch pole. I stored them immediately in the side pocket of my pack. Everything had its place. I folded the tent long ways in thirds, rolled it up, and stuffed it in its bag quietly, methodically, and efficiently, a noticeable difference from the first few times back in March.

As I climbed Bigelow Mountain, the wind picked up, the temperature dropped, and the rain stung, the type of weather that can quickly become dangerous. I followed the rock trail via cairns, barely able to discern the next one. Aware of the danger, I assessed my situation; I dealt with the conditions well enough. I reviewed my priorities; first, in poor visibility, stay on the trail, especially above the tree line. Second, stay warm. The steep climbs pumped blood powerfully through my body. I knew what to do if hypothermia surfaced, dry clothes, shelter, and a sleeping bag for the worst-case scenario. Third, do not fall and sustain an injury, a distinct possibility on this section of the trail. With no hikers nearby, it would be long before help arrived. Even then, depending on the extent of the injury, I'd have to get myself off the mountain. I slowed down, no hurry. I concentrated on the next step, chose wisely, and eliminated as much risk as possible even though the wind threatened to knock me over.

I made it to the top of Bigelow, descended a few hundred feet, then climbed to the top of Avery Peak, the last of the four-thousand footers until Katahdin. Wet, cool (but not cold), and still alone, energy coursed through me. I harbored no resentment anymore toward my crew. Being on my own triggered a deep primal response; I loved this adventure passionately. Being exposed to the elements on a remote rock face sparked a survival mechanism and a passion for life that lit me up. As I descended into the protection of the woods, I absorbed the beauty around me. The rocks, trees, and soft forest floor soothed my spirit. My energy melded with the

266

environment. On the wild and rugged rock, my energy was wild and rugged. Down in the calmer woods, my energy smoothed out.

I hit the ten-mile mark in mid-afternoon at the Little Bigelow Lean-to. I investigated the "tubs" where overheated hikers bathed or swam in the stream. I sat in the lean-to, still alone. I calculated that this would be where the crew would stay.

"Should I stay, or should I go?"

I dug out the AT Guide. Less than three miles ahead, Flagstaff Lake beckoned with two beaches and two fire pits. I desired to tent on the shore of a lake, so I considered my options. I felt really good. Tired but also at peace, I moved on. It turned out to be a great decision. I crossed East Flagstaff Road and spotted the blue roof of a pop-up tent, a good omen. Sure enough, trail magic! Former thru-hikers offered me a burger, a hot dog, soda, and chips. Extremely grateful for the hot dinner; it did wonders for my cold, wet, tired body. Plus, I sat in a chair instead of on the ground, a log, or a rock. Coincidentally, one of my super friendly hosts had developed the Guthook app.

Sitting, I hoped the other three would pass the shelter and head down here. I texted them but knew it was a long shot. Before I got too stiff and cold, I thanked the trail angels for their much-appreciated generosity and headed north to East Flagstaff Lake. Another good choice, I parked for the night on an open beach with a spectacular view. Although overcast at the lake, the sun lit up some mountains in the distance. Low clouds gently scudded by. I set up my gear and hoped to dry out my tent and sleeping bag (not completely dry since I washed it in Stratton).

Soon Voyager appeared. After dinner on the road, she set up awkwardly close to me, but I didn't mind. We chatted and discovered we had mutual acquaintances in Minnesota, a small world.

My third night in a row without the crew, all lingering resentment or self-righteousness long gone. I walked all that out miles and miles ago. Now I just missed my trail family. Rock Steady and Paradox slept a few miles ahead, the other three behind me, Sandy, and my children hundreds of miles away. As I lay in my tent, I gazed out at the water. It gently lapped against the shore. I thought of home and all the comforts. I wondered about my return. I prayed for my trail family and wished them well. As night settled, I reflected a bit on the solitude. Even though a couple of other hikers camped nearby, I felt isolated but not unhappy. I practiced acceptance and drew close to my Creator. I thanked God for getting me this far. With that thought, a loon called from far away, an enchanting, mystical sound that carried spiritual peace. Grateful, I drifted off to sleep as I listened to the loon's song.

The following day, I headed north, always north on the AT, Maine, so different from other states. I headed deeper into the wilderness. I crossed the occasional dirt road but encountered very few people. I hiked alone. I strode to impassable bogs, but trail workers cleaved logs in two and placed the round side down, providing a flat, stable path. I quietly thanked these people. I could not fathom the manpower it took to lay these paths down. I cruised peacefully through lush pine forests. The needles smoothed the trail and cushioned my feet. I breathed deeply of crisp, cool, pine-scented healing air. My body and soul thrived.

About midday, I came to the shore of East Carry Pond, the sandy beach bathed in warm sunlight. Like a cat drawn to a sunbeam, I stopped. I emptied my pack and laid all my damp gear in the hot sun. Then I waded into the pond and washed my clothes and my body. Voyager stopped by, ate, rested, and moved on. My gear dried completely. I spent two hours on the beach and hoped the others would catch me. They did not. I checked my sleeping bag, finally completely dry because the inner black liner turned a tad crispy. I loved it. I packed everything methodically and efficiently. I checked the area to make sure I left nothing behind. I found a pack of cigarettes and a lighter on a makeshift bench. I wondered if I should take them with me. I left them for another hiker. Then I shook my head as I thought about how many hikers smoked.

I reached Pierce Pond Lean-to before dark after a beautiful, peaceful, picturesque hike. I welcomed the lack of severe elevation changes. The Kennebec River loomed, requiring a ferry crossing (a guy and his canoe). It only ran certain times of the day, and I couldn't make it in time, so after an easy fifteen miles, I found an idyllic campsite, flat, pine needles, under a canopy of pine on the shore of Pierce Pond. Perfect. After setting up, I wandered around the area. Voyager, whom I passed earlier, strode in and said hello. I hung around the lean-to when I detected a disturbance in the force. Sure enough, Dr. Pickles arrived.

"Hey, Right Click! We were hoping we'd catch you here!"

"You did!" I couldn't help but smile from ear to ear.

"Where is everybody?"

"They'll be here soon."

My heart warmed. I pointed to some apparent spots for their tents. Pickles and Mockingbird set up near the water right in front of the lean-to; Just Doug near me. We started a small campfire, a rare occurrence, and caught up. We told stories of things we had seen, memorable sections of trail, and what lay ahead with one hundred fifty-five miles left, by our calculations, another ten days. Elated, without a doubt, we would finish (barring any significant injury), we looked forward eagerly.

268

Dr. Pickles and Mockingbird met a guy who broke his leg in the 100-Mile Wilderness the year before. He required emergency extraction by helicopter. The copter pilot took him by Katahdin. The hiker returned the next year and completed his thru-hike. I thought,

"Damn, that could be me."

A lot more graceful than when I started; I still took some clumsy steps now and then. It only took one to end a hike.

We arrived at the Kennebec River together, pleased to hike with the crew. The ferry (the canoe) was on the other side. The operator waved, disappeared for a bit, then made his way over. This crossing, well known for the quirky ferry service, was the only section of the AT where you don't walk. The dam up river opens randomly, the water rises quickly, and severe trouble becomes possible if you're in the river. A woman drowned when she got caught with a heavy pack on. Some hikers brag about wading the Kennebec. Not us. We decided many miles back that the risk of wading the river was not worth the reward. We used the canoe. Dr. Pickles and Mockingbird went first, then Just Doug and I. I sat in the bow and paddled, an unusual feeling to be on the water; it reminded me of the times I spent fishing from my kayak off Cape Cod. We crossed without incident.

I looked at the AT topography, and it didn't show any major steeps, but the AT Guide did not always tell the whole story. The trail surface could be smooth pine needles or jagged rock. This proved true again; the trail in this section (and most of Maine) was chock full of astonishingly slick roots, rocks, and mud. I slipped on a rock coming down Pleasant Pond Mountain and landed hard on my right hip. Downright bony, with no padding left on my frame, my hip bruised immediately and became sore to the touch. I picked myself up with barely a whimper and continued. I didn't complain. Not angry, not afraid, I noted the remarkable change in attitude.

After sixteen miles, light diminished. Dr. Pickles and Mockingbird found a stealth site. It might fit us all. Just Doug squeezed in. Noticing my doubt, Dr. Pickles responded.

"Right Click, there's another spot about one hundred yards up the trail, to the right. You could probably squeeze in there."

"Cool. I'll check it out and come back to eat with you."

The site worked. Over dinner, we talked about our resupply in two days in Monson, the 100-mile wilderness, and Katahdin; the conversation was warm, kind, and loving. We encouraged each other. The evening grew chilly. I headed up the trail to snuggle in my bag, separated from my friends. I slept securely, knowing they rested close by.

269

The camaraderie continued through the next day in weather conditions that disheartened and discouraged others. We played in the pouring rain and chilly temperatures all day long. The trail was so muddy that I abandoned any hope of tiptoeing around it. I blasted right down the middle. I developed a sixth sense when the mud might be too deep; plank bridges across the mire were a telltale sign. Once, I stood on a plank over some rich, thick, black Maine mud and tested the depth with my trekking poll. I never found the bottom of the pit, more than four feet deep. I recalled movie scenes where people fell in quicksand. If I fell in there, would I ever be found? I slowed down a little. In places, I waded through shin-deep water. I used the opportunity to rinse the mud off my socks and boots.

We arrived at Horseshoe Canyon Lean-to for the evening. We spread out and camped in the prime spots with no other hikers at the lean-to. We traveled more isolated than at any other juncture. After I set up, I noticed a few piles of moose poop a few feet away. A bit concerned but not worried about getting trampled in the middle of the night, I joined the others at the shelter for dinner. That night, I awoke to something, maybe a snort. I heard footsteps outside my tent; a giant creature neared. But everything sounded big in the woods at night. I spoke calmly.

"Hello. This is my spot. Move on."

That said, I turned my back to the receding footsteps, curled up in the fetal position, and went back to sleep.

Magical Mystery Tour

I sensed the road up ahead. ME 15 would be our ticket to Monson to resupply and then venture into the 100-Mile Wilderness, to me, the most mysterious section of the trail. More importantly, when (and if) I emerged from the 100-Mile Wilderness, I'd only have fifteen miles left to the summit of Katahdin.

Just Doug walked behind me, and we talked about our town visit. I slowed down a bit, the smooth granite slick with moisture. As I descended, I spotted the road. Then I heard feet skid and poles hit rock, and I turned to see Just Doug on his butt. He looked at his elbow, bloody.

"Are you OK?"

"No big deal." He stood up; blood dripped down his arm.

"Are you sure?"

"Yeah, I'm sure. A little embarrassed, but I'm fine."

I shook my head in awe of Doug Tough. At the parking lot, I collapsed on the ground; we covered nine miles quickly. Two ladies, one older than the other – mother and daughter, amused at my dramatic collapse, inquired.

"Are you thru-hikers?"

"Yes, we are," I said with pride.

"Can I take your picture?"

Quickly capitalizing on my celebrity status, I replied. "Sure, if you give us a ride into Monson."

"What? You want a ride?" She stuttered a bit.

"Yes. We need to get food for the next several days. This is the beginning of the 100-Mile Wilderness."

I pointed to the sign. I glanced at Dr. Pickles, who looked like, "I can't believe you just did that."

"OK. I can do that. But we'll have to take two trips. My car is small."

"OK. Thank you!"

Dr. Pickles and Mockingbird went first. Just Doug and I stayed back. The mom stayed behind and told us she once worked at the Appalachian Trail Conservancy but had never seen the trail in Maine.

"I want to see Katahdin. That's where we're headed."

I noticed a Suburban in the parking lot with Rhode Island license plates that sported several bumper stickers, the owner a hiker and saltwater fisherman. I identified many of his stickers. Had I seen this actual vehicle on a Rhode Island beach? My thoughts drifted south. The daughter returned.

Just Doug and I stuffed ourselves into the back seat with packs on our laps. The ladies seemed pleased to have a role in our adventure. They dropped us off at the store in Monson, where we found the couple. We ate a hot meal. The other three found a shower. Now wholly one with the woods, I didn't want to be bothered with washing my body. We discussed resupplying. One small store and a gas station provided slim pickings. I chose a lot of sugary, high-calorie foods. A few tuna packs sufficed for protein. As we lingered in town, we thought about staying one night but decided to head back to the trail. We crossed the road and prepared to hitchhike back. Immediately, a guy in a flatbed stopped with a cargo of two porta-potties.

"You headed to the trail?"

"Why yes. Yes! We are."

"Hop on." He pointed to the back.

We sat with our backs to the cab, interlocked our elbows to keep from falling over the side, and propped our feet on the porta-potties. I never pictured myself

271

zipping down a Maine highway staring at two blue toilets. I reached the trailhead with adrenaline flowing and gave my sincere thanks. We stood in the parking lot and contemplated the sign.

APPALACHIAN TRAIL
CAUTION
THERE ARE NO PLACES TO OBTAIN SUPPLIES OR GET HELP UNTIL ABOL BRIDGE 100 MILES NORTH. DO NOT ATTEMPT THIS SECTION UNLESS YOU HAVE A MINIMUM OF 10 DAYS SUPPLIES AND ARE FULLY EQUIPPED. THIS IS THE LONGEST WILDERNESS SECTION OF THE ENTIRE
A.T. AND ITS DIFFICULTY SHOULD NOT BE UNDERESTIMATED.
GOOD HIKING!
M.A.T.C.

Well read on the 100-Mile Wilderness; I knew roads traversed the trail in this stretch. I'd be worried if I listened to the folklore, but I assimilated no fear or trepidation. I looked forward to the test; we all did. I hiked more than two thousand miles to prepare for this.

In Monson, I learned two outfitters would drop your food off halfway through the 100-Mile Wilderness. One would meet you at a road, and the other would cache your food. Of course, they charged you to do that. The ominous sign at the trailhead recommended ten days of food. My pack, the heaviest in a long time, stored six days' worth.

I groaned under the weight of my fully loaded pack. The others did too. We decided we'd start looking for camp right away. About a mile in, we came to Bell Pond. We found one site. Pickles dropped his pack and went up ahead. I scouted the area. Hilly and overgrown, no spots materialized. We decided to squeeze all three tents into a space barely big enough for one.

I had just about settled in for the night when a peculiar sound like a colossal stone dropped in the water and commanded our attention. We heard it again, very loud. Dr. Pickles headed down to the water. I followed barefoot.

"Maybe that was a tree? It sounded enormous! Did a beaver cut it?"

"I don't know!" Excited, we scoured the pond's shore. Two beavers swam away toward the lodge in the middle. We did not see any newly felled trees.

"It must have been one of them smacking the water with its tail. I've read that's what they do, but I had no idea it could be that loud."

272

"I hope that's what it was…."

I picked my way over the rough ground. I didn't need a cut on the bottom of my foot. In times like these, I regretted sending my yellow Crocs home. I crawled back into my den (tent). As night fell, I could hear and sense how close we all lay together, not comfortable, exceedingly awkward; I couldn't fall asleep, never this close before out in the woods. With not a breath of wind, the woods eerily quiet, I lay awake listening for the deep breathing of my comrades. It never happened. I slept fitfully at best. None of us slept well. In the same mindset, we each worried about making any noise that would bother someone.

During breakfast, we resolved not to do that again. We laughed a lot. We packed up and shouldered our heavy loads. Ahead, no big climbs or descents waited for us. However, when the AT Guide showed lots of bumps and jags, I did not expect smooth hiking. We experienced many ups and downs; not too difficult to navigate, but the infamous Maine roots, rocks, and mud made the footing treacherous. I quietly thanked God for my improved balance and leg strength. Roots, whether wet or dry, are slick. The soil had washed away underneath the roots and left several inches of space. One misstep and a foot or ankle could quickly become snared and broken. We tread carefully, except for Pickles. He bounced down the trail; I ultimately conclude that Tigger would have been a more fitting trail name.

Water was plentiful in Maine, and we crossed multiple streams, some deeper than others, some with large rocks that served as a clear path across the current. When the way across was not apparent, and the distance between stones intimidated me, I proceeded cautiously. Stream crossings are also natural places for hikers to rest. At one crossing, three hikers sat on the far side. With several rocks above water, I mapped several options across. Dr. Pickles went first with exclamations.

"Whoa!" He leaped quickly to one rock. "Oh no!"

And he gracefully lit on another as he played to the crowd. He loved an audience. His athleticism gracefully got him across. Mockingbird quietly chose another route with no fanfare. I decided to follow Dr. Pickles and my long legs helped me navigate without incident. Six of us on the other side watched Just Doug take his first jump with his heavy pack. The heavy burden betrayed him on his next step. He didn't quite make it and splashed into three feet of water. Dr. Pickles exclaimed.

"Oh no!"

Just Doug slipped again, went deeper in the stream, and everything got wet. He struggled out, dripping wet. No one made a sound.

"Are you okay?" He smiled, embarrassed.

"Yeah, I am. But I don't think my camera is."

Thinking quickly, he took off his pack and removed the camera's memory card. He dried it and stashed it in a plastic bag. His camera did not work from that point forward. He loved taking photos, having taken thousands of pictures to that point. Part of me thought Just Doug's fall was quite comical, but mostly I felt compassion. I thought to myself.

"I have changed. Now would be when I'd normally crack jokes and not let it go. But it's not all that funny. I could have fallen and wouldn't have wanted to be laughed at."

I caught Just Doug's eye and received more non-verbal communication. I perceived a lot of humor, embarrassment, and a touch of just leaving it alone. I did.

"Keep going?" I asked him.

"Let's go."

We came to a gravel road late in the day; earlier, we crossed railroad tracks. Both of these sightings eased my sense of isolation. After the road, we came to yet another small river; this one traversed without incident. Hikers sat on the other side. Our planned destination, less than a mile away, I eagerly climbed the riverbank. Up top, a beautiful campsite beckoned. I tried to get my crew's attention without the other hikers seeing me. Here first, they hadn't claimed the spot yet. Finally, Dr. Pickles came up.

"Look at this. Want to stay here?"

"Looks great! Let me go another fifty yards and see what's up ahead. Just to make sure."

He dropped his pack and disappeared. I started to scout the area more closely for where I wanted to lie down, now very good at envisioning exactly where I'd place my head and then placing my tent precisely on that spot.

My tension mounted because the other hikers started to get their stuff together. They would head up the hill soon. Do we declare this spot now? But Dr. Pickles came back and, without saying a word, just waved his arm, picked up his pack, and motioned for us to follow him. He wouldn't do this unless he found something better. He did. We went up over a brief rise and descended back down to the riverbank to a flat area, the ground covered in pine needles and sheltered by tall cedars. Perfection.

"Wow, Pickles! Wow! Thanks for checking. This is way better."

"Isn't it?"

We all agreed. We set up. Just Doug hung a clothesline. We washed some mud off in the river. We ate together. We inventoried our food; then planned meals and snacks for the next four days. We flowed together as a team, peacefully, rhythmically.

274

Night fell, and I picked myself up off the ground. Stiff and sore (as usual), I made my way to my tent and crawled into my lair.

I passed the one-hundred-mile left mark right out of the gate early the following day. Only one hundred miles left. As I climbed up to Barren Ledges, I reflected on my hike.

"How had I gone this far?" It didn't seem possible; more amazed than anyone.

"Thank you, God. You are truly remarkable. I am so grateful you love me so much. I praise You."

I whispered the prayer. I thought of Sandy. God, I missed her. I prayed for her too. As I was prone to do, I prayed for all my children. My mind expanded to other thoughts. I'd be home in a week if all went according to schedule. Hard to fathom after six months in the woods.

Yet, the rugged Maine terrain rife with roots and rocks kept my mind occupied on the task at hand. I lived entirely in the moment. I felt in tune. I climbed steadily, body functioning at maximum efficiency, transformed into a hiking machine. I sweated freely, cooling all my systems. I hiked in shorts and a t-shirt. I took in vast quantities of Maine spring water, flushing all toxins. I stoked the furnace with a high number of calories that burned quickly. If I felt my body begin to bonk, I ate something to revive quickly. At this point, I consumed massive amounts and still lost weight.

Dr. Pickles took a picture of me on the Barren Ledges in brilliant sunshine with a breathtaking panorama behind. He showed me the pic. I gasped at my emaciated frame. We absorbed the expansive view of lakes, trees, and mountains. We hiked through a series of ups and downs. The landscape held me spellbound. Boulders covered in vivid green moss, topped with ferns, on one stretch, resembled green-haired giant rock heads. Another stretch sported head-high, thick, lush pine trees; I strolled through a disorganized Christmas tree farm. Next, I rose above the tree line, walked across shale rock, and gazed for miles. Trees grew out of cracks in boulders or roots wrapped around rocks in the woods. One tree grabbed a boulder with its talons. I passed another tree with a burl face that guided people along the trail.

Maybe lack of nutrition, extreme exertion, and prolonged fatigue made me delirious.

I snapped back to reality, coming down Chairback Mountain. I passed a lean-to where I said hello to two guys from Europe. They warned me about the trail ahead. I could see through the trees into empty air, a sure sign that I'd head sharply downhill. I didn't realize I'd be descending a cliff. I stood at the top and looked down in disbelief.

"Where's the trail? I don't see a trail."

I heard chuckles from the lean-to. It looked like a piece of the mountain let go, and hikers had to negotiate the remaining rockslide. Tired, late in the day, pack still on the heavy side, I considered my options. I noted to myself that fear did not cripple me. I took stock of my emotion, pleased I held healthy respect and a proper perspective for my next move. I tossed my poles down the first drop and scrambled down. I faced the cliff and used my hands. However, the further I went, the angrier I got.

"This is treacherous. Just take your time. One step at a time…"

I tested some positive self-talk, but I still directed a few F-bombs at the Maine Appalachian Trail Club. I lost the trail near the bottom, with no white blazes anywhere. I surveyed the ground; separate paths veered left, straight, and right - over, through, and around several boulders. I guessed left. After several more minutes of picking my way through the boulder field, I ended up on a soft dirt trail with a white blaze. I got fortunate. I found Dr. Pickles and Mockingbird resting at a water source in a few more minutes.

"It took me nearly an hour to go a few hundred feet! That was ridiculous."

"It was. Did you get lost? We almost took a right near the bottom."

"I almost did too." I think the same thought crossed our minds at the same time… Just Doug.

"I hope Just Doug makes it through. Should we wait?"

"It's getting dark. I think we should keep moving and start to look for a campsite."

We agreed, but no viable spots materialized for quite some time. Finally, we came upon a bit of a square clearing where Pickles and Mockingbird set up, another site close by. We waited for Just Doug. Finally, he hiked in. He had ventured to the right at the bottom of the avalanche and lost time finding the AT. He looked exhausted. Since I felt okay, I volunteered to go ahead and find a place to sleep.

"I'll see you in the morning."

"Right Click, are you sure? We could make some room."

"No, remember the other night?" They nodded. "Seriously, I'm good. I'll see you in the morning."

I headed off. The AT Guide marked a campsite two miles away, the furthest I'd have to go if I didn't find anything. I did not. Nothing. I hiked in really thick, rugged stuff on this stretch. I reached the turn-off to the campsite, another steep two-tenths of a mile. Up here, I scouted a sketchy spot just off the trail. I found a mossy area where I could lie between trees and rocks. I drew on my acquired expertise to stake out my Double Rainbow. After just a few minutes, I admired my handiwork.

276

Impressed with myself, I crawled in and wedged myself in comfortably. One of the rocks I staked over served as a ledge to put my iPhone and other gear on. Pretty sure no one had ever camped in this particular place, I drifted off to sleep, settled in between small trees and large rocks, part of the night tranquility, my breath in tune with the peaceful rhythm of the forest.

I fit in here. I fit perfectly.

We needed big miles to keep on schedule and prevent running out of food. The AT Guide showed four peaks to conquer. I set off determined. My body had bonked when I got to the third mountain. I sat down at the top of Hay Mountain, pulled out the AT Guide page, folded in a plastic Ziplock in my front shorts pocket for easy access. The last peak, White Cap, looked formidable. I sighed. I ate some food. I mixed an instant coffee/Carnation concoction and drank it down. The surge of caffeine got me to my feet and down the trail. I prepared for the rugged climb ahead.

The trail transformed. In disbelief, I climbed stairs upwards, beautiful man-made stone stairs meticulously placed by a trail crew. Yesterday, I swore at the Maine Appalachian Trail Crew. Today, I praised them. I hiked quickly, entirely enthralled by the number of person-hours it took to build these steps. At the summit, I saw several mountains, but I did not know if one of them was Katahdin, and I had no one to ask. My crew had caught up to me earlier in the day, but we separated. We'd meet later. I continued down the path and descended another set of man-made stone steps. I shouted to no one in particular.

"Thank you!"

The crew gathered after sixteen miles at another viable stealth site. Again, it would work for one or two tents, not three. Again, I volunteered to move on, another lean-to in a few miles. With about ninety minutes of light left, the trail didn't look too bad on the AT Guide, and I'd probably find a spot before then. Off I went on my own. Again.

I loved hiking in the early evening, my favorite hiking time. I did not find any suitable locations to stop. After an hour (and more than eighteen miles for the day), many hikers camped in an expansive area. Much younger than I, this group partied, talked loudly, and laughed heartily; the distinct scent of marijuana drifted to my nostrils. I neared the lean-to—a surprising amount of people nestled in and around the shelter. Eventually, I found a suitable site and settled in for the night. It felt odd to be camped among so many. Once closed in, I felt at home and at peace.

I woke up at first light. I ate and checked my dwindling supplies. I drank a dose of caffeine and then shrugged on my hiking gear. When I got out of the tent, everyone had left. What? Except for Stream Clean, from Germany. An incredibly fit and gifted hiker, he started later in the day but made time quickly. Our paths frequently crossed over the last few hundred miles. Still puzzled how all those hikers had got up so early, packed up quietly, and disappeared, I made my way to the privy for the morning poop after coffee. As I sat in the comfort of the privy, a small solid object clanged off the roof and startled me. Irritated but amused, I called out.

"Dr. Pickles, is that you?" No reply. Then two more loud thuds on the roof.

"I know it's you, Dr. Pickles. Cut it out."

No response, but I heard squirrels chatter excitedly in the tree above the privy. During their exclamations, three more brash thumps motivated me to finish up quickly. I swung the door open and expected to see Dr. Pickles standing there mischievously. No one in sight.

"What the…?"

I muttered, and another object landed on the roof. I looked up. Two red squirrels made their presence known through constant nattering. One had a green pinecone in its paws. I watched as it dropped the pinecone on the roof. I swear they gave each other high fives when it bounced off the roof. I chastised them.

"Very funny!"

They responded by elevating their chatter to a higher level; they pointed their paws at me (do squirrels have paws?). I walked away from the shameless taunting. Stream Clean calmly ate breakfast near my gear.

"Did you hear that?"

"I did Right Click. They did that to me too. And they've been doing it to anyone that goes in there."

"Incredible." I shook my head.

I headed off with big miles to do if I wanted to make it out of the 100-Mile Wilderness before running out of food. I thought about those precocious little buggers. I laughed. I hadn't gone two hundred yards when a red squirrel ran to the end of a cut log. The squirrel held an acorn in its front paws. At shoulder height, he spoke Squirrel rapidly. But I heard English.

"Hey there. Do you like my acorn?"

Two feet from me, I stopped and responded in English. Not Squirrel.

"I do. Is it this years? Or did you dig it up?" Not sure why I asked.

"It's from last year. I can't believe I found it. Look how perfect it is." He twirled the nut around in his hands. I agreed.

"It's a beauty."

"I'm so excited. I'm going to bring it home and show everyone." With that, he scurried back along the log and dove into the woods. Leaves rustled then all signs of him disappeared.

"Dude, either you are perfectly in tune with nature right now, or you are delirious from lack of nutrition. But I guess it doesn't matter."

I shook my head and kept moving. I stopped and chatted with another hiker who camped at a beautiful stealth site near a pond. A little further, a side trail beckoned to another pond. I hung an AT4Recovery bandannas on the sign to signal the crew. A cool morning, but the cloudless sky promised a warm and sunny day—time to treat myself to a bath and laundry. After shedding my pack, I waded in shoes, boots, and all. Standing waist deep, I took off my boots, rinsed out my gaiters and socks, and put them on the shore. As I floated around in deeper water, some other hikers stopped for a rest.

"Come on in. The water's great!"

"No thanks. We're good."

Dr. Pickles showed up. Guess what? He oozed enthusiasm.

"Right Click! You're here! The guy down the trail said he hadn't seen you. Happy to see your bandanna on the sign."

"Good to see you too. Didn't he see me? I talked to him for several minutes. Geez. Where's Mockingbird?"

"They're both right behind me."

Dr. Pickles took a dip too. Mockingbird and Just Doug sat on the beach. As we air-dried, we talked about the miles and where we wanted to end up.

Our day's trek took us across Jo-Mary Road, where other thru-hikers sorted through a bountiful resupply. One guy opened a massive can of beer with relish and chugged it long and hard. Another guy complained loudly about not getting something he ordered. The nerve, food delivered (weight he did not carry) in the middle of a tract called the 100-Mile Wilderness, and he complained? Before I said anything unkind, I moved on. Fortunately, the kind, serene and beautiful trail quickly soothed my irritation. Plus, I thoroughly enjoyed the lack of elevation changes.

After sixteen miles, I caught up with an excited Dr. Pickles. The Antlers Campsite boasted beautiful flat sites with spectacular views of Lower Jo-Mary lake. A young man perched on a boulder out in the water caught fish for dinner. Our planned destination was still two miles up the trail, but without any disagreement, we decided to make up the miles tomorrow and enjoy our time at this idyllic location. Another deciding factor was the strong LTE phone service, which enabled me to post a few pictures on Instagram. I lay down and rested in my tent with an unusual amount of daylight left. I talked with Just Doug. Dr. Pickles used the time to bathe more thoroughly in the lake. We checked out each other's food inventory, all extremely low. However, that meant exceptionally light packs for the nearly twenty-two miles we planned for the next day.

YES DAD

We planned to get out of camp earlier than usual. I woke up to drizzle and gray clouds; the early morning light was mystical and promised better things to come. We planned one more night in the 100-Mile Wilderness but still had to cover thirty-seven miles to our extraction point at Abol Bridge. I felt invigorated. The magnet of Katahdin drew me.

We started in high spirits. As we were prone to do, we gradually spread out. The friendly terrain enhanced the mood. As I rounded a gradual bend, the couple stood motionless and gazed into the woods. They spotted a critter of some kind, so I transitioned into stealth mode. Mockingbird pointed. I followed her point to a magnificent barred owl perched on a fallen tree just a few feet away. While we took pictures, the huge bird lifted off without a sound and flew gracefully through the thick woods.

The miles flew by. Mid-afternoon, I climbed Nesuntabunt Mountain and took the side trail to an incredible view of Mount Katahdin, sixteen miles away as the crow flew but still many more trail miles. I sat on a boulder and looked over a deep blue lake. White puffy clouds pointed toward Katahdin. The clouds dappled the deep green forest with shadows, and Katahdin's summit lit up in brilliant sunshine. The crew gathered at this beautiful spot. Pickles took my picture while I sat on the rock with Katahdin in the distance. I posted it on Instagram as we rested and enjoyed the view, likes, and comments from followers trickled in. Tough Love, my daughter, responded immediately. Her two-word response brought me to tears. I sobbed. Mockingbird responded.

"What's wrong?"

"Nothing. Look." I handed her the phone. Her eyes moistened too.

"Awww."

Samantha's capitalized words resonated deep in my soul.

"YES DAD. "

My daughter was proud of me, a reversal. I'm intensely proud of all my children, but to have them proud of me... Well, I had not thought about that at all. Usually, kids tolerate their parents, and when they become adults, they gain some appreciation

280

for parenting. Mostly, I felt encouraged. Spiritually, she sat with me on that rock and considered Katahdin, our souls connected. And if she linked with me, then others did too. I understood that this adventure had become a lot bigger than me. I contemplated the finish – the mountain in the distance. I would stand on top in a few days, and the odds rested in my favor.

I floated the rest of the way to the Rainbow Stream Lean-to. I set up near Pickles and Mockingbird in a grove of tall pines, my last night on the AT. I snapped a picture of my Double Rainbow. After a long day, we ate dinner in the dark and shared our collective enthusiasm. Our meager food supply did not dampen our zeal. We'd meet Sandy at Abol Bridge, just fifteen miles away, successfully through the 100-Mile Wilderness with just another fifteen miles left to the finish.

I crawled into my tent, an uneven floor, but I didn't care. I could sleep anywhere. I scribbled notes in my AT Guide; I walked a personal best, twenty-one point seven miles. Many hikers average that, but that was the most I had gone in a day. I fell asleep praying for all those who loved me, encouraged me, and carried me to this point. I couldn't fight off sleep, nor did I want to; my last thought…

"YES DAD. "

Three Little Skittles

A day before we planned, Sandy drove to meet us early; we'd be out of the wilderness on Monday. She would meet us at Abol Bridge. We were excited. I packed up my gear for the last time; super light with barely any food, the trail kind, and the weather perfect—brilliant blue sky, no wind, and cool temps made for highly pleasurable hiking. Mid-day, I reached the Rainbow Ledges. I hiked along the smooth granite until the ledge opened up to another outstanding view of Katahdin. I stopped, flicked off my light pack, and ate my last tuna pack. Soon, Dr. Pickles, Mockingbird, and Just Doug arrived, followed by Honey Britches and a few others.

Unbeknownst to my crew, I had stowed away a bag of Skittles. I confess I ate a few of them on the morning hike, but most of my bag remained after lunch. I poured the Skittles out into my hand, twenty-two delectable morsels left. I counted seven hikers on the ledge. I approached Pickles first.

"You can have 3." I opened my hand. He had an incredulous look as I offered him nuggets of gold.

"Are you sure?"

"Yes. I'm sure. We have six miles left to the road where I'm sure Sandy will be well supplied."

281

I smiled. Pickles carefully chose his three colors. Then Mockingbird. Then Just Doug. I approached Honey Britches. Cautiously optimistic, she checked with me.

"Right Click, are you sure?"

"Pick three." I encouraged her.

"You mean I can have a red one, an orange one, and a green one?"

"Of course!" I laughed.

"Thank you!"

Two other hikers picked too. I ate the remaining four slowly; their soury sweetness pleased all my senses. I savored the moment like the others. We found great satisfaction in little things.

We stumbled onto Golden Road at about 3:30. We found Sandy on the far side of the bridge ten minutes later. When I saw the beige Suburban, my heart leaped. She stepped out, her brilliant blue eyes beamed, and her smile warmed me. She greeted us all with loving, heartfelt enthusiasm. She drove more than four hundred miles, I hiked fifteen, and we met at the same time again. After the welcome, I instinctively looked for the cooler. We all did. Cold Cokes awaited. Snacks awaited. So happy! Sandy found a campground nearby. As we drove away, she told a harrowing tale of being chased down the Golden Road, a dirt logging road, by a monster lumber truck barreling along at seventy miles per hour with a full load. But here now, together, life was all good.

Sandy had touched base with Paradox and Rock Steady, and while we hiked to Abol Bridge, my trail sisters climbed Katahdin, my hopes of summiting with them dashed. Sandy invited them to visit us at our campsite, but not optimistic they would show. We arrived at the New England Outdoor Center, the only one booked all weekend. The caretaker showed me how to fire up the generator for lights and hot water in the bathrooms. He showed me how to shut it down too. I immediately fired it up, and we jumped into the hot shower. After all that time in the woods, layers of grit and sweat washed away. The hot water felt more than luxurious.

Situated on a beautiful site near the water, we relished a stunning view of Katahdin. It took all of us to set up the Taj Mahal, my home, for the last two nights. Sandy grilled shaved steak and cheese served on fresh rolls. We stuffed ourselves, then ate more. Sandy consistently checked the road for headlights. She hoped beyond hope that maybe the ladies might make an appearance. They did not; they had finished and were on their way home. Before we tucked in for the night, we'd leave later in the day and just cruise an easy ten miles before we summited the following day.

282

Katahdin

The next day, we slackpacked ten miles on easy, relaxing terrain. We finished in just over three hours which included a few stops.

After another feast, the Boudreaus drove up from Connecticut and joined us that evening. Just Doug bought two bundles of firewood, and we sat around a warm blaze. Al and Chris, our biggest fans, listened to story after story about life on the trail. We listened to music. I served as DJ and played different songs on the iPhone6. We talked about our journey and the miles traveled, all in disbelief that it ended the next day. We were excited and a bit sad. Bittersweet.

The next day dawned to weather perfection: cloudless sky, cool temps. Just Doug got very cold that night with only a thin foam pad and the tent floor between him and the ground. On the drive to Katahdin Stream Campground, we were navigating a dirt road to Baxter State Park when we encountered a moose. Sandy came to a sudden stop. Sandy exclaimed.

"Wow! That thing is huge!".

"That's a baby!" Four thru-hikers chimed in together, a young one, but still huge. In our excitement, no one thought to take a picture.

Other thru-hikers milled about the mountain's base and registered at the ranger station for the final hike. Honey Britches chatted with her brother, who arrived to climb with her. I sat down on a bench and re-tied my Merrells, worn out but perfectly and artistically formed to my feet.

"This is your last run, shoes; you've been very good to me," I spoke to my shoes. I kissed Sandy, hugged her a little longer than usual, and set off down the trail, white blazes beckoning.

"See you soon, honey!"

Without turning back, I raised one trekking pole. The climb up started simply enough. I anticipated the steep. Once at the bottom, the steep loomed above, spectacular in scope. The going got rough. Rock scrambling became the norm, hands and feet up the mountains' spine, unaware of the technical difficulty. In the lead, I climbed and wrestled with a nagging thought…

"I have to come back down this way."

I enjoyed the climb, a fitting finale to a fantastic adventure, the most challenging ascent of the entire Appalachian Trail. The higher I climbed, the more impressive the view; Katahdin was indeed a stand-alone mountain. In some sections, re-bar served as the only option up. That got my attention. One slip here would be catastrophic. I worked my butt off to finish the precipitous incline, with nothing but blue sky and rock in my sights. An ancient-looking dude appeared above me, at least eighty years old. Not sure about my mental stability, I cautiously questioned the possible apparition.

"Is that the top?" I pointed a few yards up. The ghost laughed.

"No, you're just about to reach the Tablelands; you have another one and a half miles."

"Damn." He laughed again.

"Enjoy your hike." He went on by. Seeing the old guy, definitely a human, encouraged me. "If he can make it up and back down, I can too."

Once again, I noted I talked to no one in particular. I went up a few more yards and discerned my final destination in the distance. I waited for the crew. They smiled broadly, appropriately amazed. I proceeded calmy over the last portion and took in the view. I paused to take many pictures. The cloudless sky and the brilliant sunshine provided an incredible day to summit. I drew closer to the finish. I heard people celebrate at the infamous Katahdin sign. As I climbed the last few yards, I choked up. I whispered.

"I'm here. I made it."

I sat next to the sign and watched Dr. Pickles and Mockingbird come up. They smiled. They cheered. They celebrated. A few minutes later, Just Doug touched the sign. Profoundly quiet, he slipped away and sat down on a rock a few yards away. A private, proud man, his shoulders heaved a few times. The trail affects everyone deeply, even someone as tough as Doug.

Others took pictures at the sign. We waited our turn. Kind Honey Britches took photos of the four of us, then we all posed individually. As I stood on the sign with eyes and hands pointed up to the heavens, I became comfortably numb, maybe too many emotions for me to process. Fatigued from the climb, I harbored some concern about making it back down in one piece. But mostly, I stood in awe that God carried me to the finish.

"Did I do this? Is it really over?"

I sat down near the summit. I posted my summit pic on Instagram with the following caption.

It is finished.
I'm pretty tired; think I'll go home now.
All glory to God.
Recovery makes all things possible.

I put the phone down. I savored the view. I sat with my thoughts. The phone vibrated. Tough Love commented instantaneously.

"DAD YOU DID IT, I'M SO PROUD, ALL GLORY TO GOD"

My daughter shared her heart from Virginia; I read her loving post and leaked again. I wiped away tears while looking at the most spectacular view of the entire Appalachian Trail. Time slipped away; now 1:00 pm, I had five miles back down. If the descent went slowly, we (or I) might need five hours, and by then, it would be dark. I didn't want to do that.

So down I started; Just Doug ahead of me. I got behind a young man and woman; the woman moved slowly. That suited me, so I followed. I picked my way down. Dr. Pickles and Mockingbird spent much longer on the summit but caught me quickly. I told them about my anxiety about getting down and asked if they would stay with me. They agreed.

Although difficult and taxing, I handled the daunting descent decently. As the trail started to flatten, a river of relief flowed through me. When I reached the base camp walking behind a dancing Dr. Pickles, I spotted Sandy, Just Doug, the Boudreaus, a huge sign congratulating us, and about a dozen other people. To the sounds of claps and cheers, I reached out for Sandy, arms opened wide and collapsed in her arms. Sobs racked my body.

Home. Finally. Home.

Epilogue

It's taken seven years to get this book done, and in some ways completing this task was more challenging than the actual thru-hike.

The first thing I have to share is that when I look back at hiking the entire Appalachian Trail, I am in just as much disbelief as the people I tell. I can't believe I did it, either. And I'm surprised that I finished this project; at times, I thought I might die with this languishing up in the iCloud, one more in billions of incomplete works. At least now it's a finished book in a sea of billions.

I'm still in touch with the crew.

I'm pretty sure I wouldn't have completed the hike without the friendship of Just Doug. We still text once in a while and have spent time together. In his late 60's, still in great shape, he hikes every year, doing sections of the Pacific Crest Trail. He has a servant's heart, loves his wife deeply, and is a wonderful dad to his six children.

While on the trail, Dr. Pickles often expressed his desire to open an art studio. We'd talk about that and my role in leading a nonprofit agency for hours. I'm happy to report that his dream became a reality. Check out Luzader Studios in Asheville, North Carolina. I must admit that when he said he was an artist, I questioned whether I'd like his work. When I saw it for the first time, my jaw dropped. Sandy, Sami (Tough Love), and I visited last year and were more impressed. He is active (rides his bike for miles and miles), funny, warm, and engaging. Mockingbird is doing well, still sweet, calm, and steady. I'm amazed at their relationship, but when you share a tiny tent for six months, you must become close or… They were instrumental in the last third of my hike, providing warm companionship, encouragement, and an abundance of understanding.

We regularly see Paradox and her husband and pick up immediately where we left off. She's like a daughter to Sandy and me. The depth of love we have for her goes beyond description. She loves the outdoors, pays attention to the little things, and seeks adventure. She's a compassionate, empathic, remarkable young woman.

I've only talked to Rock Steady a few times, but we had breakfast with her and her husband this past summer. Our reunion only reinforced the notion that what we shared on the trail was true, good, beautiful, and withstands the test of time. She has been busy doing stuff with the U.S. Army as a civilian – tasks and projects beyond my comprehension, but very cool nonetheless.

I stay in touch with many other hikers through social media; our interactions often bring a smile to my face, if not a chuckle. They bless and inspire me.

As for the family, Sandy has a new role outside of corporate America, working in a university setting. We are happily married and looking forward to the next phase. My oldest is married with two grandchildren whom we love to visit. Joshua is married, earned his doctorate in physical therapy, and lives in Kentucky. Sami (Tough Love) teaches school in Kenya. She often posts pictures of her dangling off cliffs or camping near dangerous African wildlife. Matthew (Riptide), quite athletic, is currently pursuing CrossFit while in school in Chicago, and Mary (Little Click) attends school in Boston. They seem to have an adventuresome spirit... hmmm.

And what about me?

I believe the CCAR Board of Directors invested well by approving my 'sabbatical.' To my knowledge, I was the only thru-hiker that was getting paid while on the trail. Since my return, I've increased our revenue by 400%. We established a Recovery Coach program for patients in Emergency Departments, and in the first five years, we coached more than 20,000 individuals (yes, you read that right). Our staff has also grown 4-fold. All because the Appalachian Trail transformed me into a better leader and person.

I believe that the primary goal of a leader is to create other leaders, so I still work to become better at relationships, something the people on the trail taught me. I listen better, am more curious, ask better questions, and am much more aware of my stuff. The time in the woods allowed me to become more self-aware, a process I have continued. I focus on the CCAR organizational culture – we seek to make it accepting, encouraging, supportive, compassionate, and rewarding - aspects I found within my crew on the trail.

I've become more patient. I learned to slow down and that I (we) don't have to match the frenetic pace of the world around us. The trail slows everyone down. Nature has a mystical way of doing that. When I slow down, I make better decisions.

Above all, hiking increased my confidence and humility. I possess the courage to take on new opportunities while understanding that I'm insignificant in many ways.

I've stepped on the Appalachian Trail a few times since, and the electrical current still thrums; as soon as my feet hit, energy surges into my soul. All the emotion, all the vitality returns in a rush. I love it. Someday I may return...

I believe the best is yet to come. I recently learned something about expectations from Parker J. Palmer. Today I *expect* something to delight me and I *expect* myself to be grateful. With that attitude, life is good, and I plan to... Continue.

A Note from Sandy

As of this writing, Phillip has been cancer-free for twelve years. Those years have been filled with countless kids sporting events, beach trips, graduations, birthdays, weddings, and the births of our two grandchildren. I am incredibly grateful that the chemo and radiation treatment that often appeared as though it would take his life, did what was intended and saved his life. I didn't give it much thought when he approached me with this "call" just months after an excruciatingly difficult year. He had just read Bill Bryson's book, <u>A Walk in the Woods</u>, and I assumed it was just a temporary diversion while he processed what he had experienced.

But no, it wasn't. For FOUR years, he talked about it, read about it, planned for it, and started buying gear for it. Whether at the grocery store buying food for the family or at a restaurant ordering steak and potatoes, he would drop the line "I won't be eating like this on The Trail" and wait to see if the cashier or waitress would take the bait. They almost always did. "What trail, sir?" And then, he would go into detail about his plan to hike the AT. FOUR years. Almost daily in my hearing, and who knows how often without me. So, when I dropped him at that airport and told him he couldn't come home for thirty days, no matter what – I needed a break! I didn't care if he sprained his ankle on day one and sat the thirty days out in a motel room.

I didn't know over the course of the four years of preparation that this experience would also change me. Not in the grand, awe-inspiring way hiking 2,189.2 miles did for Phil but in small, powerful ways. I knew I could manage work and family solo. The months of Phil's cancer treatment taught me that. I didn't think I could drive over twisty mountain roads looking for specific GPS coordinates to meet my favorite hiker in the middle of nowhere. I didn't know I would get to know my husband again after two decades of "partnering" as parents and individuals with high-commitment jobs. I'm not sure that "absence made my heart grow fonder." During those almost nightly phone calls, I think it was more "Oh…I remember you."

I also didn't know I would fall head over heels for his Trail Family. I remember driving south to Lickdale, PA, to see Phil for the first time in four months. I would be meeting Rock Steady and Paradox. In my mind, these were going to be two adventurous women with hairy legs and natural beauty. Two women who embraced the kind of adventure that 0% of me ever wanted to be involved in. As we drove, Samantha assured me I would like them. Phil couldn't wait for me to meet them. We pulled into the trailhead where Phil stood with his group, and as he

289

approached me, his love for me knocked me back. He thought it was the hiker funk, but it was the expression on his face seeing me in person after the longest time we had ever been apart. I did my best to set aside all my insecurities and be present for the experience. Phil and Samantha were right; I loved Rock Steady and Paradox. And I was right; they had hairy legs and natural beauty.

A few weeks later, I had my first authentic Trail Angel experience in Kent, CT. I brought a grill, chairs, and the makings for breakfast sandwiches. The kids and I journeyed west to pick Phil and five of his fellow hikers up off the trail for a weekend at home. Our chairs became occupied by thru-hikers who quietly came out of the woods with the most beatific smiles on their face when they saw that the food and chairs were for them. As with the recovery community, each generously shared their story. Their stories were inspiring and unique. While I still didn't want to hike along with them, I did wonder what God might be calling me to do next and the messages I might be missing.

I had spent a week setting up beds, filling little welcome baskets with toiletries, and stocking the fridge for these hungry hikers. The night before we were scheduled to pick them up, I sat with Matthew in the car when Phil called and asked, "Can I bring home two more?". I couldn't speak. FIVE strangers in my home were WAY out of my comfort zone. I had invested a ton of time in creating space for them, and now he wanted to invite TWO more! I didn't have enough travel toothpaste and deodorants to go around. Matthew took the phone from me and said, "Dad, what did you say to her?". Phil relayed the question, and Matthew took matters into his own hands and said, "No, Dad, no." To this day, I wonder what I missed out on by not opening my "zone" just a little bit more.

It was a wonderful weekend filled with storytelling and laughter. Dr. Pickles and Mockingbird, Just Doug, Paradox, and Rock Steady became my friends. Phillip chose his companions well, and I have no doubt he wouldn't have made it to Maine without their support at critical moments along the way. I had a chance to support them for five days in New Hampshire and the privilege of being in Maine at the end when Phil, Just Doug, Dr. Pickles, and Mockingbird finished.

The AT experience nudged me from the box I'd placed myself in, where financial insecurity drove everything about my life choices. Some thru-hikers had only loose change in their pockets, and some may have been millionaires. It didn't matter on the hike. The next footstep mattered. The next place to get water. The flat spot to lay your head at the end of the day. I began to question what mattered to me. My family. My faith. My purpose. Was my life lined up with those priorities? Yes, to family. Yes, to faith. Purpose? Nope.

290

Four years ago, I took my giant leap. I left a three-decade career for a large corporation and started working with students in recovery at our state university. I've learned a lot. I've been stretched a lot. I have a lot more to learn. But I know that for today I am exactly where I am meant to be. Working in the recovery community feels so right. Not all of us are made for hiking a couple of thousand miles, but the journey can inspire us to be aware of our surroundings, to listen for our call, and to take the first step.

Acknowledgments

I offer a heartfelt thank you to the people that helped me along the way…

All the nameless angels of the trail that provided food, beverage, transportation, and support.

Wanderbus & Safety First

Neil & Lori Campbell, Buddy, Leon & especially Jade

Richie & Amanda Tannerhill

The Giles Family

Dan Olszewski

Paul & Lori Castelli

Conrad Sienkiewicz

Pastor Frank Riley, Nate Shippee, Brian Richards, Seth Richards & Johnny Golemba

Bill & Martha Young

Al & Chris Boudreau

Arno Groot & Chris Luginbuhl

Peter Rockholz

Mark Ames

Rock & Roll Sue Juliano

Peter Wohl

Tough Love, Silent Planner, Riptide, and McPackin – I send you deep gratitude for the nights you spent in the woods with me. I will hold them in my heart forever.

Mom, Dad, Dee, and Shelly – thank you for being my biggest fans.

Colleen Marie, Joshua Alton, Samantha Helen, Matthew James, and Mary Elizabeth - I love you with a father's love. You and your loved ones will have a flat spot to pitch your tent as long as I'm alive.

Sandy – Every step taken on the trail and every word written here would not have been possible without your unconditional love and support. Your impeccable organizational skills and ability to manage a household astonish me to this day. You keep it together on the home front, rarely complain and support our family fully. In all positivity, you enabled me. This accomplishment is as much yours as mine. I am blessed that you, too, evolved into a Trail Angel extraordinaire. I love you.

God – This adventure left one set of footprints on the Appalachian Trail. They were not mine.

Gear List

Several of these items I sent home just four days into my hike. I gradually reduced the weight in my pack. Compare this list to what I carried or wore for 189 days. I also replaced some items (like clothing) as needed.

Item	Brand
Shelter	Tarptent Double Rainbow
Pack	Osprey Aether 70 XL (Bought ULA Catalyst 4 days in)
Sleeping Bag	EMS 35 degrees, Marmot 9 degrees
Sleeping Pad	Thermarest Insulated Pad
Trekking Poles	Black Diamond Trail Shock Compact
Water Filter	Sawyer Squeeze
Cook Stove	Jet Boil Zip (dropped this after 2 months)
Head	CCAR black Nike cap
	Turtle Fur Balaclava (no)
	Bug net (Dick's)
Top	Fleece, Puffy – LL Bean
	North Face full zip fleece
	Merino Wool shortsleeve Tshirt (2)
	Nike longsleeve
	Marmot Precipitation rain jacket
Hands	Light weight gloves, DeFeet International Duraglove
Bottom	Columbia fishing zip offs (pants)
	Marmot nylon hiking shorts
Underwear	Ex-Officio extra-long performance tech boxer briefs
	REI Silk Long underwear for sleeping
Socks	Darn Tough (2)
Gaiters	Dirty Gurl
Footwear	Moab Merrell Ventilators
	Camp shoes – Crocs (yellow)
First Aid Kit	ibuprofen, moleskin, immodium, cooling gel, insect repellent?, meds, vitamins
Toiletries	toothbrush, toilet paper, dental floss, soap, towel, trowel
Luxury Items	pillow

Technology	iPhone 6s + charger, Otter Box
	GoPro camera + charger (no) (sent home 4 days in)
	FluxMob BOLT battery pack (upgraded a few days in)
Fire Starter	Bic mini, 10 storm matches
Stuff Bags	Sea to Summit, Food (L) Clothes (M), Miscellaneous Gear (S)
Sunglasses	Maui Jims
Knife	Leatherman mini
Food	

Stuff I Had the Entire Hike

- ATM card
- Black Diamond trekking poles
- Bug net for the head (only worn a couple of times)
- Coin (from John Hamilton)
- Colter Abely's "copper" bracelet
- Driver's license
- Fingernail clippers
- Gold cross and necklace
- Headlamp
- iPhone6 with light blue Otter Box case
- Leatherman-mini
- Little rubber buffalo (given to me by Pat Howard)
- LLBean puff jacket
- Marmot Precip rain jacket
- Maui Jim sunglasses and case
- Nike CCAR hat
- Plastic bag the AT Passport came in – served as my wallet
- Russ Wilson's hoop earring in my left ear
- Sawyer Squeeze water filter
- Sea to Summit stuff sacks (3)
- Silver keychain tab (from CCAR staff)
- String bracelets made by Samantha and Mary
- Tarptent Double Rainbow 2-person tent
- Therm-a-Rest NeoAir XTherm sleeping pad
- Trash compactor bag (pack liner)
- Wedding band

Daily Log

Day	Date	Total	M's	Steps	Site	People	
1	3.19	8.1	8.1	9,089	Hawk Mountain Shelter	Solo	T
2	3.20	15.8	7.7	135	Gooch Mountain Shelter	RS	T
3	3.21	24.3	8.5	15,624	Lance Creek	RS	T
4	3.22	31.7	7.4	19,074	Neel Gap	RS	H
5	3.23	38.6	6.9	20,267	Hogpen Gap	RS, P, S	St
6	3.24	50.0	11.4	38,021	.5 short Blue Mountain Shelter	RS, P, S	St
7	3.25	52.9	2.9	11,403	Unicoi Gap, GA 75	Solo	M
8	3.26	63.3	10.4	30,434	Sassafras Gap	Solo	St
9	3.27	74.1	10.8	38,674	Plumorchard Gap Shelter	Solo	T
10	3.28	85.4	11.3	36,974	Deep Gap, USFS 71	C	St
11	3.29	97.6	12.2	200	Betty Creek Gap	Solo	St
12	3.30	109.8	12.2	26,175	Winding Stair Gap, US 64		M
13	3.31	109.8	0	6,029			
14	4.01	120.8	11.0	38,603	Wayah Bald Shelter	Animal	T
15	4.02	131.4	10.6	34,024	Wesser Bald Shelter		T
16	4.03	137.5	6.1	22,031	Nanatahala Outdoor Center	Solo	B
17	4.04	144.0	6.5	19,737	Sassafras Gap Shelter		T
18	4.05	156.0	12.0	41,987	Cody Gap		St
19	4.06	166.3	10.3	31,173	Fontana Dam Visitor Center	Solo	M
20	4.07	166.3	0	4,870		Solo	M
21	4.08	171.9	5.6	22,189	Birch Spring Gap	F, AW	St
22	4.09	182.7	10.8	29,748	Spence Field Shelter	F, AW	Sh
23	4.10	189.0	6.3	18,767	Derrick Knob Shelter	F, AW	T
24	4.11	196.5	7.5	21,169	Double Spring Gap Shelter	F, AW	T
25	4.12	199.6	3.1	13,596	Clingman's Dome	F, AW	Rv
26	4.13	210.3	10.7	31,892	Icewater Spring Shelter	F	Sh
27	4.14	222.9	12.6	32,657	Tri-Corner Knob Shelter	F	Sh
28	4.15	230.6	7.7	10,209	Cosby Knob Shelter	F	Sh
29	4.16	241.3	10.7	30,572	Green Corner Road	F	H
30	4.17	252.0	10.7	26,838	.9 aftr Brown Gap, USFS 148A	F	St
31	4.18	263.4	11.4	28,834	Campsite in unnamed gap	F	St
32	4.19	274.4	11.0	26,342	NC 209 + US 25/70, Ht Springs	F	H
33	4.20	274.4	0	5,266		F	H
34	4.21	281.0	6.6	20,912	.7 after Tanyard Gap	F	St
35	4.22	285.4	4.4	14,378	Spring Mountain Shelter	F	T
36	4.23	300.8	15.4	38,433	Jerry Cabin Shelter	F, RS, S	T
37	4.24	316.0	15.2	37,486	Hogback Ridge Shelter	F, RS, S	T
38	4.25	329.6	13.6	35,521	Whistling Gap	F, RS, S	St
39	4.26	342.9	13.3	22,343	River Road, Unaka Springs Rd	F, RS, S	M
40	4.27	347.2	4.3	19,754	Curley Maple Gap Shelter	F, RS, S	T

Day	Date	Total	M's	Steps	Site	People	
41	4.28	360.0	12.8	33,896	Cherry Gap Shelter	F, RS, S	T
42	4.29	372.4	12.4	32,461	Hughes Gap	F, RS, S	St
43	4.30	384.6	12.2	35,011	Overmountain Shelter	F, RS, S, P	T
44	5.01	393.8	9.2	26,540	US 19E, Roan Mountain, TN	F, RS, S, P	M
45	5.02	407.4	13.6	34,761	USFS 293	F, RS, S, P	St
46	5.03	418.5	11.1	29,236	Dennis Cove Road, USFS 50	F, RS,S,P, C	C
47	5.04	439.0	20.5	50,959	2.8 north of Vandeventer Shlter	S, G, WP,T	St
48	5.05	447.6	8.6	23,173	TN 91	TL	M
49	5.06	458.9	11.3	27,520	Abingdon Gap Shelter	TL	T
50	5.07	469.3	10.4	29,074	Laurel & Shady, Damascus, VA	TL	M
51	5.08	469.3	0	15,351		TL	M
52	5.09	484.9	15.6	31,700	Lost Mountain Shelter	TL	T
53	5.10	497.3	12.4	29,516	Thomas Knob Shelter	TL	T
54	5.11	508.5	11.2	20,827	Old Orchard Shelter	TL, RS, P	T
55	5.12	521.7	13.2	7,983	Trimpi Shelter	TL, RS, P	T
56	5.13	531.6	9.9	26,873	VA 16, Marion, VA	TL, RS, P	M
57	5.14	542.7	11.1	31,565	VA 683, US 11, I-81	TL, RS, P	M
58	5.15	557.1	14.4	35,600	Knot Maul Branch Shelter	TL, RS, P	T
59	5.16	570.0	12.9	30,465	2.6 miles south of VA 623	TL, RS, P	St
60	5.17	582.3	12.3	31,194	Laurel Creek, VA 615	TL, RS, P	St
61	5.18	603.1	20.8	47,036	.2 so Lickskillet Hllw, VA 608	TL, RS, P	St
62	5.19	616.6	13.5	35,311	Wapiti Shelter	TL, RS, P	T
63	5.20	634.9	18.3	45,431	Lane St, Pearisburg, VA	TL, RS, P	M
64	5.21	634.9	0	14,564		TL, RS, P	M
65	5.22	645.0	10.1	31,849	1.9 miles south of Symms Gap	TL, RS, P	St
66	5.23	662.2	17.2	40,094	Wind Rock	TL,RS,P,B,Q	St
67	5.24	675.6	13.4	35,202	.3 north of VA 42	TL, RS, P	St
68	5.25	685.3	9.7	24,631	Niday Shelter	TL, RS, P	T
69	5.26	695.4	10.1	25,969	Pickle Branch Shelter	TL,RS,P,VT	T
70	5.27	709.0	13.6	35,398	Johns Spring Shelter	TL,RS,P,VT	T
71	5.28	727.8	18.8	49,504	US 220, Daleville, VA	TL, RS, P	M
72	5.29	727.8	0	29,984	Daleville, VA	TL, RS, P	M
73	5.30	739.0	11.2	28,190	Wilson Creek Shelter	RS	T
74	5.31	756.0	17.0	43,475	Jennings Creek, VA 614	RS	St
75	6.01	770.0	14.0	29,984	Thunder Hill Shelter	RS, VT	T
76	6.02	782.4	12.4	30,307	Matts Creek Shelter	RS, VT	T
77	6.03	795.1	12.7	29,085	Punchbowl Shelter	RS, VT	T
78	6.04	806.4	11.3	15,362	US 60, Buena Vista, VA	RS	M
79	6.05	812.7	6.3	16,793	Hog Camp Gap	RS	T
80	6.06	827.0	14.3	38,514	The Priest Shelter	RS, P	T
81	6.07	840.8	13.8	37,333	Maupin Field Shelter	RS, P	T
82	6.08	856.6	15.8	38,103	Paul C. Wolfe Shelter	RSP, DP, M	T
83	6.09	861.7	5.1	15,548	US 250 + Blue Ridge Parkway	RS, P	M
84	6.10	879.2	17.5	41,634	Riprap Trail branches to west	RS, P	St

Day	Date	Total	M's	Steps	Site	People	
85	6.11	893.5	14.3	33,057	2.0 miles south of Pinefield Hut	RS, P, F	St
86	6.12	909.7	16.2	31,746	Former South River Shelter site	RS, P, F	St
87	6.13	924.5	14.8	39,806	Trail east Big MeadowsCmpgrd	RS, P, F	St
88	6.14	938.5	14.0	35,966	Byrd's Nest #3 Hut	RS, P, F	T
89	6.15	956.0	17.5	43,107	Gravel Springs Hut	RS, P, F	T
90	6.16	969.4	13.4	35,161	US 522, Front Royal, VA	RS, P	M
91	6.17	969.4	0	7,440	Front Royal, VA	RS, P	M
92	6.18	980.1	10.7	28,835	Manassas Gap Shelter	RS, P	T
93	6.19	995.4	15.3	38,337	2nd mountain of Roller Coaster	RS, P	St
94	6.20	1007.5	12.1	33,461	.7 miles after Roller Coaster	RS, P	St
95	6.21	1022.8	15.3	39,007	ATC, Harper's Ferry	RS, P	M
96	6.22	1022.8	0	11.045	Harper's Ferry, WV	RS, P	M
97	6.23	1033.8	11.0	28,836	Crampton Gap Shelter	RS	T
98	6.24	1054.5	20.7	48,675	Ensign Cowall Shelter	RS, F	S
99	6.25	1072.6	18.1	43,598	Tumbling Run Shelters	RS,P,LP, TV	S
100	6.26	1084.8	12.2	30,982	Quarry Gap Shelters	RS,P,LP, TV	S
101	6.27	1098.4	13.6	7,618	Toms Run Shelters	Solo	S
102	6.28	1109.3	10.9	19,511	James Fry (Tagg Run) Shelter	RS, P	T
103	6.29	1121.3	12.0	30,784	PA 174, Boiling Springs, PA	RS, P	M
104	6.30	1135.6	14.3	33,465	Darlington Shelter	RS, P	T
105	7.01	1151.2	15.6	40,559	Clarks Ferry Shelter	RS, P	T
106	7.02	1168.6	17.4	43,849	Rattling Run	RS, P	St
107	7.03	1180.6	12.0	28,425	PA 72 and cross PA 443	RS, P, family	M
108	7.04	1180.6	0	5,738	Lickdale, PA	P, family	M
109	7.05	1198.8	18.2	40,882		P	St
110	7.06	1217.5	18.7	47,745	Port Clinton, PA	P, DP, M	T
111	7.07	1232.8	15.3	40,351	.5 north of Eckvile Shelter	P	St
112	7.08	1249.7	16.9	39,608	Bake Oven Knob Shelter	Solo	T
113	7.09	1257.0	7.3	21,926	Lehigh River, PA 873	JD	M
114	7.10	1269.8	12.8	35,699	.1 north of Smith Gap Road	JD	St
115	7.11	1287.0	17.2	47,067	Kirkridge Shelter	JD	T
116	7.12	1293.4	6.4	25,677	PA 611, Delaware Water Gap	JD	M
117	7.13	1306.3	12.9	34,789	Catfish Lookout Tower	JD	St
118	7.14	1324.8	18.5	48,024	Gren Anderson Shelter	JD	T
119	7.15	1337.1	12.3	33,461	High Point State Park, NY	JD, DP, M	St
120	7.16	1350.2	13.1	32,973	Pochuck Mountain Shelter	JD, DP, M	T
121	7.17	1361.9	11.7	31,708	Wawayanda State Park	JD, DP, M,RS,P	St
122	7.18	1373.8	11.9	31,053	Wildcat Shelter	JD, DP, M,RS,P	T
123	7.19	1383.7	9.9	21,592	NY 17	JD, RS, P	M
124	7.20	1394.7	11.0	32,647	Black Mountain	JD, RS, P	St
125	7.21	1410.0	15.3	35,528	Graymoor Spiritual Life Center	JD, RS, P,DP,M	T
126	7.22	1427.5	17.5	47,765	Shenandoah Tenting Area	JD, RS, P,DP,M	T
127	7.23	1445.6	18.1	44,667	Telephone Pioneers Shelter	JD, RS, P,DP,M	T
128	7.24	1463.9	18.3	47,115	Schaghticoke Mountain Camp	JD, RS, P,DP,M	T

Day	Date	Total	M's	Steps	Site	People	
129	7.25	1467.1	3.2	10,722	CT341, Kent, CT	JD, RS, P,DP,M	Ho
130	7.26	1467.1	0	7,261	Manchester, CT	JD, RS, P,DP,M	Ho
131	7.27	1467.1	0	2,287	Manchester, CT	JD, DP, M	Ho
132	7.28	1480.8	13.7	35,040	Caesar Brook Campsite	JD, DP, M	T
133	7.29	1495.5	14.7	41,636	Limestone Spring Shelter	JD, DP, M	T
134	7.30	1511.2	15.7	41,316	Race Brook Falls Trail	JD, DP, M	T
135	7.31	1527.4	16.2	44,822	Tom Leonard Shelter	JD, DP, M	T
136	8.01	1541.6	14.2	25,027	Main Road, Tyringham, MA	JD, DP, M	Ho
137	8.02	1557.3	15.7	40,914	October Mountain Shelter	JD, DP, M	T
138	8.03	1573.3	16.0	43,563	Crystal Mountain Campsite	JD, DP, M	T
139	8.04	1589.6	16.6	42,793	Wilbur Clearing Shelter	JD, DP, M	T
140	8.05	1606.7	17.1	44,247	Congdon Shelter	JD, DP, M	T
141	8.06	1611.0	4.3	13,211	VT 9, Bennington, VT	JD	M
142	8.07	1631.6	20.6	49,438	USFS 71	JD, DP, M	St
143	8.08	1637.4	5.8	23,268	Stratton Mountain	JD, DP,M, R	Co
144	8.09	1651.1	13.7	37,008	VT 11 & 30	JD, DP, M,R	St
145	8.10	1668.7	17.6	42,773	Danby-Landgrove Rd	JD, DP, M,R	St
146	8.11	1683.5	14.8	10,133	VT 103	JD, DP, M,R	St
147	8.12	1700.9	17.4	28,761	US 4	JD, DP, M,R	M
148	8.13	1710.9	10.0	31,056	Stony Brook Shelter	JD, DP, M,R	T
149	8.14	1724.2	13.3	38,797	VT 12	JD,DP,M,R,Mc	T
150	8.15	1736.9	12.7	32,655	Quechee, West Hartford Rd	JD,DP,M,R,Mc	St
151	8.16	1747.1	10.2	26,877	Hanover, NH	JD,DP,M,R,Mc	T
152	8.17	1761.0	13.9	36,953	Goose Pond Road	JD, DP, M	T
153	8.18	1780.7	19.7	50,053	NH 25A	JD, DP, M,R	T
154	8.19	1790.5	9.8	29,551	NH 25	JD,DP,M,Mc	T
155	8.20	1799.8	9.3	28,367	NH 112, Kinsman Notch	JD,DP,M,Mc	T
156	8.21	1807.3	7.5	22,829	Eliza Brook Shelter	JD,DP,M,Mc	S
157	8.22	1816.1	8.8	31,422	Franconia Notch	JD, DP, M	St
158	8.23	1826.4	10.3	31,135	Garfield Ridge Shelter	JD, DP, M	S
159	8.24	1835.4	9.0	27,831	Whitewall Brook	DP, M	St
160	8.25	1843.8	8.4	5,272	Crawford Notch	DP, M	M
161	8.26	1852.0	8.2	23,619	Above tree line	DP, M	St
162	8.27	1862.0	10.0	36,756	Madison Spring Hut campsite	DP, M	T
163	8.28	1869.8	7.8	25,770	Pinkham Notch	DP, M	M
164	8.29	1876.9	7.1	21,694	Carter Dome	JD, DP, M	St
165	8.30	1889.0	12.1	36,236	Rattle River Shelter	JD, DP, M	T
166	8.31	1902.7	13.7	35,018	Gentian Pond Shelter	JD, DP, M	T
167	9.01	1912.3	9.6	20,600	Full Goose Shelter	JD, DP, M	T
168	9.02	1922.0	9.7	30,455	Grafton Notch, ME 26	JD, DP, M	M
169	9.03	1922.0	0	8,012	Bethel, ME	JD, DP, M	M
170	9.04	1934.2	12.2	35,422	Surplus Pond	JD, DP, M	St
171	9.05	1946.7	12.5	37,477		JD, DP, M	St
172	9.06	1961.6	14.9	43,460		Solo	St

Day	Date	Total	M's	Steps	Site	People	
173	9.07	1970.6	9.0	25,103	Piazza Rock Lean-to	JD, DP, M	T
174	9.08	1984.2	13.6	38,596	.1 north of Perham Stream	JD, DP, M	St
175	9.09	1996.9	12.7	35,236	Spring	Solo	St
176	9.10	2006.1	9.2	28,738	Horns Pond Lean-to	Solo	T
177	9.11	2018.9	12.8	32,385	East Flagstaff Lake	Solo	St
178	9.12	2034.0	15.1	38,752	Pierce Pond Lean-to	JD, DP, M	T
179	9.13	2050.2	16.2	42,995	.1 mile north of Baker Stream	JD, DP, M	St
180	9.14	2065.7	15.5	34,129	Horseshoe Canyon Lean-to	JD, DP, M	T
181	9.15	2075.9	10.2	28,137	Bell Pond	JD, DP, M	St
182	9.16	2089.1	13.2	30,172	.7 south Long Pond Lean-to	JD, DP, M	St
183	9.17	2103.3	14.2	19,251	2.6 north Chairback Gap Leanto	Solo	St
184	9.18	2121.4	18.1	26,999	East Branch Lean-to	Solo	T
185	9.19	2137.4	16.0	16,864	Antlers Campsite	JD, DP, M	T
186	9.20	2159.1	21.7	27,554	Rainbow Stream Lean-to	JD, DP, M	T
187	9.21	2174.1	15.0	13,748	Abol Bridge	JD, DP, M	T
188	9.22	2184.0	9.9	22,885	Katahdin Stream Campground	JD, DP, M	T
189	9.23	2189.2	5.2	31,669	Baxter Peak	JD, DP, M	M

*Steps – These were taken from the Health App on my iPhone6. I had no idea I was recording my footsteps until someone pointed it out to me months after I completed the hike. Occasionally, you may notice that the steps don't match the mileage. When I was very low on battery power or in terrible weather, I turned my phone completely off. It was mostly in Airplane Mode, so that I could take pictures. Total = 5,528,570 recorded footsteps over the 189 days.

Printed in Great Britain
by Amazon